Lecture Notes in Computer Science   1344

Edited by G. Goos, J. Hartmanis and J. van Leeuwen

Advisory Board: W. Brauer   D. Gries   J. Stoer

Springer
Berlin
Heidelberg
New York
Barcelona
Budapest
Hong Kong
London
Milan
Paris
Santa Clara
Singapore
Tokyo

Christine Ausnit-Hood   Kent A. Johnson
Robert G. Pettit, IV   Steven B. Opdahl (Eds.)

Ada 95
Quality and Style

 Springer

Volume Editors

Christine Ausnit-Hood
BDM International, Inc
1501 BDM Way, McLean, VA 22102-3204, USA
E-mail: CAusnit@bdm.com

Kent A. Johnson
TeraQuest Metrics, Inc.
10812 Monticello Drive, Great Falls, VA 22066-4224, USA
E-mail: k.johnson@ieee.org

Robert G. Pettit, IV
Software Productivity Consortium
2214 Rock Hill Road, Herndon, VA 20170, USA
E-mail: pettit@software.org

Steven B. Opdahl
4263-B Jefferson Oak Circle, Fairfax, VA 22033, USA
E-mail: opdahl@erols.com

Cataloging-in-Publication data applied for

Die Deutsche Bibliothek - CIP-Einheitsaufnahme

Ada 95 : quality and style / Christine Ausnit-Hood ... (ed.). - Berlin ;
Heidelberg ; New York ; Barcelona ; Budapest ; Hong Kong ;
London ; Milan ; Paris ; Santa Clara ; Singapore ; Tokyo : Springer,
1997
   (Lecture notes in computer science ; Vol. 1344)
   ISBN 3-540-63823-7

CR Subject Classification (1991): D.1-3

ISSN 0302-9743
ISBN 3-540-63823-7 Springer-Verlag Berlin Heidelberg New York

Typesetting: Camera-ready by author
SPIN 10652639   06/3142 – 5 4 3 2 1 0   Printed on acid-free paper

Software Productivity Consortium

Ada 95 Quality and Style:
Guidelines for Professional Programmers

Department of Defense Ada Joint Program Office

SPC-94093-CMC

Version 01.00.10

October 1995

Ada 95 Quality and Style:
Guidelines for Professional Programmers

SPC-94093-CMC

Version 01.00.10

October 1995

Prepared for the

Department of Defense Ada Joint Program Office

Produced by the
SOFTWARE PRODUCTIVITY CONSORTIUM

SPC Building
2214 Rock Hill Road
Herndon, Virginia 22070

PREFACE

PURPOSE

The purpose of *Ada 95 Quality and Style: Guidelines for Professional Programmer*s is to help computer professionals produce better Ada programs by identifying a set of stylistic guidelines that will directly impact the quality of their Ada 95 programs. This style guide is not intended to replace the Ada Reference Manual (1995) or Rationale (1995) or to serve as a tutorial for the Ada 95 programming language. Furthermore, this book is not intended to be a guide for transitioning from Ada 83 to Ada 95. The reader is encouraged to consult the References for sources on these related topics.

The style guide is divided into chapters that map to the major decisions that each programmer addresses when creating high-quality, reliable, reusable, and portable Ada software. Some overlap exists in the chapters because not all programming decisions can be made independently. Individual chapters address source code presentation, readability, program structure, programming practice, concurrency, portability, reusability, performance, and a new chapter on object-oriented features.

Each chapter is divided into guidelines, using a format that supports wide usage because its content is both prescriptive and tailorable. Each guideline consists of a concise statement of the principles that should be followed and a rationale explaining why the guideline is important. The guidelines also provide usage examples, in addition to possible exceptions to applying the guidelines. Many of the guidelines are specific enough to be adopted as corporate or project programming standards. Others require a managerial decision on a particular instantiation before they can be used as standards. In such cases, a sample instantiation is presented and used throughout the examples.

BACKGROUND

The Ada Joint Program Office (AJPO) funded this style guide, which was created by merging a set of guidelines for using Ada 95 with modifications to the original *Ada Quality and Style: Guidelines for Professional Programmers*, version 02.01.01 (AQ&S 83) (Software Productivity Consortium 1992), developed to support Ada 83. The Ada 95 guidelines are based on the wealth of data available from the Ada 9X Project, the AJPO library, and the Ada community at large. The Software Productivity Consortium's (Consortium's) technical staff authored the update and the Advanced Research Projects Agency (ARPA) participated in the update effort.

The preexisting AQ&S 83 presented a set of guidelines to help the programmer make disciplined use of Ada's features. In 1992, the Consortium completed the version 2.1 update to the style guide under contract to the AJPO. The AJPO referred to that style guide as "the suggested style guide for all DoD programs."

PUBLIC COMMENT

This new style guide is intended to provide a tool for both the novice and the experienced Ada programmer. To meet this objective, the Consortium directly involved both the public and the best available experts from across the Ada community. To ensure this involvement, a three-step process was defined to develop this style guide: develop a draft baseline, conduct public and expert review, and develop a final style guide.

The Consortium invites comments on this book to continue enhancing its quality and usefulness. The authors will consider suggestions for current guidelines and areas for future expansion. Examples that highlight particular points are most helpful.

---

* This material is based in part upon work sponsored by the Department of Defense Ada Joint Program Office, through the Advanced Research Projects Agency under Grant #MDA972-92-J-1018. The content does not necessarily reflect the position or the policy of the U.S. Government, and no official endorsement should be inferred.

Electronic copies of this style guide are available for downloading through the Ada Information Clearinghouse (phone: 1(800)232-4211; e-mail: `adainfo@sw-eng.falls-church.va.us`).

Please direct written comments to:

Robert G. Pettit, IV
Software Productivity Consortium
2214 Rock Hill Road
Herndon, VA 20170
e-mail: pettit@software.org
fax: (703) 742-7200

Please include your contact information in your comments.

AUTHORS AND ACKNOWLEDGMENTS

The Consortium wishes to recognize all of the nearly 100 contributors to previous versions of this style guide written to support Ada 83, including its authors, editors, and distinguished reviewers. The contributors to this version of the style guide include the authors, Ms. Christine Ausnit-Hood, Mr. Kent A. Johnson, Mr. Robert G. Pettit, and Mr. Steven B. Opdahl, and the following Distinguished Reviewers, Expert Reviewers, and Technical Advisors.

Distinguished Reviewers: Mr. Bill Beckwith, Objective Interface Systems, Inc.; Dr. Norman H. Cohen, IBM TJWatson Research Center; Dr. Robert Dewar, New York University; Dr. Charles B. Engle, Jr., Department of Computer Science, Florida Institute of Technology; Mr. Jay Ferguson, NSA, Department of Defense; Mr. Ken Garlington, Lockheed Martin, Fort Worth Company; Mr. Tim Harrison, ParcPlace-Digitalk Inc.; Mr. Ed Seidewitz, NASA, Goddard Space Flight Center; Mr. S. Tucker Taft, Intermetrics Inc.

Expert Reviewers: Mr. Brad Balfour, CACI; Dr. Bryce Bardin, Ada Consulting and Training; Mr. Philip Brashear, CTA Inc.; Dr. Ben Brosgol, Brosgol Consulting and Training; Dr. Michael B. Feldman, Department of Electrical Engineering and Computer Science, George Washington University; Mr. Gil Myers, NOSC ; Mr. Jim Moore, The MITRE Corporation; Ms. Eileen S. Quann, FASTRAK Training, Inc.; Mr. Richard Riehle, AdaWorks; Dr. Tim Teitelbaum, GrammaTech; Dr. Joyce Tokar, Tartan.

Technical Advisors: Mr. John Barnes, John Barnes Informatics; Mr. Leslie Dupaix, OO-ALC/TISE, Hill AFB; Mr. Dave Emery, The MITRE Corporation; Mr. Magnus Kempe, Kempe Software CE; Ms. Judy Kerner, The Aerospace Corporation; Mr. Alexander Miethe, CCI; LtCol Pat Lawlis, AFIT/ENG, Wright-Patterson AFB.

Thanks to the other contributors who forwarded their comments, guidelines, and examples, including Lisa Chan, Bo Sanden, Wesley Groleau, Terry D. Humphrey, Pascal Leroy, Gilles Demailly, Philippe Kipfer, Tomas Peterson, Ted Baker, Mike Dingas, Willem Treurniet, T. A. Vo, and Dave Weller.

Special Thanks to the Following:

Ed Seidewitz, Tim Harrison, Bill Beckwith, Ken Garlington, Tucker Taft, Chuck Engle, and Don Reifer for taking time from their busy schedules to attend the Distinguished Reviewer Technical Interchange Meetings.

Mike Evans and Dan Hocking from the Army Research Lab for providing electronic meeting support at the Distinguished Reviewer Technical Interchange Meetings.

Philip Brashear for rewriting Chapter 10.

Mike Feldman and Brian Kallberg for their updates to the dining philosophers problem.

John Barnes for providing extracts from his new book.

GrammaTech, Inc., who made the new version of their Ada-ASSURED product available. The examples were formatted in whole or in part using their tool.

In addition, Bobbie Troy and Mary Mallonee provided technical editing; Debbie Morgan and Lisa Smith provided word processing; and Bobbie Troy provided clean proofing.

CONTENTS

TABLES

CHAPTER 1
Introduction

Style is an often overlooked but very critical attribute of writing. The style of writing directly impacts the readability and understandability of the end product. The style of programming, as the writing of source code in a computer language, also suffers from this neglect. Programs need to be readable and understandable by humans, not just comparable by machines. This requirement is important in the creation of quality products that not only meet user needs but also can be developed on schedule and within estimated cost. This book is intended to help the computer professional produce better Ada programs. It presents a set of specific stylistic guidelines for using the powerful features of Ada 95 (Ada Reference Manual 1995) in a disciplined manner.

Each *guideline* consists of a concise statement of the principles that should be followed and a *rationale* for following the guideline. In most cases, an *example* of the use of the guideline is provided, and, in some cases, a further example is included to show the consequences of violating the guideline. Possible *exceptions* to the application of the guideline are explicitly noted, and further explanatory *notes* are provided, where appropriate. In some cases, an *instantiation* is provided to show more specific guidance that could be enforced as a standard. In selected cases, *automation notes* discuss how one could automate enforcement of the guideline.

Ada was designed to support the development of high-quality, reliable, reusable, and portable software. For a number of reasons, no programming language can ensure the achievement of these desirable objectives on its own. For example, programming must be embedded in a disciplined development process that addresses requirements analysis, design, implementation, verification, validation, and maintenance in an organized way. The use of the language must conform to good programming practices based on well-established software engineering principles. This book is intended to help bridge the gap between these principles and the actual practice of programming in Ada.

Many of the guidelines in this book are designed to promote clear source text. The goal of these guidelines is to improve the ease of program evolution, adaptation, and maintenance. Understandable source text is more likely to be correct and reliable. Easy adaptation requires a thorough understanding of the software; this is considerably facilitated by clarity. Effective code adaptation is a prerequisite to code reuse, a technique that has the potential for drastic reductions in system development cost. Finally, because maintenance (really evolution) is a costly process that continues throughout the life of a system, clarity plays a major role in keeping maintenance costs down. Over the entire life cycle, code has to be read and understood far more often than it is written; thus, the investment in writing readable, understandable code is worthwhile.

The remaining sections of this introduction discuss the organization of this book and how the material presented can be used by people in different roles, including new Ada programmers, experienced Ada programmers, object-oriented programmers, software project managers, contracting agencies, standards setting organizations, and planners of the transition to Ada 95 from existing Ada 83 (Ada Reference Manual 1983) programs.

1.1 ORGANIZATION OF THIS BOOK

The format of this book follows the well-received guideline format of the *Ada Quality and Style: Guidelines for Professional Programmers*, version 02.01.01 (AQ&S 83) (Software Productivity Consortium 1992). The style guide is divided into sections that map to the major decisions that each programmer must make when creating high-quality, reliable, reusable, and portable Ada software. Some overlap exists in the sections because not all programming decisions can be made independently.

Individual chapters address source code presentation, readability, program structure, programming practices, concurrency, portability, reusability, and performance, and a new chapter addresses object-oriented features. Each chapter ends with a *summary* of the guidelines it contains. The last chapter shows a complete implementation of the Dining Philosophers example, provided by Dr. Michael B. Feldman and Mr. Bjorn Kallberg. Many of the guidelines in this book were used to create this example. An appendix provides a cross-reference matrix between the Ada Reference Manual (1995) sections and the guidelines in this style guide.

This book is written using the general software engineering vocabulary developed over the last 20 years. Software engineering is a rapidly evolving discipline with relatively new concepts and terminology. However, to establish a common frame of reference, needed definitions are extracted from the Ada Reference Manual (1995) and Rationale (1995).

Throughout the book, references are made to other sources of information about Ada style and other Ada issues. The references are listed at the end of the book. A bibliography is also provided.

In this book, the term "Ada" refers to the latest Ada standard, released in February 1995 (sometimes also known as Ada 95). References to the earlier Ada standard are clearly denoted as "Ada 83."

1.1.1 Source Code Presentation and Readability

Chapters 2 and 3 directly address the issues of creating clear, readable, and understandable source text. Chapter 2 focuses on code formatting, and Chapter 3 addresses issues of use of comments, naming conventions, and types.

There are two main aspects of code clarity: (1) careful and consistent *layout* of the source text on the page or the screen, covered by Chapter 2, that can enhance readability dramatically; (2) careful attention to the *structure* of code, covered by Chapter 3, that can make the code easier to understand. This is true both on the small scale (e.g., by careful choice of identifier names or by disciplined use of loops) and on the large scale (e.g., by proper use of packages). These guidelines treat both layout and structure.

Code formatting and naming convention preferences tend to be very personal. You must balance your personal likes and dislikes with those of other engineers on the project so that you can agree to a consistent set of conventions that the whole project team will follow. Automatic code formatters can help in enforcing this kind of consistency.

1.1.2 Program Structure

Chapter 4 addresses overall program structure. Proper structure improves program clarity. This is analogous to readability on lower levels and includes issues of high-level structure, in particular the use of packages and child packages, visibility, and exceptions. The majority of the guidelines in this chapter are concerned with the application of sound software engineering principles, such as information hiding, abstraction, encapsulation, and separation of concerns.

1.1.3 Programming Practices

Chapter 5 presents guidelines that define consistent and logical language feature usage. These guidelines address optional parts of the syntax, types, data structures, expressions, statements, visibility, exceptions, and erroneous execution.

1.1.4 Concurrency

Chapter 6 defines the correct use of concurrency to develop predictable, reliable, reusable, and portable software. The topics include tasking, protected units, communication, and termination. One major area of enhancement of the Ada language has been better support for shared data. The task mechanism had been the only available approach to protecting shared data. The guidelines in this chapter support the use of protected types to encapsulate and synchronize access to shared data.

1.1.5 Portability and Reusability

Chapters 7 and 8 address issues of designing for change from slightly different perspectives. Chapter 7 addresses the fundamentals of portability, the ease of changing software from one computer system or environment to another, and the impact of specific feature usage on portability. Chapter 8 addresses code reusability, the extent to which code can be used in different applications with minimal change.

The portability guidelines discussed in Chapter 7 need careful attention. Adherence to them is important even if the need to port the resulting software is not currently foreseen. Following the guidelines improves the potential reusability of the resulting code in projects that use different Ada implementations. You should insist that when particular project needs force the relaxation of some of the portability guidelines, nonportable features of the source text are prominently indicated.

The reusability guidelines given in Chapter 8 are based on the principles of encapsulation and design for change. These guidelines stress that understanding and clarity, robustness, adaptability, and independence are useful and desirable, even when reuse is not expected, because the resulting code is more resistant to both planned and unplanned change.

1.1.6 Object-Oriented Features

Chapter 9 defines a set of guidelines in common objected-oriented terms that exploit some of the features of Ada 95 that are not in Ada 83. The guidelines discuss the use of the new Ada features of type extension (tagged types), abstract tagged types, and abstract subprograms to implement single inheritance, multiple inheritance, and polymorphism.

1.1.7 Performance

Chapter 10 defines a set of guidelines intended to enhance performance. It is recognized that some approaches to performance are at odds with maintainability and portability. Most of the guidelines in this chapter read ". . . when measured performance indicates." "Indicates" means that you have determined that the benefit in increased performance to your application in your environment outweighs the negative side effects on understandability, maintainability, and portability of the resulting code.

1.2 HOW TO USE THIS BOOK

This book is intended for those involved in the actual development of software systems written in Ada. The following sections discuss how to make the most effective use of the material presented. Readers with different levels of Ada experience or different roles in a software project will need to use the book in different ways.

There are a number of ways in which this book can be used: as a guide to good Ada style; as a comprehensive list of guidelines that will contribute to better Ada programs; or as a reference work to consult for usage examples of and design-tradeoff discussion on specific features of the language. The book contains many guidelines, some of which are quite complex. Learning them all at the same time should not be necessary; it is unlikely that you will be using all the features of the language at once. However, it is recommended that all programmers (and, where possible, other Ada project staff) make an effort to read and understand Chapters 2, 3, 4, and Chapter 5 up to Section 5.7. Some of the material is quite difficult (e.g., Section 4.2, which discusses visibility), but it covers issues that are fundamental to the effective use of Ada and is important for any software professional involved in building Ada systems.

This book is not intended as an introductory text on Ada or as a complete manual of the Ada language. It is assumed that you already know the syntax of Ada and have a rudimentary understanding of the semantics. With such a background, you should find the guidelines useful, informative, and often enlightening.

If you are learning Ada, you should equip yourself with a comprehensive introduction to the language. Two good introductory texts on Ada 83 are Barnes (1989) and Cohen (1986). Both authors have published new books that cover Ada 95 (Barnes 1996, Cohen 1996). Once you become familiar with these texts, you are encouraged to use them in conjunction with Rationale (1995). The Ada Reference Manual (1995) should be regarded as a companion to these books. The majority of guidelines reference the sections of the Ada Reference Manual (1995) that define the language features being discussed. Appendix A cross references sections of the Ada Language Reference Manual to the guidelines.

1.3   TO THE NEW Ada PROGRAMMER

At first sight, Ada offers a bewildering variety of features. It is a powerful tool intended to solve difficult problems, and almost every feature has a legitimate application in some context. This makes it especially important to use Ada's features in a disciplined and organized way. Following the guidelines can make learning Ada easier and help you to master its apparent complexity. From the beginning, you can write programs that exploit the best features of the language in the way that the designers intended.

Programmers experienced in using other programming languages are often tempted to use Ada as if it were their familiar language but with irritating syntactic differences. This pitfall should be avoided at all costs; it can lead to convoluted code that subverts exactly those aspects of Ada that make it so suitable for building high-quality systems. You must learn to "think Ada." Following the guidelines in this book and reading the examples of their use will help you to do this as quickly and painlessly as possible.

To some degree, novice programmers learning Ada have an advantage. Following the guidelines from the beginning helps in developing a clear programming style that effectively exploits the language. If you are in this category, it is recommended that you adopt the guidelines for those exercises you perform as part of learning Ada. Initially, developing sound programming habits by concentrating on the guidelines themselves and their supporting examples is more important than understanding the rationale for each guideline.

The rationale for many of the guidelines helps experienced programmers understand and accept the suggestions presented in the guideline. Some of the guidelines themselves are also written for the experienced programmer who must make engineering tradeoffs. This is especially true in the areas of portability, reusability, and performance. These more difficult guidelines and rationale will make you aware of the issues affecting each programming decision. You can then use that awareness to recognize the engineering tradeoffs that you will eventually be asked to make when you are the experienced Ada programmer.

1.4   TO THE EXPERIENCED Ada PROGRAMMER

As an experienced Ada programmer, you are already writing code that conforms to many of the guidelines in this book. In some areas, however, you may have adopted a personal programming style that differs from that presented here, and you might be reluctant to change. Carefully review those guidelines that are inconsistent with your current style, make sure that you understand their rationale, and consider adopting them. The overall set of guidelines in this book embodies a consistent approach to producing high-quality programs that would be weakened by too many exceptions.

Consistency is another important reason for general adoption of common guidelines. If all the staff of a project write source text in the same style, many critical project activities are easier. Consistent code simplifies formal and informal code reviews, system integration, code reuse within a project, and the provision and application of supporting tools. In practice, corporate or project standards may require deviations from the guidelines to be explicitly commented, so adopting a nonstandard approach may require extra work.

Some of the guidelines in this book, particularly in the chapters on concurrency, portability, reusability, object-oriented features, and performance, focus on design tradeoffs. These guidelines ask you to consider whether using an Ada feature is an appropriate design decision for your application. There are often several ways to implement a particular design decision, and these guidelines discuss the tradeoffs you should consider in making your decision.

1.5   TO EXPERIENCED OBJECT-ORIENTED PROGRAMMERS

As an experienced object-oriented programmer, you will appreciate the effort that has gone into elegantly extending the Ada language to include powerful object-oriented features. These new features are integrated tightly with the existing language features and vocabulary. This book is intentionally written to provide a view from the perspective of style; therefore, Ada object-oriented features are used throughout the book. Disciplined use of these features will promote programs that are easier to read and modify. These features also give you flexibility in building reusable components. Chapter 9 addresses object-oriented programming and the issues of inheritance and polymorphism. Earlier chapters cross reference the Chapter 9 guidelines.

You will find it easier to take advantage of many of the concepts in Chapter 9 if you have done an object-oriented design. The results of an object-oriented design would include a set of meaningful abstractions and hierarchy of classes. The abstractions need to include the definition of the design objects, including structure and state, the operations on the objects, and the intended encapsulation for each object. The details on designing these abstractions and the hierarchy of classes are beyond the scope of this book. A number of good sources exist for this detail, including Rumbaugh et al. (1991), Jacobson et al. (1992), the *ADARTS* ⓈⓂ *Guidebook* (Software Productivity Consortium 1993), and Booch (1994).

1.6   TO THE SOFTWARE PROJECT MANAGER

Technical management plays a key role in ensuring that the software produced in the course of a project is correct, reliable, maintainable, and portable. Management must create a project-wide commitment to the production of high-quality code; define project-specific coding standards and guidelines; foster an understanding of why uniform adherence to the chosen coding standards is critical to product quality; and establish policies and procedures to check and enforce that adherence. The guidelines contained in this book can aid such an effort.

An important activity for managers is the definition of coding standards for a project or organization. These guidelines do not, in themselves, constitute a complete set of standards; however, they can serve as a basis for standards. Several guidelines indicate a range of decisions, but they do not prescribe a particular decision. For example, the second guideline in the book (Guideline 2.1.2) advocates using a consistent number of spaces for indentation and indicates in the rationale that two to four spaces would be reasonable. With your senior technical staff, you should review each such guideline and arrive at a decision about its instantiation that will constitute your project or organizational standard.

Two other areas require managerial decisions about standardization. Guideline 3.1.4 advises you to avoid arbitrary abbreviations in object or unit names. You should prepare a glossary of acceptable abbreviations for a project that allows the use of shorter versions of application-specific terms (e.g., FFT for Fast Fourier Transform or SPN for Stochastic Petri Net). You should keep this glossary short and restrict it to terms that need to be used frequently as part of names. Having to refer continually to an extensive glossary to understand source text makes it hard to read.

The portability guidelines given in Chapter 7 need careful attention. Adherence to them is important even if the need to port the resulting software is not currently foreseen. Following the guidelines improves the potential reusability of the resulting code in projects that use different Ada implementations. You should insist that when particular project needs force the relaxation of some of the portability guidelines, nonportable features of the source text are prominently indicated. Observing the Chapter 7 guidelines requires definition and standardization of project- or organization-specific numeric types to be used in place of the (potentially nonportable) predefined numeric types.

Your decisions on standardization issues should be incorporated in a project or organization coding standards document. With coding standards in place, you need to ensure adherence to them. Gaining the wholehearted commitment of your programming staff to use the standards is critical. Given this commitment and the example of high-quality Ada being produced by your programmers, it will be far easier to conduct effective formal code reviews that check compliance to project standards.

Some general issues concerning the management of Ada projects are discussed by Hefley, et al. (1992).

1.7   TO CONTRACTING AGENCIES AND STANDARDS ORGANIZATIONS

Many of the guidelines presented here are specific enough to be adopted as corporate or project programming standards. Others require a managerial decision on a particular instantiation before they can be used as standards. In such cases, a sample instantiation is presented and used throughout the examples. Such instantiations should be recognized as weaker recommendations than the guidelines themselves. In some cases, where the examples are extracted from a published work, the author's style is used unchanged.

Other guidelines presented in this book are intentionally phrased in terms of design choices to consider. These guidelines cannot be instantiated as hard-and-fast rules that a project must follow. For example, you should not interpret Guidelines 6.1.1 and 6.1.2 to mean that a project is forbidden to use tasks. Rather, these guidelines are intended to help the designer make the tradeoffs between using protected objects and tasks, thus leading the designer to make a more informed choice between these features.

The guidelines in this document are not intended to stand alone as a standard. In some cases, it is not clear that a guideline could be enforced because it is only intended to make the engineer aware of tradeoffs. In other cases, a choice still remains about a guideline, such as how many spaces to use for each level of indentation.

When a guideline is too general to show an example, the "instantiation" section of each guideline contains more specific guidelines. These instantiations can be considered a standard and are more likely to be enforceable. Any organization that attempts to extract standards from this document needs to evaluate the complete context. Each guideline works best when related guidelines are practiced. In isolation, a guideline may have little or no benefit.

1.8   TO Ada 83 TO Ada 95 TRANSITION PLANNERS

Transitioning issues fall into two major categories: the incompatibilities between the languages, in particular, upward compatibility, and exploitation of new language features.

Upward compatibility of Ada 95 was a major design goal of the language. The small number of incompatibilities between Ada 83 and Ada 95 that are likely to occur in practice are easily overcome (see Ada 95 Rationale [1995] Appendix X entitled Upward Compatibility). Detailed information on compatibility issues can be found in Taylor (1995) and Intermetrics (1995).

The transition planner can gain insight from this book into the exploitation of language features in two ways. First, Table 1 shows the impact of new Ada 95 language features on style guide chapters. Second, Appendix A maps Ada Reference Manual (1995) sections to specific style guidelines.

1.9   TYPOGRAPHIC CONVENTIONS

This style guide uses the following typographic conventions:

Serif font	General presentation of information.
Italicized serif font	Publication titles and emphasis.
Boldfaced serif font	Section headings.
Boldfaced sans serif font	Subheadings for guideline, instantiation, example, rationale, notes, exceptions, automation notes, caution, and subheadings in Summary sections.
`Typewriter` font	Syntax of code.

Table 1. Impact of Ada 95 Features and Enhancement on Ada Style Guide Chapters

Ada 95 Features and Enhancements	Code.	Read.	Struc.	Prac.	Conc.	Port.	Reuse.	OO	Perf.
Object-Oriented Features									
Type Extension (tagged types)	✓	✓		✓			✓	✓	
Controlled Types							✓	✓	
Polymorphism				✓			✓	✓	✓
Multiple Inheritance								✓	
Abstract Types and Subprograms								✓	
Program Structure and Compilation									
Child Library Units		✓	✓						
Generics			✓				✓		
Tasking Model Revisions									
Protected Types		✓	✓		✓	✓			
Synchronization Mechanisms	✓		✓		✓	✓			
Declarations and Types									
Access-to-Subprogram Types						✓	✓		
Access Types				✓					
Other Changes									
Exceptions		✓	✓	✓		✓			
Use Type and Renaming		✓	✓						
Interfacing Foreign Languages						✓			
Specialized Annexes									
System Programming					✓	✓			
Real-Time Systems					✓	✓			✓
Distributed Systems					✓	✓			✓
Information Systems		✓		✓		✓			
Numerics		✓		✓		✓			
Safety and Security		✓		✓	✓	✓			✓

Legend: Code. = Code Presentation Read. = Readability Struct. = Program Structure
Prac. = Programming Practices Conc. = Concurrency Port. = Portability
Reuse. = Reusability OO = Object-Oriented (New) Perf. = Performance

CHAPTER 2
Source Code Presentation

The physical layout of source text on the page or screen has a strong effect on its readability. This chapter contains source code presentation guidelines intended to make the code more readable.

In addition to the general purpose guidelines, specific recommendations are made in the "instantiation" sections. If you disagree with the specific recommendations, you may want to adopt your own set of conventions that still follow the general purpose guidelines. Above all, be consistent across your entire project.

An entirely consistent layout is hard to achieve or check manually. Therefore, you may prefer to automate layout with a tool for parameterized code formatting or incorporate the guidelines into an automatic coding template. Some of the guidelines and specific recommendations presented in this chapter cannot be enforced by a formatting tool because they are based on the semantics, not the syntax, of the Ada code. More details are given in the "automation notes" sections.

2.1 CODE FORMATTING

The "code formatting" of Ada source code affects how the code looks, not what the code does. Topics included here are horizontal spacing, indentation, alignment, pagination, and line length. The most important guideline is to be consistent throughout the compilation unit as well as the project.

2.1.1 Horizontal Spacing

guideline

- Use consistent spacing around delimiters.
- Use the same spacing as you would in regular prose.

instantiation

Specifically, leave at least one blank space in the following places, as shown in the examples throughout this book. More spaces may be required for the vertical alignment recommended in subsequent guidelines.

- Before and after the following delimiters and binary operators:

```
+      -      *      /      &
<      =      >      /=     <=      >=
:=     =>     |      ..
:
<>
```

- Outside of the quotes for string (") and character (') literals, except where prohibited.
- Outside, but not inside, parentheses.
- After commas (,) and semicolons (;).

Do not leave any blank spaces in the following places, even if this conflicts with the above recommendations.

- After the plus (+) and minus (–) signs when used as unary operators.
- After a function call.
- Inside of label delimiters (<< >>).
- Before and after the exponentiation operator (**), apostrophe ('), and period (.)

- Between multiple consecutive opening or closing parentheses.

- Before commas (,) and semicolons (;).

When superfluous parentheses are omitted because of operator precedence rules, spaces may optionally be removed around the highest precedence operators in that expression.

example

```
Default_String : constant String :=
      "This is the long string returned by" &
      " default. It is broken into multiple" &
      " Ada source lines for convenience.";

type Signed_Whole_16 is range -2**15 .. 2**15 - 1;
type Address_Area  is array (Natural range <>) of Signed_Whole_16;

Register : Address_Area (16#7FF0# .. 16#7FFF#);
Memory   : Address_Area (     0 .. 16#7FEC#);

Register(Pc) := Register(A);

X := Signed_Whole_16(Radius * Sin(Angle));

Register(Index) := Memory(Base_Address + Index * Element_Length);

Get(Value => Sensor);

Error_Term := 1.0 - (Cos(Theta)**2 + Sin(Theta)**2);

Z        := X**3;
Y        := C * X + B;
Volume := Length * Width * Height;
```

rationale

It is a good idea to use white space around delimiters and operators because they are typically short sequences (one or two characters) that can easily get lost among the longer keywords and identifiers. Putting white space around them makes them stand out. Consistency in spacing also helps make the source code easier to scan visually.

However, many of the delimiters (commas, semicolons, parentheses, etc.) are familiar as normal punctuation marks. It is distracting to see them spaced differently in a computer program than in normal text. Therefore, use the same spacing as in text (no spaces before commas and semicolons, no spaces inside parentheses, etc.).

exceptions

The one notable exception is the colon (:). In Ada, it is useful to use the colon as a tabulator or a column separator (see Guideline 2.1.4). In this context, it makes sense to put spaces before and after the colon rather than only after it as in normal text.

automation notes

The guidelines in this section are easily enforced with an automatic code formatter.

2.1.2   Indentation

guideline

- Indent and align nested control structures, continuation lines, and embedded units consistently.

- Distinguish between indentation for nested control structures and for continuation lines.

- Use spaces for indentation, not the tab character (Nissen and Wallis 1984, §2.2).

instantiation

Specifically, the following indentation conventions are recommended, as shown in the examples throughout this book. Note that the minimum indentation is described. More spaces may be required for the vertical alignment recommended in subsequent guidelines.

- Use the recommended paragraphing shown in the Ada Reference Manual (1995).

- Use three spaces as the basic unit of indentation for nesting.

- Use two spaces as the basic unit of indentation for continuation lines.

A label is outdented three spaces:

```
begin
<<label>>
   <statement>
end;
```

```
<long statement with line break>
   <trailing part of same statement>
```

The if statement and the plain loop:

```
if <condition> then
   <statements>
elsif <condition> then
   <statements>
else
   <statements>
end if;
```

```
<name>:
   loop
      <statements>
      exit when <condition>;
      <statements>
   end loop <name>;
```

Loops with the for and while iteration schemes:

```
<name>:
   for <scheme> loop
      <statements>
   end loop <name>;
```

```
<name>:
   while <condition> loop
      <statements>
   end loop <name>;
```

The block and the case statement as recommended in the Ada Reference Manual (1995):

```
<name>:
   declare
      <declarations>
   begin
      <statements>
   exception
      when <choice> =>
         <statements>
      when others =>
         <statements>
   end <name>;
```

```
case <expression> is
   when <choice> =>
      <statements>
   when <choice> =>
      <statements>
   when others =>
      <statements>
end case;   --<comment>
```

These case statements save space over the Ada Reference Manual (1995) recommendation and depend on very short statement lists, respectively. Whichever you choose, be consistent:

```
case <expression> is
when <choice> =>
   <statements>
when <choice> =>
   <statements>
when others =>
   <statements>
end case;
```

```
case <expression> is
   when <choice> => <statements>
                    <statements>
   when <choice> => <statements>
   when others   => <statements>
end case;
```

The various forms of selective accept and the timed and conditional entry calls:

```
select
   when <guard> =>
      <accept statement>
      <statements>
or
   <accept statement>
   <statements>
or
   when <guard> =>
      delay <interval>;
      <statements>
or
   when <guard> =>
      terminate;
else
   <statements>
end select;
```

```
select
   <entry call>;
   <statements>
or
   delay <interval>;
   <statements>
end select;

select
   <entry call>;
   <statements>
else
   <statements>
end select;

select
   <triggering alternative>
then abort
   <abortable part>
end select;
```

The accept statement:

```
accept <specification> do
   <statements>
end <name>;
```

```
separate (<parent unit>)
<proper body>
```

A subunit:

```
separate (<parent unit>)
<proper body>
end <name>;
```

Proper bodies of program units:

```
procedure <specification> is         package body <name> is
   <declarations>                        <declarations>
begin                                 begin
   <statements>                          <statements>
exception                             exception
   when <choice> =>                      when <choice> =>
      <statements>                          <statements>
end <name>;                           end <name>;

function <specification>              task body <name> is
   return <type name> is                 <declarations>
   <declarations>                     begin
begin                                    <statements>
   <statements>                       exception
exception                                when <choice> =>
   when <choice> =>                         <statements>
      <statements>                    end <name>;
end <name>;
```

Context clauses on compilation units are arranged as a table. Generic formal parameters do not obscure the
unit itself. Function, package, and task specifications use standard indentation:

```
with <name>; use <name>;              function <specification>
with <name>;                             return <type>;
with <name>;
                                      package <name> is
                                         <declarations>
                                      private
<compilation unit>                       <declarations>
                                      end <name>;

generic                               task type <name> is
   <formal parameters>                   <entry declarations>
<compilation unit>                    end <name>;
```

Instantiations of generic units and record indentation:

```
procedure <name> is                   type ... is
   new <generic name> <actuals>          record
                                            <component list>
function <name> is                          case <discriminant name> is
   new <generic name> <actuals>                when <choice> =>
                                                   <component list>
package <name> is                              when <choice> =>
   new <generic name> <actuals>                   <component list>
                                            end case;
                                         end record;
```

Indentation for record alignment:

```
for <name> use
   record <mod clause>
      <component clause>
   end record;
```

Tagged types and type extension:

```
type ... is tagged
   record
      <component list>
   end record;

type ... is new ... with
   record
      <component list>
   end record;
```

example

```
Default_String : constant String :=
      "This is the long string returned by" &
      " default.  It is broken into multiple" &
      " Ada source lines for convenience.";
```

```
if Input_Found then
   Count_Characters;

else  --not Input_Found
   Reset_State;
   Character_Total :=
      First_Part_Total  * First_Part_Scale_Factor  +
      Second_Part_Total * Second_Part_Scale_Factor +
      Default_String'Length + Delimiter_Size;
end if;

end loop;
```

rationale

Indentation improves the readability of the code because it gives you a visual indicator of the program structure. The levels of nesting are clearly identified by indentation, and the first and last keywords in a construct can be matched visually.

While there is much discussion on the number of spaces to indent, the reason for indentation is code clarity. The fact that the code is indented consistently is more important than the number of spaces used for indentation.

Additionally, the Ada Reference Manual (1995, §1.1.4) states that the layout shown in the examples and syntax rules in the manual is the recommended code layout to be used for Ada programs: "The syntax rules describing structured constructs are presented in a form that corresponds to the recommended paragraphing .... Different lines are used for parts of a syntax rule if the corresponding parts of the construct described by the rule are intended to be on different lines .... It is recommended that all indentation be by multiples of a basic step of indentation (the number of spaces for the basic step is not defined)."

It is important to indent continuation lines differently from nested control structures to make them visually distinct. This prevents them from obscuring the structure of the code as you scan it.

Listing context clauses on individual lines allows easier maintenance; changing a context clause is less error-prone.

Indenting with spaces is more portable than indenting with tabs because tab characters are displayed differently by different terminals and printers.

exceptions

If you are using a variable width font, tabs will align better than spaces. However, depending on your tab setting, lines of successive indentation may leave you with a very short line length.

automation notes

The guidelines in this section are easily enforced with an automatic code formatter.

2.1.3   Alignment of Operators

guideline

* Align operators vertically to emphasize local program structure and semantics.

example

```
if Slot_A >= Slot_B then
   Temporary := Slot_A;
   Slot_A    := Slot_B;
   Slot_B    := Temporary;
end if;

-----------------------------------------------------------------
Numerator   := B**2 - 4.0 * A * C;
Denominator := 2.0 * A;

Solution_1 := (B + Square_Root(Numerator)) / Denominator;
Solution_2 := (B - Square_Root(Numerator)) / Denominator;
-----------------------------------------------------------------

X := A * B +
     C * D +
     E * F;

Y := (A * B + C) +  (2.0 * D - E) -  -- basic equation
     3.5;                            -- account for error factor
```

rationale

−   Alignment makes it easier to see the position of the operators and, therefore, puts visual emphasis on what the code is doing.

    The use of lines and spacing on long expressions can emphasize terms, precedence of operators, and other semantics. It can also leave room for highlighting comments within an expression.

exceptions

If vertical alignment of operators forces a statement to be broken over two lines, especially if the break is at an inappropriate spot, it may be preferable to relax the alignment guideline.

automation notes

The last example above shows a kind of "semantic alignment" that is not typically enforced or even preserved by automatic code formatters. If you break expressions into semantic parts and put each on a separate line, beware of using a code formatter later. It is likely to move the entire expression to a single line and accumulate all the comments at the end. However, there are some formatters that are intelligent enough to leave a line break intact when the line contains a comment. A good formatter will recognize that the last example above does not violate the guidelines and would, therefore, preserve it as written.

2.1.4   Alignment of Declarations

guideline

*   Use vertical alignment to enhance the readability of declarations.
*   Provide, at most, one declaration per line.
*   Indent all declarations in a single declarative part at the same level.

instantiation

For declarations not separated by blank lines, follow these alignment rules:

-   Align the colon delimiters.
-   Align the := initialization delimiter.
-   When trailing comments are used, align the comment delimiter.
-   When the declaration overflows a line, break the line and add an indentation level for those lines that wrap. The preferred places to break, in order, are: (1) the comment delimiter; (2) the initialization delimiter; (3) the colon delimiter.
-   For enumeration type declarations that do not fit on a single line, put each literal on a separate line, using the next level of indentation. When appropriate, semantically related literals can be arranged by row or column to form a table.

example

Variable and constant declarations can be laid out in a tabular format with columns separated by the symbols :, :=, and --

```
Prompt_Column  : constant         := 40;
Question_Mark  : constant String := " ? "; -- prompt on error input
Prompt_String  : constant String := " ==> ";
```

If this results in lines that are too long, they can be laid out with each part on a separate line with its unique indentation level:

```
subtype User_Response_Text_Frame is String (1 .. 72);

-- If the declaration needed a comment, it would fit here.
Input_Line_Buffer : User_Response_Text_Frame
        := Prompt_String &
           String'(1 .. User_Response_Text_Frame'Length -
                        Prompt_String'Length => ' ');
```

Declarations of enumeration literals can be listed in one or more columns as:

```
type Op_Codes_In_Column is
      (Push,
       Pop,
       Add,
       Subtract,
       Multiply,
       Divide,
       Subroutine_Call,
       Subroutine_Return,
       Branch,
       Branch_On_Zero,
       Branch_On_Negative);
```

or, to save space:

```
type Op_Codes_Multiple_Columns is
      (Push,            Pop,               Add,
       Subtract,        Multiply,          Divide,
       Subroutine_Call, Subroutine_Return, Branch,
       Branch_On_Zero,  Branch_On_Negative);
```

or, to emphasize related groups of values:

```
type Op_Codes_In_Table is
      (Push,            Pop,
       Add,             Subtract,          Multiply,       Divide,
       Subroutine_Call, Subroutine_Return,
       Branch,          Branch_On_Zero,    Branch_On_Negative);
```

rationale

Many programming standards documents require tabular repetition of names, types, initial values, and meaning in unit header comments. These comments are redundant and can become inconsistent with the code. Aligning the declarations themselves in tabular fashion (see the examples above) provides identical information to both compiler and reader; enforces, at most, one declaration per line; and eases maintenance by providing space for initializations and necessary comments. A tabular layout enhances readability, thus preventing names from "hiding" in a mass of declarations. This applies to all declarations: types, subtypes, objects, exceptions, named numbers, and so forth.

automation notes

Most of the guidelines in this section are easily enforced with an automatic code formatter. The one exception is the last enumerated type example, which is laid out in rows based on the semantics of the enumeration literals. An automatic code formatter will not be able to do this and will likely move the enumeration literals to different lines. However, tools that are checking only for violations of the guidelines should accept the tabular form of an enumeration type declaration.

2.1.5   More on Alignment

guideline

- Align parameter modes and parentheses vertically.

instantiation

Specifically, it is recommended that you:

- Place one formal parameter specification per line.

- Vertically align parameter names, colons, the reserved word in, the reserved word out, and parameter subtypes.

- Place the first parameter specification on the same line as the subprogram or entry name. If any parameter subtypes are forced beyond the line length limit, place the first parameter specification on a new line indented the same as a continuation line.

example

```
procedure Display_Menu (Title   : in     String;
                        Options : in     Menus;
                        Choice  :    out Alpha_Numerics);
```

The following two examples show alternate instantiations of this guideline:

```
procedure Display_Menu_On_Primary_Window
      (Title    : in     String;
       Options  : in     Menus;
       Choice   :    out Alpha_Numerics);
```

or:

```
procedure Display_Menu_On_Screen (
      Title    : in     String;
      Options  : in     Menus;
      Choice   :    out Alpha_Numerics
    );
```

Aligning parentheses makes complicated relational expressions more clear:

```
if not (First_Character in Alpha_Numerics and then
        Valid_Option(First_Character))          then
```

rationale

This alignment facilitates readability and understandability, and it is easy to achieve given automated support. Aligning parameter modes provides the effect of a table with columns for parameter name, mode, subtype, and, if necessary, parameter-specific comments. Vertical alignment of parameters across subprograms within a compilation unit increases the readability even more.

notes

Various options are available for subprogram layout. The second example above aligns all of the subprogram names and parameter names in a program. This has the disadvantage of occupying an unnecessary line where subprogram names are short and looking awkward if there is only one parameter.

The third example is a format commonly used to reduce the amount of editing required when parameter lines are added, deleted, or reordered. The parentheses do not have to be moved from line to line. However, the last parameter line is the only one without a semicolon.

exceptions

When an operator function has two or more formal parameters of the same type, it is more readable to declare the parameters in a single one-line list rather than to separate the formal parameter list into multiple formal parameter specifications.

```
type Color_Scheme is (Red, Purple, Blue, Green, Yellow, White, Black, Brown, Gray, Pink);
function "&" (Left, Right : Color_Scheme) return Color_Scheme;
```

automation notes

Most of the guidelines in this section are easily enforced with an automatic code formatter. The one exception is the last example, which shows vertical alignment of parentheses to emphasize terms of an expression. This is difficult to achieve with an automatic code formatter unless the relevant terms of the expression can be determined strictly through operator precedence.

2.1.6   Blank Lines

guideline

- Use blank lines to group logically related lines of text (NASA 1987).

example

```
if ... then

   for ... loop
      ...
   end loop;

end if;
```

This example separates different kinds of declarations with blank lines:

```
type Employee_Record is
   record
      Legal_Name     : Name;
      Date_Of_Birth  : Date;
      Date_Of_Hire   : Date;
      Salary         : Money;
   end record;
```

```
type Day is
     (Monday,    Tuesday,    Wednesday, Thursday,  Friday,
      Saturday,  Sunday);

subtype Weekday is Day range Monday   .. Friday;
subtype Weekend is Day range Saturday .. Sunday;
```

rationale

When blank lines are used in a thoughtful and consistent manner, sections of related code are more visible to readers.

automation notes

Automatic formatters do not enforce this guideline well because the decision on where to insert blank lines is a semantic one. However, many formatters have the ability to leave existing blank lines intact. Thus, you can manually insert the lines and not lose the effect when you run such a formatter.

2.1.7   Pagination

guideline

- Highlight the top of each package or task specification, the top of each program unit body, and the end statement of each program unit.

instantiation

Specifically, it is recommended that you:

- Use file prologues, specification headers, and body headers to highlight those structures as recommended in Guideline 3.3.

- Use a line of dashes, beginning at the same column as the current indentation to highlight the definition of nested units embedded in a declarative part. Insert the line of dashes immediately before and immediately after the definition.

- If two dashed lines are adjacent, omit the longer of the two.

example

```
with Basic_Types;

package body SPC_Numeric_Types is

   ...

   -------------------------------------------------------------------
   function Max
        (Left  : in      Basic_Types.Tiny_Integer;
         Right : in      Basic_Types.Tiny_Integer)
         return Basic_Types.Tiny_Integer is
   begin
      if Right < Left then
         return Left;
      else
         return Right;
      end if;
   end Max;

   -------------------------------------------------------------------
   function Min
        (Left  : in      Basic_Types.Tiny_Integer;
         Right : in      Basic_Types.Tiny_Integer)
         return Basic_Types.Tiny_Integer is
   begin
      if Left < Right then
         return Left;
      else
         return Right;
      end if;
   end Min;

   -------------------------------------------------------------------
   use Basic_Types;
```

```
begin  -- SPC_Numeric_Types
   Max_Tiny_Integer := Min(System_Max, Local_Max);
   Min_Tiny_Integer := Max(System_Min, Local_Min);
   -- ...
end SPC_Numeric_Types;
```

rationale

It is easy to overlook parts of program units that are not visible on the current page or screen. The page lengths of presentation hardware and software vary widely. By clearly marking the program's logical page boundaries (e.g., with a dashed line), you enable a reader to quickly check whether all of a program unit is visible. Such pagination also makes it easier to scan a large file quickly, looking for a particular program unit.

notes

This guideline does not address code layout on the physical "page" because the dimensions of such pages vary widely and no single guideline is appropriate.

automation notes

The guidelines in this section are easily enforced with an automatic code formatter.

2.1.8   Number of Statements Per Line

guideline

- Start each statement on a new line.
- Write no more than one simple statement per line.
- Break compound statements over multiple lines.

example

Use:

```
if End_Of_File then
   Close_File;
else
   Get_Next_Record;
end if;
```

rather than:

```
if End_Of_File then Close_File; else Get_Next_Record; end if;
```

exceptional case:

```
Put("A=");      Natural_IO.Put(A);      New_Line;
Put("B=");      Natural_IO.Put(B);      New_Line;
Put("C=");      Natural_IO.Put(C);      New_Line;
```

rationale

A single statement on each line enhances the reader's ability to find statements and helps prevent statements being missed. Similarly, the structure of a compound statement is clearer when its parts are on separate lines.

notes

If a statement is longer than the remaining space on the line, continue it on the next line. This guideline includes declarations, context clauses, and subprogram parameters.

According to the Ada Reference Manual (1995, §1.1.4), "The preferred places for other line breaks are after semicolons."

automation notes

The guidelines in this section are easily enforced with an automatic code formatter, with the single exception of the last example, which shows a semantic grouping of multiple statements onto a single line.

exceptions

The example of Put and New_Line statements shows a legitimate exception. This grouping of closely related statements on the same line makes the structural relationship between the groups clear.

2.1.9   Source Code Line Length

guideline

- Adhere to a maximum line length limit for source code (Nissen and Wallis 1984, §2.3).

instantiation

Specifically, it is recommended that you:

- Limit source code line lengths to a maximum of 72 characters.

rationale

When Ada code is ported from one system to another, there may be restrictions on the record size of source line statements, possibly for one of the following reasons: some operating systems may not support variable length records for tape I/O, or some printers and terminals support an 80-character line width with no line-wrap. See further rationale in the note for Guideline 7.1.2.

Source code must sometimes be published for various reasons, and letter-size paper is not as forgiving as a computer listing in terms of the number of usable columns.

In addition, there are human limitations in the width of the field of view for understanding at the level required for reading source code. These limitations correspond roughly to the 70- to 80-column range.

notes

An alternate instantiation is to limit source code length to 79 characters. The 79-character limit differentiates the code from the FORTRAN 72-character limit. It also avoids problems with 80-character width terminals where the character in the last column may not print correctly.

automation notes

The guidelines in this section are easily enforced with an automatic code formatter.

2.2   SUMMARY

code formatting

- Use consistent spacing around delimiters.
- Use the same spacing as you would in regular prose.
- Indent and align nested control structures, continuation lines, and embedded units consistently.
- Distinguish between indentation for nested control structures and for continuation lines.
- Use spaces for indentation, not the tab character (Nissen and Wallis 1984, §2.2).
- Align operators vertically to emphasize local program structure and semantics.
- Use vertical alignment to enhance the readability of declarations.
- Provide, at most, one declaration per line.
- Indent all declarations in a single declarative part at the same level.
- Align parameter modes and parentheses vertically.
- Use blank lines to group logically related lines of text (NASA 1987).
- Highlight the top of each package or task specification, the top of each program unit body, and the end statement of each program unit.
- Start each statement on a new line.
- Write no more than one simple statement per line.
- Break compound statements over multiple lines.
- Adhere to a maximum line length limit for source code (Nissen and Wallis 1984, §2.3).

CHAPTER 3
Readability

This chapter recommends ways of using Ada features to make reading and understanding code easier. There are many myths about comments and readability. The responsibility for true readability rests more with naming and code structure than with comments. Having as many comment lines as code lines does not imply readability; it more likely indicates the writer does not understand what is important to communicate.

3.1 SPELLING

Spelling conventions in source code include rules for capitalization and use of underscores, numbers, and abbreviations. If you follow these conventions consistently, the resulting code is clearer and more readable.

3.1.1 Use of Underscores

guideline

- Use underscores to separate words in a compound name.

example

```
Miles_Per_Hour
Entry_Value
```

rationale

When an identifier consists of more than one word, it is much easier to read if the words are separated by underscores. Indeed, there is precedent in English in which compound words are separated by a hyphen or a space. In addition to promoting readability of the code, if underscores are used in names, a code formatter has more control over altering capitalization. See Guideline 3.1.3.

3.1.2 Numbers

guideline

- Represent numbers in a consistent fashion.
- Represent literals in a radix appropriate to the problem.
- Use underscores to separate digits the same way commas or periods (or spaces for nondecimal bases) would be used in normal text.
- When using scientific notation, make the E consistently either uppercase or lowercase.
- In an alternate base, represent the alphabetic characters in either all uppercase or all lowercase.

instantiation

- Decimal and octal numbers are grouped by threes beginning on the left side of the radix point and by fives beginning on the right side of the radix point.
- The E is always capitalized in scientific notation.

- Use uppercase for the alphabetic characters representing digits in bases above 10.
- Hexadecimal numbers are grouped by fours beginning on either side of the radix point.

example

```
type Maximum_Samples     is range            1 ..  1_000_000;
type Legal_Hex_Address   is range    16#0000# ..    16#FFFF#;
type Legal_Octal_Address is range 8#000_000# .. 8#777_777#;

Avogadro_Number : constant := 6.02216_9E+23;
```

To represent the number 1/3 as a constant, use:

```
One_Third : constant := 1.0 / 3.0;
```

Avoid this use:

```
One_Third_As_Decimal_Approximation : constant := 0.33333_33333_3333;
```

or:

```
One_Third_Base_3 : constant := 3#0.1#;
```

rationale

Consistent use of uppercase or lowercase aids scanning for numbers. Underscores serve to group portions of numbers into familiar patterns. Consistency with common use in everyday contexts is a large part of readability.

notes

If a rational fraction is represented in a base in which it has a terminating rather than a repeating representation, as 3#0.1# does in the example above, it may have increased accuracy upon conversion to the machine base.

3.1.3   Capitalization

guideline

- Make reserved words and other elements of the program visually distinct from each other.

instantiation

- Use lowercase for all reserved words (when used as reserved words).
- Use mixed case for all other identifiers, a capital letter beginning every word separated by underscores.
- Use uppercase for abbreviations and acronyms (see automation notes).

example

```
...

type Second_Of_Day     is range 0 .. 86_400;
type Noon_Relative_Time is (Before_Noon, After_Noon, High_Noon);

subtype Morning   is Second_Of_Day range 0 .. 86_400 / 2 - 1;
subtype Afternoon is Second_Of_Day range Morning'Last + 2 .. 86_400;

...

Current_Time := Second_Of_Day(Calendar.Seconds(Calendar.Clock));

if Current_Time in Morning then
   Time_Of_Day := Before_Noon;
elsif Current_Time in Afternoon then
   Time_Of_Day := After_Noon;
else
   Time_Of_Day := High_Noon;
end if;

case Time_Of_Day is
   when Before_Noon =>   Get_Ready_For_Lunch;
   when High_Noon   =>   Eat_Lunch;
   when After_Noon  =>   Get_To_Work;
end case;

...
```

rationale

Visually distinguishing reserved words allows you to focus on program structure alone, if desired, and also aids scanning for particular identifiers.

The instantiation chosen here is meant to be more readable for the experienced Ada programmer, who does not need reserved words to leap off the page. Beginners to any language often find that reserved words should be emphasized to help them find the control structures more easily. Because of this, instructors in the classroom and books introducing the Ada language may want to consider an alternative instantiation. The Ada Reference Manual (1995) chose bold lowercase for all reserved words.

automation notes

Ada names are not case sensitive. Therefore, the names `max_limit`, `MAX_LIMIT`, and `Max_Limit` denote the same object or entity. A good code formatter should be able to automatically convert from one style to another as long as the words are delimited by underscores.

As recommended in Guideline 3.1.4, abbreviations should be project-wide. An automated tool should allow a project to specify those abbreviations and format them accordingly.

3.1.4   Abbreviations

guideline

- Do not use an abbreviation of a long word as an identifier where a shorter synonym exists.
- Use a consistent abbreviation strategy.
- Do not use ambiguous abbreviations.
- To justify its use, an abbreviation must save many characters over the full word.
- Use abbreviations that are well-accepted in the application domain.
- Maintain a list of accepted abbreviations, and use only abbreviations on that list.

example

Use:

```
Time_Of_Receipt
```

rather than:

```
Recd_Time or R_Time
```

But in an application that commonly deals with message formats that meet military standards, `DOD_STD_MSG_FMT` is an acceptable abbreviation for:

```
Department_Of_Defense_Standard_Message_Format.
```

rationale

Many abbreviations are ambiguous or unintelligible unless taken in context. As an example, `Temp` could indicate either temporary or temperature. For this reason, you should choose abbreviations carefully when you use them. The rationale in Guideline 8.1.2 provides a more thorough discussion of how context should influence the use of abbreviations.

Because very long variable names can obscure the structure of the program, especially in deeply nested (indented) control structures, it is a good idea to try to keep identifiers short and meaningful. Use short unabbreviated names whenever possible. If there is no short word that will serve as an identifier, then a well-known unambiguous abbreviation is the next best choice, especially if it comes from a list of standard abbreviations used throughout the project.

You can establish an abbreviated format for a fully qualified name using the `renames` clause. This capability is useful when a very long, fully qualified name would otherwise occur many times in a localized section of code (see Guideline 5.7.2).

A list of accepted abbreviations for a project provides a standard context for using each abbreviation.

3.2   NAMING CONVENTIONS

Choose names that clarify the object's or entity's intended use. Ada allows identifiers to be any length as long as the identifier fits on a line with all characters being significant (including underscores). Identifiers are the names used for variables, constants, program units, and other entities within a program.

3.2.1   Names

guideline

- Choose names that are as self-documenting as possible.
- Use a short synonym instead of an abbreviation (see Guideline 3.1.4).
- Use names given by the application, but do not use obscure jargon.
- Avoid using the same name to declare different kinds of identifiers.

example

In a tree-walker, using the name `Left` instead of `Left_Branch` is sufficient to convey the full meaning given the context. However, use `Time_Of_Day` instead of `TOD`.

Mathematical formulas are often given using single-letter names for variables. Continue this convention for mathematical equations where they would recall the formula, for example:

```
A*(X**2) + B*X + C.
```

With the use of child packages, a poor choice of package, subunit, and identifier names can lead to a visibility clash with subunits. See the Rationale (1995, §8.1) for a sample of the resulting, rather obscure code.

rationale

A program that follows these guidelines can be more easily comprehended. Self-documenting names require fewer explanatory comments. Empirical studies have shown that you can further improve comprehension if your variable names are not excessively long (Schneiderman 1986, 7). The context and application can help greatly. The unit of measure for numeric entities can be a source of subtype names.

You should try not to use the same name as an identifier for different declarations, such as an object and a child package. Overusing an identifier in seemingly different name spaces can, in fact, lead to visibility clashes if the enclosing program units are intended to work together.

notes

See Guideline 8.1.2 for a discussion on how to use the application domain as a guideline for selecting abbreviations.

3.2.2   Subtype Names

guideline

- Use singular, general nouns as subtype identifiers.
- Choose identifiers that describe one of the subtype's values.
- Consider using suffixes for subtype identifiers that define visible access types, visible subranges, or visible array types.
- For private types, do not use identifier constructions (e.g., suffixes) that are unique to subtype identifiers.
- Do not use the subtype names from predefined packages.

example

```
type Day is
    (Monday,    Tuesday,    Wednesday, Thursday,  Friday,
     Saturday,  Sunday);

type Day_Of_Month   is range    0 ..    31;
type Month_Number   is range    1 ..    12;
type Historical_Year is range -6_000 .. 2_500;
```

```
type Date is
   record
      Day    : Day_Of_Month;
      Month  : Month_Number;
      Year   : Historical_Year;
   end record;
```

In particular, Day should be used in preference to Days or Day_Type.

The identifier Historical_Year might appear to be specific, but it is actually general, with the adjective historical describing the range constraint:

```
-------------------------------------------------------------------------
procedure Disk_Driver is

   -- In this procedure, a number of important disk parameters are
   -- linked.
   Number_Of_Sectors  : constant :=      4;
   Number_Of_Tracks   : constant :=    200;
   Number_Of_Surfaces : constant :=     18;
   Sector_Capacity    : constant := 4_096;

   Track_Capacity   : constant := Number_Of_Sectors  * Sector_Capacity;
   Surface_Capacity : constant := Number_Of_Tracks   * Track_Capacity;
   Disk_Capacity    : constant := Number_Of_Surfaces * Surface_Capacity;

   type Sector_Range  is range 1 .. Number_Of_Sectors;
   type Track_Range   is range 1 .. Number_Of_Tracks;
   type Surface_Range is range 1 .. Number_Of_Surfaces;

   type Track_Map   is array (Sector_Range)  of ...;
   type Surface_Map is array (Track_Range)   of Track_Map;
   type Disk_Map    is array (Surface_Range) of Surface_Map;

begin   -- Disk_Driver
   ...
end Disk_Driver;
-------------------------------------------------------------------------
```

The suffixes _Capacity, _Range, and_Map help define the purpose of the above subtypes and avoid the search for synonyms for the sector, track, and surface abstractions. Without the suffixes, you would need three different names per abstraction, one to describe each of the concepts succinctly named in the suffix. This recommendation only applies to certain visible subtypes. Private types, for example, should be given a good name that reflects the abstraction being represented.

rationale

When this style and the suggested style for object identifiers are used, program code more closely resembles English (see Guideline 3.2.3). Furthermore, this style is consistent with the names of the language's predefined identifiers. They are not named Integers, Booleans, Integer_Type, or Boolean_Type.

However, using the name of a subtype from the predefined packages is sure to confuse a programmer when that subtype appears somewhere without a package qualification.

notes

This style guide tries to be consistent with the Ada Reference Manual (1995) in use of the terms "type" and "subtype name." In general, a "type" refers to the abstract concept, as in a type declaration, while the "subtype" refers to the name given to that abstract concept in an actual declaration. Thus, what was called a type name in Ada 83 (Ada Reference Manual 1983) is now called a subtype name.

3.2.3   Object Names

guideline

- Use predicate clauses or adjectives for Boolean objects.
- Use singular, specific nouns as object identifiers.
- Choose identifiers that describe the object's value during execution.
- Use singular, general nouns as identifiers for record components.

example

Non-Boolean objects:

```
Today            : Day;
Yesterday        : Day;
Retirement_Date : Date;
```

Boolean objects:

```
User_Is_Available : Boolean;    -- predicate clause
List_Is_Empty     : Boolean;    -- predicate clause
Empty             : Boolean;    -- adjective
Bright            : Boolean;    -- adjective
```

rationale

Using specific nouns for objects establishes a context for understanding the object's value, which is one of the general values described by the subtype's name (see Guideline 3.2.2). Object declarations become very English-like with this style. For example, the first declaration above is read as "Today is a Day."

General nouns, rather than specific, are used for record components because a record object's name will supply the context for understanding the component. Thus, the following component is understood as "the year of retirement":

```
Retirement_Date.Year
```

Following conventions that relate object types and parts of speech makes code read more like text. For example, because of the names chosen, the following code segment needs no comments:

```
if List_Is_Empty then
    Number_Of_Elements := 0;
else
    Number_Of_Elements := Length_Of_List;
end if;
```

notes

If it is difficult to find a specific noun that describes an object's value during the entire execution of a program, the object is probably serving multiple purposes. Multiple objects should be used in such a case.

3.2.4   Naming of Tagged Types and Associated Packages

guideline

- Use a consistent naming convention for tagged types and associated packages.

instantiation

Naming conventions spark "religious wars"; therefore, two different instantiations are presented. The first instantiation integrates the use of object-oriented features. Except for two special cases, it applies the same naming conventions to declarations, independent of whether they use an object-oriented feature:

- Name tagged types no differently than subtype names (see Guideline 3.2.2).
- Use the prefix Abstract_ for packages that export an abstraction for which you intend to provide multiple implementations (see Guideline 9.2.4).
- Use the suffix _Mixin for packages that provide units of functionality that can be "mixed in" to core abstractions.

The second instantiation highlights the use of object-oriented features through special names or suffixes:

- Name class packages after the object they represent, without a suffix (Rosen 1995).
- Name mixin packages after the facet they represent, appending the suffix _Facet (Rosen 1995).
- Name the main tagged type Instance (Rosen 1995).
- Follow the declaration of the specific type with a subtype named Class for the corresponding class-wide type (Rosen 1995).

example

The following two-part example from the Rationale (1995, §§4.4.4 and 4.6.2) applies the naming conventions of the first instantiation.

For the first part of this example, assume the type Set_Element was declared elsewhere:

```
package Abstract_Sets is

    type Set is abstract tagged private;
```

```
      -- empty set
      function Empty return Set is abstract;

      -- build set with 1 element
      function Unit (Element: Set_Element) return Set is abstract;

      -- union of two sets
      function Union (Left, Right: Set) return Set is abstract;

      -- intersection of two sets
      function Intersection (Left, Right: Set) return Set is abstract;

      -- remove an element from a set
      procedure Take (From     : in out Set;
                      Element :    out set_Element) is abstract;

   Element_Too_Large : exception;
private
   type Set is abstract tagged null record;
end Abstract_Sets;

with Abstract_Sets;
package Bit_Vector_Sets is    -- one implementation of set abstraction

   type Bit_Set is new Abstract_Sets.Set with private;
   ...
private
   Bit_Set_Size : constant := 64;
   type Bit_Vector is ...
   type Bit_Set is new Abstract_Sets.Set with
      record
         Data : Bit_Vector;
      end record;
end Bit_Vector_Sets;

with Abstract_Sets;
package Sparse_Sets  -- alternate implementation of set abstraction

   type Sparse_Set is new Abstract_Sets.Set with private;
   ...
private
   ...
end Bit_Vector_Sets;
```

The second part of this example applies the naming convention to mixin packages that support a windowing system:

```
   -- assume you have type Basic_Window is tagged limited private;

generic
   type Some_Window is abstract new Basic_Window with private;
package Label_Mixin is
   type Window_With_Label is abstract new Some_Window with private;
   ...
private
   ...
end Label_Mixin;

generic
   type Some_Window is abstract new Basic_Window with private;
package Border_Mixin is
   type Window_With_Label is abstract new Some_Window with private;
   ...
private
   ...
end Border_Mixin;
```

The following example applies the naming conventions of the second instantiation, as discussed in Rosen (1995):

```
package Shape is
   subtype Side_Count is range 0 .. 100;
   type Instance (Sides: Side_Count) is tagged private;
   subtype Class is Instance'Class;
   . . .
   -- operations on Shape.Instance
private
   . . .
end Shape;
```

```
with Shape; use Shape;
package Line is
    type Instance is new Shape.Instance with private;
    subtype Class is Instance'Class;
      . . .
    -- Overridden or new operations
private
    . . .
end Line;

with Shape; use Shape;
generic
    type Origin is new Shape.Instance;
package With_Color_Facet is
    type Instance is new Origin with private;
    subtype Class is Instance'Class;
    -- operations for colored shapes
private
    . . .
end With_Color_Facet;

with Line; use Line;
with With_Color_Facet;
package Colored_Line is new With_Color_Facet (Line.Instance);
```

Sample declarations might look like:

```
Red_Line : Colored_Line.Instance;

procedure Draw (What : Shape.Instance);
```

The above scheme works whether you use full names or a use clause. As long as you use the same name for all the specific types (i.e., type Instance) and class-wide types, the unqualified names will always hide one another. Thus, the compiler will insist you use full name qualification to resolve the ambiguity introduced by the use clause (Rosen 1995).

rationale

You want to use a naming scheme that is consistent and readable and conveys the intent of the abstraction. Ideally, the naming scheme should be uniform in how it handles the different ways in which tagged types are used to create classes. If the naming convention is too rigid, however, you will write code fragments that appear stilted from a readability point of view. By using a similar naming convention for type extension through derivation and through generic mixin (see also Guideline 9.5.1), you achieve readable declarations of objects and procedures.

notes

A naming convention for classes draws a hard line between object-oriented abstractions and other kinds of abstractions. Given that engineers have been defining abstract data types in Ada 83 (Ada Reference Manual 1983) for over 10 years, you may not want to change the naming convention just for the sake of using type extension with a type. You must consider how important it is to call out uses of inheritance in the overall use of abstractions in your program. If you prefer to emphasize abstraction, in general, over the mechanism used to implement the abstraction (i.e., inheritance, type-extension, and polymorphism), you may not want to impose such a stringent naming convention. You do not hamper quality by favoring a smoother transition in naming conventions from abstractions developed without inheritance to those developed with inheritance.

If you choose a naming convention that highlights the use of object-oriented features and later decide to change the declaration to one that does not use an object-oriented feature, the change may be expensive. You must naturally change all occurrences of the names and must be careful not to introduce errors as you update the names. If you choose a naming convention that prohibits the use of suffixes or prefixes to characterize the declaration, you lose the opportunity to convey the intended usage of the declared item.

3.2.5   Program Unit Names

guideline

- Use action verbs for procedures and entries.
- Use predicate clauses for Boolean functions.
- Use nouns for non-Boolean functions.

- Give packages names that imply a higher level of organization than subprograms. Generally, these are noun phrases that describe the abstraction provided.
- Give tasks names that imply an active entity.
- Use nouns descriptive of the data being protected for protected units.
- Consider naming generic subprograms as if they were nongeneric subprograms.
- Consider naming generic packages as if they were nongeneric packages.
- Make the generic names more general than the instantiated names.

example

The following are sample names for elements that compose an Ada program:

Sample procedure names:

```
procedure Get_Next_Token        -- get is a transitive verb
procedure Create                -- create is a transitive verb
```

Sample function names for Boolean-valued functions:

```
function Is_Last_Item           -- predicate clause
function Is_Empty               -- predicate clause
```

Sample function names for non-Boolean-valued functions:

```
function Successor              -- common noun
function Length                 -- attribute
function Top                    -- component
```

Sample package names:

```
package Terminals is            -- common noun
package Text_Routines is        -- common noun
```

Sample protected objects:

```
protected Current_Location is   -- data being protected
protected type Guardian is      -- noun implying protection
```

Sample task names:

```
task Terminal_Resource_Manager is  -- common noun that shows action
```

The following sample piece of code shows the clarity that results from using the parts-of-speech naming conventions:

```
Get_Next_Token(Current_Token);

case Current_Token is
   when Identifier =>        Process_Identifier;
   when Numeric    =>        Process_Numeric;
end case;  -- Current_Token

if Is_Empty(Current_List) then
   Number_Of_Elements := 0;
else
   Number_Of_Elements := Length(Current_List);
end if;
```

When packages and their subprograms are named together, the resulting code is very descriptive:

```
if Stack.Is_Empty(Current_List) then
   Current_Token := Stack.Top(Current_List);
end if;
```

rationale

Using these naming conventions creates understandable code that reads much like natural language. When verbs are used for actions, such as subprograms, and nouns are used for objects, such as the data that the subprogram manipulates, code is easier to read and understand. This models a medium of communication already familiar to a reader. Where the pieces of a program model a real-life situation, using these conventions reduces the number of translation steps involved in reading and understanding the program. In a sense, your choice of names reflects the level of abstraction from computer hardware toward application requirements.

See also Guideline 3.2.4 for the use of special-purpose suffixes in packages associated with tagged types.

notes

There are some conflicting conventions in current use for task entries. Some programmers and designers advocate naming task entries with the same conventions used for subprograms to blur the fact that a task is involved. Their reasoning is that if the task is reimplemented as a package, or vice versa, the names need not change. Others prefer to make the fact of a task entry as explicit as possible to ensure that the existence of a task with its presumed overhead is recognizable. Project-specific priorities may be useful in choosing between these conventions.

3.2.6   Constants and Named Numbers

guideline

- Use symbolic values instead of literals, wherever possible.
- Use the predefined constants `Ada.Numerics.Pi` and `Ada.Numerics.e` for the mathematical constants `Pi` and `e`.
- Use constants instead of variables for constant values.
- Use a constant when the value is specific to a type or when the value must be static.
- Use named numbers instead of constants, whenever possible.
- Use named numbers to replace numeric literals whose type or context is truly universal.
- Use constants for objects whose values cannot change after elaboration (United Technologies 1987).
- Show relationships between symbolic values by defining them with static expressions.
- Use linearly independent sets of literals.
- Use attributes like `'First` and `'Last` instead of literals, wherever possible.

example

```
3.14159_26535_89793                             -- literal
Max_Entries : constant Integer        := 400;   -- constant
Avogadros_Number  : constant := 6.022137 * 10**23;  -- named number
Avogadros_Number / 2                            -- static expression
Avogadros_Number                                -- symbolic value
```

Declaring `Pi` as a named number (assuming a `with` clause for the predefined package `Ada.Numerics` in the Ada Reference Manual [1995, §A.5] allows it to be referenced symbolically in the assignment statement below:

```
Area :=      Pi * Radius**2;     -- if radius is known.
```

instead of:

```
Area := 3.14159 * Radius**2;     -- Needs explanatory comment.
```

Also, `Ada.Characters.Latin_1.Bel` is more expressive than `Character'Val(8#007#)`.

Clarity of constant and named number declarations can be improved by using other constant and named numbers. For example:

```
Bytes_Per_Page    : constant := 512;
Pages_Per_Buffer  : constant := 10;
Buffer_Size       : constant := Pages_Per_Buffer * Bytes_Per_Page;
```

is more self-explanatory and easier to maintain than:

```
Buffer_Size : constant := 5_120;   -- ten pages
```

The following literals should be constants:

```
if New_Character  = '$' then  -- "constant" that may change
...
if Current_Column = 7 then    -- "constant" that may change
```

rationale

Using identifiers instead of literals makes the purpose of expressions clear, reducing the need for comments. Constant declarations consisting of expressions of numeric literals are safer because they do not need to be computed by hand. They are also more enlightening than a single numeric literal because there is more opportunity for embedding explanatory names. Clarity of constant declarations can be improved further by using other related constants in static expressions defining new constants. This is not less efficient because static expressions of named numbers are computed at compile time.

A constant has a type. A named number can only be a universal type: universal_integer or universal_real. Strong typing is enforced for constants but not for named numbers or literals. Named numbers allow compilers to generate more efficient code than for constants and to perform more complete error checking at compile time. If the literal contains a large number of digits (as Pi in the example above), the use of an identifier reduces keystroke errors. If keystroke errors occur, they are easier to locate either by inspection or at compile time.

Independence of literals means that the few literals that are used do not depend on one another and that any relationship between constant or named values is shown in the static expressions. Linear independence of literal values gives the property that if one literal value changes, all of the named numbers of values dependent on that literal are automatically changed.

See Guideline 4.1.4 for additional guidelines on choosing a parameterless function versus a constant.

notes

There are some gray areas where the literal is actually more self-documenting than a name. These are application-specific and generally occur with universally familiar, unchangeable values such as the following relationship:

```
Fahrenheit := 32.0 + (9.0 * Celsius) / 5.0;
```

3.2.7 Exceptions

guideline

• Use a name that indicates the kind of problem the exception represents.

example

```
Invalid_Name: exception;

Stack_Overflow: exception;
```

rationale

Naming exceptions according to the kind of problem they are detecting enhances the readability of the code. You should name your exceptions as precisely as you can so that the maintainer of the code understands why the exception might be raised. A well-named exception should be meaningful to the clients of the package declaring the exception.

3.2.8 Constructors

guideline

• Include a prefix like New, Make, or Create in naming constructors (in this sense, operations to create and/or initialize an object).

• Use names indicative of their content for child packages containing constructors.

instantiation

- Name a child package containing constructors <whatever>.Constructor.

example

```
function Make_Square (Center : Cartesian_Coordinates;
                      Side   : Positive)
   return Square;
```

rationale

Including a word like New, Make, or Create in a constructor name makes its purpose clear. You may want to restrict the use of the prefix New to constructors that return an access value because the prefix suggests the internal use of an allocator.

Putting all constructors in a child package, even when they return access values, is a useful organizational principle.

For information regarding the use of Ada constructors, refer to Guideline 9.3.3.

3.3 COMMENTS

Comments in source text are a controversial issue. There are arguments both for and against the view that comments enhance readability. In practice, the biggest problem with comments is that people often fail to update them when the associated source text is changed, thereby making the commentary misleading. Commentary should be reserved for expressing needed information that cannot be expressed in code and highlighting cases where there are overriding reasons to violate one of the guidelines. If possible, source text should use self-explanatory names for objects and program units, and it should use simple, understandable program structures so that little additional commentary is needed. The extra effort in selecting (and entering) appropriate names and the extra thought needed to design clean and understandable program structures are fully justified.

Use comments to state the intent of the code. Comments that provide an overview of the code help the maintenance programmer see the forest for the trees. The code itself is the detailed "how" and should not be paraphrased in the comments.

Comments should be minimized. They should provide needed information that cannot be expressed in the Ada language, emphasize the structure of code, and draw attention to deliberate and necessary violations of the guidelines. Comments are present either to draw attention to the real issue being exemplified or to compensate for incompleteness in the sample program.

Maintenance programmers need to know the causal interaction of noncontiguous pieces of code to get a global, more or less complete sense of the program. They typically acquire this kind of information from mental simulation of parts of the code. Comments should be sufficient enough to support this process (Soloway et al. 1986).

This section presents general guidelines about how to write good comments. It then defines several different classes of comments with guidelines for the use of each. The classes are file headers, program unit specification headers, program unit body headers, data comments, statement comments, and marker comments.

3.3.1 General Comments

guideline

- Make the code as clear as possible to reduce the need for comments.
- Never repeat information in a comment that is readily available in the code.
- Where a comment is required, make it concise and complete.
- Use proper grammar and spelling in comments.
- Make comments visually distinct from the code.
- Structure comments in headers so that information can be automatically extracted by a tool.

rationale

The structure and function of well-written code is clear without comments. Obscured or badly structured code is hard to understand, maintain, or reuse regardless of comments. *Bad code should be improved, not explained.* Reading the code itself is the only way to be absolutely positive about what the code does; therefore, the code should be made as readable as possible.

Using comments to duplicate information in the code is a bad idea for several reasons. First, it is unnecessary work that decreases productivity. Second, it is very difficult to correctly maintain the duplication as the code is modified. When changes are made to existing code, it is compiled and tested to make sure that it is once again correct. However, there is no automatic mechanism to make sure that the comments are correctly updated to reflect the changes. Very often, the duplicate information in a comment becomes obsolete at the first code change and remains so through the life of the software. Third, when comments about an entire system are written from the limited point of view of the author of a single subsystem, the comments are often incorrect from the start.

Comments are necessary to reveal information difficult or impossible to obtain from the code. Subsequent chapters of this book contain examples of such comments. Completely and concisely present the required information.

The purpose of comments is to help readers understand the code. Misspelled, ungrammatical, ambiguous, or incomplete comments defeat this purpose. If a comment is worth adding, it is worth adding correctly in order to increase its usefulness.

Making comments visually distinct from the code by indenting them, grouping them together into headers, or highlighting them with dashed lines is useful because it makes the code easier to read. Subsequent chapters of this book elaborate on this point.

automation notes

The guideline about storing redundant information in comments applies only to manually generated comments. There are tools that automatically maintain information about the code (e.g., calling units, called units, cross-reference information, revision histories, etc.), storing it in comments in the same file as the code. Other tools read comments but do not update them, using the information from the comments to automatically generate detailed design documents and other reports.

The use of such tools is encouraged and may require that you structure your header comments so they can be automatically extracted and/or updated. Beware that tools that modify the comments in a file are only useful if they are executed frequently enough. Automatically generated obsolete information is even more dangerous than manually generated obsolete information because it is more trusted by the reader.

Revision histories are maintained much more accurately and completely by configuration management tools. With no tool support, it is very common for an engineer to make a change and forget to update the revision history. If your configuration management tool is capable of maintaining revision histories as comments in the source file, then take advantage of that capability, regardless of any compromise you might have to make about the format or location of the revision history. It is better to have a complete revision history appended to the end of the file than to have a partial one formatted nicely and embedded in the file header.

3.3.2   File Headers

guideline

- Put a file header on each source file.

- Place ownership, responsibility, and history information for the file in the file header.

instantiation

- Put a copyright notice in the file header.

- Put the author's name and department in the file header.

- Put a revision history in the file header, including a summary of each change, the date, and the name of the person making the change.

example

```
-------------------------------------------------------------------------
--        Copyright (c) 1991, Software Productivity Consortium, Inc.
--        All rights reserved.

-- Author: J. Smith

-- Department:System Software Department

-- Revision History:
--    7/9/91 J. Smith
--       - Added function Size_Of to support queries of node sizes.
--       - Fixed bug in Set_Size which caused overlap of large nodes.
--    7/1/91 M. Jones
--       - Optimized clipping algorithm for speed.
--    6/25/91 J. Smith
--       - Original version.
-------------------------------------------------------------------------
```

rationale

Ownership information should be present in each file if you want to be sure to protect your rights to the software. Furthermore, for high visibility, it should be the first thing in the file.

Responsibility and revision history information should be present in each file for the sake of future maintainers; this is the header information most trusted by maintainers because it accumulates. It does not evolve. There is no need to ever go back and modify the author's name or the revision history of a file. As the code evolves, the revision history should be updated to reflect each change. At worst, it will be incomplete; it should rarely be wrong. Also, the number and frequency of changes and the number of different people who made the changes over the history of a unit can be good indicators of the integrity of the implementation with respect to the design.

Information about how to find the original author should be included in the file header, in addition to the author's name, to make it easier for maintainers to find the author in case questions arise. However, detailed information like phone numbers, mail stops, office numbers, and computer account user names are too volatile to be very useful. It is better to record the department for which the author was working when the code was written. This information is still useful if the author moves offices, changes departments, or even leaves the company because the department is likely to retain responsibility for the original version of the code.

notes

With modern configuration management systems, explicitly capturing version history as header comments may be superfluous. The configuration management tool maintains a more reliable and consistent (from a content point of view) change history. Some systems can re-create earlier versions of a unit.

3.3.3   Program Unit Specification Headers

guideline

- Put a header on the specification of each program unit.
- Place information required by the user of the program unit in the specification header.
- Do not repeat information (except unit name) in the specification header that is present in the specification.
- Explain what the unit does, not how or why it does it.
- Describe the complete interface to the program unit, including any exceptions it can raise and any global effects it can have.
- Do not include information about how the unit fits into the enclosing software system.
- Describe the performance (time and space) characteristics of the unit.

instantiation

- Put the name of the program unit in the header.
- Briefly explain the purpose of the program unit.
- For packages, describe the effects of the visible subprograms on each other and how they should be used together.
- List all exceptions that can be raised by the unit.
- List all global effects of the unit.
- List preconditions and postconditions of the unit.
- List hidden tasks activated by the unit.
- Do not list the names of parameters of a subprogram.
- Do not list the names of package subprograms just to list them.
- Do not list the names of all other units used by the unit.
- Do not list the names of all other units that use the unit.

example

```
------------------------------------------------------------------------
    -- AUTOLAYOUT
```

```
-- Purpose:
--   This package computes positional information for nodes and arcs
--   of a directed graph.  It encapsulates a layout algorithm which is
--   designed to minimize the number of crossing arcs and to emphasize
--   the primary direction of arc flow through the graph.

-- Effects:
--   - The expected usage is:
--       1. Call Define for each node and arc to define the graph.
--       2. Call Layout to assign positions to all nodes and arcs.
--       3. Call Position_Of for each node and arc to determine the
--          assigned coordinate positions.
--   - Layout can be called multiple times, and recomputes the
--     positions of all currently defined nodes and arcs each time.
--   - Once a node or arc has been defined, it remains defined until
--     Clear is called to delete all nodes and arcs.

-- Performance:
--   This package has been optimized for time, in preference to space.
--   Layout times are on the order of N*log(N) where N is the number
--   of nodes, but memory space is used inefficiently.
---------------------------------------------------------------------

package Autolayout is

    ...

---------------------------------------------------------------------
-- Define

-- Purpose:
--   This procedure defines one node of the current graph.
-- Exceptions:
--   Node_Already_Defined
---------------------------------------------------------------------
procedure Define
       (New_Node : in     Node);

---------------------------------------------------------------------
-- Layout

-- Purpose:
--   This procedure assigns coordinate positions to all defined
--   nodes and arcs.
-- Exceptions:
--   None.
---------------------------------------------------------------------
procedure Layout;

---------------------------------------------------------------------
-- Position_Of

-- Purpose:
--   This function returns the coordinate position of the
--   specified node.  The default position (0,0) is returned if no
--   position has been assigned yet.
-- Exceptions:
--   Node_Not_Defined
---------------------------------------------------------------------
function Position_Of (Current : in     Node)
       return Position;

    ...

end Autolayout;
```

rationale

The purpose of a header comment on the specification of a program unit is to help the user understand how to use the program unit. From reading the program unit specification and header, a user should know everything necessary to use the unit. It should not be necessary to read the body of the program unit. Therefore, there should be a header comment on each program unit specification, and each header should contain all usage information not expressed in the specification itself. Such information includes the units' effects on each other and on shared resources, exceptions raised, and time/space characteristics. None of this information can be determined from the Ada specification of the program unit.

When you duplicate information in the header that can be readily obtained from the specification, the information tends to become incorrect during maintenance. For example, do not make a point of listing all parameter names, modes, or subtypes when describing a procedure. This information is already available from the procedure specification. Similarly, do not list all subprograms of a package in the header unless this is necessary to make some important statement about the subprograms.

Do not include information in the header that the user of the program unit does not need. In particular, do not include information about how a program unit performs its function or why a particular algorithm was used. This information should be hidden in the body of the program unit to preserve the abstraction defined by the unit. If the user knows such details and makes decisions based on that information, the code may suffer when that information is later changed.

When describing the purpose of the unit, avoid referring to other parts of the enclosing software system. It is better to say "this unit does . . ." than to say "this unit is called by Xyz to do . . . ." The unit should be written in such a way that it does not know or care which unit is calling it. This makes the unit much more general purpose and reusable. In addition, information about other units is likely to become obsolete and incorrect during maintenance.

Include information about the performance (time and space) characteristics of the unit. Much of this information is not present in the Ada specification, but it is required by the user. To integrate the unit into a system, the user needs to understand the resource usage (CPU, memory, etc.) of the unit. It is especially important to note that when a subprogram call causes activation of a task hidden in a package body, the task may continue to consume resources after the subroutine ends.

notes

Some projects have deferred most of the commentary to the end rather than at the beginning of the program unit. Their rationale is that program units are written once and read many times and that long header comments make the start of the specification difficult to find.

exceptions

Where a group of program units are closely related or simple to understand, it is acceptable to use a single header for the entire group of program units. For example, it makes sense to use a single header to describe the behavior of Max and Min functions; Sin, Cos, and Tan functions; or a group of functions to query related attributes of an object encapsulated in a package. This is especially true when each function in the set is capable of raising the same exceptions.

3.3.4   Program Unit Body Headers

guideline

- Place information required by the maintainer of the program unit in the body header.
- Explain how and why the unit performs its function, not what the unit does.
- Do not repeat information (except unit name) in the header that is readily apparent from reading the code.
- Do not repeat information (except unit name) in the body header that is available in the specification header.

Instantiation

- Put the name of the program unit in the header.
- Record portability issues in the header.
- Summarize complex algorithms in the header.
- Record reasons for significant or controversial implementation decisions.
- Record discarded implementation alternatives, along with the reason for discarding them.
- Record anticipated changes in the header, especially if some work has already been done to the code to make the changes easy to accomplish.

example

```
----------------------------------------------------------------
-- Autolayout
```

```
-- Implementation Notes:
--    - This package uses a heuristic algorithm to minimize the number
--      of arc crossings.  It does not always achieve the true minimum
--      number which could theoretically be reached.  However it does a
--      nearly perfect job in relatively little time.  For details about
--      the algorithm, see ...

-- Portability Issues:
--    - The native math package Math_Lib is used for computations of
--      coordinate positions.
--    - 32-bit integers are required.
--    - No operating system specific routines are called.

-- Anticipated Changes:
--    - Coordinate_Type below could be changed from integer to float
--      with little effort.  Care has been taken to not depend on the
--      specific characteristics of integer arithmetic.
-------------------------------------------------------------------
package body Autolayout is

    ...

-------------------------------------------------------------------
-- Define

-- Implementation Notes:
--    - This routine stores a node in the general purpose Graph data
--      structure, not the Fast_Graph structure because ...
-------------------------------------------------------------------
procedure Define
        (New_Node : in      Node) is
begin
    ...
end Define;

-------------------------------------------------------------------
-- Layout

-- Implementation Notes:
--    - This routine copies the Graph data structure (optimized for
--      fast random access) into the Fast_Graph data structure
--      (optimized for fast sequential iteration), then performs the
--      layout, and copies the data back to the Graph structure.  This
--      technique was introduced as an optimization when the algorithm
--      was found to be too slow, and it produced an order of
--      magnitude improvement.
-------------------------------------------------------------------
procedure Layout is
begin
    ...
end Layout;

-------------------------------------------------------------------
-- Position_Of
-------------------------------------------------------------------
function Position_Of (Current : in      Node)
        return Position is
begin

    ...
end Position_Of;

    ...

end Autolayout;
```

rationale

The purpose of a header comment on the body of a program unit is to help the maintainer of the program unit to understand the implementation of the unit, including tradeoffs among different techniques. Be sure to document all decisions made during implementation to prevent the maintainer from making the same mistakes you made. One of the most valuable comments to a maintainer is a clear description of why a change being considered will not work.

The header is also a good place to record portability concerns. The maintainer may have to port the software to a different environment and will benefit from a list of nonportable features. Furthermore, the act of collecting and recording portability issues focuses attention on these issues and may result in more portable code from the start.

Summarize complex algorithms in the header if the code is difficult to read or understand without such a summary, but do not merely paraphrase the code. Such duplication is unnecessary and hard to maintain. Similarly, do not repeat the information from the header of the program unit specification.

notes

It is often the case that a program unit is self-explanatory so that it does not require a body header to explain how it is implemented or why. In such a case, omit the header entirely, as in the case with `Position_Of` above. Be sure, however, that the header you omit truly contains no information. For example, consider the difference between the two header sections:

```
-- Implementation Notes:  None.
```

and:

```
-- NonPortable Features:  None.
```

The first is a message from the author to the maintainer saying "I can't think of anything else to tell you," while the second may mean "I guarantee that this unit is entirely portable."

3.3.5   Data Comments

guideline

- Comment on all data types, objects, and exceptions unless their names are self-explanatory.

- Include information on the semantic structure of complex, pointer-based data structures.

- Include information about relationships that are maintained between data objects.

- Omit comments that merely repeat the information in the name.

- Include information on redispatching for tagged types in cases where you intend the specializations (i.e., derived types) to override these redispatching operations.

example

Objects can be grouped by purpose and commented as:

```
   ...

----------------------------------------------------------------------
-- Current position of the cursor in the currently selected text
-- buffer, and the most recent position explicitly marked by the
-- user.

-- Note:  It is necessary to maintain both current and desired
--        column positions because the cursor cannot always be
--        displayed in the desired position when moving between
--        lines of different lengths.
----------------------------------------------------------------------

Desired_Column  : Column_Counter;
Current_Column  : Column_Counter;
Current_Row     : Row_Counter;
Marked_Column   : Column_Counter;
Marked_Row      : Row_Counter;
```

The conditions under which an exception is raised should be commented:

```
----------------------------------------------------------------------
-- Exceptions
----------------------------------------------------------------------
Node_Already_Defined : exception;    -- Raised when an attempt is made
                                     --|    to define a node with an
                                     --|    identifier which already
                                     --|    defines a node.
Node_Not_Defined     : exception;    -- Raised when a reference is
                                     --|    made to a node which has
                                     --|    not been defined.
```

Here is a more complex example, involving multiple record and access types that are used to form a complex data structure:

```
----------------------------------------------------------------------
-- These data structures are used to store the graph during the
-- layout process. The overall organization is a sorted list of
-- "ranks," each containing a sorted list of nodes, each containing
-- a list of incoming arcs and a list of outgoing arcs.
```

```
-- The lists are doubly linked to support forward and backward
-- passes for sorting. Arc lists do not need to be doubly linked
-- because order of arcs is irrelevant.

-- The nodes and arcs are doubly linked to each other to support
-- efficient lookup of all arcs to/from a node, as well as efficient
-- lookup of the source/target node of an arc.
------------------------------------------------------------------

type Arc;
type Arc_Pointer is access Arc;

type Node;
type Node_Pointer is access Node;

type Node is
   record
      Id       : Node_Pointer;-- Unique node ID supplied by the user.
      Arc_In   : Arc_Pointer;
      Arc_Out  : Arc_Pointer;
      Next     : Node_Pointer;
      Previous : Node_Pointer;
   end record;

type Arc is
   record
      ID       : Arc_ID;        -- Unique arc ID supplied by the user.
      Source   : Node_Pointer;
      Target   : Node_Pointer;
      Next     : Arc_Pointer;
   end record;

type Rank;
type Rank_Pointer is access Rank;

type Rank is
   record
      Number     : Level_ID;  -- Computed ordinal number of the rank.
      First_Node : Node_Pointer;
      Last_Node  : Node_Pointer;
      Next       : Rank_Pointer;
      Previous   : Rank_Pointer;
   end record;

First_Rank : Rank_Pointer;
Last_Rank  : Rank_Pointer;
```

rationale

It is very useful to add comments explaining the purpose, structure, and semantics of the data structures. Many maintainers look at the data structures first when trying to understand the implementation of a unit. Understanding the data that can be stored, along with the relationships between the different data items and the flow of data through the unit, is an important first step in understanding the details of the unit.

In the first example above, the names Current_Column and Current_Row are relatively self-explanatory. The name Desired_Column is also well chosen, but it leaves the reader wondering what the relationship is between the current column and the desired column. The comment explains the reason for having both.

Another advantage of commenting on the data declarations is that the single set of comments on a declaration can replace multiple sets of comments that might otherwise be needed at various places in the code where the data is manipulated. In the first example above, the comment briefly expands on the meaning of "current" and "marked." It states that the "current" position is the location of the cursor, the "current" position is in the current buffer, and the "marked" position was marked by the user. This comment, along with the mnemonic names of the variables, greatly reduces the need for comments at individual statements throughout the code.

It is important to document the full meaning of exceptions and under what conditions they can be raised, as shown in the second example above, especially when the exceptions are declared in a package specification. The reader has no other way to find out the exact meaning of the exception (without reading the code in the package body).

Grouping all the exceptions together, as shown in the second example, can provide the reader with the effect of a "glossary" of special conditions. This is useful when many different subprograms in the package can raise the same exceptions. For a package in which each exception can be raised by only one subprogram, it may be better to group related subprograms and exceptions together.

When commenting exceptions, it is better to describe the exception's meaning in general terms than to list all the subprograms that can cause the exception to be raised; such a list is harder to maintain. When a new routine is added, it is likely that these lists will not be updated. Also, this information is already present in the comments describing the subprograms, where all exceptions that can be raised by the subprogram should be listed. Lists of exceptions by subprogram are more useful and easier to maintain than lists of subprograms by exception.

In the third example, the names of the record fields are short and mnemonic, but they are not completely self-explanatory. This is often the case with complex data structures involving access types. There is no way to choose the record and field names so that they completely explain the overall organization of the records and pointers into a nested set of sorted lists. The comments shown are useful in this case. Without them, the reader would not know which lists are sorted, which lists are doubly linked, or why. The comments express the intent of the author with respect to this complex data structure. The maintainer still has to read the code if he wants to be sure that the double links are all properly maintained. Keeping this in mind when reading the code makes it much easier for the maintainer to find a bug where one pointer is updated and the opposite one is not.

See Guideline 9.3.1 for the rationale for documenting the use of redispatching operations. (Redispatching means converting an argument of one primitive operation to a class-wide type and making a dispatching call to another primitive operation.) The rationale in Guideline 9.3.1 discusses whether such documentation should be in the specification or the body.

3.3.6   Statement Comments

guideline

- Minimize comments embedded among statements.
- Use comments only to explain parts of the code that are not obvious.
- Comment intentional omissions from the code.
- Do not use comments to paraphrase the code.
- Do not use comments to explain remote pieces of code, such as subprograms called by the current unit.
- Where comments are necessary, make them visually distinct from the code.

example

The following is an example of very poorly commented code:

```
...

-- Loop through all the strings in the array Strings, converting
-- them to integers by calling Convert_To_Integer on each one,
-- accumulating the sum of all the values in Sum, and counting them
-- in Count.  Then divide Sum by Count to get the average and store
-- it in Average. Also, record the maximum number in the global
-- variable Max_Number.

for I in Strings'Range loop
    -- Convert each string to an integer value by looping through
    -- the characters which are digits, until a nondigit is found,
    -- taking the ordinal value of each, subtracting the ordinal value
    -- of '0', and multiplying by 10 if another digit follows.  Store
    -- the result in Number.
    Number := Convert_To_Integer(Strings(I));
    -- Accumulate the sum of the numbers in Total.
    Sum := Sum + Number;
    -- Count the numbers.
    Count := Count + 1;

    -- Decide whether this number is more than the current maximum.
    if Number > Max_Number then
        -- Update the global variable Max_Number.
        Max_Number := Number;
    end if;

end loop;
-- Compute the average.
Average := Sum / Count;
```

The following is improved by not repeating things in the comments that are obvious from the code, not describing the details of what goes in inside of Convert_To_Integer, deleting an erroneous comment (the one on the statement that accumulates the sum), and making the few remaining comments more visually distinct from the code.

```
Sum_Integers_Converted_From_Strings:
    for I in Strings'Range loop
        Number := Convert_To_Integer(Strings(I));
        Sum := Sum + Number;
        Count := Count + 1;

        -- The global Max_Number is computed here for efficiency.
        if Number > Max_Number then
            Max_Number := Number;
        end if;

    end loop Sum_Integers_Converted_From_Strings;

Average := Sum / Count;
```

rationale

The improvements shown in the example are not improvements merely by reducing the total number of comments; they are improvements by reducing the number of useless comments.

Comments that paraphrase or explain obvious aspects of the code have no value. They are a waste of effort for the author to write and the maintainer to update. Therefore, they often end up becoming incorrect. Such comments also clutter the code, hiding the few important comments.

Comments describing what goes on inside another unit violate the principle of information hiding. The details about Convert_To_Integer (deleted above) are irrelevant to the calling unit, and they are better left hidden in case the algorithm ever changes. Examples explaining what goes on elsewhere in the code are very difficult to maintain and almost always become incorrect at the first code modification.

The advantage of making comments visually distinct from the code is that it makes the code easier to scan, and the few important comments stand out better. Highlighting unusual or special code features indicates that they are intentional. This assists maintainers by focusing attention on code sections that are likely to cause problems during maintenance or when porting the program to another implementation.

Comments should be used to document code that is nonportable, implementation-dependent, environment-dependent, or tricky in any way. They notify the reader that something unusual was put there for a reason. A beneficial comment would be one explaining a work around for a compiler bug. If you use a lower level (not "ideal" in the software engineering sense) solution, comment on it. Information included in the comments should state why you used that particular construct. Also include documentation on the failed attempts, for example, using a higher level structure. This kind of comment is useful to maintainers for historical purposes. You show the reader that a significant amount of thought went into the choice of a construct.

Finally, comments should be used to explain what is not present in the code as well as what is present. If you make a conscious decision to not perform some action, like deallocating a data structure with which you appear to be finished, be sure to add a comment explaining why not. Otherwise, a maintainer may notice the apparent omission and "correct" it later, thus introducing an error.

See also Guideline 9.3.1 for a discussion of what kind of documentation you should provide regarding tagged types and redispatching.

notes

Further improvements can be made on the above example by declaring the variables Count and Sum in a local block so that their scope is limited and their initializations occur near their usage, e.g., by naming the block Compute_Average or by moving the code into a function called Average_Of. The computation of Max_Number can also be separated from the computation of Average. However, those changes are the subject of other guidelines; this example is only intended to illustrate the proper use of comments.

3.3.7   Marker Comments

guideline

- Use pagination markers to mark program unit boundaries (see Guideline 2.1.7).
- Repeat the unit name in a comment to mark the begin of a package body, subprogram body, task body, or block if the begin is preceded by declarations.

- For long or heavily nested `if` and `case` statements, mark the end of the statement with a comment summarizing the condition governing the statement.
- For long or heavily nested `if` statements, mark the `else` part with a comment summarizing the conditions governing this portion of the statement.

example

```
if    A_Found then
   ...
elsif B_Found then
   ...

else  -- A and B were both not found
   ...

   if Count = Max then
      ...

   end if;

   ...
end if;  -- A_Found
------------------------------------------------------------------
package body Abstract_Strings is
   ...

------------------------------------------------------------------
   procedure Concatenate (...) is
   begin
      ...
   end Concatenate;
------------------------------------------------------------------

   ...
begin  -- Abstract_Strings
   ...
end Abstract_Strings;
------------------------------------------------------------------
```

rationale

Marker comments emphasize the structure of code and make it easier to scan. They can be lines that separate sections of code or descriptive tags for a construct. They help the reader resolve questions about the current position in the code. This is more important for large units than for small ones. A short marker comment fits on the same line as the reserved word with which it is associated. Thus, it adds information without clutter.

The `if`, `elsif`, `else`, and `end if` of an `if` statement are often separated by long sequences of statements, sometimes involving other `if` statements. As shown in the first example, marker comments emphasize the association of the keywords of the same statement over a great visual distance. Marker comments are not necessary with the block statement and loop statement because the syntax of these statements allows them to be named with the name repeated at the end. Using these names is better than using marker comments because the compiler verifies that the names at the beginning and end match.

The sequence of statements of a package body is often very far from the first line of the package. Many subprogram bodies, each containing many `begin` lines, may occur first. As shown in the second example, the marker comment emphasizes the association of the `begin` with the package.

notes

Repeating names and noting conditional expressions clutters the code if overdone. It is visual distance, especially page breaks, that makes marker comments beneficial.

3.4   USING TYPES

Strong typing promotes reliability in software. The type definition of an object defines all legal values and operations and allows the compiler to check for and identify potential errors during compilation. In addition, the rules of type allow the compiler to generate code to check for violations of type constraints at execution time. Using these Ada compiler's features facilitates earlier and more complete error detection than that which is available with less strongly typed languages.

3.4.1   Declaring Types

guideline

- Limit the range of scalar types as much as possible.
- Seek information about possible values from the application.
- Do not reuse any of the subtype names in package `standard`.
- Use subtype declarations to improve program readability (Booch 1987).
- Use derived types and subtypes in concert (see Guideline 5.3.1).

example

```
subtype Card_Image is String (1 .. 80);

Input_Line : Card_Image := (others => ' ');

-- restricted integer type:
type    Day_Of_Leap_Year     is                  range 1 .. 366;
subtype Day_Of_Non_Leap_Year is Day_Of_Leap_Year range 1 .. 365;
```

By the following declaration, the programmer means, "I haven't the foggiest idea how many," but the actual base range will show up buried in the code or as a system parameter:

```
Employee_Count : Integer;
```

rationale

Eliminating meaningless values from the legal range improves the compiler's ability to detect errors when an object is set to an invalid value. This also improves program readability. In addition, it forces you to carefully think about each use of objects declared to be of the subtype.

Different implementations provide different sets of values for most of the predefined types. A reader cannot determine the intended range from the predefined names. This situation is aggravated when the predefined names are overloaded.

The names of an object and its subtype can clarify their intended use and document low-level design decisions. The example above documents a design decision to restrict the software to devices whose physical parameters are derived from the characteristics of punch cards. This information is easy to find for any later changes, thus enhancing program maintainability.

You can rename a type by declaring a subtype without a constraint (Ada Reference Manual 1995, §8.5). You cannot overload a subtype name; overloading only applies to callable entities. Enumeration literals are treated as parameterless functions and so are included in this rule.

Types can have highly constrained sets of values without eliminating useful values. Usage as described in Guideline 5.3.1 eliminates many flag variables and type conversions within executable statements. This renders the program more readable while allowing the compiler to enforce strong typing constraints.

notes

Subtype declarations do not define new types, only constraints for existing types.

Any deviation from this guideline detracts from the advantages of the strong typing facilities of the Ada language.

exceptions

There are cases where you do not have a particular dependence on any range of numeric values. Such situations occur, for example, with array indices (e.g., a list whose size is not fixed by any particular semantics). See Guideline 7.2.1 for a discussion of appropriate uses of predefined types.

3.4.2   Enumeration Types

guideline

- Use enumeration types instead of numeric codes.
- Only if absolutely necessary, use representation clauses to match requirements of external devices.

example

Use:

```
type Color is (Blue, Red, Green, Yellow);
```

rather than:

```
Blue    : constant := 1;
Red     : constant := 2;
Green   : constant := 3;
Yellow  : constant := 4;
```

and add the following if necessary:

```
for Color use (Blue   => 1,
               Red    => 2,
               Green  => 3,
               Yellow => 4);
```

rationale

Enumerations are more robust than numeric codes; they leave less potential for errors resulting from incorrect interpretation and from additions to and deletions from the set of values during maintenance. Numeric codes are holdovers from languages that have no user-defined types.

In addition, Ada provides a number of attributes ('Pos, 'Val, 'Succ, 'Pred, 'Image, and 'Value) for enumeration types that, when used, are more reliable than user-written operations on encodings.

A numeric code may at first seem appropriate to match external values. Instead, these situations call for a representation clause on the enumeration type. The representation clause documents the "encoding." If the program is properly structured to isolate and encapsulate hardware dependencies (see Guideline 7.1.5), the numeric code ends up in an interface package where it can be easily found and replaced if the requirements change.

In general, avoid using representation clauses for enumeration types. When there is no obvious ordering of the enumeration literals, an enumeration representation can create portability problems if the enumeration type must be reordered to accommodate a change in representation order on the new platform.

3.5   SUMMARY

spelling

- Use underscores to separate words in a compound name.
- Represent numbers in a consistent fashion.
- Represent literals in a radix appropriate to the problem.
- Use underscores to separate digits the same way commas or periods (or spaces for nondecimal bases) would be used in normal text.
- When using scientific notation, make the e consistently either uppercase or lowercase.
- In an alternate base, represent the alphabetic characters in either all uppercase or all lowercase.
- Make reserved words and other elements of the program visually distinct from each other.
- Do not use an abbreviation of a long word as an identifier where a shorter synonym exists.
- Use a consistent abbreviation strategy.
- Do not use ambiguous abbreviations.
- To justify its use, an abbreviation must save many characters over the full word.
- Use abbreviations that are well-accepted in the application domain.
- Maintain a list of accepted abbreviations, and use only abbreviations on that list.

naming conventions

- Choose names that are as self-documenting as possible.
- Use a short synonym instead of an abbreviation.
- Use names given by the application, but do not use obscure jargon.

- Avoid using the same name to declare different kinds of identifiers.
- Use singular, general nouns as subtype identifiers.
- Choose identifiers that describe one of the subtype's values.
- Consider using suffixes for subtype identifiers that define visible access types, visible subranges, or visible array types.
- For private types, do not use identifier constructions (e.g., suffixes) that are unique to subtype identifiers.
- Do not use the subtype names from predefined packages.
- Use predicate clauses or adjectives for Boolean objects.
- Use singular, specific nouns as object identifiers.
- Choose identifiers that describe the object's value during execution.
- Use singular, general nouns as identifiers for record components.
- Use a consistent naming convention for tagged types and associated packages.
- Use action verbs for procedures and entries.
- Use predicate clauses for Boolean functions.
- Use nouns for non-Boolean functions.
- Give packages names that imply a higher level of organization than subprograms. Generally, these are noun phrases that describe the abstraction provided.
- Give tasks names that imply an active entity.
- Use nouns descriptive of the data being protected for protected units.
- Consider naming generic subprograms as if they were nongeneric subprograms.
- Consider naming generic packages as if they were nongeneric packages.
- Make the generic names more general than the instantiated names.
- Use symbolic values instead of literals, wherever possible.
- Use the predefined constants `Ada.Numerics.Pi` and `Ada.Numerics.e` for the mathematical constants `Pi` and `e`.
- Use constants instead of variables for constant values.
- Use a constant when the value is specific to a type or when the value must be static.
- Use named numbers instead of constants, whenever possible.
- Use named numbers to replace numeric literals whose type or context is truly universal.
- Use constants for objects whose values cannot change after elaboration (United Technologies 1987).
- Show relationships between symbolic values by defining them with static expressions.
- Use linearly independent sets of literals.
- Use attributes like `'First` and `'Last` instead of literals, wherever possible.
- Use a name that indicates the kind of problem the exception represents.
- Include a prefix like `New`, `Make`, or `Create` in naming constructors (in this sense, operations to create and/or initialize an object).
- Use names indicative of their content for child packages containing constructors.

comments

- Make the code as clear as possible to reduce the need for comments.
- Never repeat information in a comment that is readily available in the code.
- Where a comment is required, make it concise and complete.
- Use proper grammar and spelling in comments.
- Make comments visually distinct from the code.
- Structure comments in headers so that information can be automatically extracted by a tool.

- Put a file header on each source file.
- Place ownership, responsibility, and history information for the file in the file header.
- Put a header on the specification of each program unit.
- Place information required by the user of the program unit in the specification header.
- Do not repeat information (except unit name) in the specification header that is present in the specification.
- Explain what the unit does, not how or why it does it.
- Describe the complete interface to the program unit, including any exceptions it can raise and any global effects it can have.
- Do not include information about how the unit fits into the enclosing software system.
- Describe the performance (time and space) characteristics of the unit.
- Place information required by the maintainer of the program unit in the body header.
- Explain how and why the unit performs its function, not what the unit does.
- Do not repeat information (except unit name) in the header that is readily apparent from reading the code.
- Do not repeat information (except unit name) in the body header that is available in the specification header.
- Comment on all data types, objects, and exceptions unless their names are self-explanatory.
- Include information on the semantic structure of complex, pointer-based data structures.
- Include information about relationships that are maintained between data objects.
- Omit comments that merely repeat the information in the name.
- Include information on redispatching for tagged types in cases where you intend the specializations (i.e., derived types) to override these redispatching operations.
- Minimize comments embedded among statements.
- Use comments only to explain parts of the code that are not obvious.
- Comment intentional omissions from the code.
- Do not use comments to paraphrase the code.
- Do not use comments to explain remote pieces of code, such as subprograms called by the current unit.
- Where comments are necessary, make them visually distinct from the code.
- Use pagination markers to mark program unit boundaries.
- Repeat the unit name in a comment to mark the `begin` of a package body, subprogram body, task body, or block if the `begin` is preceded by declarations.
- For long or heavily nested `if` and `case` statements, mark the end of the statement with a comment summarizing the condition governing the statement.
- For long or heavily nested `if` statements, mark the `else` part with a comment summarizing the conditions governing this portion of the statement.

using types

- Limit the range of scalar types as much as possible.
- Seek information about possible values from the application.
- Do not reuse any of the subtype names in package `standard`.
- Use subtype declarations to improve program readability (Booch 1987).
- Use derived types and subtypes in concert.
- Use enumeration types instead of numeric codes.
- Only if absolutely necessary, use representation clauses to match requirements of external devices.

CHAPTER 4
Program Structure

Proper structure improves program clarity. This is analogous to readability on lower levels and facilitates the use of the readability guidelines (Chapter 3). The various program structuring facilities provided by Ada were designed to enhance overall clarity of design. These guidelines show how to use these facilities for their intended purposes.

The concept of child packages supports the concept of subsystem, where a subsystem is represented in Ada as a hierarchy of library units. In general, a large system should be structured as a series of subsystems. Subsystems should be used to represent logically related library units, which together implement a single, high-level abstraction or framework.

Abstraction and encapsulation are supported by the package concept and by private types. Related data and subprograms can be grouped together and seen by a higher level as a single entity. Information hiding is enforced via strong typing and by the separation of package and subprogram specifications from their bodies. Exceptions and tasks are additional Ada language elements that impact program structure.

4.1 HIGH-LEVEL STRUCTURE

Well-structured programs are easily understood, enhanced, and maintained. Poorly structured programs are frequently restructured during maintenance just to make the job easier. Many of the guidelines listed below are often given as general program design guidelines.

4.1.1 Separate Compilation Capabilities

guideline

- Place the specification of each library unit package in a separate file from its body.
- Avoid defining library unit subprograms that are not intended to be used as main programs. If such subprograms are defined, then create an explicit specification, in a separate file, for each library unit subprogram.
- Minimize the use of subunits.
- In preference to subunits, use child library units to structure a subsystem into manageable units.
- Place each subunit in a separate file.
- Use a consistent file naming convention.
- In preference to nesting in a package body, use a private child and with it to the parent body.
- Use private child unit specifications for data and subprograms that are required by (other) child units that extend a parent unit's abstraction or services.

example

The file names below illustrate one possible file organization and associated consistent naming convention. The library unit name uses the adb suffix for the body. The suffix ads indicates the specification, and any files containing subunits use names constructed by separating the body name from the subunit name with an underscore:

```
text_io.ads                      -- the specification
text_io.adb                      -- the body
text_io_integer_io.adb           -- a subunit
text_io_fixed_io.adb             -- a subunit
text_io_float_io.adb             -- a subunit
text_io_enumeration_io.adb       -- a subunit
```

Depending on what characters your file system allows you to use in file names, you could show the distinction between parent and subunit name more clearly in the file name. If your file system allows the "#" character, for example, you could separate the body name from the subunit name with a #:

```
text_io.ads                      -- the specification
text_io.adb                      -- the body
text_io#integer_io.adb           -- a subunit
text_io#fixed_io.adb             -- a subunit
text_io#float_io.adb             -- a subunit
text_io#enumeration_io.adb       -- a subunit
```

Some operating systems are case sensitive, although Ada itself is not a case-sensitive language. For example, you could choose a convention of all lowercase file names.

rationale

The main reason for the emphasis on separate files in this guideline is to minimize the amount of recompilation required after each change. Typically, during software development, bodies of units are updated far more often than specifications. If the body and specification reside in the same file, then the specification will be compiled each time the body is compiled, even though the specification has not changed. Because the specification defines the interface between the unit and all of its users, this recompilation of the specification typically makes recompilation of all users necessary in order to verify compliance with the specification. If the specifications and bodies of the users also reside together, then any users of these units will also have to be recompiled and so on. The ripple effect can force a huge number of compilations that could have been avoided, severely slowing the development and test phase of a project. This is why you should place specifications of all library units (nonnested units) in separate files from their bodies.

Library unit subprograms should be minimized. The only real use for library unit subprograms is as the main subprogram. In almost all other cases, it is better to embed the subprogram into a package. This provides a place (the package body) to localize data needed by the subprogram. Moreover, it cuts down on the number of separate modules in the system.

In general, you should use a separate specification for any library subprogram that is mentioned in a with clause. This makes the with'ing unit dependent on the library subprogram specification, not its body.

You should minimize the use of subunits because they create maintenance problems. Declarations appearing in the parent body are visible in the subunit, increasing the amount of data global to the subunit and, thus, increasing the potential ripple effect of changes. Subunits hinder reuse because they provide an incentive to put otherwise reusable code in the subunit directly rather than in a common routine called from multiple subprograms.

With the availability of child library units in Ada 95, you can avoid most uses of subunits. For example, instead of using a subunit for a large nested body, you should try to encapsulate this code in a child library unit and add the necessary context clauses. You can modify the body of the child unit without having to recompile any of the other units in a subsystem.

An additional benefit of using multiple, separate files is that it allows different implementors to modify different parts of the system at the same time with conventional editors, which do not allow multiple concurrent updates to a single file.

Finally, keeping bodies and specifications separate makes it possible to have multiple bodies for the same specification or multiple specifications for the same body. Although Ada requires that there be exactly one specification per body in a system at any given time, it can still be useful to maintain multiple bodies or multiple specifications for use in different builds of a system. For example, a single specification may have multiple bodies, each of which implements the same functionality with a different tradeoff of time versus space efficiency, or, for machine-dependent code, there may be one body for each target machine. Maintaining multiple package specifications can also be useful during development and test. You may develop one specification for delivery to your customer and another for unit testing. The first one would export only those subprograms intended to be called from outside of the package during normal operation of the system. The second one would export all subprograms of the package so that each of them could be independently tested.

A consistent file naming convention is recommended to make it easier to manage the large number of files that may result from following this guideline.

In implementing the abstraction defined in a package specification, you often need to write supporting subprograms that manipulate the internal representation of the data. These subprograms should not be exported on the interface. You have a choice of whether to place them in the package body of the parent program or in a child package named in a context clause of the parent package body. When you place them in the parent package body, you make them inaccessible to all clients of the parent, including extensions of the parent declared in child packages. If these subprograms are needed to implement extensions of the parent abstraction, you would be forced to modify both the parent specification and the body because you would have to declare the extensions within the parent specification. This technique would then force recompilation of the entire package (specification and body) as well as all its clients.

Alternatively, you can implement the supporting subprograms in a private child package. Because the parent unit's specification is not modified, neither it nor its clients need to be recompiled. The data and subprograms that might have declared in the parent unit body must now be declared in the private child unit's specification to make them visible to both the parent unit body and to any child units that extend the parent unit's services or abstractions. (See also Guidelines 4.1.6 and 4.2.) This use of private child units will generally minimize recompilations within the unit family and among its clients.

In declaring the child package private, you achieve a similar effect to declaring it in the parent package body to the extent that clients of the parent cannot name the private child in a context clause. You gain flexibility because now you can extend the parent abstraction using child packages without having to recompile the parent specification or its body, assuming that you do not otherwise modify the parent or its body. This added flexibility will usually compensate for the increased dependency between units, in this case, the additional context clause on the parent body (and other child package bodies) that names the private child package of supporting subprograms.

4.1.2   Configuration Pragmas

guideline

- When possible, express configuration pragmas through compiler options or other means that do not require modifications to the source code.

- When configuration pragmas must be placed in source code, consider isolating them to one compilation unit per partition; if specified, the main subprogram for the partition is recommended.

rationale

Configuration pragmas are generally used to select a partition-wide or system-wide option. Usually, they reflect either high-level software architecture decisions (e.g., pragma Task_Dispatching_Policy) or the use of the software in a particular application domain (e.g., safety-critical software). If a configuration pragma is embedded within a software component and that component is reused in a different context where the pragma is no longer appropriate, then it may cause problems in the new application. Such problems can include the rejection by the compilation system of otherwise legal source code or unexpected behavior at run-time. These problems can be significant given the wide scope of a configuration pragma. In addition, maintenance of the original system may require that some of these system-wide decisions be changed. If the configuration pragmas are scattered throughout the software, it may be difficult to locate the lines that need to change.

As a result, it is recommended that all configuration pragmas be kept in a single compilation unit if possible to make them easy to locate and modify as needed. If this compilation unit is unlikely to be reused (e.g., a main subprogram), then the likelihood of conflicts with future reusers is reduced. Finally, if these system-wide decisions are indicated without embedding them in the code at all, such as through a compiler option, then the problems described above are even less likely to occur.

exceptions

Certain pragmas (e.g., pragma Suppress) can be used in several forms, including as a configuration pragma. This guideline does not apply to such pragmas when they are not used as a configuration pragma.

4.1.3   Subprograms

guideline

- Use subprograms to enhance abstraction.
- Restrict each subprogram to the performance of a single action.

example

Your program is required to draw a menu of user options as part of a menu-driven user interface package. Because the contents of the menu can vary depending on the user state, the proper way to do this is to write a subprogram to draw the menu. This way, the output subprogram has one purpose and the way to determine the menu content is described elsewhere.

```
   ...
----------------------------------------------------------------------
procedure Draw_Menu
        (Title   : in    String;
         Options : in    Menu) is

    ...

begin   -- Draw_Menu

    Ada.Text_IO.New_Page;
    Ada.Text_IO.New_Line;
    Ada.Text_IO.Set_Col (Right_Column);
    Ada.Text_IO.Put_Line (Title);
    Ada.Text_IO.New_Line;

    for Choice in Alpha_Numeric loop

      if Options (Choice) /= Empty_Line then
         Valid_Option (Choice) := True;
         Ada.Text_IO.Set_Col (Left_Column);
         Ada.Text_IO.Put (Choice & " -- ");
         Ada.Text_IO.Put_Line (Options (Choice));
      end if;
      ...

    end loop;

end Draw_Menu;
----------------------------------------------------------------------
```

rationale

Subprograms are an extremely effective and well-understood abstraction technique. Subprograms increase program readability by hiding the details of a particular activity. It is not necessary that a subprogram be called more than once to justify its existence.

notes

Guideline 10.7.1 discusses dealing with the overhead of subroutine calls.

4.1.4   Functions

guideline

- Use a function when the subprogram's primary purpose is to provide a single value.
- Minimize the side effect of a function.
- Consider using a parameterless function when the value does not need to be static.
- Use a parameterless function (instead of a constant) if the value should be inherited by types derived from the type.
- Use a parameterless function if the value itself is subject to change.

example

Although reading a character from a file will change what character is read next, this is accepted as a minor side effect compared to the primary purpose of the following function:

```
function Next_Character return Character is separate;
```

However, the use of a function like this could lead to a subtle problem. Any time the order of evaluation is undefined, the order of the values returned by the function will effectively be undefined. In this example, the order of the characters placed in word and the order that the following two characters are given to the suffix parameters are unknown. No implementation of the Next_Character function can guarantee which character will go where:

```
    Word : constant String := String'(1 .. 5 => Next_Character);

  begin   -- Start_Parsing

    Parse(Keyword => Word,
          Suffix1 => Next_Character,
          Suffix2 => Next_Character);
  end Start_Parsing;
```

Of course, if the order is unimportant (as in a random number generator), then the order of evaluation is unimportant.

The following example shows the use of a parameterless function instead of a constant:

```
type T is private;
function Nil return T;          -- This function is a derivable operation of type T
function Default return T;      -- Also derivable, and the value can be changed by
                                -- recompiling the body of the function
```

This same example could have been written using constants:

```
type T is private;
Nil : constant T;
Default : constant T;
```

rationale

A side effect is a change to any variable that is not local to the subprogram. This includes changes to variables by other subprograms and entries during calls from the function if the changes persist after the function returns. Side effects are discouraged because they are difficult to understand and maintain. Additionally, the Ada language does not define the order in which functions are evaluated when they occur in expressions or as actual parameters to subprograms. Therefore, a program that depends on the order in which side effects of functions occur is erroneous. Avoid using side effects anywhere.

4.1.5   Packages

guideline

- Use packages for information hiding.
- Use packages with tagged types and private types for abstract data types.
- Use packages to model abstract entities appropriate to the problem domain.
- Use packages to group together related type and object declarations (e.g., common declarations for two or more library units).
- Encapsulate machine dependencies in packages. Place a software interface to a particular device in a package to facilitate a change to a different device.
- Place low-level implementation decisions or interfaces in subprograms within packages.
- Use packages and subprograms to encapsulate and hide program details that may change (Nissen and Wallis 1984).

example

Reading the names and other attributes of external files is highly machine dependent. A package called Directory could contain type and subprogram declarations to support a generalized view of an external directory that contains external files. Its internals may, in turn, depend on other packages more specific to the hardware or operating system:

```
package Directory is

   type Directory_Listing is limited private;

   procedure Read_Current_Directory (D : in out Directory_Listing);

   generic
      with procedure Process (Filename : in String);
   procedure Iterate (Over : in Directory_Listing);

   ...

private

   type Directory_Listing is ...

end Directory;

------------------------------------------------------------------

package body Directory is

   -- This procedure is machine dependent
   procedure Read_Current_Directory (D : in out Directory_Listing) is separate;

   procedure Iterate (Over : in Directory_Listing) is
      ...
   begin
      ...

      Process (Filename);

      ...
   end Iterate;

   ...

end Directory;
```

rationale

Packages are the principal structuring facility in Ada. They are intended to be used as direct support for abstraction, information hiding, and modularization. For example, they are useful for encapsulating machine dependencies as an aid to portability. A single specification can have multiple bodies isolating implementation-specific information so other parts of the code do not need to change.

Encapsulating areas of potential change helps to minimize the effort required to implement that change by preventing unnecessary dependencies among unrelated parts of the system.

notes

The most prevalent objection to this guideline usually involves performance penalties. See Guideline 10.7.1 for a discussion about subprogram overhead.

4.1.6   Child Library Units

guideline

- If a new library unit represents a logical extension to the original abstraction, define it as a child library unit.
- If a new library unit is independent (e.g., introduces a new abstraction that depends only in part on the existing one), then encapsulate the new abstraction in a separate library unit.
- Use child packages to implement a subsystem.
- Use public child units for those parts of a subsystem that should be visible to clients of the subsystem.
- Use private child units for those parts of a subsystem that should not be visible to clients of the subsystem.
- Use private child units for local declarations used only in implementing the package specification.
- Use child packages to implement constructors, even when they return access values.

example

The following example of a windowing system is taken from Cohen et al. (1993) and illustrates some of the uses of child units in designing subsystems. The parent (root) package declares the types, subtypes, and constants that its clients and subsystems need. Individual child packages provide specific parts of the windowing abstraction, such as atoms, fonts, graphic output, cursors, and keyboard information:

```
package X_Windows is
   ...
private
   ...
end X_Windows;


package X_Windows.Atoms is
   type Atom is private;
   ...
private
   ...
end X_Windows.Atoms;


package X_Windows.Fonts is
   type Font is private;
   ...
private
   ...
end X_Windows.Fonts;


package X_Windows.Graphic_Output is
   type Graphic_Context is private;
   type Image is private;
   ...
private
   ...
end X_Windows.Graphic_Output;


package X_Windows.Cursors is
   ...
end X_Windows.Cursors;


package X_Windows.Keyboard is
   ...
end X_Windows.Keyboard;
```

rationale

The user can create more precise packages with less cluttered interfaces, using child library packages to extend the interfaces as needed. The parent contains only the relevant functionality. The parent provides a general-purpose interface, while the child units provide more complete programming interfaces, tailored to that aspect of an abstraction that they are extending or defining.

Child packages build on the modular strength of Ada where "the distinct specification and body decouple the user interface to a package (the specification) from its implementation (the body)" (Rationale 1995, §II.7). Child packages provide the added capability of being able to extend a parent package without recompiling the parent or the parent's clients.

Child packages allow you to write logically distinct packages that share a private type. The visibility rules give the private part of the child specification and the body of the child visibility into the private part of the parent. Thus, you can avoid creating a monolithic package for the sake of developing abstractions that share a private type and need to know its representation. The private representation is not available to clients of the package, so the abstraction in the package and its children is maintained.

Using private child packages for local declarations enables you to have available the support declarations you need when implementing both the parent package and extensions to the parent package. You enhance the maintainability of your program by using a common set of support declarations (data representations, data manipulation subprograms). You can modify the internal representation and the implementation of the support subprograms without modifying or recompiling the rest of your subsystem because these support subprograms are implemented in the body of the private child package. See also Guidelines 4.1.1, 4.2.1, 8.4.1, and 8.4.8.

See also Guideline 9.4.1 for a discussion of the use of child library units in creating a tagged type hierarchy.

4.1.7   Cohesion

guideline

- Make each package serve a single purpose.
- Use packages to group related data, types, and subprograms.
- Avoid collections of unrelated objects and subprograms (NASA 1987; Nissen and Wallis 1984).
- Consider restructuring a system to move two highly related units into the same package (or package hierarchy) or to move relatively independent units into separate packages.

example

As a bad example, a package named `Project_Definitions` is obviously a "catch all" for a particular project and is likely to be a jumbled mess. It probably has this form to permit project members to incorporate a single `with` clause into their software.

Better examples are packages called `Display_Format_Definitions`, containing all the types and constants needed by some specific display in a specific format, and `Cartridge_Tape_Handler`, containing all the types, constants, and subprograms that provide an interface to a special-purpose device.

rationale

The degree to which the entities in a package are related has a direct impact on the ease of understanding packages and programs made up of packages. There are different criteria for grouping, and some criteria are less effective than others. Grouping the class of data or activity (e.g., initialization modules) or grouping data or activities based on their timing characteristics is less effective than grouping based on function or need to communicate through data (Charette 1986).

The "correct" structuring of a system can make a tremendous difference in the maintainability of a system. Although it may seem painful at the time, it is important to restructure if the initial structuring is not quite right.

See also Guideline 5.4.2 on heterogeneous data.

notes

Traditional subroutine libraries often group functionally unrelated subroutines. Even such libraries should be broken into a collection of packages, each containing a logically cohesive set of subprograms.

4.1.8   Data Coupling

guideline

- Avoid declaring variables in package specifications.

example

This is part of a compiler. Both the package handling error messages and the package containing the code generator need to know the current line number. Rather than storing this in a shared variable of type `Natural`, the information is stored in a package that hides the details of how such information is represented and makes it available with access routines:

```
-----------------------------------------------------------------------
package Compilation_Status is
    type Line_Number is range 1 .. 2_500_000;
    function Source_Line_Number return Line_Number;
end Compilation_Status;
-----------------------------------------------------------------------

with Compilation_Status;
package Error_Message_Processing is
    -- Handle compile-time diagnostic.
end Error_Message_Processing;
-----------------------------------------------------------------------
```

```
with Compilation_Status;

package Code_Generation is
    -- Operations for code generation.
end Code_Generation;
```
----

rationale

Strongly coupled program units can be difficult to debug and very difficult to maintain. By protecting shared data with access functions, the coupling is lessened. This prevents dependence on the data structure, and access to the data can be controlled.

notes

The most prevalent objection to this guideline usually involves performance penalties. When a variable is moved to the package body, subprograms to access the variable must be provided and the overhead involved during each call to those subprograms is introduced. See Guideline 10.7.1 for a discussion about subprogram overhead.

4.1.9 Tasks

guideline

- Use tasks to model abstract, asynchronous entities within the problem domain.
- Use tasks to define concurrent algorithms for multiprocessor architectures.
- Use tasks to perform concurrent, cyclic, or prioritized activities (NASA 1987).

rationale

The rationale for this guideline is given under Guideline 6.1.2. Chapter 6 discusses tasking in more detail.

4.1.10 Protected Types

guideline

- Use protected types to control or synchronize access to data or devices.
- Use protected types to implement synchronization tasks, such as a passive resource monitor.

example

See example in Guideline 6.1.1.

rationale

The rationale for this guideline is given under Guideline 6.1.1. Chapter 6 discusses concurrency and protected types in more detail.

4.2 VISIBILITY

Ada's ability to enforce information hiding and separation of concerns through its visibility controlling features is one of the most important advantages of the language, particularly when "pieces of a large system are being developed separately." Subverting these features, for example, by excessive reliance on the use clause, is wasteful and dangerous. See also Guidelines 5.7 and 9.4.1.

4.2.1 Minimization of Interfaces

guideline

- Put only what is needed for the use of a package into its specification.
- Minimize the number of declarations in package specifications.
- Do not include extra operations simply because they are easy to build.
- Minimize the context (with) clauses in a package specification.
- Reconsider subprograms that seem to require large numbers of parameters.

- Do not manipulate global data within a subprogram or package merely to limit the number of parameters.
- Avoid unnecessary visibility; hide the implementation details of a program unit from its users.
- Use child library units to control the visibility of parts of a subsystem interface.
- Use private child packages for those declarations that should not be used outside the subsystem.
- Use child library units to present different views of an entity to different clients.
- Design (and redesign) interfaces after having worked out the logic of various expected clients of the interface.

example

```
-------------------------------------------------------------------------
package Telephone_Book is

   type Listing is limited private;

   procedure Set_Name (New_Name : in      String;
                        Current  : in out Listing);

   procedure Insert (Name    : in      String;
                     Current : in out Listing);
   procedure Delete (Obsolete : in      String;
                     Current  : in out Listing);

private

   type Information;
   type Listing is access Information;

end Telephone_Book;

-------------------------------------------------------------------------

package body Telephone_Book is

   -- Full details of record for a listing
   type Information is
      record
         ...
         Next : Listing;
      end record;

   First : Listing;

   procedure Set_Name (New_Name : in      String;
                        Current  : in out Listing) is separate;
   procedure Insert (Name    : in      String;
                     Current : in out Listing) is separate;
   procedure Delete (Obsolete : in      String;
                     Current  : in out Listing) is separate;

end Telephone_Book;
-------------------------------------------------------------------------
```

rationale

For each entity in the specification, give careful consideration to whether it could be moved to a child package or to the parent package body. The fewer the extraneous details, the more understandable the program, package, or subprogram. It is important to maintainers to know exactly what a package interface is so that they can understand the effects of changes. Interfaces to a subprogram extend beyond the parameters. Any modification of global data from within a package or subprogram is an undocumented interface to the "outside" as well.

Minimize the context clauses on a specification by moving unnecessary clauses to the body. This technique makes the reader's job easier, localizes the recompilation required when library units change, and helps prevent a ripple effect during modifications. See also Guideline 4.2.3.

Subprograms with large numbers of parameters often indicate poor design decisions (e.g., the functional boundaries of the subprogram are inappropriate or parameters are structured poorly). Conversely, subprograms with no parameters are likely to be accessing global data.

Objects visible within package specifications can be modified by any unit that has visibility to them. The object cannot be protected or represented abstractly by its enclosing package. Objects that must persist should be declared in package bodies. Objects whose value depends on program units external to their enclosing package are probably either in the wrong package or are better accessed by a subprogram specified in the package specification.

Child library units can provide distinct views of the hierarchical library. The engineer can provide a different view for the client than for the implementor (Rationale 1995, §10.1). By creating private child packages, the engineer can provide facilities that are only available inside the subsystem rooted at the parent library unit. The declarations inside a private child package specification are not exported outside the subsystem. Thus, the engineer can declare utilities needed to implement an abstraction in a private child package (e.g., debugging utilities [Cohen et al. 1993]) and be certain that users of the abstraction (i.e., the clients) cannot access these utilities.

Different clients may have different needs for essentially the same resource. Instead of having multiple versions of the resources, consider having child units that export different views for different purposes.

Designing an interface based strictly on predicting what clients "might" need can produce a bloated and inappropriate interface. What then happens is that clients try to "live" with the interface and work around the inappropriate interfaces, repeating code that logically should be part of the shared abstraction. See Guideline 8.3.1 for a discussion of interfaces from the reusability perspective.

notes

In some cases, subroutine libraries look like large, monolithic packages. In such cases, it may be beneficial to break these up into smaller packages, grouping them according to category (e.g., trigonometric functions).

4.2.2   Nested Packages

guideline

- Use child packages rather than nested packages to present different views of the same abstraction.
- Nest package specifications within another package specification only for grouping operations or hiding common implementation details.

example

Annex A of the Ada Reference Manual (1995) gives an example of package specification nesting. The specification of the generic package Generic_Bounded_Length is nested inside the specification of package Ada.Strings.Bounded. The nested package is a generic, grouping closely related operations.

rationale

Grouping package specifications into an encompassing package emphasizes a relationship of commonality among those packages. It also allows them to share common implementation details resulting from the relationship. Nesting packages allows you to organize the name space of the package in contrast to the semantic effect of nesting inside of subprograms or task bodies.

An abstraction occasionally needs to present different views to different classes of users. Building one view upon another as an additional abstraction does not always suffice because the functionality of the operations presented by the views may be only partially disjointed. Nesting specifications groups the facilities of the various views, yet associates them with the abstraction they present. Abusive mixing of the views by another unit would be easy to detect due to the multiple use clauses or an incongruous mix of qualified names.

See the rationale discussed in Guideline 4.2.1.

4.2.3   Restricting Visibility

guideline

- Consider using private child packages in lieu of nesting.
- Restrict the visibility of program units as much as possible by nesting them inside package bodies (Nissen and Wallis 1984) if you cannot use a private child package.
- Minimize nesting program units inside subprograms and tasks.
- Minimize the scope within which with clauses apply.
- Only with those units directly needed.

example

This program illustrates the use of child library units to restrict visibility. The procedure `Rational_Numbers.Reduce` is nested inside the body of `Rational_Numbers` to restrict its visibility to the implementation of this abstraction. Rather than make the text input/output facilities visible to the entire rational number hierarchy, it is only available to the body of the child library `Rational_Numbers.IO`. This example is adapted from the Ada Reference Manual (1995, §§7.1, 7.2, and 10.1.1):

```
------------------------------------------------------------------------
package Rational_Numbers is

    type Rational is private;

    function "=" (X, Y: Rational) return Boolean;

    function "/" (X, Y: Integer)  return Rational;   -- construct a rational number

    function "+" (X, Y: Rational) return Rational;
    function "-" (X, Y: Rational) return Rational;
    function "*" (X, Y: Rational) return Rational;
    function "/" (X, Y: Rational) return Rational;   -- rational division

private
    ...
end Rational_Numbers;

package body Rational_Numbers is

    procedure Reduce (R :in out Rational) is . . . end Reduce;

    . . .

end Rational_Numbers;

package Rational_Numbers.IO is

    procedure Put (R : in  Rational);
    procedure Get (R : out Rational);

end Rational_Numbers.IO;

with Ada.Text_IO;
with Ada.Integer_Text_IO;
package body Rational_Numbers.IO is    -- has visibility to parent private type declaration

    procedure Put (R : in  Rational) is
    begin
        Ada.Integer_Text_IO.Put (Item => R.Numerator, Width => 0);
        Ada.Text_IO.Put ("/");
        Ada.Integer_Text_IO.Put (Item => R.Denominator, Width => 0);
    end Put;

    procedure Get (R : out Rational) is . . . end Get;

end Rational_Numbers.IO;
```

rationale

Restricting visibility of a program unit ensures that the program unit is not called from some part of the system other than that which was intended. This is done by nesting it inside the only unit that uses it, by hiding it inside a package body rather than declaring it in the package specification, or by declaring it as a private child unit. This avoids errors and eases the job of maintainers by guaranteeing that a local change in that unit will not have an unforeseen global effect.

Restricting visibility of a library unit by using `with` clauses on subunits rather than on the entire parent unit is useful in the same way. In the example above, it is clear that the package `Text_IO` is used only by the `Listing_Facilities` package of the compiler.

Nesting inside subprograms and tasks is discouraged because it leads to unreusable components. These components are essentially unreusable because they make undesirable up-level references into the defining context. Unless you truly want to ensure that the program unit is not called from some unintended part of the system, you should minimize this form of nesting.

See also Guideline 4.2.1 for a discussion of the use of child units.

notes

One way to minimize the coverage of a with clause is to use it only with subunits that really need it. Consider making those subunits separate compilation units when the need for visibility to a library unit is restricted to a subprogram or two.

4.2.4   Hiding Tasks

guideline

- Carefully consider encapsulation of tasks.

example

```
----------------------------------------------------------------------
package Disk_Head_Scheduler is

    type Words       is ...

    type Track_Number is ...

    procedure Transmit (Track : in    Track_Number;
                        Data  : in    Words);

    ...
end Disk_Head_Scheduler;
----------------------------------------------------------------------

package body Disk_Head_Scheduler is

    ...
    task Control is
       entry Sign_In (Track : in    Track_Number);

       ...
    end Control;
    ----------------------------------------------------------------
    task Track_Manager is
       entry Transfer(Track_Number) (Data : in    Words);
    end Track_Manager;
    ----------------------------------------------------------------
    ...

    procedure Transmit (Track : in    Track_Number;
                        Data  : in    Words) is
    begin

       Control.Sign_In(Track);
       Track_Manager.Transfer(Track)(Data);

    end Transmit;

    ----------------------------------------------------------------
    ...
end Disk_Head_Scheduler;
----------------------------------------------------------------------
```

rationale

The decision whether to declare a task in the specification or body of an enclosing package is not a simple one. There are good arguments for both.

Hiding a task specification in a package body and exporting (via subprograms) only required entries reduces the amount of extraneous information in the package specification. It allows your subprograms to enforce any order of entry calls necessary to the proper operation of the tasks. It also allows you to impose defensive task communication practices (see Guideline 6.2.2) and proper use of conditional and timed entry calls. Finally, it allows the grouping of entries into sets for export to different classes of users (e.g., producers versus consumers) or the concealment of entries that should not be made public at all (e.g., initialization, completion, signals). Where performance is an issue and there are no ordering rules to enforce, the entries can be renamed as subprograms to avoid the overhead of an extra procedure call.

An argument, which can be viewed as an advantage or disadvantage, is that hiding the task specification in a package body hides the fact of a tasking implementation from the user. If the application is such that a change to or from a tasking implementation or a reorganization of services among tasks need not concern users of the package, then this is an advantage. However, if the package user must know about the tasking implementation to reason about global tasking behavior, then it is better not to hide the task completely. Either move it to the package specification or add comments stating that there is a tasking implementation, describing when a call may block, etc. Otherwise, it is the package implementor's responsibility to ensure that users of the package do not have to concern themselves with behaviors such as deadlock, starvation, and race conditions.

Finally, keep in mind that hiding tasks behind a procedural interface prevents the usage of conditional and timed entry calls and entry families, unless you add parameters and extra code to the procedures to make it possible for callers to direct the procedures to use these capabilities.

4.3   EXCEPTIONS

This section addresses the issue of exceptions in the context of program structures. It discusses how exceptions should be used as part of the interface to a unit, including what exceptions to declare and raise and under what conditions to raise them. Information on how to handle, propagate, and avoid raising exceptions is found in Guideline 5.8. Guidelines on how to deal with portability issues are in Guideline 7.5.

4.3.1   Using Exceptions to Help Define an Abstraction

guideline

*   For unavoidable internal errors for which no user recovery is possible, declare a single user-visible exception. Inside the abstraction, provide a way to distinguish between the different internal errors.
*   Do not borrow an exception name from another context.
*   Export (declare visibly to the user) the names of all exceptions that can be raised.
*   In a package, document which exceptions can be raised by each subprogram and task entry.
*   Do not raise exceptions for internal errors that can be avoided or corrected within the unit.
*   Do not raise the same exception to report different kinds of errors that are distinguishable by the user of the unit.
*   Provide interrogative functions that allow the user of a unit to avoid causing exceptions to be raised.
*   When possible, avoid changing state information in a unit before raising an exception.
*   Catch and convert or handle all predefined and compiler-defined exceptions at the earliest opportunity.
*   Do not explicitly raise predefined or implementation-defined exceptions.
*   Never let an exception propagate beyond its scope.

example

This package specification defines two exceptions that enhance the abstraction:

```
generic
   type Element is private;
package Stack is

   function Stack_Empty return Boolean;
   function Stack_Full  return Boolean;

   procedure Pop  (From_Top :    out Element);
   procedure Push (Onto_Top : in     Element);

   -- Raised when Pop is used on empty stack.
   Underflow : exception;

   -- Raised when Push is used on full stack.
   Overflow  : exception;

end Stack;
```

```
   ...
------------------------------------------------------------------------
procedure Pop (From_Top :    out Element) is
begin
   ...

   if Stack_Empty then
      raise Underflow;

   else -- Stack contains at least one element
      Top_Index := Top_Index - 1;
      From_Top  := Data(Top_Index + 1);

   end if;
end Pop;
------------------------------------------------------------------------
   ...
```

rationale

Exceptions should be used as part of an abstraction to indicate error conditions that the abstraction is unable to prevent or correct. Because the abstraction is unable to correct such an error, it must report the error to the user. In the case of a usage error (e.g., attempting to invoke operations in the wrong sequence or attempting to exceed a boundary condition), the user may be able to correct the error. In the case of an error beyond the control of the user, the user may be able to work around the error if there are multiple mechanisms available to perform the desired operation. In other cases, the user may have to abandon use of the unit, dropping into a degraded mode of limited functionality. In any case, the user must be notified.

Exceptions are a good mechanism for reporting such errors because they provide an alternate flow of control for dealing with errors. This allows error-handling code to be kept separate from the code for normal processing. When an exception is raised, the current operation is aborted and control is transferred directly to the appropriate exception handler.

Several of the guidelines above exist to maximize the ability of the user to distinguish and correct different kinds of errors. Declaring new exception names, rather than raising exceptions declared in other packages, reduces the coupling between packages and also makes different exceptions more distinguishable. Exporting the names of all exceptions that a unit can raise, rather than declaring them internally to the unit, makes it possible for users of the unit to refer to the names in exception handlers. Otherwise, the user would be able to handle the exception only with an others handler. Finally, use comments to document exactly which of the exceptions declared in a package can be raised by each subprogram or task entry making it possible for the user to know which exception handlers are appropriate in each situation.

In situations where there are errors for which the abstraction user can take no intelligent action (e.g., there is no workaround or degraded mode), it is better to export a single internal error exception. Within the package, you should consider distinguishing between the different internal errors. For instance, you could record or handle different kinds of internal error in different ways. When you propagate the error to the user, however, you should use a special internal error exception, indicating that no user recovery is possible. You should also provide relevant information when you propagate the error, using the facilities provided in Ada.Exceptions. Thus, for any abstraction, you effectively provide N + 1 different exceptions: N different recoverable errors and one irrecoverable error for which there is no mapping to the abstraction. Both the application requirements and what the client needs/wants in terms of error information help you identify the appropriate exceptions for an abstraction.

Because they cause an immediate transfer of control, exceptions are useful for reporting unrecoverable errors, which prevent an operation from being completed, but not for reporting status or modes incidental to the completion of an operation. They should not be used to report internal errors that a unit was able to correct invisibly to the user.

To provide the user with maximum flexibility, it is a good idea to provide interrogative functions that the user can call to determine whether an exception would be raised if a subprogram or task entry were invoked. The function Stack_Empty in the above example is such a function. It indicates whether Underflow would be raised if Pop were called. Providing such functions makes it possible for the user to avoid triggering exceptions.

To support error recovery by its user, a unit should try to avoid changing state during an invocation that raises an exception. If a requested operation cannot be completely and correctly performed, then the unit should either detect this before changing any internal state information or should revert to the state at the time of the request. For example, after raising the exception Underflow, the stack package in the above example should remain in exactly the same state it was in when Pop was called. If it were to partially update its internal data structures for managing the stack, then future Push and Pop operations would not perform correctly. This is always desirable, but not always possible.

User-defined exceptions should be used instead of predefined or compiler-defined exceptions because they are more descriptive and more specific to the abstraction. The predefined exceptions are very general and can be triggered by many different situations. Compiler-defined exceptions are nonportable and have meanings that are subject to change even between successive releases of the same compiler. This introduces too much uncertainty for the creation of useful handlers.

If you are writing an abstraction, remember that the user does not know about the units you use in your implementation. That is an effect of information hiding. If any exception is raised within your abstraction, you must catch it and handle it. The user is not able to provide a reasonable handler if the original exception is allowed to propagate out of the body of your abstraction. You can still convert the exception into a form intelligible to the user if your abstraction cannot effectively recover on its own.

Converting an exception means raising a user-defined exception in the handler for the original exception. This introduces a meaningful name for export to the user of the unit. Once the error situation is couched in terms of the application, it can be handled in those terms.

4.4   SUMMARY

high-level structure

- Place the specification of each library unit package in a separate file from its body.
- Avoid defining library unit subprograms that are not intended to be used as main programs. If such subprograms are defined, then create an explicit specification, in a separate file, for each library unit subprogram.
- Minimize the use of subunits.
- In preference to subunits, use child library units to structure a subsystem into manageable units.
- Place each subunit in a separate file.
- Use a consistent file naming convention.
- In preference to nesting in a package body, use a private child and with it to the parent body.
- Use private child unit specifications for data and subprograms that are required by (other) child units that extend a parent unit's abstraction or services.
- When possible, express configuration pragmas through compiler options or other means that do not require modifications to the source code. .
- When configuration pragmas must be placed in source code, consider isolating them to one compilation unit per partition; if specified, the main subprogram for the partition is recommended.
- Use subprograms to enhance abstraction.
- Restrict each subprogram to the performance of a single action.
- Use a function when the subprogram's primary purpose is to provide a single value.
- Minimize the side effect of a function.
- Consider using a parameterless function when the value does not need to be static.
- Use a parameterless function (instead of a constant) if the value should be inherited by types derived from the type.
- Use a parameterless function if the value itself is subject to change.
- Use packages for information hiding.
- Use packages with tagged types and private types for abstract data types.
- Use packages to model abstract entities appropriate to the problem domain.

- Use packages to group together related type and object declarations (e.g., common declarations for two or more library units).
- Encapsulate machine dependencies in packages. Place a software interface to a particular device in a package to facilitate a change to a different device.
- Place low-level implementation decisions or interfaces in subprograms within packages.
- Use packages and subprograms to encapsulate and hide program details that may change (Nissen and Wallis 1984).
- If a new library unit represents a logical extension to the original abstraction, define it as a child library unit.
- If a new library unit is independent (e.g., introduces a new abstraction that depends only in part on the existing one), then encapsulate the new abstraction in a separate library unit.
- Use child packages to implement a subsystem.
- Use public child units for those parts of a subsystem that should be visible to clients of the subsystem.
- Use private child units for those parts of a subsystem that should not be visible to clients of the subsystem.
- Use private child units for local declarations used only in implementing the package specification.
- Use child packages to implement constructors, even when they return access values.
- Make each package serve a single purpose.
- Use packages to group related data, types, and subprograms.
- Avoid collections of unrelated objects and subprograms (NASA 1987; Nissen and Wallis 1984).
- Consider restructuring a system to move two highly related units into the same package (or package hierarchy) or to move relatively independent units into separate packages.
- Avoid declaring variables in package specifications.
- Use tasks to model abstract, asynchronous entities within the problem domain.
- Use tasks to define concurrent algorithms for multiprocessor architectures.
- Use tasks to perform concurrent, cyclic, or prioritized activities (NASA 1987).
- Use protected types to control or synchronize access to data or devices.
- Use protected types to implement synchronization tasks, such as a passive resource monitor.

visibility

- Put only what is needed for the use of a package into its specification.
- Minimize the number of declarations in package specifications.
- Do not include extra operations simply because they are easy to build.
- Minimize the context (with) clauses in a package specification.
- Reconsider subprograms that seem to require large numbers of parameters.
- Do not manipulate global data within a subprogram or package merely to limit the number of parameters.
- Avoid unnecessary visibility; hide the implementation details of a program unit from its users.
- Use child library units to control the visibility of parts of a subsystem interface.
- Use private child packages for those declarations that should not be used outside the subsystem.
- Use child library units to present different views of an entity to different clients.
- Design (and redesign) interfaces after having worked out the logic of various expected clients of the interface.
- Use child packages rather than nested packages to present different views of the same abstraction.
- Nest package specifications within another package specification only for grouping operations or hiding common implementation details.
- Consider using private child packages in lieu of nesting.

- Restrict the visibility of program units as much as possible by nesting them inside package bodies (Nissen and Wallis 1984) if you cannot use a private child package.
- Minimize nesting program units inside subprograms and tasks.
- Minimize the scope within which `with` clauses apply.
- Only `with` those units directly needed.
- Carefully consider encapsulation of tasks.

exceptions

- For unavoidable internal errors for which no user recovery is possible, declare a single user-visible exception. Inside the abstraction, provide a way to distinguish between the different internal errors.
- Do not borrow an exception name from another context.
- Export (declare visibly to the user) the names of all exceptions that can be raised.
- In a package, document which exceptions can be raised by each subprogram and task entry.
- Do not raise exceptions for internal errors that can be avoided or corrected within the unit.
- Do not raise the same exception to report different kinds of errors that are distinguishable by the user of the unit.
- Provide interrogative functions that allow the user of a unit to avoid causing exceptions to be raised.
- When possible, avoid changing state information in a unit before raising an exception.
- Catch and convert or handle all predefined and compiler-defined exceptions at the earliest opportunity.
- Do not explicitly raise predefined or implementation-defined exceptions.
- Never let an exception propagate beyond its scope.

CHAPTER 5
Programming Practices

Software is always subject to change. The need for this change, euphemistically known as "maintenance" arises from a variety of sources. Errors need to be corrected as they are discovered. System functionality may need to be enhanced in planned or unplanned ways. Inevitably, the requirements change over the lifetime of the system, forcing continual system evolution. Often, these modifications are conducted long after the software was originally written, usually by someone other than the original author.

Easy and successful modification requires that the software be readable, understandable, and structured according to accepted practice. If a software component cannot be easily understood by a programmer who is familiar with its intended function, that software component is not maintainable. Techniques that make code readable and comprehensible enhance its maintainability. Previous chapters presented techniques such as consistent use of naming conventions, clear and well-organized commentary, and proper modularization. This chapter presents consistent and logical use of language features.

Correctness is one aspect of reliability. While style guidelines cannot enforce the use of correct algorithms, they can suggest the use of techniques and language features known to reduce the number or likelihood of failures. Such techniques include program construction methods that reduce the likelihood of errors or that improve program predictability by defining behavior in the presence of errors.

5.1   OPTIONAL PARTS OF THE SYNTAX

Parts of the Ada syntax, while optional, can enhance the readability of the code. The guidelines given below concern use of some of these optional features.

5.1.1   Loop Names

guideline

- Associate names with loops when they are nested (Booch 1986, 1987).
- Associate names with any loop that contains an `exit` statement.

example

```
Process_Each_Page:
   loop

      Process_All_The_Lines_On_This_Page:
         loop

            . . .
            exit Process_All_The_Lines_On_This_Page when Line_Number = Max_Lines_On_Page;

            . . .
            Look_For_Sentinel_Value:
               loop

                  . . .
                  exit Look_For_Sentinel_Value when Current_Symbol = Sentinel;

                  . . .
               end loop Look_For_Sentinel_Value;
```

```
         ...
      end loop Process_All_The_Lines_On_This_Page;

   ...
   exit Process_Each_Page when Page_Number = Maximum_Pages;

   ...
end loop Process_Each_Page;
```

rationale

When you associate a name with a loop, you must include that name with the associated end for that loop (Ada Reference Manual 1995). This helps readers find the associated end for any given loop. This is especially true if loops are broken over screen or page boundaries. The choice of a good name for the loop documents its purpose, reducing the need for explanatory comments. If a name for a loop is very difficult to choose, this could indicate a need for more thought about the algorithm.

Regularly naming loops helps you follow Guideline 5.1.3. Even in the face of code changes, for example, adding an outer or inner loop, the exit statement does not become ambiguous.

It can be difficult to think up a name for every loop; therefore, the guideline specifies nested loops. The benefits in readability and second thought outweigh the inconvenience of naming the loops.

5.1.2   Block Names

guideline

- Associate names with blocks when they are nested.

example

```
Trip:
   declare
      ...
   begin  -- Trip

      Arrive_At_Airport:
         declare
            ...
         begin  -- Arrive_At_Airport

            Rent_Car;
            Claim_Baggage;
            Reserve_Hotel;

            ...
         end Arrive_At_Airport;
      Visit_Customer:
         declare
            ...
         begin  -- Visit_Customer
            -- again a set of activities...
            ...
         end Visit_Customer;
      Departure_Preparation:
         declare
            ...
         begin  -- Departure_Preparation
            Return_Car;
            Check_Baggage;
            Wait_For_Flight;

            ...
         end Departure_Preparation;

      Board_Return_Flight;
   end Trip;
```

rationale

When there is a nested block structure, it can be difficult to determine which end corresponds to which block. Naming blocks alleviates this confusion. The choice of a good name for the block documents its purpose, reducing the need for explanatory comments. If a name for the block is very difficult to choose, this could indicate a need for more thought about the algorithm.

This guideline is also useful if nested blocks are broken over a screen or page boundary.

It can be difficult to think up a name for each block; therefore, the guideline specifies nested blocks. The benefits in readability and second thought outweigh the inconvenience of naming the blocks.

5.1.3   Exit Statements

guideline

- Use loop names on all exit statements from nested loops.

example

See the example in Guideline 5.1.1.

rationale

An exit statement is an implicit goto. It should specify its source explicitly. When there is a nested loop structure and an exit statement is used, it can be difficult to determine which loop is being exited. Also, future changes that may introduce a nested loop are likely to introduce an error, with the exit accidentally exiting from the wrong loop. Naming loops and their exits alleviates this confusion. This guideline is also useful if nested loops are broken over a screen or page boundary.

5.1.4   Naming End Statements

guideline

- Include the defining program unit name at the end of a package specification and body.
- Include the defining identifier at the end of a task specification and body.
- Include the entry identifier at the end of an accept statement.
- Include the designator at the end of a subprogram body.
- Include the defining identifier at the end of a protected unit declaration.

example

```
-----------------------------------------------------------------------
package Autopilot is

    function Is_Engaged return Boolean;

    procedure Engage;
    procedure Disengage;

end Autopilot;
-----------------------------------------------------------------------

package body Autopilot is

    ...

-----------------------------------------------------------------------
    task Course_Monitor is
        entry Reset (Engage : in      Boolean);
    end Course_Monitor;

-----------------------------------------------------------------------
    function Is_Engaged return Boolean is
    ...
    end Is_Engaged;

-----------------------------------------------------------------------
    procedure Engage is
    ...
    end Engage;

-----------------------------------------------------------------------
    procedure Disengage is
    ...
    end Disengage;

-----------------------------------------------------------------------
    task body Course_Monitor is
    ...
        accept Reset (Engage : in      Boolean) do

            ...
```

```
        end Reset;

    ...
    end Course_Monitor;

    ------------------------------------------------------------------
    end Autopilot;
    ------------------------------------------------------------------
```

rationale

> Repeating names on the end of these compound statements ensures consistency throughout the code. In addition, the named end provides a reference for the reader if the unit spans a page or screen boundary or if it contains a nested unit.

5.2   PARAMETER LISTS

A subprogram or entry parameter list is the interface to the abstraction implemented by the subprogram or entry. It is important that it is clear and that it is expressed in a consistent style. Careful decisions about formal parameter naming and ordering can make the purpose of the subprogram easier to understand, which can make it easier to use.

5.2.1   Formal Parameters

guideline

- Name formal parameters descriptively to reduce the need for comments.

example

```
List_Manager.Insert (Element     => New_Employee,
                     Into_List   => Probationary_Employees,
                     At_Position => 1);
```

rationale

> Following the variable naming guidelines (Guidelines 3.2.1 and 3.2.3) for formal parameters can make calls to subprograms read more like regular prose, as shown in the example above, where no comments are necessary. Descriptive names of this sort can also make the code in the body of the subprogram more clear.

5.2.2   Named Association

guideline

- Use named parameter association in calls of infrequently used subprograms or entries with many formal parameters.
- Use named association when instantiating generics.
- Use named association for clarification when the actual parameter is any literal or expression.
- Use named association when supplying a nondefault value to an optional parameter.

instantiation

- Use named parameter association in calls of subprograms or entries called from less than five places in a single source file or with more than two formal parameters.

example

```
Encode_Telemetry_Packet (Source         => Power_Electronics,
                         Content        => Temperature,
                         Value          => Read_Temperature_Sensor(Power_Electronics),
                         Time           => Current_Time,
                         Sequence       => Next_Packet_ID,
                         Vehicle        => This_Spacecraft,
                         Primary_Module => True);
```

rationale

> Calls of infrequently used subprograms or entries with many formal parameters can be difficult to understand without referring to the subprogram or entry code. Named parameter association can make these calls more readable.

When the formal parameters have been named appropriately, it is easier to determine exactly what purpose the subprogram serves without looking at its code. This reduces the need for named constants that exist solely to make calls more readable. It also allows variables used as actual parameters to be given names indicating what they are without regard to why they are being passed in a call. An actual parameter, which is an expression rather than a variable, cannot be named otherwise.

Named association allows subprograms to have new parameters inserted with minimal ramifications to existing calls.

notes

The judgment of when named parameter association improves readability is subjective. Certainly, simple or familiar subprograms, such as a swap routine or a sine function, do not require the extra clarification of named association in the procedure call.

caution

A consequence of named parameter association is that the formal parameter names may not be changed without modifying the text of each call.

5.2.3   Default Parameters

guideline

- Provide default parameters to allow for occasional, special use of widely used subprograms or entries.
- Place default parameters at the end of the formal parameter list.
- Consider providing default values to new parameters added to an existing subprogram.

example

Annex A of the Ada Reference Manual (1995) contains many examples of this practice.

rationale

Often, the majority of uses of a subprogram or entry need the same value for a given parameter. Providing that value, as the default for the parameter, makes the parameter optional on the majority of calls. It also allows the remaining calls to customize the subprogram or entry by providing different values for that parameter.

Placing default parameters at the end of the formal parameter list allows the caller to use positional association on the call; otherwise, defaults are available only when named association is used.

Often during maintenance activities, you increase the functionality of a subprogram or entry. This requires more parameters than the original form for some calls. New parameters may be required to control this new functionality. Give the new parameters default values that specify the old functionality. Calls needing the old functionality need not be changed; they take the defaults. This is true if the new parameters are added to the end of the parameter list, or if named association is used on all calls. New calls needing the new functionality can specify that by providing other values for the new parameters.

This enhances maintainability in that the places that use the modified routines do not themselves have to be modified, while the previous functionality levels of the routines are allowed to be "reused."

exceptions

Do not go overboard. If the changes in functionality are truly radical, you should be preparing a separate routine rather than modifying an existing one. One indicator of this situation would be that it is difficult to determine value combinations for the defaults that uniquely and naturally require the more restrictive of the two functions. In such cases, it is better to go ahead with creation of a separate routine.

5.2.4   Mode Indication

guideline

- Show the mode indication of all procedure and entry parameters (Nissen and Wallis 1984).
- Use the most restrictive parameter mode applicable to your application.

example

```
procedure Open_File (File_Name  : in      String;
                     Open_Status :      out Status_Codes);

entry Acquire (Key      : in      Capability;
               Resource :     out Tape_Drive);
```

rationale

By showing the mode of parameters, you aid the reader. If you do not specify a parameter mode, the default mode is in. Explicitly showing the mode indication of all parameters is a more assertive action than simply taking the default mode. Anyone reviewing the code later will be more confident that you intended the parameter mode to be in.

Use the mode that reflects the actual use of the parameter. You should avoid the tendency to make all parameters in out mode because out mode parameters may be examined as well as updated.

exceptions

It may be necessary to consider several alternative implementations for a given abstraction. For example, a bounded stack can be implemented as a pointer to an array. Even though an update to the object being pointed to does not require changing the pointer value itself, you may want to consider making the mode in out to allow changes to the implementation and to document more accurately what the operation is doing. If you later change the implementation to a simple array, the mode will have to be in out, potentially causing changes to all places that the routine is called.

5.3   TYPES

In addition to determining the possible values for variables and subtype names, type distinctions can be very valuable aids in developing safe, readable, and understandable code. Types clarify the structure of your data and can limit or restrict the operations performed on that data. "Keeping types distinct has been found to be a very powerful means of detecting logical mistakes when a program is written and to give valuable assistance whenever the program is being subsequently maintained" (Pyle 1985). Take advantage of Ada's strong typing capability in the form of subtypes, derived types, task types, protected types, private types, and limited private types.

The guidelines encourage much code to be written to ensure strong typing. While it might appear that there would be execution penalties for this amount of code, this is usually not the case. In contrast to other conventional languages, Ada has a less direct relationship between the amount of code that is written and the size of the resulting executable program. Most of the strong type checking is performed at compilation time rather than execution time, so the size of the executable code is not greatly affected.

For guidelines on specific kinds of data structures and tagged types, see Guidelines 5.4 and 9.2.1, respectively.

5.3.1   Derived Types and Subtypes

guideline

- Use existing types as building blocks by deriving new types from them.
- Use range constraints on subtypes.
- Define new types, especially derived types, to include the largest set of possible values, including boundary values.
- Constrain the ranges of derived types with subtypes, excluding boundary values.
- Use type derivation rather than type extension when there are no meaningful components to add to the type.

example

Type Table is a building block for the creation of new types:

```
type Table is
   record
      Count : List_Size  := Empty;
      List  : Entry_List := Empty_List;
   end record;
```

```
type Telephone_Directory  is new Table;
type Department_Inventory is new Table;
```

The following are distinct types that cannot be intermixed in operations that are not programmed explicitly to use them both:

```
type Dollars is new Number;
type Cents   is new Number;
```

Below, `Source_Tail` has a value outside the range of `Listing_Paper` when the line is empty. All the indices can be mixed in expressions, as long as the results fall within the correct subtypes:

```
type Columns           is range First_Column - 1 .. Listing_Width + 1;

subtype Listing_Paper is Columns range First_Column .. Listing_Width;
subtype Dumb_Terminal is Columns range First_Column .. Dumb_Terminal_Width;

type Line             is array (Columns range <>) of Bytes;
subtype Listing_Line is Line (Listing_Paper);
subtype Terminal_Line is Line (Dumb_Terminal);

Source_Tail : Columns       := Columns'First;
Source      : Listing_Line;
Destination : Terminal_Line;

...

Destination(Destination'First .. Source_Tail - Destination'Last) :=
    Source(Columns'Succ(Destination'Last) .. Source_Tail);
```

rationale

The name of a derived type can make clear its intended use and avoid proliferation of similar type definitions. Objects of two derived types, even though derived from the same type, cannot be mixed in operations unless such operations are supplied explicitly or one is converted to the other explicitly. This prohibition is an enforcement of strong typing.

Define new types, derived types, and subtypes cautiously and deliberately. The concepts of subtype and derived type are not equivalent, but they can be used to advantage in concert. A subtype limits the range of possible values for a type but does not define a new type.

Types can have highly constrained sets of values without eliminating useful values. Used in concert, derived types and subtypes can eliminate many flag variables and type conversions within executable statements. This renders the program more readable, enforces the abstraction, and allows the compiler to enforce strong typing constraints.

Many algorithms begin or end with values just outside the normal range. If boundary values are not compatible within subexpressions, algorithms can be needlessly complicated. The program can become cluttered with flag variables and special cases when it could just test for zero or some other sentinel value just outside normal range.

The type `Columns` and the subtype `Listing_Paper` in the example above demonstrate how to allow sentinel values. The subtype `Listing_Paper` could be used as the type for parameters of subprograms declared in the specification of a package. This would restrict the range of values that could be specified by the caller. Meanwhile, the type `Columns` could be used to store such values internally to the body of the package, allowing `First_Column - 1` to be used as a sentinel value. This combination of types and subtypes allows compatibility between subtypes within subexpressions without type conversions as would happen with derived types.

The choice between type derivation and type extension depends on what kind of changes you expect to occur to objects in the type. In general, type derivation is a very simple form of inheritance: the derived types inherit the structure, operations, and values of the parent type (Rationale 1995, §4.2). Although you can add operations, you cannot augment the data structure. You can derive from either scalar or composite types.

Type extension is a more powerful form of inheritance, only applied to `tagged` records, in which you can augment both the type's components and operations. When the record implements an abstraction with the potential for reuse and/or extension, it is a good candidate for making it `tagged`. Similarly, if the abstraction is a member of a family of abstractions with well-defined variable and common properties, you should consider a `tagged` record.

notes

The price of the reduction in the number of independent type declarations is that subtypes and derived types change when the base type is redefined. This trickle-down of changes is sometimes a blessing and sometimes a curse. However, usually it is intended and beneficial.

5.3.2   Anonymous Types

guideline

- Avoid anonymous array types.
- Use anonymous array types for array variables only when no suitable type exists or can be created and the array will not be referenced as a whole (e.g., used as a subprogram parameter).
- Use access parameters and access discriminants to guarantee that the parameter or discriminant is treated as a constant.

example

Use:

```
type Buffer_Index is range 1 .. 80;
type Buffer      is array (Buffer_Index) of Character;

Input_Line : Buffer;
```

rather than:

```
Input_Line : array (Buffer_Index) of Character;
```

rationale

Although Ada allows anonymous types, they have limited usefulness and complicate program modification. For example, except for arrays, a variable of anonymous type can never be used as an actual parameter because it is not possible to define a formal parameter of the same type. Even though this may not be a limitation initially, it precludes a modification in which a piece of code is changed to a subprogram. Although you can declare the anonymous array to be aliased, you cannot use this access value as an actual parameter in a subprogram because the subprogram's formal parameter declaration requires a type mark. Also, two variables declared using the same anonymous type declaration are actually of different types.

Even though the implicit conversion of array types during parameter passing is supported in Ada, it is difficult to justify not using the type of the parameter. In most situations, the type of the parameter is visible and easily substituted in place of an anonymous array type. The use of an anonymous array type implies that the array is only being used as a convenient way to implement a collection of values. It is misleading to use an anonymous type, and then treat the variable as an object.

When you use an access parameter or access discriminant, the anonymous type is essentially declared inside the subprogram or object itself (Rationale 1995, §3.7.1). Thus, you have no way of declaring another object of the same type, and the object is treated as a constant. In the case of a self-referential data structure (see Guideline 5.4.6), you need the access parameter to be able to manipulate the data the discriminant accesses (Rationale 1995, §3.7.1).

notes

For anonymous task types, see Guideline 6.1.4.

exceptions

If you are creating a unique table, for example, the periodic table of the elements, consider using an anonymous array type.

5.3.3   Private Types

guideline

- Derive from controlled types in preference to using limited private types.
- Use limited private types in preference to private types.
- Use private types in preference to nonprivate types.
- Explicitly export needed operations rather than easing restrictions.

example

```
--------------------------------------------------------------------------
with Ada.Finalization;
package Packet_Telemetry is

    type Frame_Header is new Ada.Finalization.Controlled with private;
    type Frame_Data   is private;
    type Frame_Codes  is (Main_Bus_Voltage, Transmitter_1_Power);

    ...
private

    type Frame_Header is new Ada.Finalization.Controlled with
        record
        ...
        end record;

    -- override adjustment and finalization to get correct assignment semantics
    procedure Adjust (Object : in out Frame_Header);
    procedure Finalize (Object : in out Frame_Header);

    type Frame_Data is
        record
        ...
        end record;

    ...
end Packet_Telemetry;
--------------------------------------------------------------------------
```

rationale

Limited private types and private types support abstraction and information hiding better than nonprivate types. The more restricted the type, the better information hiding is served. This, in turn, allows the implementation to change without affecting the rest of the program. While there are many valid reasons to export types, it is better to try the preferred route first, loosening the restrictions only as necessary. If it is necessary for a user of the package to use a few of the restricted operations, it is better to export the operations explicitly and individually via exported subprograms than to drop a level of restriction. This practice retains the restrictions on other operations.

Limited private types have the most restricted set of operations available to users of a package. Of the types that must be made available to users of a package, as many as possible should be derived from the controlled types or limited private. Controlled types give you the ability to adjust assignment and to finalize values, so you no longer need to create limited private types to guarantee a client that assignment and equality obey deep copy/comparison semantics. Therefore, it is possible to export a slightly less restrictive type (i.e., private type that extends Ada.Finalization.Controlled) that has an adjustable assignment operator and overridable equality operator. See also Guideline 5.4.5.

The operations available to limited private types are membership tests, selected components, components for the selections of any discriminant, qualification and explicit conversion, and attributes 'Base and 'Size. Objects of a limited private type also have the attribute 'Constrained if there are discriminants. None of these operations allows the user of the package to manipulate objects in a way that depends on the structure of the type.

notes

The predefined packages Direct_IO and Sequential_IO do not accept limited private types as generic parameters. This restriction should be considered when I/O operations are needed for a type.

See Guideline 8.3.3 for a discussion of the use of private and limited private types in generic units.

5.3.4   Subprogram Access Types

guideline

- Use access-to-subprogram types for indirect access to subprograms.
- Wherever possible, use abstract tagged types and dispatching rather than access-to-subprogram types to implement dynamic selection and invocation of subprograms.

example

The following example is taken from the Rationale (1995, §3.7.2):

```
generic
   type Float_Type is digits <>;
package Generic_Integration is
   type Integrand is access function (X : Float_Type) return Float_Type;
   function Integrate (F        : Integrand;
                       From     : Float_Type;
                       To       : Float_Type;
                       Accuracy : Float_Type := 10.0*Float_Type'Model_Epsilon)
      return Float_Type;
end Generic_Integration;

with Generic_Integration;
procedure Try_Estimate (External_Data : in     Data_Type;
                        Lower         : in     Float;
                        Upper         : in     Float;
                        Answer        :    out Float) is
   -- external data set by other means

   function Residue (X : Float) return Float is
      Result : Float;
   begin  -- Residue
      -- compute function value dependent upon external data
      return Result;
   end Residue;

   package Float_Integration is
      new Generic_Integration (Float_Type => Float);

   use Float_Integration;

begin -- Try_Estimate
   ...
   Answer := Integrate (F    => Residue'Access,
                        From => Lower,
                        To   => Upper);
end Try_Estimate;
```

rationale

Access-to-subprogram types allow you to create data structures that contain subprogram references. There are many uses for this feature, for instance, implementing state machines, call backs in the X Window System, iterators (the operation to be applied to each element of a list), and numerical algorithms (e.g., integration function) (Rationale 1995, §3.7.2).

You can achieve the same effect as access-to-subprogram types for dynamic selection by using abstract tagged types. You declare an abstract type with one abstract operation and then use an access-to-class-wide type to get the dispatching effect. This technique provides greater flexibility and type safety than access-to-subprogram types (Ada Reference Manual 1995, §3.10.2).

Access-to-subprogram types are useful in implementing dynamic selection. References to the subprograms can be stored directly in the data structure. In a finite state machine, for example, a single data structure can describe the action to be taken on state transitions. Strong type checking is maintained because Ada 95 requires that the designated subprogram has the same parameter/result profile as the one specified in the subprogram access type.

See also Guideline 7.3.2.

5.4   DATA STRUCTURES

The data structuring capabilities of Ada are a powerful resource; therefore, use them to model the data as closely as possible. It is possible to group logically related data and let the language control the abstraction and operations on the data rather than requiring the programmer or maintainer to do so. Data can also be organized in a building block fashion. In addition to showing how a data structure is organized (and possibly giving the reader an indication as to why it was organized that way), creating the data structure from smaller components allows those components to be reused. Using the features that Ada provides can increase the maintainability of your code.

5.4.1 Discriminated Records

guideline

- When declaring a discriminant, use as constrained a subtype as possible (i.e., subtype with as specific a range constraint as possible).
- Use a discriminated record rather than a constrained array to represent an array whose actual values are unconstrained.

example

An object of type Name_Holder_1 could potentially hold a string whose length is Natural'Last:

```
type Number_List is array (Integer range <>) of Integer;

type Number_Holder_1 (Current_Length : Natural := 0) is
   record
      Numbers : Number_List (1 .. Current_Length);
   end record;
```

An object of type Name_Holder_2 imposes a more reasonable restriction on the length of its string component:

```
type    Number_List is array (Integer range <>) of Integer;
subtype Max_Numbers is Natural range 0 .. 42;

type Number_Holder_2 (Current_Length : Max_Numbers := 0) is
   record
      Numbers : Number_List (1 .. Current_Length);
   end record;
```

rationale

When you use the discriminant to constrain an array inside a discriminated record, the larger the range of values the discriminant can assume, the more space an object of the type might require. Although your program may compile and link, it will fail at execution when the run-time system is unable to create an object of the potential size required.

The discriminated record captures the intent of an array whose bounds may vary at run-time. A simple constrained array definition (e.g., type Number_List is array (1 .. 42) of Integer;) does not capture the intent that there are at most 42 possible numbers in the list.

5.4.2 Heterogeneous Related Data

guideline

- Use records to group heterogeneous but related data.
- Consider records to map to I/O device data.

example

```
type Propulsion_Method is (Sail, Diesel, Nuclear);

type Craft is
   record
      Name    : Common_Name;
      Plant   : Propulsion_Method;
      Length  : Feet;
      Beam    : Feet;
      Draft   : Feet;
   end record;

type Fleet is array (1 .. Fleet_Size) of Craft;
```

rationale

You help the maintainer find all of the related data by gathering it into the same construct, simplifying any modifications that apply to all rather than part. This, in turn, increases reliability. Neither you nor an unknown maintainer is liable to forget to deal with all the pieces of information in the executable statements, especially if updates are done with aggregate assignments whenever possible.

The idea is to put the information a maintainer needs to know where it can be found with the minimum of effort. For example, if all information relating to a given Craft is in the same place, the relationship is clear both in the declarations and especially in the code accessing and updating that information. But, if it is scattered among several data structures, it is less obvious that this is an intended relationship as opposed to a coincidental one. In the latter case, the declarations may be grouped together to imply intent, but it may not be possible to group the accessing and updating code that way. Ensuring the use of the same index to access the corresponding element in each of several parallel arrays is difficult if the accesses are at all scattered.

If the application must interface directly to hardware, the use of records, especially in conjunction with record representation clauses, could be useful to map onto the layout of the hardware in question.

notes

It may seem desirable to store heterogeneous data in parallel arrays in what amounts to a FORTRAN-like style. This style is an artifact of FORTRAN's data structuring limitations. FORTRAN only has facilities for constructing homogeneous arrays.

exceptions

If the application must interface directly to hardware, and the hardware requires that information be distributed among various locations, then it may not be possible to use records.

5.4.3　Heterogeneous Polymorphic Data

guideline

- Use access types to class-wide types to implement heterogeneous polymorphic data structures.
- Use tagged types and type extension rather than variant records (in combination with enumeration types and case statements).

example

An array of type `Employee_List` can contain pointers to part-time and full-time employees (and possibly other kinds of employees in the future):

```
--------------------------------------------------------------------------------
package Personnel is
    type Employee  is tagged limited private;
    type Reference is access all Employee'Class;
    ...
private
    ...
end Personnel;

--------------------------------------------------------------------------------
with Personnel;
package Part_Time_Staff is
    type Part_Time_Employee is new Personnel.Employee with
        record
            ...
        end record;
    ...
end Part_Time_Staff;

--------------------------------------------------------------------------------
with Personnel;
package Full_Time_Staff is
    type Full_Time_Employee is new Personnel.Employee with
        record
            ...
        end record;
    ...
end Full_Time_Staff;

--------------------------------------------------------------------------------

...

type Employee_List is array (Positive range <>) of Personnel.Reference;

Current_Employees : Employee_List (1..10);

...

Current_Employees(1) := new Full_Time_Staff.Full_Time_Employee;
Current_Employees(2) := new Part_Time_Staff.Part_Time_Employee;
...
```

rationale

Polymorphism is a means of factoring out the differences among a collection of abstractions so that programs may be written in terms of the common properties. Polymorphism allows the different objects in a heterogeneous data structure to be treated the same way, based on dispatching operations defined on the root tagged type. This eliminates the need for case statements to select the processing required for each specific type. Guideline 5.6.3 discusses the maintenance impact of using case statements.

Enumeration types, variant records, and case statements are hard to maintain because the expertise on a given variant of the data type tends to be spread all over the program. When you create a tagged type hierarchy (tagged types and type extension), you can avoid the variant records, case statement, and single enumeration type that only supports the variant record discriminant. Moreover, you localize the "expertise" about the variant within the data structure by having all the corresponding primitives for a single operation call common "operation-specific" code.

See also Guideline 9.2.1 for a more detailed discussion of tagged types.

exceptions

In some instances, you may want to use a variant record approach to organize modularity around operations. For graphic output, for example, you may find it more maintainable to use variant records. You must make the tradeoff of whether adding a new operation will be less work than adding a new variant.

5.4.4   Nested Records

guideline

- Record structures should not always be flat. Factor out common parts.
- For a large record structure, group related components into smaller subrecords.
- For nested records, pick element names that read well when inner elements are referenced.
- Consider using type extension to organize large data structures.

example

```
type Coordinate is
   record
      Row      : Local_Float;
      Column   : Local_Float;
   end record;

type Window is
   record
      Top_Left      : Coordinate;
      Bottom_Right  : Coordinate;
   end record;
```

rationale

You can make complex data structures understandable and comprehensible by composing them of familiar building blocks. This technique works especially well for large record types with parts that fall into natural groupings. The components factored into separately declared records, based on a common quality or purpose, correspond to a lower level of abstraction than that represented by the larger record.

When designing a complex data structure, you must consider whether type composition or type extension is the best suited technique. Type composition refers to creating a record component whose type is itself a record. You will often need a hybrid of these techniques, that is, some components you include through type composition and others you create through type extension. Type extension may provide a cleaner design if the "intermediate" records are all instances of the same abstraction family. See also Guidelines 5.4.2 and 9.2.1.

notes

A carefully chosen name for the component of the larger record that is used to select the smaller enhances readability, for example:

```
if Window1.Bottom_Right.Row > Window2.Top_Left.Row then . . .
```

5.4.5   Dynamic Data

guideline

- Differentiate between static and dynamic data. Use dynamically allocated objects with caution.
- Use dynamically allocated data structures only when it is necessary to create and destroy them dynamically or to be able to reference them by different names.
- Do not drop pointers to undeallocated objects.
- Do not leave dangling references to deallocated objects.
- Initialize all access variables and components within a record.
- Do not rely on memory deallocation.
- Deallocate explicitly.
- Use length clauses to specify total allocation size.
- Provide handlers for storage_Error.
- Use controlled types to implement private types that manipulate dynamic data.
- Avoid unconstrained record objects unless your run-time environment reliably reclaims dynamic heap storage.
- Unless your run-time environment reliably reclaims dynamic heap storage, declare the following items only in the outermost, unnested declarative part of either a library package, a main subprogram, or a permanent task:
  - Access types
  - Constrained composite objects with nonstatic bounds
  - Objects of an unconstrained composite type other than unconstrained records
  - Composite objects large enough (at compile time) for the compiler to allocate implicitly on the heap
- Unless your run-time environment reliably reclaims dynamic heap storage or you are creating permanent, dynamically allocated tasks, avoid declaring tasks in the following situations:
  - Unconstrained array subtypes whose components are tasks
  - Discriminated record subtypes containing a component that is an array of tasks, where the array size depends on the value of the discriminant
  - Any declarative region other than the outermost, unnested declarative part of either a library package or a main subprogram
  - Arrays of tasks that are not statically constrained

example

These lines show how a dangling reference might be created:

```
P1 := new Object;
P2 := P1;
Unchecked_Object_Deallocation(P2);
```

This line can raise an exception due to referencing the deallocated object:

```
X := P1.all;
```

In the following three lines, if there is no intervening assignment of the value of P1 to any other pointer, the object created on the first line is no longer accessible after the third line. The only pointer to the allocated object has been dropped:

```
P1 := new Object;
...
P1 := P2;
```

The following code shows an example of using Finalize to make sure that when an object is finalized (i.e., goes out of scope), the dynamically allocated elements are chained on a free list:

```
with Ada.Finalization;
package List is
    type Object is private;
    function "=" (Left, Right : Object) return Boolean;   -- element-by-element comparison
    ... -- Operations go here
private
    type Handle is access List.Object;
    type Object is new Ada.Finalization.Controlled with
        record
            Next : List.Handle;
            ... -- Useful information go here
        end record;
    procedure Adjust (L : in out List.Object);
    procedure Finalize (L : in out List.Object);
end List;

package body List is
    Free_List : List.Handle;
    ...
    procedure Adjust (L : in out List.Object) is
    begin
        L := Deep_Copy (L);
    end Adjust;

    procedure Finalize (L : in out List.Object) is
    begin
        -- Chain L to Free_List
    end Finalize;

end List;
```

rationale

See also Guidelines 5.9.1, 5.9.2, 6.1.5, and 6.3.2 for variations on these problems. A dynamically allocated object is an object created by the execution of an allocator (new). Allocated objects referenced by access variables allow you to generate aliases, which are multiple references to the same object. Anomalous behavior can arise when you reference a deallocated object by another name. This is called a dangling reference. Totally disassociating a still-valid object from all names is called dropping a pointer. A dynamically allocated object that is not associated with a name cannot be referenced or explicitly deallocated.

A dropped pointer depends on an implicit memory manager for reclamation of space. It also raises questions for the reader as to whether the loss of access to the object was intended or accidental.

An Ada environment is not required to provide deallocation of dynamically allocated objects. If provided, it may be provided implicitly (objects are deallocated when their access type goes out of scope), explicitly (objects are deallocated when Ada.Unchecked_Deallocation is called), or both. To increase the likelihood of the storage space being reclaimed, it is best to call Ada.Unchecked_Deallocation explicitly for each dynamically created object when you are finished using it. Calls to Ada.Unchecked_Deallocation also document a deliberate decision to abandon an object, making the code easier to read and understand. To be absolutely certain that space is reclaimed and reused, manage your own "free list." Keep track of which objects you are finished with, and reuse them instead of dynamically allocating new objects later.

The dangers of dangling references are that you may attempt to use them, thereby accessing memory that you have released to the memory manager and that may have been subsequently allocated for another purpose in another part of your program. When you read from such memory, unexpected errors may occur because the other part of your program may have previously written totally unrelated data there. Even worse, when you write to such memory you can cause errors in an apparently unrelated part of the code by changing values of variables dynamically allocated by that code. This type of error can be very difficult to find. Finally, such errors may be triggered in parts of your environment that you did not write, for example, in the memory management system itself, which may dynamically allocate memory to keep records about your dynamically allocated memory.

Keep in mind that any unreset component of a record or array can also be a dangling reference or carry a bit pattern representing inconsistent data. Components of an access type are always initialized by default to null; however, you should not rely on this default initialization. To enhance readability and maintainability, you should include explicit initialization.

Whenever you use dynamic allocation, it is possible to run out of space. Ada provides a facility (a length clause) for requesting the size of the pool of allocation space at compile time. Anticipate that you can still run out at run time. Prepare handlers for the exception Storage_Error, and consider carefully what alternatives you may be able to include in the program for each such situation.

There is a school of thought that dictates avoidance of all dynamic allocation. It is largely based on the fear of running out of memory during execution. Facilities, such as length clauses and exception handlers for `Storage_Error`, provide explicit control over memory partitioning and error recovery, making this fear unfounded.

When implementing a complex data structure (tree, list, sparse matrices, etc.), you often use access types. If you are not careful, you can consume all your storage with these dynamically allocated objects. You could export a deallocate operation, but it is impossible to ensure that it is called at the proper places; you are, in effect, trusting the clients. If you derive from controlled types (see Guidelines 5.3.3, 5.9.6, 8.3.1, 8.3.3, and 9.2.3 for more information), you can use finalization to deal with deallocation of dynamic data, thus avoiding storage exhaustion. User-defined storage pools give better control over the allocation policy.

A related but distinct issue is that of shared versus copy semantics: even if the data structure is implemented using access types, you do not necessarily want shared semantics. In some instances you really want `:=` to create a copy, not a new reference, and you really want `=` to compare the contents, not the reference. You should implement your structure as a controlled type. If you want copy semantics, you can redefine `Adjust` to perform a deep copy and `=` to perform a comparison on the contents. You can also redefine `Finalize` to make sure that when an object is finalized (i.e., goes out of scope) the dynamically allocated elements are chained on a free list (or deallocated by `Ada.Unchecked_Deallocation`).

The implicit use of dynamic (heap) storage by an Ada program during execution poses significant risks that software failures may occur. An Ada run-time environment may use implicit dynamic (heap) storage in association with composite objects, dynamically created tasks, and catenation. Often, the algorithms used to manage the dynamic allocation and reclamation of heap storage cause fragmentation or leakage, which can lead to storage exhaustion. It is usually very difficult or impossible to recover from storage exhaustion or `Storage_Error` without reloading and restarting the Ada program. It would be very restrictive to avoid all uses of implicit allocation. On the other hand, preventing both explicit and implicit deallocation significantly reduces the risks of fragmentation and leakage without overly restricting your use of composite objects, access values, task objects, and catenation.

exceptions

If a composite object is large enough to be allocated on the heap, you can still declare it as an `in` or `in out` formal parameter. The guideline is meant to discourage declaring the object in an object declaration, a formal `out` parameter, or the value returned by a function.

You should monitor the leakage and/or fragmentation from the heap. If they become steady-state and do not continually increase during program or partition execution, you can use the constructs described in the guidelines.

5.4.6   Aliased Objects

guideline

*   Minimize the use of aliased variables.
*   Use aliasing for statically created, ragged arrays (Rationale 1995, §3.7.1).
*   Use aliasing to refer to part of a data structure when you want to hide the internal connections and bookkeeping information.

example

```
package Message_Services is
   type Message_Code_Type is range 0 .. 100;

   subtype Message is String;

   function Get_Message (Message_Code: Message_Code_Type)
      return Message;

   pragma Inline (Get_Message);
end Message_Services;

package body Message_Services is
   type Message_Handle is access constant Message;
```

```
Message_0 : aliased constant Message := "OK";
Message_1 : aliased constant Message := "Up";
Message_2 : aliased constant Message := "Shutdown";
Message_3 : aliased constant Message := "Shutup";
. . .

type Message_Table_Type is array (Message_Code_Type) of Message_Handle;

Message_Table : Message_Table_Type :=
  (0 => Message_0'Access,
   1 => Message_1'Access,
   2 => Message_2'Access,
   3 => Message_3'Access,
   -- etc.
   );

function Get_Message (Message_Code : Message_Code_Type)
  return Message is
begin
  return Message_Table (Message_Code).all;
end Get_Message;
end Message_Services;
```

The following code fragment shows a use of aliased objects, using the attribute 'Access to implement a generic component that manages hashed collections of objects:

```
generic
  type Hash_Index is mod <>;
  type Object is tagged private;
  type Handle is access all Object;
  with function Hash (The_Object : in Object) return Hash_Index;
package Collection is

  function Insert (Object : in Collection.Object) return Collection.Handle;
  function Find (Object : in Collection.Object) return Collection.Handle;

  Object_Not_Found : exception;

  ...
private

  type Cell;
  type Access_Cell is access Cell;

end Collection;

package body Collection is

  type Cell is
  record
    Value : aliased Collection.Object;
    Link  : Access_Cell;
  end record;

  type Table_Type is array (Hash_Index) of Access_Cell;

  Table : Table_Type;

  -- Go through the collision chain and return an access to the useful data.
  function Find (Object : in Collection.Object;
                 Index  : in Hash_Index) return Handle is
    Current : Access_Cell := Table (Index);
  begin
    while Current /= null loop
      if Current.Value = Object then
        return Current.Value'Access;
      else
        Current := Current.Link;
      end if;
    end loop;
    raise Object_Not_Found;
  end Find;

  -- The exported one
  function Find (Object : in Collection.Object) return Collection.Handle is
    Index : constant Hash_Index := Hash (Object);
  begin
    return Find (Object, Index);
  end Find;

  ...
end Collection;
```

rationale

Aliasing allows the programmer to have indirect access to declared objects. Because you can update aliased objects through more than one path, you must exercise caution to avoid unintended updates. When you restrict the aliased objects to being constant, you avoid having the object unintentionally modified. In the example above, the individual message objects are aliased constant message strings so their values cannot be changed. The ragged array is then initialized with references to each of these constant strings.

Aliasing allows you to manipulate objects using indirection while avoiding dynamic allocation. For example, you can insert an object onto a linked list without dynamically allocating the space for that object (Rationale 1995, §3.7.1).

Another use of aliasing is in a linked data structure in which you try to hide the enclosing container. This is essentially the inverse of a self-referential data structure (see Guideline 5.4.7). If a package manages some data using a linked data structure, you may only want to export access values that denote the "useful" data. You can use an access-to-object to return an access to the useful data, excluding the pointers used to chain objects.

5.4.7   Access Discriminants

guideline

- Use access discriminants to create self-referential data structures, i.e., a data structure one of whose components points to the enclosing structure.

example

See the examples in Guidelines 8.3.6 (using access discriminants to build an iterator) and 9.5.1 (using access discriminants in multiple inheritance).

rationale

The access discriminant is essentially a pointer of an anonymous type being used as a discriminant. Because the access discriminant is of an anonymous access type, you cannot declare other objects of the type. Thus, once you initialize the discriminant, you create a "permanent" (for the lifetime of the object) association between the discriminant and the object it accesses. When you create a self-referential structure, that is, a component of the structure is initialized to point to the enclosing object, the "constant" behavior of the access discriminant provides the right behavior to help you maintain the integrity of the structure.

See also Rationale (1995, §4.6.3) for a discussion of access discriminants to achieve multiple views of an object.

See also Guideline 6.1.3 for an example of an access discriminant for a task type.

5.4.8   Modular Types

guideline

- Use modular types rather than Boolean arrays when you create data structures that need bit-wise operations, such as and and or.

example

```
with Interfaces;
procedure Main is

   type Unsigned_Byte is mod 255;

   X : Unsigned_Byte;
   Y : Unsigned_Byte;
   Z : Unsigned_Byte;

   X1 : Interfaces.Unsigned_16;

begin -- Main
   Z := X or Y;   -- does not cause overflow
-- show example of left shift
   X1 := 16#FFFF#;
   for Counter in 1 .. 16 loop
      X1 := Interfaces.Shift_Left (Value => X1, Amount => 1);
   end loop;

end Main;
```

rationale

Modular types are preferred when the number of bits is known to be fewer than the number of bits in a word and/or performance is a serious concern. Boolean arrays are appropriate when the number of bits is not particularly known in advance and performance is not a serious issue. See also Guideline 10.6.3.

5.5 EXPRESSIONS

Properly coded expressions can enhance the readability and understandability of a program. Poorly coded expressions can turn a program into a maintainer's nightmare.

5.5.1 Range Values

guideline

- Use 'First or 'Last instead of numeric literals to represent the first or last values of a range.

- Use 'Range or the subtype name of the range instead of 'First .. 'Last.

example

```
type Temperature      is range All_Time_Low .. All_Time_High;
type Weather_Stations is range            1 ..  Max_Stations;

Current_Temperature : Temperature := 60;
Offset              : Temperature;

...
for I in Weather_Stations loop
   Offset := Current_Temperature - Temperature'First;

   ...
end loop;
```

rationale

In the example above, it is better to use Weather_Stations in the for loop than to use Weather_Stations'First .. Weather_Stations'Last or 1 .. Max_Stations because it is clearer, less error-prone, and less dependent on the definition of the type Weather_Stations. Similarly, it is better to use Temperature'First in the offset calculation than to use All_Time_Low because the code will still be correct if the definition of the subtype Temperature is changed. This enhances program reliability.

caution

When you implicitly specify ranges and attributes like this, be careful that you use the correct subtype name. It is easy to refer to a very large range without realizing it. For example, given the declarations:

```
type    Large_Range is new Integer;
subtype Small_Range is Large_Range range 1 .. 10;

type Large_Array is array (Large_Range) of Integer;
type Small_Array is array (Small_Range) of Integer;
```

then the first declaration below works fine, but the second one is probably an accident and raises an exception on most machines because it is requesting a huge array (indexed from the smallest integer to the largest one):

```
Array_1 : Small_Array;
Array_2 : Large_Array;
```

5.5.2 Array Attributes

guideline

- Use array attributes 'First, 'Last, or 'Length instead of numeric literals for accessing arrays.
- Use the 'Range of the array instead of the name of the index subtype to express a range.
- Use 'Range instead of 'First .. 'Last to express a range.

example

```
subtype Name_String is String (1 .. Name_Length);

File_Path : Name_String := (others => ' ');
```

```
...
for I in File_Path'Range loop
   ...
end loop;
```

rationale

In the example above, it is better to use `Name_String'Range` in the `for` loop than to use `Name_String_Size`, `Name_String'First .. Name_String'Last`, or `1 .. 30` because it is clearer, less error-prone, and less dependent on the definitions of `Name_String` and `Name_String_Size`. If `Name_String` is changed to have a different index type or if the bounds of the array are changed, this will still work correctly. This enhances program reliability.

5.5.3   Parenthetical Expressions

guideline

- Use parentheses to specify the order of subexpression evaluation to clarify expressions (NASA 1987).
- Use parentheses to specify the order of evaluation for subexpressions whose correctness depends on left to right evaluation.

example

```
(1.5 * X**2)/A - (6.5*X + 47.0)

2*I + 4*Y + 8*Z + C
```

rationale

The Ada rules of operator precedence are defined in the Ada Reference Manual (1995, §4.5) and follow the same commonly accepted precedence of algebraic operators. The strong typing facility in Ada combined with the common precedence rules make many parentheses unnecessary. However, when an uncommon combination of operators occurs, it may be helpful to add parentheses even when the precedence rules apply. The expression:

```
5 + ((Y ** 3) mod 10)
```

is clearer, and equivalent to:

```
5 + Y**3 mod 10
```

The rules of evaluation do specify left to right evaluation for operators with the same precedence level. However, it is the most commonly overlooked rule of evaluation when checking expressions for correctness.

5.5.4   Positive Forms of Logic

guideline

- Avoid names and constructs that rely on the use of negatives.
- Choose names of flags so they represent states that can be used in positive form.

example

Use:

```
if Operator_Missing then
```

rather than either:

```
if not Operator_Found then
```

or:

```
if not Operator_Missing then
```

rationale

Relational expressions can be more readable and understandable when stated in a positive form. As an aid in choosing the name, consider that the most frequently used branch in a conditional construct should be encountered first.

exceptions

There are cases in which the negative form is unavoidable. If the relational expression better reflects what is going on in the code, then inverting the test to adhere to this guideline is not recommended.

5.5.5   Short Circuit Forms of the Logical Operators

guideline

* Use short-circuit forms of the logical operators to specify the order of conditions when the failure of one condition means that the other condition will raise an exception.

example

Use:

```
if Y /= 0 or else (X/Y) /= 10 then
```

or:

```
if Y /= 0 then
   if (X/Y) /= 10 then
```

rather than either:

```
if Y /= 0 and (X/Y) /= 10 then
```

or:

```
if (X/Y) /= 10 then
```

to avoid `Constraint_Error`.
Use:

```
if Target /= null and then Target.Distance < Threshold then
```

rather than:

```
if Target.Distance < Threshold then
```

to avoid referencing a field in a nonexistent object.

rationale

The use of short-circuit control forms prevents a class of data-dependent errors or exceptions that can occur as a result of expression evaluation. The short-circuit forms guarantee an order of evaluation and an `exit` from the sequence of relational expressions as soon as the expression's result can be determined.

In the absence of short-circuit forms, Ada does not provide a guarantee of the order of expression evaluation, nor does the language guarantee that evaluation of a relational expression is abandoned when it becomes clear that it evaluates to `False` (for and) or `True` (for or).

notes

If it is important that all parts of a given expression always be evaluated, the expression probably violates Guideline 4.1.4, which limits side-effects in functions.

5.5.6   Accuracy of Operations With Real Operands

guideline

* Use <= and >= in relational expressions with real operands instead of =.

example

```
Current_Temperature   : Temperature :=      0.0;
Temperature_Increment : Temperature := 1.0 / 3.0;
Maximum_Temperature   : constant    :=    100.0;
...
loop
   ...
   Current_Temperature :=
         Current_Temperature + Temperature_Increment;
   ...
   exit when Current_Temperature >= Maximum_Temperature;
   ...
end loop;
```

rationale

Fixed- and floating-point values, even if derived from similar expressions, may not be exactly equal. The imprecise, finite representations of real numbers in hardware always have round-off errors so that any variation in the construction path or history of two real numbers has the potential for resulting in different numbers, even when the paths or histories are mathematically equivalent.

The Ada definition of model intervals also means that the use of <= is more portable than either < or =.

notes

Floating-point arithmetic is treated in Guideline 7.2.7.

exceptions

If your application must test for an exact value of a real number (e.g., testing the precision of the arithmetic on a certain machine), then the = would have to be used. But never use = on real operands as a condition to exit a loop.

5.6 STATEMENTS

Careless or convoluted use of statements can make a program hard to read and maintain even if its global structure is well organized. You should strive for simple and consistent use of statements to achieve clarity of local program structure. Some of the guidelines in this section counsel use or avoidance of particular statements. As pointed out in the individual guidelines, rigid adherence to those guidelines would be excessive, but experience has shown that they generally lead to code with improved reliability and maintainability.

5.6.1 Nesting

guideline

- Minimize the depth of nested expressions (Nissen and Wallis 1984).
- Minimize the depth of nested control structures (Nissen and Wallis 1984).
- Try using simplification heuristics (see the following Notes).

instantiation

- Do not nest expressions or control structures beyond a nesting level of five.

example

The following section of code:
```
if not Condition_1 then

    if Condition_2 then
        Action_A;
    else   -- not Condition_2
        Action_B;
    end if;

else   -- Condition_1
    Action_C;
end if;
```

can be rewritten more clearly and with less nesting as:
```
if Condition_1 then
    Action_C;
elsif Condition_2 then
    Action_A;

else   -- not (Condition_1 or Condition_2)
    Action_B;
end if;
```

rationale

Deeply nested structures are confusing, difficult to understand, and difficult to maintain. The problem lies in the difficulty of determining what part of a program is contained at any given level. For expressions, this is important in achieving the correct placement of balanced grouping symbols and in achieving the desired operator precedence. For control structures, the question involves what part is controlled. Specifically, is a given statement at the proper level of nesting, that is, is it too deeply or too shallowly nested, or is the given statement associated with the proper choice, for example, for if or case statements? Indentation helps, but it is not a panacea. Visually inspecting alignment of indented code (mainly intermediate levels) is an uncertain job at best. To minimize the complexity of the code, keep the maximum number of nesting levels between three and five.

notes

Ask yourself the following questions to help you simplify the code:

-   Can some part of the expression be put into a constant or variable?
-   Does some part of the lower nested control structures represent a significant and, perhaps, reusable computation that I can factor into a subprogram?
-   Can I convert these nested if statements into a case statement?
-   Am I using else if where I could be using elsif?
-   Can I reorder the conditional expressions controlling this nested structure?
-   Is there a different design that would be simpler?

exceptions

If deep nesting is required frequently, there may be overall design decisions for the code that should be changed. Some algorithms require deeply nested loops and segments controlled by conditional branches. Their continued use can be ascribed to their efficiency, familiarity, and time-proven utility. When nesting is required, proceed cautiously and take special care with the choice of identifiers and loop and block names.

5.6.2   Slices

guideline

•   Use slices rather than a loop to copy part of an array.

example

```
First  : constant Index := Index'First;
Second : constant Index := Index'Succ(First);
Third  : constant Index := Index'Succ(Second);

type Vector is array (Index range <>) of Element;

subtype Column_Vector is Vector (Index);
type    Square_Matrix is array  (Index) of Column_Vector;

subtype Small_Range is Index range First .. Third;
subtype Diagonals   is Vector (Small_Range);
type    Tri_Diagonal is array  (Index) of Diagonals;

Markov_Probabilities : Square_Matrix;
Diagonal_Data        : Tri_Diagonal;

. . .

-- Remove diagonal and off diagonal elements.
Diagonal_Data(Index'First)(First) := Null_Value;
Diagonal_Data(Index'First)(Second .. Third) :=
    Markov_Probabilities(Index'First)(First .. Second);

for I in Second .. Index'Pred(Index'Last) loop
   Diagonal_Data(I) :=
        Markov_Probabilities(I)(Index'Pred(I) .. Index'Succ(I));
end loop;

Diagonal_Data(Index'Last)(First .. Second) :=
    Markov_Probabilities(Index'Last)(Index'Pred(Index'Last) .. Index'Last);
Diagonal_Data(Index'Last)(Third) := Null_Value;
```

rationale

An assignment statement with slices is simpler and clearer than a loop and helps the reader see the intended action. See also Guideline 10.5.7 regarding possible performance issues of slice assignments versus loops.

5.6.3 Case Statements

guideline

- Minimize the use of an `others` choice in a `case` statement.
- Do not use ranges of enumeration literals in `case` statements.
- Use `case` statements rather than `if`/`elsif` statements, wherever possible.
- Use type extension and dispatching rather than `case` statements if, possible.

example

```
type Color is (Red, Green, Blue, Purple);
Car_Color : Color := Red;

...

case Car_Color is
    when Red .. Blue => ...
    when Purple      => ...
end case;   -- Car_Color
```

Now consider a change in the type:

```
type Color is (Red, Yellow, Green, Blue, Purple);
```

This change may have an unnoticed and undesired effect in the `case` statement. If the choices had been enumerated explicitly, as `when Red | Green | Blue =>` instead of `when Red .. Blue =>`, then the `case` statement would not have compiled. This would have forced the maintainer to make a conscious decision about what to do in the case of `Yellow`.

In the following example, assume that a menu has been posted, and the user is expected to enter one of the four choices. Assume that `User_Choice` is declared as a `Character` and that `Terminal_IO.Get` handles errors in user input. The less readable alternative with the `if`/`elsif` statement is shown after the `case` statement:

```
Do_Menu_Choices_1:
    loop
        ...

        case User_Choice is
            when 'A'   => Item := Terminal_IO.Get ("Item to add");
            when 'D'   => Item := Terminal_IO.Get ("Item to delete");
            when 'M'   => Item := Terminal_IO.Get ("Item to modify");
            when 'Q'   => exit Do_Menu_Choices_1;

            when others => -- error has already been signaled to user
                        null;
        end case;
    end loop Do_Menu_Choices_1;


Do_Menu_Choices_2:
    loop
        ...

        if User_Choice = 'A' then
            Item := Terminal_IO.Get ("Item to add");

        elsif User_Choice = 'D' then
            Item := Terminal_IO.Get ("Item to delete");

        elsif User_Choice = 'M' then
            Item := Terminal_IO.Get ("Item to modify");

        elsif User_Choice = 'Q' then
            exit Do Menu Choices 2;

        end if;
    end loop Do_Menu_Choices_2;
```

rationale

All possible values for an object should be known and should be assigned specific actions. Use of an `others` clause may prevent the developer from carefully considering the actions for each value. A compiler warns the user about omitted values if an `others` clause is not used.

You may not be able to avoid the use of `others` in a `case` statement when the subtype of the case expression has many values, for example, `universal_integer`, `Wide_Character`, or `Character`). If your choice of values is small compared to the range of the subtype, you should consider using an `if`/`elsif` statement. Note that you must supply an `others` alternative when your `case` expression is of a generic type.

Each possible value should be explicitly enumerated. Ranges can be dangerous because of the possibility that the range could change and the `case` statement may not be reexamined. If you have declared a subtype to correspond to the range of interest, you can consider using this named subtype.

In many instances, `case` statements enhance the readability of the code. See Guideline 10.5.3 for a discussion of the performance considerations. In many implementations, `case` statements may be more efficient.

Type extension and dispatching ease the maintenance burden when you add a new variant to a data structure. See also Guidelines 5.4.2 and 5.4.4.

notes

Ranges that are needed in `case` statements can use constrained subtypes to enhance maintainability. It is easier to maintain because the declaration of the range can be placed where it is logically part of the abstraction, not buried in a `case` statement in the executable code:

```
subtype Lower_Case is Character range 'a' .. 'z';
subtype Upper_Case is Character range 'A' .. 'Z';
subtype Control    is Character range Ada.Characters.Latin_1.NUL ..
                                      Ada.Characters.Latin_1.US;
subtype Numbers    is Character range '0' .. '9';

...
case Input_Char is
   when Lower_Case => Capitalize(Input_Char);
   when Upper_Case => null;
   when Control    => raise Invalid_Input;
   when Numbers    => null;
   ...
end case;
```

exceptions

It is acceptable to use ranges for possible values only when the user is certain that new values will never be inserted among the old ones, as for example, in the range of ASCII characters: `'a' .. 'z'`.

5.6.4   Loops

guideline

- Use `for` loops, whenever possible.
- Use `while` loops when the number of iterations cannot be calculated before entering the loop but a simple continuation condition can be applied at the top of the loop.
- Use plain loops with `exit` statements for more complex situations.
- Avoid `exit` statements in `while` and `for` loops.
- Minimize the number of ways to `exit` a loop.

example

To iterate over all elements of an array:

```
for I in Array_Name'Range loop
   ...
end loop;
```

To iterate over all elements in a linked list:

```
Pointer := Head_Of_List;
while Pointer /= null loop
   ...
   Pointer := Pointer.Next;
end loop;
```

Situations requiring a "loop and a half" arise often. For this, use:

```
P_And_Q_Processing:
   loop
      P;
      exit P_And_Q_Processing when Condition_Dependent_On_P;
      Q;
   end loop P_And_Q_Processing;
```

rather than:

```
P;
while not Condition_Dependent_On_P loop
   Q;
   P;
end loop;
```

rationale

A `for` loop is bounded, so it cannot be an "infinite loop." This is enforced by the Ada language, which requires a finite range in the loop specification and does not allow the loop counter of a `for` loop to be modified by a statement executed within the loop. This yields a certainty of understanding for the reader and the writer not associated with other forms of loops. A `for` loop is also easier to maintain because the iteration range can be expressed using attributes of the data structures upon which the loop operates, as shown in the example above where the range changes automatically whenever the declaration of the array is modified. For these reasons, it is best to use the `for` loop whenever possible, that is, whenever simple expressions can be used to describe the first and last values of the loop counter.

The `while` loop has become a very familiar construct to most programmers. At a glance, it indicates the condition under which the loop continues. Use the `while` loop whenever it is not possible to use the `for` loop but when there is a simple Boolean expression describing the conditions under which the loop should continue, as shown in the example above.

The plain loop statement should be used in more complex situations, even if it is possible to contrive a solution using a `for` or `while` loop in conjunction with extra flag variables or `exit` statements. The criteria in selecting a loop construct are to be as clear and maintainable as possible. It is a bad idea to use an `exit` statement from within a `for` or `while` loop because it is misleading to the reader after having apparently described the complete set of loop conditions at the top of the loop. A reader who encounters a plain loop statement expects to see `exit` statements.

There are some familiar looping situations that are best achieved with the plain loop statement. For example, the semantics of the Pascal `repeat until` loop, where the loop is always executed at least once before the termination test occurs, are best achieved by a plain loop with a single `exit` at the end of the loop. Another common situation is the "loop and a half" construct, shown in the example above, where a loop must terminate somewhere within the sequence of statements of the body. Complicated "loop and a half" constructs simulated with `while` loops often require the introduction of flag variables or duplication of code before and during the loop, as shown in the example. Such contortions make the code more complex and less reliable.

Minimize the number of ways to `exit` a loop to make the loop more understandable to the reader. It should be rare that you need more than two exit paths from a loop. When you do, be sure to use `exit` statements for all of them, rather than adding an `exit` statement to a `for` or `while` loop.

5.6.5   Exit Statements

guideline

- Use `exit` statements to enhance the readability of loop termination code (NASA 1987).
- Use `exit when` ... rather than `if` ... `then exit` whenever possible (NASA 1987).
- Review `exit` statement placement.

example

See the examples in Guidelines 5.1.1 and 5.6.4.

rationale

It is more readable to use `exit` statements than to try to add Boolean flags to a `while` loop condition to simulate exits from the middle of a loop. Even if all `exit` statements would be clustered at the top of the loop body, the separation of a complex condition into multiple exit statements can simplify and make it more readable and clear. The sequential execution of two exit statements is often more clear than the short-circuit control forms.

The exit when form is preferable to the if ... then exit form because it makes the word exit more visible by not nesting it inside of any control construct. The if ... then exit form is needed only in the case where other statements, in addition to the exit statement, must be executed conditionally. For example:

```
Process_Requests:
   loop
      if Status = Done then

         Shut_Down;
         exit Process_Requests;

      end if;

      ...

   end loop Process_Requests;
```

Loops with many scattered exit statements can indicate fuzzy thinking regarding the loop's purpose in the algorithm. Such an algorithm might be coded better some other way, for example, with a series of loops. Some rework can often reduce the number of exit statements and make the code clearer.

See also Guidelines 5.1.3 and 5.6.4.

5.6.6   Recursion and Iteration Bounds

guideline

- Consider specifying bounds on loops.
- Consider specifying bounds on recursion.

example

Establishing an iteration bound:

```
Safety_Counter := 0;

Process_List:
   loop
      exit when Current_Item = null;

      ...
      Current_Item := Current_Item.Next;

      ...
      Safety_Counter := Safety_Counter + 1;
      if Safety_Counter > 1_000_000 then
         raise Safety_Error;
      end if;

   end loop Process_List;
```

Establishing a recursion bound:

```
subtype Recursion_Bound is Natural range 0 .. 1_000;

procedure Depth_First (Root          : in    Tree;
                       Safety_Counter : in    Recursion_Bound
                                           := Recursion_Bound'Last) is
begin
   if Root /= null then

      if Safety_Counter = 0 then
         raise Recursion_Error;
      end if;

      Depth_First (Root           => Root.Left_Branch,
                   Safety_Counter => Safety_Counter - 1);

      Depth_First (Root           => Root.Right_Branch,
                   Safety_Counter => Safety_Counter - 1);

      ... -- normal subprogram body
   end if;

end Depth_First;
```

Following are examples of this subprogram's usage. One call specifies a maximum recursion depth of 50. The second takes the default (1,000). The third uses a computed bound:

```
Depth_First(Root => Tree_1, Safety_Counter => 50);
Depth_First(Tree_2);
Depth_First(Root => Tree_3, Safety_Counter => Current_Tree_Height);
```

rationale

Recursion, and iteration using structures other than `for` statements, can be infinite because the expected terminating condition does not arise. Such faults are sometimes quite subtle, may occur rarely, and may be difficult to detect because an external manifestation might be absent or substantially delayed.

By including counters and checks on the counter values, in addition to the loops themselves, you can prevent many forms of infinite loops. The inclusion of such checks is one aspect of the technique called Safe Programming (Anderson and Witty 1978).

The bounds of these checks do not have to be exact, just realistic. Such counters and checks are not part of the primary control structure of the program but a benign addition functioning as an execution-time "safety net," allowing error detection and possibly recovery from potential infinite loops or infinite recursion.

notes

If a loop uses the `for` iteration scheme (Guideline 5.6.4), it follows this guideline.

exceptions

Embedded control applications have loops that are intended to be infinite. Only a few loops within such applications should qualify as exceptions to this guideline. The exceptions should be deliberate (and documented) policy decisions.

This guideline is most important to safety critical systems. For other systems, it may be overkill.

5.6.7   Goto Statements

guideline

* Do not use `goto` statements.

rationale

A `goto` statement is an unstructured change in the control flow. Worse, the label does not require an indicator of where the corresponding `goto` statement(s) are. This makes code unreadable and makes its correct execution suspect.

Other languages use `goto` statements to implement loop exits and exception handling. Ada's support of these constructs makes the `goto` statement extremely rare.

notes

If you should ever use a `goto` statement, highlight both it and the label with blank space. Indicate at the label where the corresponding `goto` statement(s) may be found.

5.6.8   Return Statements

guideline

* Minimize the number of `return` statements from a subprogram (NASA 1987).

* Highlight `return` statements with comments or white space to keep them from being lost in other code.

example

The following code fragment is longer and more complex than necessary:

```
if Pointer /= null then

   if Pointer.Count > 0 then
      return True;

   else  -- Pointer.Count = 0
      return False;
   end if;
```

```
else  -- Pointer = null
   return False;
end if;
```

It should be replaced with the shorter, more concise, and clearer equivalent line:

```
return Pointer /= null and then Pointer.Count > 0;
```

rationale

Excessive use of returns can make code confusing and unreadable. Only use `return` statements where warranted. Too many returns from a subprogram may be an indicator of cluttered logic. If the application requires multiple returns, use them at the same level (i.e., as in different branches of a `case` statement), rather than scattered throughout the subprogram code. Some rework can often reduce the number of `return` statements to one and make the code more clear.

exceptions

Do not avoid `return` statements if it detracts from natural structure and code readability.

5.6.9   Blocks

guideline

- Use blocks to localize the scope of declarations.
- Use blocks to perform local renaming.
- Use blocks to define local exception handlers.

example

```
with Motion;
with Accelerometer_Device;
...

    ----------------------------------------------------------------------
    function Maximum_Velocity return Motion.Velocity is

        Cumulative : Motion.Velocity := 0.0;

    begin  -- Maximum_Velocity

        -- Initialize the needed devices
        ...

        Calculate_Velocity_From_Sample_Data:
            declare
                use type Motion.Acceleration;

                Current      : Motion.Acceleration := 0.0;
                Time_Delta   : Duration;

            begin  -- Calculate_Velocity_From_Sample_Data
                for I in 1 .. Accelerometer_Device.Sample_Limit loop

                    Get_Samples_And_Ignore_Invalid_Data:
                        begin
                            Accelerometer_Device.Get_Value(Current, Time_Delta);
                        exception
                            when Constraint_Error =>
                                null; -- Continue trying

                            when Accelerometer_Device.Failure =>
                                raise Accelerometer_Device_Failed;
                        end Get_Samples_And_Ignore_Invalid_Data;

                    exit when Current <= 0.0; -- Slowing down
```

```
            Update_Velocity:
               declare
                  use type Motion.Velocity;
                  use type Motion.Acceleration;

               begin
                  Cumulative := Cumulative + Current * Time_Delta;

               exception
                  when Constraint_Error =>
                     raise Maximum_Velocity_Exceeded;
               end Update_Velocity;

         end loop;
      end Calculate_Velocity_From_Sample_Data;

   return Cumulative;

end Maximum_Velocity;
------------------------------------------------------------------------
...
```

rationale

Blocks break up large segments of code and isolate details relevant to each subsection of code. Variables that are only used in a particular section of code are clearly visible when a declarative block delineates that code.

Renaming may simplify the expression of algorithms and enhance readability for a given section of code. But it is confusing when a renames clause is visually separated from the code to which it applies. The declarative region allows the renames to be immediately visible when the reader is examining code that uses that abbreviation. Guideline 5.7.1 discusses a similar guideline concerning the use clause.

Local exception handlers can catch exceptions close to the point of origin and allow them to be either handled, propagated, or converted.

5.6.10   Aggregates

guideline

- Use an aggregate instead of a sequence of assignments to assign values to all components of a record.
- Use an aggregate instead of a temporary variable when building a record to pass as an actual parameter.
- Use positional association only when there is a conventional ordering of the arguments.

example

It is better to use aggregates:

```
Set_Position((X, Y));

Employee_Record := (Number     => 42,
                    Age        => 51,
                    Department => Software_Engineering);
```

than to use consecutive assignments or temporary variables:

```
Temporary_Position.X := 100;
Temporary_Position.Y := 200;
Set_Position(Temporary_Position);

Employee_Record.Number     := 42;
Employee_Record.Age        := 51;
Employee_Record.Department := Software_Engineering;
```

rationale

Using aggregates during maintenance is beneficial. If a record structure is altered, but the corresponding aggregate is not, the compiler flags the missing field in the aggregate assignment. It would not be able to detect the fact that a new assignment statement should have been added to a list of assignment statements.

Aggregates can also be a real convenience in combining data items into a record or array structure required for passing the information as a parameter. Named component association makes aggregates more readable.

See Guideline 10.4.5 for the performance impact of aggregates.

5.7 VISIBILITY

As noted in Guideline 4.2, Ada's ability to enforce information hiding and separation of concerns through its visibility controlling features is one of the most important advantages of the language. Subverting these features, for example, by too liberal use of the use clause, is wasteful and dangerous.

5.7.1 The Use Clause

guideline

- When you need to provide visibility to operators, use the use type clause.
- Avoid/minimize the use of the use clause (Nissen and Wallis 1984).
- Consider using a package renames clause rather than a use clause for a package.
- Consider using the use clause in the following situations:
  - When standard packages are needed and no ambiguous references are introduced
  - When references to enumeration literals are needed
- Localize the effect of all use clauses.

example

This is a modification of the example from Guideline 4.2.3. The effect of a use clause is localized:

```
-------------------------------------------------------------------------------
package Rational_Numbers is

    type Rational is private;

    function "=" (X, Y : Rational) return Boolean;

    function "/" (X, Y : Integer)  return Rational;   -- construct a rational number

    function "+" (X, Y : Rational) return Rational;
    function "-" (X, Y : Rational) return Rational;
    function "*" (X, Y : Rational) return Rational;
    function "/" (X, Y : Rational) return Rational;   -- rational division

private
    ...
end Rational_Numbers;

-------------------------------------------------------------------------------
package body Rational_Numbers is

    procedure Reduce (R : in out Rational) is . . . end Reduce;

    . . .

end Rational_Numbers;

-------------------------------------------------------------------------------
package Rational_Numbers.IO is

    ...

    procedure Put (R : in  Rational);
    procedure Get (R : out Rational);

end Rational_Numbers.IO;

-------------------------------------------------------------------------------
with Rational_Numbers;
with Rational_Numbers.IO;
with Ada.Text_IO;
procedure Demo_Rationals is

    package R_IO renames Rational_Numbers.IO;

    use type Rational_Numbers.Rational;
    use R_IO;
    use Ada.Text_IO;

    X : Rational_Numbers.Rational;
    Y : Rational_Numbers.Rational;
```

```
begin   -- Demo_Rationals
    Put ("Please input two rational numbers: ");
    Get (X);
    Skip_Line;
    Get (Y);
    Skip_Line;
    Put ("X / Y = ");
    Put (X / Y);
    New_Line;
    Put ("X * Y = ");
    Put (X * Y);
    New_Line;
    Put ("X + Y = ");
    Put (X + Y);
    New_Line;
    Put ("X - Y = ");
    Put (X - Y);
    New_Line;
end Demo_Rationals;
```

rationale

These guidelines allow you to maintain a careful balance between maintainability and readability. Use of the use clause may indeed make the code read more like prose text. However, the maintainer may also need to resolve references and identify ambiguous operations. In the absence of tools to resolve these references and identify the impact of changing use clauses, fully qualified names are the best alternative.

Avoiding the use clause forces you to use fully qualified names. In large systems, there may be many library units named in with clauses. When corresponding use clauses accompany the with clauses and the simple names of the library packages are omitted (as is allowed by the use clause), references to external entities are obscured and identification of external dependencies becomes difficult.

In some situations, the benefits of the use clause are clear. A standard package can be used with the obvious assumption that the reader is very familiar with those packages and that additional overloading will not be introduced.

The use type clause makes both infix and prefix operators visible without the need for renames clauses. You enhance readability with the use type clause because you can write statements using the more natural infix notation for operators. See also Guideline 5.7.2.

You can minimize the scope of the use clause by placing it in the body of a package or subprogram or by encapsulating it in a block to restrict visibility.

notes

Avoiding the use clause completely can cause problems with enumeration literals, which must then be fully qualified. This problem can be solved by declaring constants with the enumeration literals as their values, except that such constants cannot be overloaded like enumeration literals.

An argument defending the use clause can be found in Rosen (1987).

automation notes

There are tools that can analyze your Ada source code, resolve overloading of names, and automatically convert between the use clause or fully qualified names.

5.7.2   The Renames Clause

guideline

- Limit the scope of a renaming declaration to the minimum necessary scope.
- Rename a long, fully qualified name to reduce the complexity if it becomes unwieldy (see Guideline 3.1.4).
- Use renaming to provide the body of a subprogram if this subprogram merely calls the first subprogram.
- Rename declarations for visibility purposes rather than using the use clause, except for operators (see Guideline 5.7.1).
- Rename parts when your code interfaces to reusable components originally written with nondescriptive or inapplicable nomenclature.

- Use a project-wide standard list of abbreviations to rename common packages.

- Provide a use type rather than a renames clause to provide visibility to operators.

example

```
procedure Disk_Write (Track_Name : in      Track;
                      Item        : in      Data) renames
        System_Specific.Device_Drivers.Disk_Head_Scheduler.Transmit;
```

See also the example in Guideline 5.7.1, where a package-level renames clause provides an abbreviation for the package Rational_Numbers_IO.

rationale

If the renaming facility is abused, the code can be difficult to read. A renames clause can substitute an abbreviation for a qualifier or long package name locally. This can make code more readable yet anchor the code to the full name. You can use the renames clause to evaluate a complex name once or to provide a new "view" of an object (regardless of whether it is tagged). However, the use of renames clauses can often be avoided or made obviously undesirable by carefully choosing names so that fully qualified names read well.

When a subprogram body calls another subprogram without adding local data or other algorithmic content, it is more readable to have this subprogram body rename the subprogram that actually does the work. Thus, you avoid having to write code to "pass through" a subprogram call (Rationale 1995, §II.12).

The list of renaming declarations serves as a list of abbreviation definitions (see Guideline 3.1.4). As an alternative, you can rename a package at the library level to define project-wide abbreviations for packages and then with the renamed packages. Often the parts recalled from a reuse library do not have names that are as general as they could be or that match the new application's naming scheme. An interface package exporting the renamed subprograms can map to your project's nomenclature. See also Guideline 5.7.1.

The method described in the Ada Reference Manual (1995) for renaming a type is to use a subtype (see Guideline 3.4.1).

The use type clause eliminates the need for renaming infix operators. Because you no longer need to rename each operator explicitly, you avoid errors such as renaming a + to a -. See also Guideline 5.7.1.

notes

You should choose package names to be minimally meaningful, recognizing that package names will be widely used as prefixes (e.g., Pkg.Operation or Object : Pkg.Type_Name;). If you rename every package to some abbreviation, you defeat the purpose of choosing meaningful names, and it becomes hard to keep track of what all the abbreviations represent.

For upward compatibility of Ada 83 programs in an Ada 95 environment, the environment includes library-level renamings of the Ada 83 library level packages (Ada Reference Manual 1995, §J.1). It is not recommended that you use these renamings in Ada 95 code.

5.7.3   Overloaded Subprograms

guideline

- Limit overloading to widely used subprograms that perform similar actions on arguments of different types (Nissen and Wallis 1984).

example

```
function Sin (Angles : in     Matrix_Of_Radians) return Matrix;
function Sin (Angles : in     Vector_Of_Radians) return Vector;
function Sin (Angle  : in     Radians)            return Small_Real;
function Sin (Angle  : in     Degrees)            return Small_Real;
```

rationale

Excessive overloading can be confusing to maintainers (Nissen and Wallis 1984, 65). There is also the danger of hiding declarations if overloading becomes habitual. Attempts to overload an operation may actually hide the original operation if the parameter profile is not distinct. From that point on, it is not clear whether invoking the new operation is what the programmer intended or whether the programmer intended to invoke the hidden operation and accidentally hid it.

notes

This guideline does not prohibit subprograms with identical names declared in different packages.

5.7.4   Overloaded Operators

guideline

- Preserve the conventional meaning of overloaded operators (Nissen and Wallis 1984).
- Use "+" to identify adding, joining, increasing, and enhancing kinds of functions.
- Use "-" to identify subtraction, separation, decreasing, and depleting kinds of functions.
- Use operator overloading sparingly and uniformly when applied to tagged types.

example

```
function "+" (X : in    Matrix;
              Y : in    Matrix)
   return Matrix;

...
Sum := A + B;
```

rationale

Subverting the conventional interpretation of operators leads to confusing code.

The advantage of operator overloading is that the code can become more clear and written more compactly (and readably) when it is used. This can make the semantics simple and natural. However, it can be easy to misunderstand the meaning of an overloaded operator, especially when applied to descendants. This is especially true if the programmer has not applied natural semantics. Thus, do not use overloading if it cannot be used uniformly and if it is easily misunderstood.

notes

There are potential problems with any overloading. For example, if there are several versions of the "+" operator and a change to one of them affects the number or order of its parameters, locating the occurrences that must be changed can be difficult.

5.7.5   Overloading the Equality Operator

guideline

- Define an appropriate equality operator for private types.
- Consider redefining the equality operator for a private type.
- When overloading the equality operator for types, maintain the properties of an algebraic equivalence relation.

rationale

The predefined equality operation provided with private types depends on the data structure chosen to implement that type. If access types are used, then equality will mean the operands have the same pointer value. If discrete types are used, then equality will mean the operands have the same value. If a floating-point type is used, then equality is based on Ada model intervals (see Guideline 7.2.7). You should, therefore, redefine equality to provide the meaning expected by the client. If you implement a private type using an access type, you should redefine equality to provide a deep equality. For floating-point types, you may want to provide an equality that tests for equality within some application-dependent epsilon value.

Any assumptions about the meaning of equality for private types will create a dependency on the implementation of that type. See Gonzalez (1991) for a detailed discussion.

When the definition of "=" is provided, there is a conventional algebraic meaning implied by this symbol. As described in Baker (1991), the following properties should remain true for the equality operator:

- Reflexive: $a = a$
- Symmetric: $a = b ==> b = a$
- Transitive: $a = b$ and $b = c ==> a = c$

In redefining equality, you are not required to have a result type of `standard.Boolean`. The Rationale (1995, §6.3) gives two examples where your result type is a user-defined type. In a three-valued logic abstraction, you redefine equality to return one of `True`, `False`, or `Unknown`. In a vector processing application, you can define a component-wise equality operator that returns a vector of Boolean values. In both these instances, you should also redefine inequality because it is not the Boolean complement of the equality function.

5.8   USING EXCEPTIONS

Ada exceptions are a reliability-enhancing language feature designed to help specify program behavior in the presence of errors or unexpected events. Exceptions are not intended to provide a general purpose control construct. Further, liberal use of exceptions should not be considered sufficient for providing full software fault tolerance (Melliar-Smith and Randell 1987).

This section addresses the issues of how and when to avoid raising exceptions, how and where to handle them, and whether to propagate them. Information on how to use exceptions as part of the interface to a unit includes what exceptions to declare and raise and under what conditions to raise them. Other issues are addressed in the guidelines in Sections 4.3 and 7.5.

5.8.1   Handling Versus Avoiding Exceptions

guideline

- When it is easy and efficient to do so, avoid causing exceptions to be raised.
- Provide handlers for exceptions that cannot be avoided.
- Use exception handlers to enhance readability by separating fault handling from normal execution.
- Do not use exceptions and exception handlers as `goto` statements.
- Do not evaluate the value of an object (or a part of an object) that has become abnormal because of the failure of a language-defined check.

rationale

In many cases, it is possible to detect easily and efficiently that an operation you are about to perform would raise an exception. In such a case, it is a good idea to check rather than allowing the exception to be raised and handling it with an exception handler. For example, check each pointer for `null` when traversing a linked list of records connected by pointers. Also, test an integer for 0 before dividing by it, and call an interrogative function `Stack_Is_Empty` before invoking the `pop` procedure of a stack package. Such tests are appropriate when they can be performed easily and efficiently as a natural part of the algorithm being implemented.

However, error detection in advance is not always so simple. There are cases where such a test is too expensive or too unreliable. In such cases, it is better to attempt the operation within the scope of an exception handler so that the exception is handled if it is raised. For example, in the case of a linked list implementation of a list, it is very inefficient to call a function `Entry_Exists` before each call to the procedure `Modify_Entry` simply to avoid raising the exception `Entry_Not_Found`. It takes as much time to search the list to avoid the exception as it takes to search the list to perform the update. Similarly, it is much easier to attempt a division by a real number within the scope of an exception handler to handle numeric overflow than to test, in advance, whether the dividend is too large or the divisor too small for the quotient to be representable on the machine.

In concurrent situations, tests done in advance can also be unreliable. For example, if you want to modify an existing file on a multiuser system, it is safer to attempt to do so within the scope of an exception handler than to test in advance whether the file exists, whether it is protected, whether there is room in the file system for the file to be enlarged, etc. Even if you tested for all possible error conditions, there is no guarantee that nothing would change after the test and before the modification operation. You still need the exception handlers, so the advance testing serves no purpose.

Whenever such a case does not apply, normal and predictable events should be handled by the code without the abnormal transfer of control represented by an exception. When fault handling and only fault handling code is included in exception handlers, the separation makes the code easier to read. The reader can skip all the exception handlers and still understand the normal flow of control of the code. For this reason, exceptions should never be raised and handled within the same unit, as a form of a `goto` statement to exit from a `loop`, `if`, `case`, or `block` statement.

Evaluating an abnormal object results in erroneous execution (Ada Reference Manual 1995, §13.9.1). The failure of a language-defined check raises an exception. In the corresponding exception handler, you want to perform appropriate cleanup actions, including logging the error (see the discussion on exception occurrences in Guideline 5.8.2) and/or reraising the exception. Evaluating the object that put you into the exception handling code will lead to erroneous execution, where you do not know whether your exception handler has executed completely or correctly. See also Guideline 5.9.1, which discusses abnormal objects in the context of `Ada.Unchecked_Conversion`.

5.8.2   Handlers for Others

guideline

- When writing an exception handler for `others`, capture and return additional information about the exception through the `Exception_Name`, `Exception_Message`, or `Exception_Information` subprograms declared in the predefined package `Ada.Exceptions`.

- Use `others` only to catch exceptions you cannot enumerate explicitly, preferably only to flag a potential abort.

- During development, trap `others`, capture the exception being handled, and consider adding an explicit handler for that exception.

example

The following simplified example gives the user one chance to enter an integer in the range 1 to 3. In the event of an error, it provides information back to the user. For an integer value that is outside the expected range, the function reports the name of the exception. For any other error, the function provides more complete traceback information. The amount of traceback information is implementation dependent.

```
with Ada.Exceptions;
with Ada.Text_IO;
with Ada.Integer_Text_IO;
function Valid_Choice return Positive is

    subtype Choice_Range is Positive range 1..3;

    Choice : Choice_Range;

begin

    Ada.Text_IO.Put ("Please enter your choice: 1, 2, or 3: ");
    Ada.Integer_Text_IO.Get (Choice);

    if Choice in Choice_Range then    -- else garbage returned
        return Choice;
    end if;


    when Out_of_Bounds : Constraint_Error =>
        Ada.Text_IO.Put_Line ("Input choice not in range.");
        Ada.Text_IO.Put_Line (Ada.Exceptions.Exception_Name (Out_of_Bounds));
        Ada.Text_IO.Skip_Line;
    when The_Error : others =>
        Ada.Text_IO.Put_Line ("Unexpected error.");
        Ada.Text_IO.Put_Line (Ada.Exceptions.Exception_Information (The_Error));
        Ada.Text_IO.Skip_Line;

end Valid_Choice;
```

rationale

The predefined package `Ada.Exceptions` allows you to log an exception, including its name and traceback information. When writing a handler for `others`, you should provide information about the exception to facilitate debugging. Because you can access information about an exception occurrence, you can save information suitable for later analysis in a standard way. By using exception occurrences, you can identify the particular exception and either log the details or take corrective action.

Providing a handler for `others` allows you to follow the other guidelines in this section. It affords a place to catch and convert truly unexpected exceptions that were not caught by the explicit handlers. While it may be possible to provide "fire walls" against unexpected exceptions being propagated without providing handlers in every block, you can convert the unexpected exceptions as soon as they arise. The others handler cannot discriminate between different exceptions, and, as a result, any such handler must treat the exception as a disaster. Even such a disaster can still be converted into a user-defined exception at that point. Because a handler for others catches any exception not otherwise handled explicitly, one placed in the frame of a task or of the main subprogram affords the opportunity to perform final cleanup and to shut down cleanly.

Programming a handler for others requires caution. You should name it in the handler (e.g., Error : others;) to discriminate either which exception was actually raised or precisely where it was raised. In general, the others handler cannot make any assumptions about what can be or even what needs to be "fixed."

The use of handlers for others during development, when exception occurrences can be expected to be frequent, can hinder debugging unless you take advantage of the facilities in Ada.Exceptions. It is much more informative to the developer to see a traceback with the actual exception information as captured by the Ada.Exceptions subprograms. Writing a handler without these subprograms limits the amount of error information you may see. For example, you may only see the converted exception in a traceback that does not list the point where the original exception was raised.

notes

It is possible, but not recommended, to use Exception_Id to distinguish between different exceptions in an others handler. The type Exception_Id is implementation defined. Manipulating values of type Exception_Id reduces the portability of your program and makes it harder to understand.

5.8.3   Propagation

guideline

- Handle all exceptions, both user and predefined.
- For every exception that might be raised, provide a handler in suitable frames to protect against undesired propagation outside the abstraction.

rationale

The statement that "it can never happen" is not an acceptable programming approach. You must assume it can happen and be in control when it does. You should provide defensive code routines for the "cannot get here" conditions.

Some existing advice calls for catching and propagating any exception to the calling unit. This advice can stop a program. You should catch the exception and propagate it or a substitute only if your handler is at the wrong abstraction level to effect recovery. Effecting recovery can be difficult, but the alternative is a program that does not meet its specification.

Making an explicit request for termination implies that your code is in control of the situation and has determined that to be the only safe course of action. Being in control affords opportunities to shut down in a controlled manner (clean up loose ends, close files, release surfaces to manual control, sound alarms) and implies that all available programmed attempts at recovery have been made.

5.8.4   Localizing the Cause of an Exception

guideline

- Do not rely on being able to identify the fault-raising, predefined, or implementation-defined exceptions.
- Use the facilities defined in Ada.Exceptions to capture as much information as possible about an exception.
- Use blocks to associate localized sections of code with their own exception handlers.

example

See Guideline 5.6.9.

rationale

In an exception handler, it is very difficult to determine exactly which statement and which operation within that statement raised an exception, particularly the predefined and implementation-defined exceptions. The predefined and implementation-defined exceptions are candidates for conversion and propagation to higher abstraction levels for handling there. User-defined exceptions, being more closely associated with the application, are better candidates for recovery within handlers.

User-defined exceptions can also be difficult to localize. Associating handlers with small blocks of code helps to narrow the possibilities, making it easier to program recovery actions. The placement of handlers in small blocks within a subprogram or task body also allows resumption of the subprogram or task after the recovery actions. If you do not handle exceptions within blocks, the only action available to the handlers is to shut down the task or subprogram as prescribed in Guideline 5.8.3.

As discussed in Guideline 5.8.2, you can log run-time system information about the exception. You can also attach a message to the exception. During code development, debugging, and maintenance, this information should be useful to localize the cause of the exception.

notes

The optimal size for the sections of code you choose to protect by a block and its exception handlers is very application-dependent. Too small a granularity forces you to expend more effort in programming for abnormal actions than for the normal algorithm. Too large a granularity reintroduces the problems of determining what went wrong and of resuming normal flow.

5.9 ERRONEOUS EXECUTION AND BOUNDED ERRORS

Ada 95 introduces the category of bounded errors. Bounded errors are cases where the behavior is not deterministic but falls within well-defined bounds (Rationale 1995, §1.4). The consequence of a bounded error is to limit the behavior of compilers so that an Ada environment is not free to do whatever it wants in the presence of errors. The Ada Reference Manual (1995) defines a set of possible outcomes for the consequences of undefined behavior, as in an uninitialized value or a value outside the range of its subtype. For example, the executing program may raise the predefined exception Program_Error, Constraint_Error, or it may do nothing.

An Ada program is erroneous when it generates an error that is not required to be detected by the compiler or run-time environments. As stated in the Ada Reference Manual (1995, §1.1.5), "The effects of erroneous execution are unpredictable." If the compiler does detect an instance of an erroneous program, its options are to indicate a compile time error; to insert the code to raise Program_Error, possibly to write a message to that effect; or to do nothing at all.

Erroneousness is not a concept unique to Ada. The guidelines below describe or explain some specific instances of erroneousness defined in the Ada Reference Manual (1995). These guidelines are not intended to be all-inclusive but rather emphasize some commonly overlooked problem areas. Arbitrary order dependencies are not, strictly speaking, a case of erroneous execution; thus, they are discussed in Guideline 7.1.9 as a portability issue.

5.9.1 Unchecked Conversion

guideline

- Use Ada.Unchecked_Conversion only with the utmost care (Ada Reference Manual 1995, §13.9).
- Consider using the 'Valid attribute to check the validity of scalar data.
- Ensure that the value resulting from Ada.Unchecked_Conversion properly represents a value of the parameter's subtype.
- Isolate the use of Ada.Unchecked_Conversion in package bodies.

example

The following example shows how to use the 'Valid attribute to check validity of scalar data:

```
-------------------------------------------------------------------------
with Ada.Unchecked_Conversion;
with Ada.Text_IO;
with Ada.Integer_Text_IO;

procedure Test is

    type Color is (Red, Yellow, Blue);
    for Color'Size use Integer'Size;

    function Integer_To_Color is
        new Ada.Unchecked_Conversion (Source => Integer,
                                      Target => Color);

    Possible_Color : Color;
    Number         : Integer;

begin  -- Test

    Ada.Integer_Text_IO.Get (Number);
    Possible_Color := Integer_To_Color (Number);

    if Possible_Color'Valid then
        Ada.Text_IO.Put_Line(Color'Image(Possible_Color));
    else
        Ada.Text_IO.Put_Line("Number does not correspond to a color.");
    end if;

end Test;
-------------------------------------------------------------------------
```

rationale

An unchecked conversion is a bit-for-bit copy without regard to the meanings attached to those bits and bit positions by either the source or the destination type. The source bit pattern can easily be meaningless in the context of the destination type. Unchecked conversions can create values that violate type constraints on subsequent operations. Unchecked conversion of objects mismatched in size has implementation-dependent results.

Using the 'Valid attribute on scalar data allows you to check whether it is in range without raising an exception if it is out of range. There are several cases where such a validity check enhances the readability and maintainability of the code:

- Data produced through an unchecked conversion
- Input data
- Parameter values returned from a foreign language interface
- Aborted assignment (during asynchronous transfer of control or execution of an abort statement)
- Disrupted assignment from failure of a language-defined check
- Data whose address has been specified with the 'Address attribute

An access value should not be assumed to be correct when obtained without compiler or run-time checks. When dealing with access values, use of the 'Valid attribute helps prevent the erroneous dereferencing that might occur after using Ada.Unchecked_Deallocation, Unchecked_Access, or Ada.Unchecked_Conversion.

In the case of a nonscalar object used as an actual parameter in an unchecked conversion, you should ensure that its value on return from the procedure properly represents a value in the subtype. This case occurs when the parameter is of mode out or in out. It is important to check the value when interfacing to foreign languages or using a language-defined input procedure. The Ada Reference Manual (1995, §13.9.1) lists the full rules concerning data validity.

5.9.2 Unchecked Deallocation

guideline

- Isolate the use of Ada.Unchecked_Deallocation in package bodies.
- Ensure that no dangling reference to the local object exists after exiting the scope of the local object.

rationale

Most of the reasons for using Ada.Unchecked_Deallocation with caution have been given in Guideline 5.4.5. When this feature is used, no checking is performed to verify that there is only one access path to the storage being deallocated. Thus, any other access paths are not made null. Depending on the value of these other access paths could result in erroneous execution.

If your Ada environment implicitly uses dynamic heap storage but does not fully and reliably reclaim and reuse heap storage, you should not use Ada.Unchecked_Deallocation.

5.9.3   Unchecked Access

guideline

- Minimize the use of the attribute Unchecked_Access, preferably isolating it to package bodies.

- Use the attribute Unchecked_Access only on data whose lifetime/scope is "library level."

rationale

The accessibility rules are checked statically at compile time (except for access parameters, which are checked dynamically). These rules ensure that the access value cannot outlive the object it designates. Because these rules are not applied in the case of Unchecked_Access, an access path could be followed to an object no longer in scope.

Isolating the use of the attribute Unchecked_Access means to isolate its use from clients of the package. You should not apply it to an access value merely for the sake of returning a now unsafe value to clients.

When you use the attribute Unchecked_Access, you are creating access values in an unsafe manner. You run the risk of dangling references, which in turn lead to erroneous execution (Ada Reference Manual 1995, §13.9.1).

exceptions

The Ada Reference Manual (1995, §13.10) defines the following potential use for this otherwise dangerous attribute. "This attribute is provided to support the situation where a local object is to be inserted into a global linked data structure, when the programmer knows that it will always be removed from the data structure prior to exiting the object's scope."

5.9.4   Address Clauses

guideline

- Use address clauses to map variables and entries to the hardware device or memory, not to model the FORTRAN "equivalence" feature.

- Ensure that the address specified in an attribute definition clause is valid and does not conflict with the alignment.

- If available in your Ada environment, use the package Ada.Interrupts to associate handlers with interrupts.

- Avoid using the address clause for nonimported program units.

example

```
Single_Address : constant System.Address := System.Storage_Elements.To_Address(...);

Interrupt_Vector_Table : Hardware_Array;
for Interrupt_Vector_Table'Address use Single_Address;
```

rationale

The result of specifying a single address for multiple objects or program units is undefined, as is specifying multiple addresses for a single object or program unit. Specifying multiple address clauses for an interrupt is also undefined. It does not necessarily overlay objects or program units, or associate a single entry with more than one interrupt.

You are responsible for ensuring the validity of an address you specify. Ada requires that the object of an address be an integral multiple of its alignment.

In Ada 83 (Ada Reference Manual 1983) you had to use values of type System.Address to attach an interrupt entry to an interrupt. While this technique is allowed in Ada 95, you are using an obsolete feature. You should use a protected procedure and the appropriate pragmas (Rationale 1995, §C.3.2).

5.9.5 Suppression of Exception Check

guideline

- Do not suppress exception checks during development.
- If necessary, during operation, introduce blocks that encompass the smallest range of statements that can safely have exception checking removed.

rationale

If you disable exception checks and program execution results in a condition in which an exception would otherwise occur, the program execution is erroneous. The results are unpredictable. Further, you must still be prepared to deal with the suppressed exceptions if they are raised in and propagated from the bodies of subprograms, tasks, and packages you call.

By minimizing the code that has exception checking removed, you increase the reliability of the program. There is a rule of thumb that suggests that 20% of the code is responsible for 80% of the CPU time. So, once you have identified the code that actually needs exception checking removed, it is wise to isolate it in a block (with appropriate comments) and leave the surrounding code with exception checking in effect.

5.9.6 Initialization

guideline

- Initialize all objects prior to use.
- Use caution when initializing access values.
- Do not depend on default initialization that is not part of the language.
- Derive from a controlled type and override the primitive procedure to ensure automatic initialization.
- Ensure elaboration of an entity before using it.
- Use function calls in declarations cautiously.

example

The first example illustrates the potential problem with initializing access values:

```
procedure Mix_Letters (Of_String : in out String) is
   type String_Ptr is access String;
   Ptr : String_Ptr := new String'(Of_String);   -- could raise Storage_Error in caller
begin -- Mix_Letters
   ...
exception
   ...   -- cannot trap Storage_Error raised during elaboration of Ptr declaration
end Mix_Letters;
```

The second example illustrates the issue of ensuring the elaboration of an entity before its use:

```
-------------------------------------------------------------------------
package Robot_Controller is
   ...
   function Sense return Position;
   ...
end Robot_Controller;

-------------------------------------------------------------------------
package body Robot_Controller is
   ...
   Goal : Position := Sense;        -- This raises Program_Error
   ...

-------------------------------------------------------------------------
   function Sense return Position is
   begin
      ...
   end Sense;
-------------------------------------------------------------------------
```

```
begin  -- Robot_Controller
   Goal := Sense;                    -- The function has been elaborated.

   ...
end Robot_Controller;
```
----

rationale

Ada does not define an initial default value for objects of any type other than access types, whose initial default value is null. If you are initializing an access value at the point at which it is declared and the allocation raises the exception Storage_Error, the exception is raised in the calling not the called procedure. The caller is unprepared to handle this exception because it knows nothing about the problem-causing allocation.

Operating systems differ in what they do when they allocate a page in memory: one operating system may zero out the entire page; a second may do nothing. Therefore, using the value of an object before it has been assigned a value causes unpredictable (but bounded) behavior, possibly raising an exception. Objects can be initialized implicitly by declaration or explicitly by assignment statements. Initialization at the point of declaration is safest as well as easiest for maintainers. You can also specify default values for components of records as part of the type declarations for those records.

Ensuring initialization does not imply initialization at the declaration. In the example above, Goal must be initialized via a function call. This cannot occur at the declaration because the function Sense has not yet been elaborated, but it can occur later as part of the sequence of statements of the body of the enclosing package.

An unelaborated function called within a declaration (initialization) raises the exception, Program_Error, that must be handled outside of the unit containing the declarations. This is true for any exception the function raises even if it has been elaborated.

If an exception is raised by a function call in a declaration, it is not handled in that immediate scope. It is raised to the enclosing scope. This can be controlled by nesting blocks.

See also Guideline 9.2.3.

notes

Sometimes, elaboration order can be dictated with pragma Elaborate_All. Pragma Elaborate_All applied to a library unit causes the elaboration of the transitive closure of the unit and its dependents. In other words, all bodies of library units reachable from this library unit's body are elaborated, preventing an access-before-elaboration error (Rationale 1995, §10.3). Use the pragma Elaborate_Body when you want the body of a package to be elaborated immediately after its declaration.

5.9.7   Direct_IO and Sequential_IO

guideline

* Ensure that values obtained from Ada.Direct_IO and Ada.Sequential_IO are in range.
* Use the 'Valid attribute to check the validity of scalar values obtained through Ada.Direct_IO and Ada.Sequential_IO.

rationale

The exception Data_Error can be propagated by the Read procedures found in these packages if the element read cannot be interpreted as a value of the required subtype (Ada Reference Manual 1995, §A.13). However, if the associated check is too complex, an implementation need not propagate Data_Error. In cases where the element read cannot be interpreted as a value of the required subtype but Data_Error is not propagated, the resulting value can be abnormal, and subsequent references to the value can lead to erroneous execution.

notes

It is sometimes difficult to force an optimizing compiler to perform the necessary checks on a value that the compiler believes is in range. Most compiler vendors allow the option of suppressing optimization, which can be helpful.

5.9.8 Exception Propagation

guideline

- Prevent exceptions from propagating outside any user-defined Finalize or Adjust procedure by providing handlers for all predefined and user-defined exceptions at the end of each procedure.

rationale

Using Finalize or Adjust to propagate an exception results in a bounded error (Ada Reference Manual 1995, §7.6.1). Either the exception will be ignored or a Program_Error exception will be raised.

5.9.9 Protected Objects

guideline

- Do not invoke a potentially blocking operation within a protected entry, a protected procedure, or a protected function.

rationale

The Ada Reference Manual (1995, §9.5.1) lists the potentially blocking operations:

- Select statement
- Accept statement
- Entry-call statement
- Delay statement
- Abort statement
- Task creation or activation
- External call on a protected subprogram (or an external requeue) with the same target object as that of the protected action
- Call on a subprogram whose body contains a potentially blocking operation

Invoking any of these potentially blocking operations could lead either to a bounded error being detected or to a deadlock situation. In the case of bounded error, the exception Program_Error is raised. In addition, avoid calling routines within a protected entry, procedure, or function that could directly or indirectly invoke operating system primitives or similar operations that can cause blocking that is not visible to the Ada runtime system.

5.9.10 Abort Statement

guideline

- Do not use an asynchronous select statement within abort-deferred operations.
- Do not create a task that depends on a master that is included entirely within the execution of an abort-deferred operation.

rationale

An abort-deferred operation is one of the following:

- Protected entry, protected procedure, or protected function
- User-defined Initialize procedure used as the last step of a default initialization of a controlled object
- User-defined Finalize procedure used in finalization of a controlled object
- User-defined Adjust procedure used in assignment of a controlled object

The Ada Reference Manual (1995, §9.8) states that the practices discouraged in the guidelines result in bounded error. The exception Program_Error is raised if the implementation detects the error. If the implementation does not detect the error, the operations proceed as they would outside an abort-deferred operation. An abort statement itself may have no effect.

5.10   SUMMARY

optional parts of the syntax

- Associate names with loops when they are nested (Booch 1986, 1987).
- Associate names with any loop that contains an `exit` statement.
- Associate names with blocks when they are nested.
- Use loop names on all `exit` statements from nested loops.
- Include the defining program unit name at the end of a package specification and body.
- Include the defining identifier at the end of a task specification and body.
- Include the entry identifier at the end of an `accept` statement.
- Include the designator at the end of a subprogram body.
- Include the defining identifier at the end of a protected unit declaration.

parameter lists

- Name formal parameters descriptively to reduce the need for comments.
- Use named parameter association in calls of infrequently used subprograms or entries with many formal parameters.
- Use named association when instantiating generics.
- Use named association for clarification when the actual parameter is any literal or expression.
- Use named association when supplying a nondefault value to an optional parameter.
- Provide default parameters to allow for occasional, special use of widely used subprograms or entries.
- Place default parameters at the end of the formal parameter list.
- Consider providing default values to new parameters added to an existing subprogram.
- Show the mode indication of all procedure and entry parameters (Nissen and Wallis 1984).
- Use the most restrictive parameter mode applicable to your application.

types

- Use existing types as building blocks by deriving new types from them.
- Use range constraints on subtypes.
- Define new types, especially derived types, to include the largest set of possible values, including boundary values.
- Constrain the ranges of derived types with subtypes, excluding boundary values.
- Use type derivation rather than type extension when there are no meaningful components to add to the type.
- Avoid anonymous array types.
- Use anonymous array types for array variables only when no suitable type exists or can be created and the array will not be referenced as a whole (e.g., used as a subprogram parameter).
- Use access parameters and access discriminants to guarantee that the parameter or discriminant is treated as a constant.
- Derive from controlled types in preference to using limited private types.
- Use limited private types in preference to private types.
- Use private types in preference to nonprivate types.
- Explicitly export needed operations rather than easing restrictions.
- Use access-to-subprogram types for indirect access to subprograms.
- Wherever possible, use abstract tagged types and dispatching rather than access-to-subprogram types to implement dynamic selection and invocation of subprograms.

data structures

- When declaring a discriminant, use as constrained a subtype as possible (i.e., subtype with as specific a range constraint as possible).
- Use a discriminated record rather than a constrained array to represent an array whose actual values are unconstrained.
- Use records to group heterogeneous but related data.
- Consider records to map to I/O device data.
- Use access types to class-wide types to implement heterogeneous polymorphic data structures.
- Use tagged types and type extension rather than variant records (in combination with enumeration types and case statements).
- Record structures should not always be flat. Factor out common parts.
- For a large record structure, group related components into smaller subrecords.
- For nested records, pick element names that read well when inner elements are referenced.
- Consider using type extension to organize large data structures.
- Differentiate between static and dynamic data. Use dynamically allocated objects with caution.
- Use dynamically allocated data structures only when it is necessary to create and destroy them dynamically or to be able to reference them by different names.
- Do not drop pointers to undeallocated objects.
- Do not leave dangling references to deallocated objects.
- Initialize all access variables and components within a record.
- Do not rely on memory deallocation.
- Deallocate explicitly.
- Use length clauses to specify total allocation size.
- Provide handlers for Storage_Error.
- Use controlled types to implement private types that manipulate dynamic data.
- Avoid unconstrained record objects unless your run-time environment reliably reclaims dynamic heap storage.
- Unless your run-time environment reliably reclaims dynamic heap storage, declare the following items only in the outermost, unnested declarative part of either a library package, a main subprogram, or a permanent task:
  - Access types
  - Constrained composite objects with nonstatic bounds
  - Objects of an unconstrained composite type other than unconstrained records
  - Composite objects large enough (at compile time) for the compiler to allocate implicitly on the heap
- Unless your run-time environment reliably reclaims dynamic heap storage or you are creating permanent, dynamically allocated tasks, avoid declaring tasks in the following situations:
  - Unconstrained array subtypes whose components are tasks
  - Discriminated record subtypes containing a component that is an array of tasks, where the array size depends on the value of the discriminant
  - Any declarative region other than the outermost, unnested declarative part of either a library package or a main subprogram
  - Arrays of tasks that are not statically constrained
- Minimize the use of aliased variables.
- Use aliasing for statically created, ragged arrays (Rationale 1995, §3.7.1).
- Use aliasing to refer to part of a data structure when you want to hide the internal connections and bookkeeping information.

- Use access discriminants to create self-referential data structures, i.e., a data structure one of whose components points to the enclosing structure.
- Use modular types rather than a Boolean arrays when you create data structures that need bit-wise operations, such as and and or.

expressions

- Use 'First or 'Last instead of numeric literals to represent the first or last values of a range.
- Use 'Range or the subtype name of the range instead of 'First .. 'Last.
- Use array attributes 'First, 'Last, or 'Length instead of numeric literals for accessing arrays.
- Use the 'Range of the array instead of the name of the index subtype to express a range.
- Use 'Range instead of 'First .. 'Last to express a range.
- Use parentheses to specify the order of subexpression evaluation to clarify expressions (NASA 1987).
- Use parentheses to specify the order of evaluation for subexpressions whose correctness depends on left to right evaluation.
- Avoid names and constructs that rely on the use of negatives.
- Choose names of flags so they represent states that can be used in positive form.
- Use short-circuit forms of the logical operators to specify the order of conditions when the failure of one condition means that the other condition will raise an exception.
- Use <= and >= in relational expressions with real operands instead of =.

statements

- Minimize the depth of nested expressions (Nissen and Wallis 1984).
- Minimize the depth of nested control structures (Nissen and Wallis 1984).
- Try using simplification heuristics.
- Use slices rather than a loop to copy part of an array.
- Minimize the use of an others choice in a case statement.
- Do not use ranges of enumeration literals in case statements.
- Use case statements rather than if/elsif statements, wherever possible.
- Use type extension and dispatching rather than case statements, if possible.
- Use for loops, whenever possible.
- Use while loops when the number of iterations cannot be calculated before entering the loop but a simple continuation condition can be applied at the top of the loop.
- Use plain loops with exit statements for more complex situations.
- Avoid exit statements in while and for loops.
- Minimize the number of ways to exit a loop.
- Use exit statements to enhance the readability of loop termination code (NASA 1987).
- Use exit when ... rather than if ... then exit whenever possible (NASA 1987).
- Review exit statement placement.
- Consider specifying bounds on loops.
- Consider specifying bounds on recursion.
- Do not use goto statements.
- Minimize the number of return statements from a subprogram (NASA 1987).
- Highlight return statements with comments or white space to keep them from being lost in other code.
- Use blocks to localize the scope of declarations.
- Use blocks to perform local renaming.
- Use blocks to define local exception handlers.

- Use an aggregate instead of a sequence of assignments to assign values to all components of a record.
- Use an aggregate instead of a temporary variable when building a record to pass as an actual parameter.
- Use positional association only when there is a conventional ordering of the arguments.

visibility

- When you need to provide visibility to operators, use the use type clause.
- Avoid/minimize the use of the use clause (Nissen and Wallis 1984).
- Consider using a package renames clause rather than a use clause for a package.
- Consider using the use clause in the following situations:
  - When standard packages are needed and no ambiguous references are introduced
  - When references to enumeration literals are needed
- Localize the effect of all use clauses.
- Limit the scope of a renaming declaration to the minimum necessary scope.
- Rename a long, fully qualified name to reduce the complexity if it becomes unwieldy.
- Use renaming to provide the body of a subprogram if this subprogram merely calls the first subprogram.
- Rename declarations for visibility purposes rather than using the use clause, except for operators.
- Rename parts when your code interfaces to reusable components originally written with nondescriptive or inapplicable nomenclature.
- Use a project-wide standard list of abbreviations to rename common packages.
- Provide a use type rather than a renames clause to provide visibility to operators.
- Limit overloading to widely used subprograms that perform similar actions on arguments of different types (Nissen and Wallis 1984).
- Preserve the conventional meaning of overloaded operators (Nissen and Wallis 1984).
- Use "+" to identify adding, joining, increasing, and enhancing kinds of functions.
- Use "-" to identify subtraction, separation, decreasing, and depleting kinds of functions.
- Use operator overloading sparingly and uniformly when applied to tagged types.
- Define an appropriate equality operator for private types.
- Consider redefining the equality operator for a private type.
- When overloading the equality operator for types, maintain the properties of an algebraic equivalence relation.

using exceptions

- When it is easy and efficient to do so, avoid causing exceptions to be raised.
- Provide handlers for exceptions that cannot be avoided.
- Use exception handlers to enhance readability by separating fault handling from normal execution.
- Do not use exceptions and exception handlers as goto statements.
- Do not evaluate the value of an object (or a part of an object) that has become abnormal because of the failure of a language-defined check.
- When writing an exception handler for others, capture and return additional information about the exception through the Exception_Name, Exception_Message, or Exception_Information subprograms declared in the predefined package Ada.Exceptions.
- Use others only to catch exceptions you cannot enumerate explicitly, preferably only to flag a potential abort.
- During development, trap others, capture the exception being handled, and consider adding an explicit handler for that exception.
- Handle all exceptions, both user and predefined.

- For every exception that might be raised, provide a handler in suitable frames to protect against undesired propagation outside the abstraction.
- Do not rely on being able to identify the fault-raising, predefined, or implementation-defined exceptions.
- Use the facilities defined in Ada.Exceptions to capture as much information as possible about an exception.
- Use blocks to associate localized sections of code with their own exception handlers.

erroneous execution and bounded errors

- Use Ada.Unchecked_Conversion only with the utmost care (Ada Reference Manual 1995, §13.9).
- Consider using the 'Valid attribute to check the validity of scalar data).
- Ensure that the value resulting from Ada.Unchecked_Conversion properly represents a value of the parameter's subtype.
- Isolate the use of Ada.Unchecked_Conversion in package bodies.
- Isolate the use of Ada.Unchecked_Deallocation in package bodies.
- Ensure that no dangling reference to the local object exists after exiting the scope of the local object.
- Minimize the use of the attribute Unchecked_Access, preferably isolating it to package bodies.
- Use the attribute Unchecked_Access only on data whose lifetime/scope is "library level."
- Use address clauses to map variables and entries to the hardware device or memory, not to model the FORTRAN "equivalence" feature.
- Ensure that the address specified in an attribute definition clause is valid and does not conflict with the alignment.
- If available in your Ada environment, use the package Ada.Interrupts to associate handlers with interrupts.
- Avoid using the address clause for nonimported program units.
- Do not suppress exception checks during development.
- If necessary, during operation, introduce blocks that encompass the smallest range of statements that can safely have exception checking removed.
- Initialize all objects, including access values, prior to use.
- Use caution when initializing access values.
- Do not depend on default initialization that is not part of the language.
- Derive from a controlled type and override the primitive procedure to ensure automatic initialization.
- Ensure elaboration of an entity before using it.
- Use function calls in declarations cautiously.
- Ensure that values obtained from Ada.Direct_IO and Ada.Sequential_IO are in range.
- Use the 'Valid attribute to check the validity of scalar values obtained through Ada.Direct_IO and Ada.Sequential_IO.
- Prevent exceptions from propagating outside any user-defined Finalize or Adjust procedure by providing handlers for all predefined and user-defined exceptions at the end of each procedure.
- Do not invoke a potentially blocking operation within a protected entry, a protected procedure, or a protected function.
- Do not use an asynchronous select statement within abort-deferred operations.
- Do not create a task that depends on a master that is included entirely within the execution of an abort-deferred operation.

CHAPTER 6
Concurrency

Concurrency exists as either apparent concurrency or real concurrency. In a single processor environment, apparent concurrency is the result of interleaved execution of concurrent activities. In a multiprocessor environment, real concurrency is the result of overlapped execution of concurrent activities.

Concurrent programming is more difficult and error prone than sequential programming. The concurrent programming features of Ada are designed to make it easier to write and maintain concurrent programs that behave consistently and predictably and avoid such problems as deadlock and starvation. The language features themselves cannot guarantee that programs have these desirable properties. They must be used with discipline and care, a process supported by the guidelines in this chapter.

The correct usage of Ada concurrency features results in reliable, reusable, and portable software. Protected objects (added in Ada 95) encapsulate and provide synchronized access to their private data (Rationale 1995, §II.9). Protected objects help you manage shared data without incurring a performance penalty. Tasks model concurrent activities and use the rendezvous to synchronize between cooperating concurrent tasks. Much of the synchronization required between tasks involves data synchronization, which can be accomplished most efficiently, in general, using protected objects. Misuse of language features results in software that is unverifiable and difficult to reuse or port. For example, using task priorities or delays to manage synchronization is not portable. It is also important that a reusable component not make assumptions about the order or speed of task execution (i.e., about the compiler's tasking implementation).

Although concurrent features such as tasks and protected objects are supported by the core Ada language, care should be taken when using these features with implementations that do not specifically support Annex D (Real-Time Systems). If Annex D is not specifically supported, features required for real-time applications might not be implemented.

Guidelines in this chapter are frequently worded "consider . . ." because hard and fast rules cannot apply in all situations. The specific choice you make in a given situation involves design tradeoffs. The rationale for these guidelines is intended to give you insight into some of these tradeoffs.

6.1   CONCURRENCY OPTIONS

Many problems map naturally to a concurrent programming solution. By understanding and correctly using the Ada language concurrency features, you can produce solutions that are largely independent of target implementation. Tasks provide a means, within the Ada language, of expressing concurrent, asynchronous threads of control and relieving programmers from the problem of explicitly controlling multiple concurrent activities. Protected objects serve as a building block to support other synchronization paradigms.

Tasks cooperate to perform the required activities of the software. Synchronization and mutual exclusion are required between individual tasks. The Ada rendezvous and protected objects provide powerful mechanisms for both synchronization and mutual exclusion.

6.1.1 Protected Objects

guideline

- Consider using protected objects to provide mutually exclusive access to data.
- Consider using protected objects to control or synchronize access to data shared by multiple tasks.
- Consider using protected objects to implement synchronization, such as a passive resource monitor.
- Consider encapsulating protected objects in the private part or body of a package.
- Consider using a protected procedure to implement an interrupt handler.
- Do not attach a protected procedure handler to a hardware interrupt if that interrupt has a maximum priority greater than the ceiling priority assigned to the handler.
- Avoid the use of global variables in entry barriers.
- Avoid the use of barrier expressions with side effects.

example

```
generic
   type Item is private;
   Maximum_Buffer_Size : in Positive;
package Bounded_Buffer_Package is

   subtype Buffer_Index is Positive range 1..Maximum_Buffer_Size;
   subtype Buffer_Count is Natural  range 0..Maximum_Buffer_Size;
   type    Buffer_Array is array (Buffer_Index) of Item;

   protected type Bounded_Buffer is
      entry Get (X : out Item);
      entry Put (X : in Item);
   private
      Get_Index : Buffer_Index := 1;
      Put_Index : Buffer_Index := 1;
      Count     : Buffer_Count := 0;
      Data      : Buffer_Array;
   end Bounded_Buffer;

end Bounded_Buffer_Package;

-------------------------------------------------------------------

package body Bounded_Buffer_Package is

   protected body Bounded_Buffer is

      entry Get (X : out Item) when Count > 0 is
      begin
         X := Data(Get_Index);
         Get_Index := (Get_Index mod Maximum_Buffer_Size) + 1;
         Count := Count - 1;
      end Get;

      entry Put (X : in Item) when Count < Maximum_Buffer_Size is
      begin
         Data(Put_Index) := X;
         Put_Index := (Put_Index mod Maximum_Buffer_Size) + 1;
         Count := Count + 1;
      end Put;

   end Bounded_Buffer;

end Bounded_Buffer_Package;
```

rationale

Protected objects are intended to provide a "lightweight" mechanism for mutual exclusion and data synchronization. You should use a task only when you need to introduce explicitly a new, concurrent thread of control (see Guideline 6.1.2).

Protected objects offer a low overhead, efficient means to coordinate access to shared data. A protected type declaration is similar to a program unit and consists of both a specification and a body. The data to be protected must be declared in the specification, as well as the operations that can be used to manipulate this data. If some operations are only allowed conditionally, entries must be provided. Ada 95 rules require that entry barriers be evaluated at the end of procedure calls and entry calls on protected objects. Entry barriers should avoid referring to global variables so that the underlying assumptions of the state of the protected object are not violated. Protected procedures and entries should be used to change the state of a protected object.

Most clients of an abstraction do not need to know how it is implemented, whether it is a regular abstraction or a shared abstraction. A protected type is inherently a limited type, and you can use protected types to implement a limited private type exported by a package. As pointed out in Guideline 5.3.3, abstractions are best implemented using private types (possibly derived from controlled types) or limited private types, providing appropriate operations that overcome the restrictiveness imposed by the use of private types.

The Rationale (1995, §9.1) describes the interrupt handling features that make the protected procedure the recommended building block:

> A protected procedure is very well suited to act as an interrupt handler for a number of reasons; they both typically have a short bounded execution time, do not arbitrarily block, have a limited context and finally they both have to integrate with the priority model. The nonblocking critical region matches the needs of an interrupt handler, as well as the needs of non-interrupt-level code to synchronize with an interrupt handler. The entry barrier construct allows an interrupt handler to signal a normal task by changing the state of a component of the protected object and thereby making a barrier true.

When using protected procedures for interrupt handling, you must ensure that the ceiling priority of the handler is at least as high as the maximum possible priority of the interrupt to be handled. With priority-ceiling locking, the delivery of an interrupt with a higher priority than the ceiling priority of the handler will result in erroneous execution (Ada Reference Manual 1995, §C.3.1).

A global variable could be changed by another task or even by a call of a protected function. These changes will not be acted upon promptly. Therefore, you should not use a global variable in an entry barrier.

Side effects in barrier expressions can cause undesirable dependencies. Therefore, you should avoid the use of barrier expressions that can cause side effects.

See also Guideline .

exceptions

If the client of the abstraction containing the protected object must use a `select` statement with an entry call, you must expose the protected object on the package interface.

6.1.2   Tasks

guideline

- Use tasks to model selected asynchronous threads of control within the problem domain.
- Consider using tasks to define concurrent algorithms.
- Consider using rendezvous when your application requires synchronous unbuffered communication.

example

The naturally concurrent objects within the problem domain can be modeled as Ada tasks.

```
-- The following example of a stock exchange simulation shows how naturally
-- concurrent objects within the problem domain can be modeled as Ada tasks.

-------------------------------------------------------------------------

-- Protected objects are used for the Display and for the Transaction_Queue
-- because they only need a mutual exclusion mechanism.

protected Display is
    entry Shift_Tape_Left;
    entry Put_Character_On_Tape (C : in Character);
end Display;

protected Transaction_Queue is
    entry Put (T : in     Transaction);
    entry Get (T :     out Transaction);
    function Is_Empty return Boolean;
end Transaction_Queue;

-------------------------------------------------------------------------
```

```
-- A task is needed for the Ticker_Tape because it has independent cyclic
-- activity.  The Specialist and the Investor are best modeled with tasks
-- since they perform different actions simultaneously, and should be
-- asynchronous threads of control.

task Ticker_Tape;

task Specialist is
   entry Buy  (Order : in Order_Type);
   entry Sell (Order : in Order_Type);
end Specialist;

task Investor;
--------------------------------------------------------------------------
task body Ticker_Tape is
   ...
begin
   loop
      Display.Shift_Tape_Left;

      if not More_To_Send (Current_Tape_String) and then
         not Transaction_Queue.Is_Empty
      then
         Transaction_Queue.Get (Current_Tape_Transaction);
         ... -- convert Transaction to string
      end if;

      if More_To_Send (Current_Tape_String) then
         Display.Put_Character_On_Tape (Next_Char);
      end if;

      delay until Time_To_Shift_Tape;
      Time_To_Shift_Tape := Time_To_Shift_Tape + Shift_Interval;
   end loop;
end Ticker_Tape;

task body Specialist is
   ...

   loop
      select
         accept Buy  (Order : in Order_Type) do
            ...
         end Buy;
         ...
      or
         accept Sell (Order : in Order_Type) do
            ...
         end Sell;
         ...
      else
         -- match orders
         ...
         Transaction_Queue.Put (New_Transaction);
         ...
      end select;
   end loop;

end Specialist;


task body Investor is
   ...
begin

   loop
      -- some algorithm that determines whether the investor
      -- buys or sells, quantity, price, etc

      ...

      if ... then
         Specialist.Buy (Order);
      end if;

      if ... then
         Specialist.Sell (Order);
      end if;
   end loop;

end Investor;
```

Multiple tasks that implement the decomposition of a large, matrix multiplication algorithm are an example of an opportunity for real concurrency in a multiprocessor target environment. In a single processor target environment, this approach may not be justified due to the overhead incurred from context switching and the sharing of system resources.

A task that updates a radar display every 30 milliseconds is an example of a cyclic activity supported by a task.

A task that detects an over-temperature condition in a nuclear reactor and performs an emergency shutdown of the systems is an example of a task to support a high-priority activity.

rationale

These guidelines reflect the intended uses of tasks. They all revolve around the fact that a task has its own thread of control separate from the main subprogram (or environment task) of a partition. The conceptual model for a task is a separate program with its own virtual processor. This provides the opportunity to model entities from the problem domain in terms more closely resembling those entities and the opportunity to handle physical devices as a separate concern from the main algorithm of the application. Tasks also allow naturally concurrent activities that can be mapped to multiple processors within a partition when available.

You should use tasks for separate threads of control. When you synchronize tasks, you should use the rendezvous mechanism only when you are trying to synchronize actual processes (e.g., specify a time-sensitive ordering relationship or tightly coupled interprocess communication). For most synchronization needs, however, you should use protected objects (see Guideline 6.1.1), which are more flexible and can minimize unnecessary bottlenecks. Additionally, passive tasks are probably better modeled through protected objects than active tasks.

Resources shared between multiple tasks, such as devices, require control and synchronization because their operations are not atomic. Drawing a circle on a display might require that many low-level operations be performed without interruption by another task. A display manager would ensure that no other task accesses the display until all these operations are complete.

6.1.3   Discriminants

guideline

- Consider using discriminants to minimize the need for an explicit initialization operation (Rationale 1995, §9.1).
- Consider using discriminants to control composite components of the protected objects, including setting the size of an entry family (Rationale 1995, §9.1).
- Consider using a discriminant to set the priority of a protected object (Rationale 1995, §9.1).
- Consider using a discriminant to identify an interrupt to a protected object (Rationale 1995, §9.1).
- Consider declaring a task type with a discriminant to indicate (Rationale 1995, §9.6):
    - Priority, storage size, and size of entry families of individual tasks of a type
    - Data associated with a task (through an access discriminant)

example

The following code fragment shows how a task type with discriminant can be used to associate data with a task (Rationale 1995, §9.6):

```
type Task_Data is
   record
      ... -- data for task to work on
   end record;

task type Worker (D : access Task_Data) is
   ...
end;

-- When you declare a task object of type Worker, you explicitly associate this task with
-- its data through the discriminant D

Data_for_Worker_X : aliased Task_Data := ...;

X : Worker (Data_for_Worker_X'Access);
```

The following example shows how to use discriminants to associate data with tasks, thus allowing the tasks to be parameterized when they are declared and eliminating the need for an initial rendezvous with the task:

```
task type Producer (Channel : Channel_Number; ID : ID_Number);

task body Producer is
begin

   loop

      ... -- generate an item

      Buffer.Put (New_Item);

   end loop;
end Producer;

...

Keyboard : Producer (Channel => Keyboard_Channel, ID => 1);
Mouse    : Producer (Channel => Mouse_Channel,    ID => 2);
```

The next example shows how an initial rendezvous can be used to associate data with tasks. This is more complicated and more error prone than the previous example. This method is no longer needed in Ada 95 due to the availability of discriminants with task types and protected types:

```
task type Producer is
    entry Initialize (Channel : in Channel_Number; ID : in ID_Number);
end Producer;

task body Producer is
    IO_Channel  : Channel_Number;
    Producer_ID : ID_Number;
begin

    accept Initialize (Channel : in Channel_Number; ID : in ID_Number) do
       IO_Channel  := Channel;
       Producer_ID := ID;
    end;

    loop

       ... -- generate an item

       Buffer.Put (New_Item);

    end loop;
end Producer;

...

Keyboard : Producer;
Mouse    : Producer;

...

begin
    ...
    Keyboard.Initialize (Channel => Keyboard_Channel, ID => 1);
    Mouse.Initialize    (Channel => Mouse_Channel,    ID => 2);
    ...
```

rationale

Using discriminants to parameterize protected objects provides a low-overhead way of specializing the protected object. You avoid having to declare and call special subprograms solely for the purpose of passing this information to the protected object.

Task discriminants provide a way for you to identify or parameterize a task without the overhead of an initial rendezvous. For example, you can use this discriminant to initialize a task or tell it who it is (from among an array of tasks) (Rationale 1995, §II.9). More importantly, you can associate the discriminant with specific data. When you use an access discriminant, you can bind the data securely to the task because the access discriminant is constant and cannot be detached from the task (Rationale 1995, §9.6). This reduces and might eliminate bottlenecks in the parallel activation of tasks (Rationale 1995, §9.6).

notes

Using an access discriminant to initialize a task has a potential danger in that the data being referenced could change after the rendezvous. This possibility and its effects should be considered and, if necessary, appropriate actions taken (e.g., copy the referenced data and not rely on the data pointed to by the discriminant after initialization).

6.1.4   Anonymous Task Types and Protected Types

guideline

- Consider using single task declarations to declare unique instances of concurrent tasks.
- Consider using single protected declarations to declare unique instances of protected objects.

example

The following example illustrates the syntactic differences between the kinds of tasks and protected objects discussed here. Buffer is static, but its type is anonymous. No type name is declared to enable you to declare further objects of the same type.

```
task        Buffer;
```

Because it is declared explicitly, the task type Buffer_Manager is not anonymous. Channel is static and has a name, and its type is not anonymous.

```
task type Buffer_Manager;
Channel : Buffer_Manager;
```

rationale

The use of anonymous tasks and protected objects of anonymous type avoids a proliferation of task and protected types that are only used once, and the practice communicates to maintainers that there are no other tasks or protected objects of that type. If the need arises later to have additional tasks or protected objects of the same type, then the work required to convert an anonymous task to a task type or an anonymous protected object to a protected type is minimal.

The consistent and logical use of task and protected types, when necessary, contributes to understandability. Identical tasks can be declared using a common task type. Identical protected objects can be declared using a common protected type. Dynamically allocated task or protected structures are necessary when you must create and destroy tasks or protected objects dynamically or when you must reference them by different names.

notes

Though changing the task or protected object from an anonymous type to a declared type is trivial, structural changes to the software architecture might not be trivial. Introduction of multiple tasks or protected objects of the declared type might require the scope of the type to change and might change the behavior of the network of synchronizing tasks and protected objects.

6.1.5   Dynamic Tasks

guideline

- Minimize dynamic creation of tasks because of the potentially high startup overhead; reuse tasks by having them wait for new work on some appropriate entry queue.

example

The approach used in the following example is not recommended. The example shows why caution is required with dynamically allocated task and protected objects. It illustrates how a dynamic task can be disassociated from its name:

```
task type Radar_Track;
type      Radar_Track_Pointer is access Radar_Track;

Current_Track : Radar_Track_Pointer;
```

```
task body Radar_Track is
begin
   loop
      -- update tracking information
      ...
      -- exit when out of range
      delay 1.0;
   end loop;

...
end Radar_Track;
----------------------------------------------------------------------

...
loop
   ...

   -- Radar_Track tasks created in previous passes through the loop
   -- cannot be accessed from Current_Track after it is updated.
   -- Unless some code deals with non-null values of Current_Track,
   -- (such as an array of existing tasks)
   -- this assignment leaves the existing Radar_Track task running with
   -- no way to signal it to abort or to instruct the system to
   -- reclaim its resources.

   Current_Track := new Radar_Track;

   ...
end loop;
```

rationale

Starting up a task has significant overhead in many implementations. If an application has a need for dynamically created tasks, the tasks should be implemented with a top-level loop so that after such a task completes its given job, it can cycle back and wait for a new job.

You can use dynamically allocated tasks and protected objects when you need to allow the number of tasks and protected objects to vary during execution. When you must ensure that tasks are activated in a particular order, you should use dynamically allocated tasks because the Ada language does not define an activation order for statically allocated task objects. In using dynamically allocated tasks and protected objects, you face the same issues as with any use of the heap.

6.1.6   Priorities

guideline

- Do not rely on pragma `Priority` unless your compiler supports the Real-Time Annex (Ada Reference Manual 1995, Annex D) and priority scheduling.
- Minimize risk of priority inversion by use of protected objects and ceiling priority.
- Do not rely upon task priorities to achieve a particular sequence of task execution.

example

For example, let the tasks have the following priorities:

```
task T1 is
   pragma Priority (High);
end T1;

task T2 is
   pragma Priority (Medium);
end T2;

task Server is
   entry Operation (...);
end Server;

----------------------------

task body T1 is
begin
   ...
   Server.Operation (...);
   ...
end T1;
```

```
task body T2 is
begin
   ...
   Server.Operation (...);
   ...
end T2;

task body Server is
begin
   ...
   accept Operation (...);
   ...
end Server;
```

At some point in its execution, T1 is blocked. Otherwise, T2 and Server might never execute. If T1 is blocked, it is possible for T2 to reach its call to Server's entry (Operation) before T1. Suppose this has happened and that T1 now makes its entry call before Server has a chance to accept T2's call.

This is the timeline of events so far:

```
T1 blocks
T2 calls Server.Operation
T1 unblocks
T1 calls Server.Operation

-- Does Server accept the call from T1 or from T2?
```

You might expect that, due to its higher priority, T1's call would be accepted by Server before that of T2. However, entry calls are queued in first-in-first-out (FIFO) order and not queued in order of priority (unless pragma Queueing_Policy is used). Therefore, the synchronization between T1 and Server is not affected by T1's priority. As a result, the call from T2 is accepted first. This is a form of *priority inversion*. (Annex D can change the default policy of FIFO queues.)

A solution might be to provide an entry for a High priority user and an entry for a Medium priority user.

```
------------------------------------------------------------------------
task Server is
   entry Operation_High_Priority;
   entry Operation_Medium_Priority;
   ...
end Server;

------------------------------------------------------------------------
task body Server is
begin

   loop
      select
         accept Operation_High_Priority do
            Operation;
         end Operation_High_Priority;
      else  -- accept any priority

         select
            accept Operation_High_Priority do
               Operation;
            end Operation_High_Priority;
         or
            accept Operation_Medium_Priority do
               Operation;
            end Operation_Medium_Priority;
         or
            terminate;
         end select;
      end select;

   end loop;

   ...
end Server;
------------------------------------------------------------------------
```

However, in this approach, T1 still waits for one execution of Operation when T2 has already gained control of the task Server. In addition, the approach increases the communication complexity (see Guideline 6.2.6).

rationale

The pragma Priority allows relative priorities to be placed on tasks to accomplish scheduling. Precision becomes a critical issue with hard-deadline scheduling. However, there are certain problems associated with using priorities that warrant caution.

Priority inversion occurs when lower priority tasks are given service while higher priority tasks remain blocked. In the first example, this occurred because entry queues are serviced in FIFO order, not by priority. There is another situation referred to as a *race condition*. A program like the one in the first example might often behave as expected as long as T1 calls Server.Operation only when T2 is not already using Server.Operation or waiting. You cannot rely on T1 always winning the race because that behavior would be due more to fate than to the programmed priorities. Race conditions change when either adding code to an unrelated task or porting this code to a new target.

You should not rely upon task priorities to achieve an exact sequence of execution or rely upon them to achieve mutual exclusion. Although the underlying dispatching model is common to all Ada 95 implementations, there might be differences in dispatching, queuing, and locking policies for tasks and protected objects. All of these factors might lead to different sequences of execution. If you need to ensure a sequence of execution, you should make use of Ada's synchronization mechanisms, i.e., protected objects or rendezvous.

notes

Work is being done to minimize these problems, including the introduction of a scheduling algorithm known as the priority ceiling protocol (Goodenough and Sha 1988). The priority ceiling protocol reduces the blocking time that causes *priority inversion* to only one critical region (defined by the entries in a task). The protocol also eliminates deadlock (unless a task recursively tries to access a critical region) by giving a ceiling priority to each task accessing a resource that is as high as the priority of any task that ever accesses that resource. This protocol is based on priority inheritance and, thus, deviates from the standard Ada tasking paradigm, which supports priority ceiling emulation instead of the priority ceiling blocking that occurs with priority inheritance.

Priorities are used to control when tasks run relative to one another. When both tasks are not blocked waiting at an entry, the highest priority task is given precedence. However, the most critical tasks in an application do not always have the highest priority. For example, support tasks or tasks with small periods might have higher priorities because they need to run frequently.

All production-quality validated Ada 95 compilers will probably support pragma Priority. However, you should use caution unless Annex D is specifically supported.

There is currently no universal consensus on how to apply the basic principles of rate monotonic scheduling (RMS) to the Ada 95 concurrency model. One basic principle of RMS is to arrange all periodic tasks so that tasks with shorter periods have higher priorities than tasks with longer periods. However, with Ada 95, it might be faster to raise the priorities of tasks whose jobs suddenly become critical than to wait for an executive task to reschedule them. In this case, priority inversion can be minimized using a protected object with pragma Locking_Policy(Ceiling_Locking) as the server instead of a task.

6.1.7   Delay Statements

guideline

- Do not depend on a particular delay being achievable (Nissen and Wallis 1984).
- Use a delay until not a delay statement to delay until a specific time has been reached.
- Avoid using a busy waiting loop instead of a delay.

example

The phase of a periodic task is the fraction of a complete cycle elapsed as measured from a specified reference point. In the following example, an inaccurate delay causes the phase of the periodic task to drift over time (i.e., the task starts later and later in the cycle):

```
Periodic:
   loop
      delay Interval;
      ...
   end loop Periodic;
```

To avoid an inaccurate delay drift, you should use the delay until statement. The following example (Rationale 1995, §9.3) shows how to satisfy a periodic requirement with an average period:

```
task body Poll_Device is
   use type Ada.Real_Time.Time;
   use type Ada.Real_Time.Time_Span;

   Poll_Time  :           Ada.Real_Time.Time := ...; -- time to start polling
   Period     : constant Ada.Real_Time.Time_Span := Ada.Real_Time.Milliseconds (10);
begin
   loop
      delay until Poll_Time;
      ... -- Poll the device
      Poll_Time := Poll_Time + Period;
   end loop;
end Poll_Device;
```

rationale

There are two forms of `delay` statement. The `delay` will cause a delay for at least a specified time interval. The `delay until` causes a delay until an absolute wake-up time. You should choose the form appropriate to your application.

The Ada language definition only guarantees that the delay time is a minimum. The meaning of a `delay` or `delay until` statement is that the task is not scheduled for execution before the interval has expired. In other words, a task becomes eligible to resume execution as soon as the amount of time has passed. However, there is no guarantee of when (or if) it is scheduled after that time because the required resources for that task might not be available at the expiration of the delay.

A busy wait can interfere with processing by other tasks. It can consume the very processor resource necessary for completion of the activity for which it is waiting. Even a loop with a delay can have the impact of busy waiting if the planned wait is significantly longer then the delay interval. If a task has nothing to do, it should be blocked at an `accept` or `select` statement, an entry call, or an appropriate delay.

The expiration time for a relative delay is rounded up to the nearest clock tick. If you use the real-time clock features provided by Annex D, however, clock ticks are guaranteed to be no greater than one millisecond (Ada Reference Manual 1995, §D.8).

notes

You need to ensure the arithmetic precision of the calculation `Poll_Time := Poll_Time + Period;` to avoid drift.

6.1.8   Extensibility and Concurrent Structures

guideline

- Carefully consider the placement of components of protected types within a tagged type inheritance hierarchy.

- Consider using generics to provide extensibility of data types requiring the restrictions provided by protected objects.

rationale

Once a component of a protected type is added to an inheritance hierarchy of an abstract data type, further extensibility of that data type is impaired. When you constrain the concurrent behavior of a type (i.e., introduce a protected type component), you lose the ability to modify that behavior in subsequent derivations. Therefore, when the need arises for a version of an abstract data type to impose the restrictions provided by protected objects, the opportunity for reuse is maximized by adding the protected objects at the leaves of the inheritance hierarchy.

The reusability of common protected operations (e.g., mutually exclusive read/write operations) can be maximized by using generic implementations of abstract data types. These generic implementations then provide templates that can be instantiated with data types specific to individual applications.

notes

You can address synchronization within an inheritance hierarchy in one of three ways:

-    You can declare the root as a limited tagged type with a component that belongs to a protected type and give the tagged type primitive operations that work by invoking the protected operations of that component.

- Given a tagged type implementing an abstract data type (perhaps resulting from several extensions), you can declare a protected type with a component belonging to the tagged type. The body of each protected operation would then invoke the corresponding operation of the abstract data type. The protected operations provide mutual exclusion.

- You can use a hybrid approach where you declare a protected type with a component of some tagged type. You then use this protected type to implement a new root tagged type (not a descendant of the original tagged type).

6.2   COMMUNICATION

The need for tasks to communicate gives rise to most of the problems that make concurrent programming so difficult. Used properly, Ada's intertask communication features can improve the reliability of concurrent programs; used thoughtlessly, they can introduce subtle errors that can be difficult to detect and correct.

6.2.1   Efficient Task Communication

guideline

- Minimize the work performed during a rendezvous.
- Minimize the work performed in the selective accept loop of a task.
- Consider using protected objects for data synchronization and communication.

example

In the following example, the statements in the accept body are performed as part of the execution of both the caller task and the task Server, which contains Operation and Operation2. The statements after the accept body are executed before Server can accept additional calls to Operation or Operation2.

```
...
loop
   select
      accept Operation do

         -- These statements are executed during rendezvous.
         -- Both caller and server are blocked during this time.
         ...
      end Operation;

      ...
      -- These statements are not executed during rendezvous.
      -- The execution of these statements increases the time required
      --    to get back to the accept and might be a candidate for another task.

   or
      accept Operation_2 do

         -- These statements are executed during rendezvous.
         -- Both caller and server are blocked during this time.
         ...
      end Operation_2;

   end select;
   -- These statements are also not executed during rendezvous,
   -- The execution of these statements increases the time required
   --    to get back to the accept and might be a candidate for another task.

end loop;
```

rationale

To minimize the time required to rendezvous, only work that needs to be performed during a rendezvous, such as saving or generating parameters, should be allowed in the accept bodies.

When work is removed from the accept body and placed later in the selective accept loop, the additional work might still suspend the caller task. If the caller task calls entry Operation again before the server task completes its additional work, the caller is delayed until the server completes the additional work. If the potential delay is unacceptable and the additional work does not need to be completed before the next service of the caller task, the additional work can form the basis of a new task that will not block the caller task.

Operations on protected objects incur less execution overhead than tasks and are more efficient for data synchronization and communication than the rendezvous. You must design protected operations to be bounded, short, and not potentially blocking.

notes

In some cases, additional functions can be added to a task. For example, a task controlling a communication device might be responsible for a periodic function to ensure that the device is operating correctly. This type of addition should be done with care, realizing that the response time of the task might be impacted (see the above rationale).

Minimizing the work performed during a rendezvous or selective accept loop of a task can increase the rate of execution only when it results in additional overlaps in processing between the caller and callee or when other tasks can be scheduled due to the shorter period of execution. Therefore, the largest increases in execution rates will be seen in multiprocessor environments. In single-processor environments, the increased execution rate will not be as significant and there might even be a small net loss. The guideline is still applicable, however, if the application could ever be ported to a multiprocessor environment.

6.2.2 Defensive Task Communication

guideline

- Provide a handler for exception `Program_Error` whenever you cannot avoid a selective `accept` statement whose alternatives can all be closed (Honeywell 1986).
- Make systematic use of handlers for `Tasking_Error`.
- Be prepared to handle exceptions during a rendezvous.
- Consider using a `when others` exception handler.

example

This block allows recovery from exceptions raised while attempting to communicate a command to another task:

```
Accelerate:
   begin
       Throttle.Increase(Step);

   exception
       when Tasking_Error     =>    ...
       when Constraint_Error  =>    ...
       when Throttle_Too_Wide =>    ...

       ...
   end Accelerate;
```

In this `select` statement, if all the guards happen to be closed, the program can continue by executing the `else` part. There is no need for a handler for `Program_Error`. Other exceptions can still be raised while evaluating the guards or attempting to communicate. You will also need to include an exception handler in the task `Throttle` so that it can continue to execute after an exception is raised during the rendezvous:

```
   ...
Guarded:
   begin
       select
          when Condition_1 =>
             accept Entry_1;

       or
          when Condition_2 =>
             accept Entry_2;

       else  -- all alternatives closed
          ...
       end select;
   exception
       when Constraint_Error =>
          ...
   end Guarded;
```

In this `select` statement, if all the guards happen to be closed, exception `Program_Error` will be raised. Other exceptions can still be raised while evaluating the guards or attempting to communicate:

```
Guarded:
   begin
      select
         when Condition_1 =>
            accept Entry_1;

      or
         when Condition_2 =>
            delay Fraction_Of_A_Second;
      end select;

      exception
         when Program_Error    =>  ...
         when Constraint_Error =>  ...
      end Guarded;
   ...
```

rationale

The exception Program_Error is raised if a selective accept statement (select statement containing accepts) is reached, all of whose alternatives are closed (i.e., the guards evaluate to False and there are no alternatives without guards), unless there is an else part. When all alternatives are closed, the task can never again progress, so there is by definition an error in its programming. You must be prepared to handle this error should it occur.

Because an else part cannot have a guard, it can never be closed off as an alternative action; thus, its presence prevents Program_Error. However, an else part, a delay alternative, and a terminate alternative are all mutually exclusive, so you will not always be able to provide an else part. In these cases, you must be prepared to handle Program_Error.

The exception Tasking_Error can be raised in the calling task whenever it attempts to communicate. There are many situations permitting this. Few of them are preventable by the calling task.

If an exception is raised during a rendezvous and not handled in the accept statement, it is propagated to both tasks and must be handled in two places (see Guideline 5.8).

The handling of the others exception can be used to avoid propagating unexpected exceptions to callers (when this is the desired effect) and to localize the logic for dealing with unexpected exceptions in the rendezvous. After handling, an unknown exception should normally be raised again because the final decision of how to deal with it might need to be made at the outermost scope of the task body.

notes

There are other ways to prevent Program_Error at a selective accept. These involve leaving at least one alternative unguarded or proving that at least one guard will evaluate True under all circumstances. The point here is that you or your successors will make mistakes in trying to do this, so you should prepare to handle the inevitable exception.

6.2.3   Attributes 'Count, 'Callable, and 'Terminated

guideline

- Do not depend on the values of the task attributes 'Callable or 'Terminated (Nissen and Wallis 1984).
- Do not depend on attributes to avoid Tasking_Error on an entry call.
- For tasks, do not depend on the value of the entry attribute 'Count.
- Using the 'Count attribute with protected entries is more reliable than using the 'Count attribute with task entries.

example

In the following examples, Dispatch'Callable is a Boolean expression, indicating whether a call can be made to the task Intercept without raising the exception Tasking_Error. Dispatch'Count indicates the number of callers currently waiting at entry Transmit. Dispatch'Terminated is a Boolean expression, indicating whether the task Dispatch is in a terminated state.

This task is badly programmed because it relies upon the values of the 'Count attributes not changing between evaluating and acting upon them:

```
task body Dispatch is
   ...

   select
      when Transmit'Count > 0 and Receive'Count = 0 =>
         accept Transmit;
         ...

   or
      accept Receive;
      ...
   end select;

   ...
end Dispatch;
```

If the following code is preempted between evaluating the condition and initiating the call, the assumption that the task is still callable might no longer be valid:

```
...
if Dispatch'Callable then
   Dispatch.Receive;
end if;
...
```

rationale

Attributes 'Callable, 'Terminated, and 'Count are all subject to race conditions. Between the time you reference an attribute and the time you take action, the value of the attribute might change. Attributes 'Callable and 'Terminated convey reliable information once they become False and True, respectively. If 'Callable is False, you can expect the callable state to remain constant. If 'Terminated is True, you can expect the task to remain terminated. Otherwise, 'Terminated and 'Callable can change between the time your code tests them and the time it responds to the result.

The Ada Reference Manual (1995, §9.9) itself warns about the asynchronous increase and decrease of the value of 'Count. A task can be removed from an entry queue due to execution of an abort statement as well as expiration of a timed entry call. The use of this attribute in guards of a selective accept statement might result in the opening of alternatives that should not be opened under a changed value of 'Count.

The value of the attribute 'Count is stable for protected units because any change to an entry queue is itself a protected action, which will not occur while any other protected action is already proceeding. Nevertheless, when you use 'Count within an entry barrier of a protected unit, you should remember that the condition of the barrier is evaluated both before and after queueing a given caller.

6.2.4   Unprotected Shared Variables

guideline

- Use calls on protected subprograms or entries to pass data between tasks rather than unprotected shared variables.

- Do not use unprotected shared variables as a task synchronization device.

- Do not reference nonlocal variables in a guard.

- If an unprotected shared variable is necessary, use the pragma Volatile or Atomic.

example

This code will either print the same line more than once, fail to print some lines, or print garbled lines (part of one line followed by part of another) nondeterministically. This is because there is no synchronization or mutual exclusion between the task that reads a command and the one that acts on it. Without knowledge about their relative scheduling, the actual results cannot be predicted:

```
task body Line_Printer_Driver is
   ...
begin
   loop
      Current_Line := Line_Buffer;
      -- send to device
   end loop;
end Line_Printer_Driver;
```

```
task body Spool_Server is
   ...
begin
   loop
      Disk_Read (Spool_File, Line_Buffer);
   end loop;
end Spool_Server;
```

The following example shows a vending machine that dispenses the amount requested into an appropriately sized container. The guards reference the global variables Num_Requested and Item_Count, leading to a potential problem in the wrong amount being dispensed into an inappropriately sized container:

```
Num_Requested : Natural;
Item_Count    : Natural := 1000;

task type Request_Manager (Personal_Limit : Natural := 1) is
   entry Make_Request (Num : Natural);
   entry Get_Container;
   entry Dispense;
end Request_Manager;

task body Request_Manager is
begin
   loop
      select
         accept Make_Request (Num : Natural) do
            Num_Requested := Num;
         end Make_Request;
      or

         when Num_Requested < Item_Count =>
            accept Get_Container;
            ...

      or
         when Num_Requested < Item_Count =>
            accept Dispense do
               if Num_Requested <= Personal_Limit then
                  Ada.Text_IO.Put_Line ("Please pick up items.");
               else
                  Ada.Text_IO.Put_Line ("Sorry! Requesting too many items.");
               end if;
            end Dispense;

      end select;
   end loop;
end Request_Manager;

R1 : Request_Manager (Personal_Limit => 10);
R2 : Request_Manager (Personal_Limit => 2);
```

The interleaving of the execution of R1 and R2 can lead to Num_Requested being changed before the entry call to Dispense is accepted. Thus, R1 might receive fewer items than requested or R2's request might be bounced because the request manager thinks that what R2 is requesting exceeds R2's personal limit. By using the local variable, you will dispense the correct amount. Furthermore, by using the pragma Volatile (Ada Reference Manual 1995, §C.6), you ensure that the Item_Count is reevaluated when the guards are evaluated. Given that the variable Item_Count is not updated in this task body, the compiler might otherwise have optimized the code and not generated code to reevaluate Item_Count every time it is read:

```
Item_Count : Natural := 1000;
pragma Volatile (Item_Count);

task body Request_Manager is
   Local_Num_Requested : Natural := 0;
begin
   loop
      select
         accept Make_Request (Num : Natural) do
            Local_Num_Requested := Num;
         end Make_Request;

      or
         when Local_Num_Requested <= Personal_Limit =>
            accept Get_Container;
            ...
```

```
         or
            when Local_Num_Requested < Item_Count =>
               accept Dispense do
                  ... -- output appropriate message if couldn't service request
               end Dispense;
               Item_Count := Item_Count - Local_Num_Requested;
         end select;
      end loop;
   end Request_Manager;
```

rationale

There are many techniques for protecting and synchronizing data access. You must program most of them yourself to use them. It is difficult to write a program that shares unprotected data correctly. If it is not done correctly, the reliability of the program suffers.

Ada provides protected objects that encapsulate and provide synchronized access to protected data that is shared between tasks. Protected objects are expected to provide better performance than the rendezvous that usually requires introduction of an additional task to manage the shared data. The use of unprotected shared variables is more error-prone than the protected objects or rendezvous because the programmer must ensure that the unprotected shared variables are independently addressable and that the actions of reading or updating the same unprotected shared variable are sequential (Ada Reference Manual 1995, §9.10; Rationale 1995, §II.9).

The first example above has a race condition requiring perfect interleaving of execution. This code can be made more reliable by introducing a flag that is set by Spool_Server and reset by Line_Printer_Driver. An if (condition flag) then delay ... else would be added to each task loop in order to ensure that the interleaving is satisfied. However, notice that this approach requires a delay and the associated rescheduling. Presumably, this rescheduling overhead is what is being avoided by not using the rendezvous.

You might need to use an object in shared memory to communicate data between (Rationale 1995, §C.5):

- Ada tasks
- An Ada program and concurrent non-Ada processes
- An Ada program and hardware devices

If your environment supports the Systems Programming Annex (Ada Reference Manual 1995, Annex C), you should indicate whether loads and stores to the shared object must be indivisible. If you specify the pragma Atomic, make sure that the object meets the underlying hardware requirements for size and alignment.

Multiple tasks sharing the predefined random number generator and certain input/output subprograms can lead to problems with unprotected updates to shared state. The Ada Reference Manual (1995, §A.5.2) points out the need for tasks to synchronize their access to the random number generators (packages Ada.Numerics.Float_Random and Ada.Numerics.Discrete_Random). See Guideline 7.7.5 for the I/O issue.

6.2.5   Selective Accepts and Entry Calls

guideline

- Use caution with conditional entry calls to task entries.
- Use caution with selective accepts with else parts.
- Do not depend upon a particular delay in timed entry calls to task entries.
- Do not depend upon a particular delay in selective accepts with delay alternatives.
- Consider using protected objects instead of the rendezvous for data-oriented synchronization.

example

The conditional entry call in the following code results in a potential race condition that might degenerate into a busy waiting loop (i.e., perform the same calculation over and over). The task Current_Position containing entry Request_New_Coordinates might never execute if the loop-containing task (shown in the following code fragment) has a higher priority than Current_Position because it does not release the processing resource:

```
task body Calculate_Flightpath is
begin
   ...
   loop

      select
         Current_Position.Request_New_Coordinates (X, Y);
         -- calculate projected location based on new coordinates
         ...

      else
         -- calculate projected location based on last locations
         ...
      end select;

   end loop;
   ...
end Calculate_Flightpath;
```

The addition of a delay, as shown, may allow Current_Position to execute until it reaches an accept for Request_New_Coordinates:

```
task body Calculate_Flightpath is
begin
   ...
   loop

      select
         Current_Position.Request_New_Coordinates(X, Y);
         -- calculate projected location based on new coordinates
         ...

      else
         -- calculate projected location based on last locations
         ...

         delay until Time_To_Execute;
         Time_To_Execute := Time_To_Execute + Period;
      end select;

   end loop;
   ...
end Calculate_Flightpath;
```

The following selective accept with else again does not degenerate into a busy wait loop only because of the addition of a delay statement:

```
task body Buffer_Messages is

   ...

begin

   ...

   loop
      delay until Time_To_Execute;

      select
         accept Get_New_Message (Message : in       String) do
            -- copy message to parameters
            ...
         end Get_New_Message;
      else  -- Don't wait for rendezvous
         -- perform built in test Functions
         ...
      end select;

      Time_To_Execute := Time_To_Execute + Period;
   end loop;

   ...

end Buffer_Messages;
```

The following timed entry call might be considered an unacceptable implementation if lost communications with the reactor for over 25 milliseconds results in a critical situation:

```
task body Monitor_Reactor is
   ...
begin
   ...
   loop

      select
         Reactor.Status(OK);

      or
         delay 0.025;
         -- lost communication for more that 25 milliseconds
         Emergency_Shutdown;
      end select;

         -- process reactor status
         ...
   end loop;
      ...
end Monitor_Reactor;
```

In the following "selective accept with delay" example, the accuracy of the coordinate calculation function is bounded by time. For example, the required accuracy cannot be obtained unless Period is within + or − 0.005 seconds. This period cannot be guaranteed because of the inaccuracy of the delay statement:

```
task body Current_Position is
begin
   ...
   loop

      select
         accept Request_New_Coordinates (X :    out Integer;
                                         Y :    out Integer) do
            -- copy coordinates to parameters
            ...
         end Request_New_Coordinates;

      or
         delay until Time_To_Execute;
      end select;

      Time_To_Execute := Time_To_Execute + Period;
      -- Read Sensors
      -- execute coordinate transformations
   end loop;
      ...
end Current_Position;
```

rationale

Use of these constructs always poses a risk of race conditions. Using them in loops, particularly with poorly chosen task priorities, can have the effect of busy waiting.

These constructs are very much implementation dependent. For conditional entry calls and selective accepts with else parts, the Ada Reference Manual (1995, §9.7) does not define "immediately." For timed entry calls and selective accepts with delay alternatives, implementors might have ideas of time that differ from each other and from your own. Like the delay statement, the delay alternative on the select construct might wait longer than the time required (see Guideline 6.1.7).

Protected objects offer an efficient means for providing data-oriented synchronization. Operations on protected objects incur less execution overhead than tasks and are more efficient for data synchronization and communication than the rendezvous. See Guideline 6.1.1 for an example of this use of protected objects.

6.2.6   Communication Complexity

guideline

- Minimize the number of accept and select statements per task.
- Minimize the number of accept statements per entry.

example

Use:

```
accept A;
if Mode_1 then
    -- do one thing
else   -- Mode_2
    -- do something different
end if;
```

rather than:

```
if Mode_1 then
    accept A;
    -- do one thing

else   -- Mode_2
    accept A;
    -- do something different
end if;
```

rationale

This guideline reduces conceptual complexity. Only entries necessary to understand externally observable task behavior should be introduced. If there are several different accept and select statements that do not modify task behavior in a way important to the user of the task, there is unnecessary complexity introduced by the proliferation of select/accept statements. Externally observable behavior important to the task user includes task timing behavior, task rendezvous initiated by the entry calls, prioritization of entries, or data updates (where data is shared between tasks).

notes

Sanden (1994) argues that you need to trade off the complexity of the guards associated with the accept statements against the number of select/accept statements. Sanden (1994) shows an example of a queue controller for bank tellers where there are two modes, open and closed. You can implement this scenario with one loop and two select statements, one for the open mode and the other for the closed mode. Although you are using more select/accept statements, Sanden (1994) argues that the resulting program is easier to understand and verify.

6.3   TERMINATION

The ability of tasks to interact with each other using Ada's intertask communication features makes it especially important to manage planned or unplanned (e.g., in response to a catastrophic exception condition) termination in a disciplined way. To do otherwise can lead to a proliferation of undesired and unpredictable side effects as a result of the termination of a single task.

The guidelines on termination focus on the termination of tasks. Wherever possible, you should use protected objects (see Guideline 6.1.1), thus avoiding the termination problems associated with tasks.

6.3.1   Avoiding Undesired Termination

guideline

- Consider using an exception handler for a rendezvous within the main loop inside each task.

example

In the following example, an exception raised using the primary sensor is used to change Mode to Degraded still allowing execution of the system:

```
...
loop

    Recognize_Degraded_Mode:
        begin

            case Mode is
                when Primary =>

                    select
                        Current_Position_Primary.Request_New_Coordinates (X, Y);
```

```
            or
                delay 0.25;
                -- Decide whether to switch modes;
            end select;

        when Degraded =>

            Current_Position_Backup.Request_New_Coordinates (X, Y);

      end case;

      ...
    exception
        when Tasking_Error | Program_Error =>
            Mode := Degraded;
    end Recognize_Degraded_Mode;

end loop;
...
```

rationale

Allowing a task to terminate might not support the requirements of the system. Without an exception handler for the rendezvous within the main task loop, the functions of the task might not be performed.

notes

The use of an exception handler is the only way to guarantee recovery from an entry call to an abnormal task. Use of the 'Terminated attribute to test a task's availability before making the entry call can introduce a race condition where the tested task fails after the test but before the entry call (see Guideline 6.2.3).

6.3.2   Normal Termination

guideline

- Do not create nonterminating tasks unintentionally.

- Explicitly shut down tasks that depend on library packages.

- Confirm that a task is terminated before freeing it with Ada.Unchecked_Deallocation.

- Consider using a select statement with a terminate alternative rather than an accept statement alone.

- Consider providing a terminate alternative for every selective accept that does not require an else part or a delay.

- Do not declare or create a task within a user-defined Finalize procedure after the environment task has finished waiting for other tasks.

example

This task will never terminate:

```
-------------------------------------------------------------------
task body Message_Buffer is
    ...
begin  -- Message_Buffer
    loop
        select
            when Head /= Tail => -- Circular buffer not empty
                accept Retrieve (Value :    out Element) do
                    ...
                end Retrieve;

        or
            when not ((Head = Index'First and then
                       Tail = Index'Last) or else
                      (Head /= Index'First and then
                       Tail = Index'Pred(Head))    )
                => -- Circular buffer not full
                accept Store (Value : in     Element);
        end select;
    end loop;
    ...
end Message_Buffer;
-------------------------------------------------------------------
```

rationale

The implicit environment task does not terminate until all other tasks have terminated. The environment task serves as a master for all other tasks created as part of the execution of the partition; it awaits termination of all such tasks in order to perform finalization of any remaining objects of the partition. Thus, a partition will exist until all library tasks are terminated.

A nonterminating task is a task whose body consists of a nonterminating loop with no selective accept with terminate or a task that depends on a library package. Execution of a subprogram or block containing a task cannot complete until the task terminates. Any task that calls a subprogram containing a nonterminating task will be delayed indefinitely.

A task that depends on a library package cannot be forced to terminate using a selective accept construct with alternative and should be terminated explicitly during program shutdown. One way to explicitly shut down tasks that depend on library packages is to provide them with exit entries and have the main subprogram call the exit entry just before it terminates.

The Ada Reference Manual (1995, §13.11.2) states that a bounded error results from freeing a discriminated, unterminated task object. The danger lies in deallocating the discriminants as a result of freeing the task object. The effect of unterminated tasks containing bounded errors at the end of program execution is undefined.

Execution of an accept statement or of a selective accept statement without an else part, a delay, or a terminate alternative cannot proceed if no task ever calls the entry(s) associated with that statement. This could result in deadlock. Following the guideline to provide a terminate alternative for every selective accept without an else or a delay entails programming multiple termination points in the task body. A reader can easily "know where to look" for the normal termination points in a task body. The termination points are the end of the body's sequence of statements and alternatives to select statements.

When the environment task has been terminated, either normally or abnormally, the language does not specify whether to await a task activated during finalization of the controlled objects in a partition. While the environment task is waiting for all other tasks in the partition to complete, starting up a new task during finalization results in a bounded error (Ada Reference Manual 1995, §10.2). The exception Program_Error can be raised during creation or activation of such a task.

exceptions

If you are implementing a cyclic executive, you might need a scheduling task that does not terminate. It has been said that no real-time system should be programmed to terminate. This is extreme. Systematic shutdown of many real-time systems is a desirable safety feature.

If you are considering programming a task not to terminate, be certain that it is not a dependent of a block or subprogram from which the task's caller(s) will ever expect to return. Because entire programs can be candidates for reuse (see Chapter 8), note that the task (and whatever it depends upon) will not terminate. Also be certain that for any other task that you do wish to terminate, its termination does not await this task's termination. Reread and fully understand the Ada Reference Manual (1995, §9.3) on "Task Dependence—Termination of Tasks."

6.3.3 The Abort Statement

guideline

- Avoid using the abort statement.
- Consider using the asynchronous select statement rather than the abort statement.
- Minimize uses of the asynchronous select statement.
- Avoid assigning nonatomic global objects from a task or from the abortable part of an asynchronous select statement.

example

If required in the application, provide a task entry for orderly shutdown.

The following example of asynchronous transfer of control shows a database transaction. The database operation may be cancelled (through a special input key) unless the commit transaction has begun. The code is extracted from the Rationale (1995, §9.4):

```
with Ada.Finalization;
package Txn_Pkg is

    type Txn_Status is (Incomplete, Failed, Succeeded);
    type Transaction is new Ada.Finalization.Limited_Controlled with private;

    procedure Finalize (Txn : in out transaction);
    procedure Set_Status (Txn    : in out Transaction;
                          Status : in     Txn_Status);

private
    type Transaction is new Ada.Finalization.Limited_Controlled with
        record
            Status : Txn_Status := Incomplete;
            pragma Atomic (Status);
            . . . -- More components
        end record;
end Txn_Pkg;

---------------------------------------------------------------------------

package body Txn_Pkg is

    procedure Finalize (Txn : in out Transaction) is
    begin
        -- Finalization runs with abort and ATC deferred
        if Txn.Status = Succeeded then
            Commit (Txn);
        else
            Rollback (Txn);
        end if;
    end Finalize;

    . . . -- body of procedure Set_Status

end Txn_Pkg;

---------------------------------------------------------------------------

-- sample code block showing how Txn_Pkg could be used:

declare
    Database_Txn : Transaction;
    -- declare a transaction, will commit or abort during finalization

begin
    select  -- wait for a cancel key from the input device
        Input_Device.Wait_For_Cancel;
        -- the Status remains Incomplete, so that the transaction will not commit

    then abort  -- do the transaction
        begin
            Read (Database_Txn, . . .);
            Write (Database_Txn, . . .);
            . . .
            Set_Status (Database_Txn, Succeeded);
            -- set status to ensure the transaction is committed
        exception
            when others =>
                Ada.Text_IO.Put_Line ("Operation failed with unhandled exception:");
                Set_Status (Database_Txn, Failed);
        end;
    end select;

    -- Finalize on Database_Txn will be called here and, based on the recorded
    -- status, will either commit or abort the transaction.
end;
```

rationale

When an abort statement is executed, there is no way to know what the targeted task was doing beforehand. Data for which the target task is responsible might be left in an inconsistent state. The overall effect on the system of aborting a task in such an uncontrolled way requires careful analysis. The system design must ensure that all tasks depending on the aborted task can detect the termination and respond appropriately.

Tasks are not aborted until they reach an abort completion point such as beginning or end of elaboration, a delay statement, an accept statement, an entry call, a select statement, task allocation, or the execution of an exception handler. Consequently, the abort statement might not release processor resources as soon as you might expect. It also might not stop a runaway task because the task might be executing an infinite loop containing no abort completion points. There is no guarantee that a task will not abort until an abort completion point in multiprocessor systems, but the task will almost always stop running right away.

An asynchronous `select` statement allows an external event to cause a task to begin execution at a new point, without having to abort and restart the task (Rationale 1995, §9.3). Because the triggering statement and the abortable statement execute in parallel until one of them completes and forces the other to be abandoned, you need only one thread of control. The asynchronous `select` statement improves maintainability because the abortable statements are clearly delimited and the transfer cannot be mistakenly redirected.

In task bodies and in the abortable part of an asynchronous `select`, you should avoid assigning to nonatomic global objects, primarily because of the risk of an abort occurring before the nonatomic assignment completes. If you have one or more `abort` statements in your application and the assignment is disrupted, the target object can become abnormal, and subsequent uses of the object lead to erroneous execution (Ada Reference Manual 1995, §9.8). In the case of scalar objects, you can use the attribute `'Valid`, but there is no equivalent attribute for nonscalar objects. (See Guideline 5.9.1 for a discussion of the `'Valid` attribute.) You also can still safely assign to local objects and call operations of global protected objects.

6.3.4   Abnormal Termination

guideline

- Place an exception handler for `others` at the end of a task body.
- Consider having each exception handler at the end of a task body report the task's demise.
- Do not rely on the task status to determine whether a rendezvous can be made with the task.

example

This is one of many tasks updating the positions of blips on a radar screen. When started, it is given part of the name by which its parent knows it. Should it terminate due to an exception, it signals the fact in one of its parent's data structures:

```
task type Track (My_Index : Track_Index) is
   ...
end Track;
-----------------------------------------------------------------------
task body Track is

     Neutral : Boolean := True;

begin  -- Track

   select
      accept ...
      ...

   or
      terminate;
   end select;

   ...
exception
   when others =>
      if not Neutral then
         Station(My_Index).Status := Dead;
      end if;

end Track;
-----------------------------------------------------------------------
```

rationale

A task will terminate if an exception is raised within it for which it has no handler. In such a case, the exception is not propagated outside of the task (unless it occurs during a rendezvous). The task simply dies with no notification to other tasks in the program. Therefore, providing exception handlers within the task, and especially a handler for `others`, ensures that a task can regain control after an exception occurs. If the task cannot proceed normally after handling an exception, this affords it the opportunity to shut itself down cleanly and to notify tasks responsible for error recovery necessitated by the abnormal termination of the task.

You should not use the task status to determine whether a rendezvous can be made with the task. If Task A depends on Task B and Task A checks the status flag before it rendezvouses with Task B, there is a potential that Task B fails between the status test and the rendezvous. In this case, Task A must provide an exception handler to handle the `Tasking_Error` exception raised by the call to an entry of an abnormal task (see Guideline 6.3.1).

6.3.5   Circular Task Calls

guideline

- Do not call a task entry that directly or indirectly results in a call to an entry of the original calling task.

rationale

A software failure known as *task deadlock* will occur if a task calls one of its own entries directly or indirectly via a circular chain of calls.

6.3.6   Setting Exit Status

guideline

- Avoid race conditions in setting an exit status code from the main program when using the procedure `Ada.Command_Line.Set_Exit_Status`.

- In a program with multiple tasks, encapsulate, serialize, and check calls to the procedure `Ada.Command_Line.Set_Exit_Status`.

rationale

In accordance with the rules of Ada, tasks in library-level packages may terminate after the main program task. If the program permits multiple tasks to use `Set_Exit_Status`, then there can be no guarantee that any particular status value is the one actually returned.

6.4   SUMMARY

concurrency options

- Consider using protected objects to provide mutually exclusive access to data.
- Consider using protected objects to control or synchronize access to data shared by multiple tasks.
- Consider using protected objects to implement synchronization, such as a passive resource monitor.
- Consider encapsulating protected objects in the private part or body of a package.
- Consider using a protected procedure to implement an interrupt handler.
- Do not attach a protected procedure handler to a hardware interrupt if that interrupt has a maximum priority greater than the ceiling priority assigned to the handler.
- Avoid the use of global variables in entry barriers.
- Avoid the use of barrier expressions with side effects.
- Use tasks to model selected asynchronous threads of control within the problem domain.
- Consider using tasks to define concurrent algorithms.
- Consider using rendezvous when your application requires synchronous unbuffered communication.
- Consider using discriminants to minimize the need for an explicit initialization operation (Rationale 1995, §9.1).
- Consider using discriminants to control composite components of the protected objects, including setting the size of an entry family (Rationale 1995, §9.1).
- Consider using a discriminant to set the priority of a protected object (Rationale 1995, §9.1).
- Consider using a discriminant to identify an interrupt to a protected object (Rationale 1995, §9.1).
- Consider declaring a task type with a discriminant to indicate (Rationale 1995, §9.6):
    - Priority, storage size, and size of entry families of individual tasks of a type
    - Data associated with a task (through an access discriminant)
- Consider using single task declarations to declare unique instances of concurrent tasks.
- Consider using single protected declarations to declare unique instances of protected objects.

- Minimize dynamic creation of tasks because of the potentially high startup overhead; reuse tasks by having them wait for new work on some appropriate entry queue.
- Do not rely on pragma `Priority` unless your compiler supports the Real-Time Annex (Ada Reference Manual 1995, Annex D) and priority scheduling.
- Minimize risk of priority inversion by use of protected objects and ceiling priority.
- Do not rely upon task priorities to achieve a particular sequence of task execution.
- Do not depend on a particular delay being achievable (Nissen and Wallis 1984).
- Use a `delay until` not a `delay` statement to delay until a specific time has been reached.
- Avoid using a busy waiting loop instead of a delay.
- Carefully consider the placement of components of protected types within a tagged type inheritance hierarchy.
- Consider using generics to provide extensibility of data types requiring the restrictions provided by protected objects.

communication

- Minimize the work performed during a rendezvous.
- Minimize the work performed in the selective `accept` loop of a task.
- Consider using protected objects for data synchronization and communication.
- Provide a handler for exception `Program_Error` whenever you cannot avoid a selective `accept` statement whose alternatives can all be closed (Honeywell 1986).
- Make systematic use of handlers for `Tasking_Error`.
- Be prepared to handle exceptions during a rendezvous.
- Consider using a `when others` exception handler.
- Do not depend on the values of the task attributes `'Callable` or `'Terminated` (Nissen and Wallis 1984).
- Do not depend on attributes to avoid `Tasking_Error` on an entry call.
- For tasks, do not depend on the value of the entry attribute `'Count`.
- Using the `'Count` attribute with protected entries is more reliable than using the `'Count` attribute with task entries.
- Use calls on protected subprograms or entries to pass data between tasks rather than unprotected shared variables.
- Do not use unprotected shared variables as a task synchronization device.
- Do not reference nonlocal variables in a guard.
- If an unprotected shared variable is necessary, use the pragma `Volatile` or `Atomic`.
- Use caution with conditional entry calls to task entries.
- Use caution with selective `accepts` with `else` parts.
- Do not depend upon a particular delay in timed entry calls to task entries.
- Do not depend upon a particular delay in selective `accepts` with `delay` alternatives.
- Consider using protected objects instead of the rendezvous for data-oriented synchronization.
- Minimize the number of `accept` and `select` statements per task.
- Minimize the number of `accept` statements per entry.

termination

- Consider using an exception handler for a rendezvous within the main loop inside each task.
- Do not create nonterminating tasks unintentionally.
- Explicitly shut down tasks that depend on library packages.
- Confirm that a task is terminated before freeing it with `Ada.Unchecked_Deallocation`.
- Consider using a `select` statement with a `terminate` alternative rather than an `accept` statement alone.

- Consider providing a `terminate` alternative for every selective `accept` that does not require an `else` part or a delay.

- Do not declare or create a task within a user-defined `Finalize` procedure after the environment task has finished waiting for other tasks.

- Avoid using the `abort` statement.

- Consider using the asynchronous `select` statement rather than the `abort` statement.

- Minimize uses of the asynchronous `select` statement.

- Avoid assigning nonatomic global objects from a task or from the abortable part of an asynchronous `select` statement.

- Place an exception handler for `others` at the end of a task body.

- Consider having each exception handler at the end of a task body report the task's demise.

- Do not rely on the task status to determine whether a rendezvous can be made with the task.

- Do not call a task entry that directly or indirectly results in a call to an entry of the original calling task.

- Avoid race conditions in setting an exit status code from the main program when using the procedure `Ada.Command_Line.Set_Exit_Status`.

- In a program with multiple tasks, encapsulate, serialize, and check calls to the procedure `Ada.Command_Line.Set_Exit_Status`.

CHAPTER 7
Portability

Discussions concerning portability usually concentrate on the differences in computer systems, but the development and run-time environment may also change:

> **portability** (software). The ease with which software can be transferred from one computer system or environment to another (IEEE Dictionary 1984).

Most portability problems are not pure language issues. Portability involves hardware (byte order, device I/O) and software (utility libraries, operating systems, run-time libraries). This chapter will not address these challenging design issues.

This chapter does identify the more common portability problems that are specific to Ada when moving from one platform or compiler to another. It also suggests ways that nonportable code can be isolated. By using the implementation hiding features of Ada, the cost of porting can be significantly reduced.

In fact, many language portability issues are solved by the strict definition of the Ada language itself. In most programming languages, different dialects are prevalent as vendors extend or dilute a language for various reasons: conformance to a programming environment or features for a particular application domain. The Ada Compiler Validation Capability (ACVC) was developed by the U.S. Department of Defense at the Ada Validation Facility, ASD/SIDL, Wright-Patterson Air Force Base, to ensure that implementors strictly adhered to the Ada standard.

As part of the strict definition of Ada, certain constructs are defined to be erroneous, and the effect of executing an erroneous construct is unpredictable. Therefore, erroneous constructs are obviously not portable. Erroneous constructs and bounded errors are discussed in Guideline 5.9.1 through 5.9.10 and are not repeated in this chapter.

Most programmers new to the language expect Ada to eliminate all portability problems; it definitely does not. Certain areas of Ada are not yet covered by validation. The definition of Ada leaves certain details to the implementor. The compiler implementor's choices, with respect to these details, affect portability.

The revisions to the Ada language approved in the 1995 standard generate a new area of portability concerns. Some programs are intended to have a long life and may start in Ada 83 (Ada Reference Manual 1983) but transition to Ada 95 (Ada Reference Manual 1995). Although this style guide focuses on the current Ada standard and does not address transition issues, there are portability issues relating to using certain features of the language. These issues revolve around the language features designated as obsolescent in Annex J of the Ada Reference Manual (1995).

The constructs of the language have been developed to satisfy a series of needs. These constructs can legitimately be used even though they may impact portability. There are some general principles to enhancing portability that are exemplified by many of the guidelines in this chapter. They are:

- Recognize those Ada constructs that may adversely affect portability on the relevant implementations or platforms.

- Rely on those Ada constructs that depend on characteristics shared by all relevant implementations. Avoid the use of those constructs whose implementation characteristics vary on the relevant platforms.

- Localize and encapsulate nonportable features of a program if their use is essential.

- Highlight the use of constructs that may cause portability problems.

These guidelines cannot be applied thoughtlessly. Many of them involve a detailed understanding of the Ada model and its implementation. In many cases, you will have to make carefully considered tradeoffs between efficiency and portability. Reading this chapter should improve your insight into the tradeoffs involved.

The material in this chapter was largely acquired from three sources: the Ada Run-Time Environments Working Group (ARTEWG) *Catalogue of Ada Runtime Implementation Dependencies* (ARTEWG 1986); the Nissen and Wallis book on *Portability and Style in Ada* (Nissen and Wallis 1984); and a paper written for the U.S. Air Force by SofTech on *Ada Portability Guidelines* (Pappas 1985). The last of these sources (Pappas 1985) encompasses the other two and provides an in-depth explanation of the issues, numerous examples, and techniques for minimizing portability problems. Conti (1987) is a valuable reference for understanding the latitude allowed for implementors of Ada and the criteria often used to make decisions.

This chapter's purpose is to provide a summary of portability issues in the guideline format of this book. The chapter does not include all issues identified in the references but only the most significant. For an in-depth presentation, see Pappas (1985). A few additional guidelines are presented here and others are elaborated upon where applicable. For further reading on Ada I/O portability issues, see Matthews (1987), Griest (1989), and CECOM (1989).

Some of the guidelines in this chapter cross reference and place stricter constraints on other guidelines in this book. These constraints apply when portability is being emphasized.

Guidelines in this chapter are frequently worded "consider . . ." because hard and fast rules cannot apply in all situations. The specific choice you make in a given situation involves design tradeoffs. The rationale for these guidelines is intended to give you insight into some of these tradeoffs.

7.1   FUNDAMENTALS

This section introduces some generally applicable principles of writing portable Ada programs. It includes guidelines about the assumptions you should make with respect to a number of Ada features and their implementations and guidelines about the use of other Ada features to ensure maximum portability.

7.1.1   Obsolescent Features

guideline

- In programs or components intended to have a long life, avoid using the features of Ada declared as "obsolescent" by Annex J of the Ada Reference Manual (1995), unless the use of the feature is needed for backward compatibility with Ada 83 (Ada Reference Manual 1983).
- Document the use of any obsolescent features.
- Avoid using the following features:
  - The short renamings of the packages in the predefined environment (e.g., `Text_IO` as opposed to `Ada.Text_IO`)
  - The character replacements of ! for |, : for #, and % for quotation marks
  - Reduced accuracy subtypes of floating-point types
  - The `'Constrained` attribute as applied to private types
  - The predefined package `ASCII`
  - The exception `Numeric_Error`
  - Various representation specifications, including `at` clauses, `mod` clauses, interrupt entries, and the `Storage_Size` attribute

rationale

Ten years of reflection on the use of Ada 83 led to the conclusion that some features of the original language are not as useful as originally intended. These features have been replaced with others in the Ada 95 revision. It would have been desirable to remove the obsolescent features completely, but that would have prevented the upward compatible transition of programs from Ada 83 to Ada 95. Thus, the obsolescent features remain in the language and are explicitly labeled as such in Annex J of the Ada Reference Manual (1995). The features listed in Annex J are candidates for removal from the language during its next revision.

If a program's lifetime may extend beyond the next language revision, it should avoid the obsolescent language features unless backward compatibility with Ada 83 forces their use.

exceptions

When you instantiate Ada.Text_IO.Float_IO, the values of the Default_Fore and Default_Aft fields are set from the values of the 'Fore and 'Aft attributes of the actual floating-point type used in the instantiation. If you declare a reduced accuracy floating-point type that you then use to instantiate Ada.Text_IO.Float_IO, the output field widths are determined from the reduced accuracy type, although the implementation accuracy is unchanged (Rationale 1995, §3.3).

7.1.2   Global Assumptions

guideline

- Make informed assumptions about the support provided for the following on potential target platforms:
    - Number of bits available for type Integer (range constraints)
    - Number of decimal digits of precision available for floating-point types
    - Number of bits available for fixed-point types (delta and range constraints)
    - Number of characters per line of source text
    - Number of bits for Root_Integer expressions
    - Number of seconds for the range of Duration
    - Number of milliseconds for Duration'Small
    - Minimum and maximum scale for decimal types
- Avoid assumptions about the values and the number of values included in the type Character.

instantiation

These are minimum values (or minimum precision in the case of Duration'Small) that a project or application might assume that an implementation provides. There is no guarantee that a given implementation provides more than the minimum, so these would be treated by the project or application as maximum values also.

- 16 bits available for type Integer (-2**15 .. 2**15 - 1)
- 6 decimal digits of precision available for floating-point types
- 24 bits available for fixed-point types
- 200 characters per line of source text
- 16 bits for expressions
- -86_400 .. 86_400 seconds (1 day) for the range of Duration (as specified in Ada Reference Manual [1995, §9.6])
- 20 milliseconds for Duration'Small (as specified in Ada Reference Manual [1995, §9.6])

rationale

Some assumptions must be made with respect to certain implementation-specific values. The exact values assumed should cover the majority of the target equipment of interest. Choosing the lowest common denominator for values improves portability.

Implementations may supply an alternate character set specific to a locale or environment. For instance, the implementation on an IBM-compatible PC may support that machine's native character set rather than Latin 1. As a result, some character values may or may not be supported, for example, the smiley face.

notes

Of the microcomputers currently available for incorporation within embedded systems, 16-bit and 32-bit processors are prevalent. Using current representation schemes, 6 decimal digits of floating point accuracy imply a representation mantissa at least 21 bits wide, leaving 11 bits for exponent and sign within a 32-bit representation. This correlates with the data widths of floating point hardware currently available for the embedded systems market. A 32-bit minimum on fixed-point numbers correlates with the accuracy and storage requirements of floating point numbers. The 16-bit example for Root_Integer expressions matches that for Integer storage. (The 32-bit integers can be assumed if the application will only be considered for 32-bit processors with a corresponding 32-bit operating system and supporting compiler.)

The values for the range and accuracy of values of the predefined type Duration are the limits expressed in the Ada Reference Manual (1995, §9.6). You should not expect an implementation to provide a wider range or a finer granularity.

A standard-mode Ada character set of Latin 1 can be assumed in most cases for the contents and internal behavior of type Character and packages Character.Latin_1, Character.Handling, and Strings.Maps. However, this does not mean that the target hardware platform is capable of displaying the entire character set. You should not use a nonstandard Ada character set unless intentionally producing a nonportable user interface with a specific purpose.

7.1.3   Comments

guideline

- Use highlighting comments for each package, subprogram, and task where any nonportable features are present.
- For each nonportable feature employed, describe the expectations for that feature.

example

```
------------------------------------------------------------------------
package Memory_Mapped_IO is

    -- WARNING - This package is implementation specific.
    -- It uses absolute memory addresses to interface with the I/O
    -- system. It assumes a particular printer's line length.
    -- Change memory mapping and printer details when porting.

    Printer_Line_Length : constant := 132;

    type Data is array (1 .. Printer_Line_Length) of Character;

    procedure Write_Line (Line : in    Data);

end Memory_Mapped_IO;
------------------------------------------------------------------------
with System;
with System.Storage_Elements;
package body Memory_Mapped_IO is

    -- WARNING: Implementation specific memory address

    Buffer_Address : constant System.Address
        := System.Storage_Elements.To_Address(16#200#);


    ------------------------------------------------------------------------
    procedure Write_Line (Line : in    Data) is

        Buffer : Data;
        for Buffer'Address use Buffer_Address;

    begin   -- Write_Line
        -- perform output operation through specific memory locations.
        ...
    end Write_Line;
    ------------------------------------------------------------------------

end Memory_Mapped_IO;
------------------------------------------------------------------------
```

rationale

Explicitly commenting each breach of portability will raise its visibility and aid in the porting process. A description of the nonportable feature's expectations covers the common case where vendor documentation of the original implementation is not available to the person performing the porting process.

7.1.4   Main Subprogram

guideline

- Consider using only a parameterless procedure as the main subprogram.

- Consider using Ada.Command_Line for accessing values from the environment, but recognize that this package's behavior and even its specification are nonportable (see Guideline 7.1.6).

- Encapsulate and document all uses of package Ada.Command_Line.

example

The following example encapsulates the arguments for a hypothetical "execution mode" argument passed from the environment. It encapsulates both the expected position and the expected values of the argument, as well as provides a default in cases where the environment was unable to provide the information:

```
package Environment is

    type Execution_Mode is (Unspecified, Interactive, Batch);

    function Execution_Argument return Execution_Mode;

    ...

end Environment;
---------------------------------------------------------------------
with Ada.Command_Line;       use Ada.Command_Line;
with Ada.Strings.Unbounded;  use Ada.Strings.Unbounded;

package body Environment is

    function Execution_Argument return Execution_Mode is

        Execution_Argument_Number : constant := 1;

        Interactive_Mode_String : constant String := "-i";
        Batch_Mode_String       : constant String := "-b";

    begin
        if Argument_Count < Execution_Argument_Number then
            return Unspecified;
        elsif To_Unbounded_String (Argument (Execution_Argument_Number)) =
                    Interactive_Mode_String then
            return Interactive;
        elsif To_Unbounded_String (Argument (Execution_Argument_Number)) =
                    Batch_Mode_String then
            return Batch;
        else
            return Unspecified;
        end if;
    end Execution_Argument;

end Environment;
```

rationale

The predefined language environment declares the package Ada.Command_Line, providing a standardized way for a program to obtain the values of a command line. Because all Ada compilers must implement the packages in the predefined language environment, you can create a program that is more portable, maintainable, and readable by using this package. You should, however, be aware that even though the language defines the objects and type profiles of this package, it does not force a relationship between the function results and any other entity or operation, and thus, allows the possibility of a nonportable behavior and specification.

The value returned by the function Ada.Command_Line.Argument_Count is implementation-dependent. Different operating systems follow different conventions regarding the parsing and meaning of command line parameters. To enhance your program's portability, assume the simplest case: that the external execution environment does not support passing arguments to a program.

Some operating systems are capable of acquiring and interpreting returned integer values near 0 from a function, but many others cannot. Further, many real-time, embedded systems will not be designed to terminate, so a function or a procedure having parameters with modes out or in out will be inappropriate to such applications.

This leaves procedures with in parameters. Although some operating systems can pass parameters into a program as it starts, others are not. Also, an implementation may not be able to perform type checking on such parameters even if the surrounding environment is capable of providing them.

notes

Real-time, embedded applications may not have an "operator" initiating the program to supply the parameters, in which case it would be more appropriate for the program to have been compiled with a package containing the appropriate constant values or for the program to read the necessary values from switch settings or a downloaded auxiliary file. In any case, the variation in surrounding initiating environments is far too great to depend upon the kind of last-minute (program) parameterization implied by (subprogram) parameters to the main subprogram.

POSIX 5 provides a standard operating system command line interface that might be a more appropriate alternative to the Ada command line facility depending on the implementation family of an application.

7.1.5   Encapsulating Implementation Dependencies

guideline

- Create packages specifically designed to isolate hardware and implementation dependencies and designed so that their specification will not change when porting.
- Clearly indicate the objectives if machine or solution efficiency is the reason for hardware or implementation-dependent code.
- For the packages that hide implementation dependencies, maintain different package bodies for different target environments.
- Isolate interrupt receiving tasks into implementation-dependent packages.
- Refer to Annex M of the Ada Reference Manual (1995) for a list of implementation-dependent features.

example

See Guideline 7.1.3.

rationale

Encapsulating hardware and implementation dependencies in a package allows the remainder of the code to ignore them and, thus, to be fully portable. It also localizes the dependencies, making it clear exactly which parts of the code may need to change when porting the program.

Some implementation-dependent features may be used to achieve particular performance or efficiency objectives. Commenting these objectives ensures that the programmer can find an appropriate way to achieve them when porting to a different implementation or explicitly recognize that they cannot be achieved.

Interrupt entries are implementation-dependent features that may not be supported (e.g., VAX Ada uses pragmas to assign system traps to "normal" rendezvous). However, interrupt entries cannot be avoided in most embedded, real-time systems, and it is reasonable to assume that they are supported by an Ada implementation. The value for an interrupt is implementation-defined. Isolate it.

notes

You can use Ada to write machine-dependent programs that take advantage of an implementation in a manner consistent with the Ada model but that make particular choices where Ada allows implementation freedom. These machine dependencies should be treated in the same way as any other implementation-dependent features of the code.

7.1.6   Implementation-Added Features

guideline

- Avoid the use of vendor-supplied packages.
- Avoid the use of features added to the predefined packages that are not specified in the Ada language definition or Specialized Needs Annexes.

rationale

Vendor-added features are not likely to be provided by other implementations. Even if a majority of vendors eventually provide similar additional features, they are unlikely to have identical formulations. Indeed, different vendors may use the same formulation for (semantically) entirely different features. See Guideline 7.5.2 for further information on vendor-supplied exceptions.

Ada has introduced a number of new pragmas and attributes that were not present in Ada 83 (Ada Reference Manual 1983). These new pragmas and attributes may clash with implementation-defined pragmas and attributes.

exceptions

There are many kinds of applications that require the use of these features. Examples include multilingual systems that standardize on a vendor's file system, applications that are closely integrated with vendor products (i.e., user interfaces), and embedded systems for performance reasons. Isolate the use of these features into packages.

If a vendor-supplied package is provided in compilable source code form, use of the package does not make a program nonportable provided that the package does not contain any nonportable code and can be lawfully included in your program.

7.1.7 Specialized Needs Annexes

guideline

- Use features defined in the Specialized Needs Annexes rather than vendor-defined features.

- Document clearly the use of any features from the Specialized Needs Annexes (systems programming, real-time systems, distributed systems, information systems, numerics, and safety and security).

rationale

The Specialized Needs Annexes define standards for specific application areas without extending the syntax of the language. You can port a program with specific domain needs (e.g., distributed systems, information systems) across vendor implementations more easily if they support the features standardized in an annex rather than rely on specific vendor extensions. The purpose of the annexes is to provide a consistent and uniform way to address issues faced in several application areas where Ada is expected to be used. Because different compilers will support different sets of annexes if any, you may have portability problems if you rely on the features defined in any given annex.

The Specialized Needs Annexes provide special capabilities that go beyond the core language definition. Because compilers are not required to support the special-purpose annexes, you should localize your use of these features where possible. By documenting their usage, you are leaving a record of potential porting difficulties for future programmers.

7.1.8 Dependence on Parameter Passing Mechanism

guideline

- Do not write code whose correct execution depends on the particular parameter passing mechanism used by an implementation (Ada Reference Manual 1995, §6.2; Cohen 1986).

- If a subprogram has more than one formal parameter of a given subtype, at least one of which is [in] out, make sure that the subprogram can properly handle the case when both formal parameters denote the same actual object.

example

The output of this program depends on the particular parameter passing mechanism that was used:

```
------------------------------------------------------------------------
with Ada.Integer_Text_IO;

procedure Outer is

   type Coordinates is
      record
         X : Integer := 0;
         Y : Integer := 0;
      end record;
```

```
Outer_Point : Coordinates;

--------------------------------------------------------------------
procedure Inner (Inner_Point : in out Coordinates) is
begin
    Inner_Point.X := 5;

    -- The following line causes the output of the program to
    -- depend on the parameter passing mechanism.
    Ada.Integer_Text_IO.Put(Outer_Point.X);
end Inner;
--------------------------------------------------------------------

begin   -- Outer
    Ada.Integer_Text_IO.Put(Outer_Point.X);
    Inner(Outer_Point);
    Ada.Integer_Text_IO.Put(Outer_Point.X);
end Outer;
--------------------------------------------------------------------
```

If the parameter passing mechanism is by copy, the results on the standard output file are:

```
0 0 5
```

If the parameter passing mechanism is by reference, the results are:

```
0 5 5
```

The following code fragment shows where there is a potential for bounded error when a procedure is called with actual parameters denoting the same object:

```
procedure Test_Bounded_Error (Parm_1 : in out    Integer;
                              Parm_2 : in out Integer) is

    procedure Inner (Parm : in out Integer) is
    begin
        Parm := Parm * 10;
    end Inner;

begin
    Parm_2 := 5;
    Inner (Parm_1);
end Test_Bounded_Error;
```

In executing the procedure Test_Bounded_Error, both Parm_1 and Parm_2 denote the object Actual_Parm. After executing the first statement, the object Actual_Parm has the value 5. When the procedure Inner is called, its formal parameter Parm denotes Actual_Parm. It cannot be determined whether it denotes the old value of Parm_1, in this case 1, or the new value, in this case 5.

```
Actual_Parm : Integer := 1;

. . .

Test_Bounded_Error (Actual_Parm, Actual_Parm);   -- potential bounded error
```

rationale

Certain composite types (untagged records and arrays) can be passed either by copy or by reference. If there are two or more formal parameters of the same type, one or more of which is writable, then you should document whether you assume that these formal parameters do not denote the same actual object. Similarly, if a subprogram that has a formal parameter of a given subtype also makes an up-level reference to an object of this same type, you should document whether you assume that the formal parameter denotes a different object from the object named in the up-level reference. In these situations where an object can be accessed through distinct formal parameter paths, the exception Program_Error may be raised, the new value may be read, or the old value of the object may be used (Ada Reference Manual 1995, §6.2).

See also Guideline 8.2.7.

exceptions

Frequently, when interfacing Ada to foreign code, dependence on parameter-passing mechanisms used by a particular implementation is unavoidable. In this case, isolate the calls to the foreign code in an interface package that exports operations that do not depend on the parameter-passing mechanism.

7.1.9   Arbitrary Order Dependencies

guideline

- Avoid depending on the order in which certain constructs in Ada are evaluated.

example

The output of this program depends upon the order of evaluation of subprogram parameters, but the Ada Reference Manual (1995, §6.4) specifies that these evaluations are done in an arbitrary order:

```
package Utilities is
    function Unique_ID return Integer;
end Utilities;

package body Utilities is

    ID : Integer := 0;

    function Unique_ID return Integer is
    begin
        ID := ID + 1;
        return ID;
    end Unique_ID;

end Utilities;
-------------------------------------------------------------------------------
with Ada.Text_IO;
with Utilities; use Utilities;
procedure P is
begin
    Ada.Text_IO.Put_Line (Integer'Image(Unique_ID) & Integer'Image(Unique_ID));
end P;
```

If the parameters to the "&" function are evaluated in textual order, the output is:

```
1 2
```

If the parameters are evaluated in the reverse order, the output is:

```
2 1
```

rationale

The Ada language defines certain evaluations to occur in arbitrary order (e.g., subprogram parameters). While a dependency on the order of evaluation may not adversely affect the program on a certain implementation, the code might not execute correctly when it is ported. For example, if two actual parameters of a subprogram call have side effects, the effect of the program could depend on the order of evaluation (Ada Reference Manual 1995, §1.1.4). Avoid arbitrary order dependencies, but also recognize that even an unintentional error of this kind could prohibit portability.

7.2   NUMERIC TYPES AND EXPRESSIONS

A great deal of care was taken with the design of the Ada features related to numeric computations to ensure that the language could be used in embedded systems and mathematical applications where precision was important. As far as possible, these features were made portable. However, there is an inevitable tradeoff between maximally exploiting the available precision of numeric computation on a particular machine and maximizing the portability of Ada numeric constructs. This means that these Ada features, particularly numeric types and expressions, must be used with great care if full portability of the resulting program is to be guaranteed.

7.2.1   Predefined Numeric Types

guideline

- Avoid using the predefined numeric types in package standard. Use range and digits declarations and let the implementation pick the appropriate representation.

- For programs that require greater accuracy than that provided by the global assumptions, define a package that declares a private type and operations as needed; see Pappas (1985) for a full explanation and examples.
- Consider using predefined numeric types (Integer, Natural, Positive) for:
  - Indexes into arrays where the index type is not significant, such as type String
  - "Pure" numbers, that is, numbers with no associated physical unit (e.g., exponents)
  - Values whose purpose is to control a repeat or iteration count

example

The second and third examples below are not representable as subranges of Integer on a machine with a 16-bit word. The first example below allows a compiler to choose a multiword representation, if necessary.

Use:

```
type    Second_Of_Day is            range 0 .. 86_400;
```

rather than:

```
type    Second_Of_Day is new Integer range 1 .. 86_400;
```

or:

```
subtype Second_Of_Day is       Integer range 1 .. 86_400;
```

rationale

An implementor is free to define the range of the predefined numeric types. Porting code from an implementation with greater accuracy to one of lesser accuracy is a time consuming and error-prone process. Many of the errors are not reported until run-time.

This applies to more than just numerical computation. An easy-to-overlook instance of this problem occurs if you neglect to use explicitly declared types for integer discrete ranges (array sizes, loop ranges, etc.) (see Guidelines 5.5.1 and 5.5.2). If you do not provide an explicit type when specifying index constraints and other discrete ranges, a predefined integer type is assumed.

The predefined numeric types are useful when you use them wisely. You should not use them to avoid declaring numeric types—then you lose the benefits of strong typing. When your application deals with different kinds of quantities and units, you should definitely separate them through the use of distinct numeric types. However, if you are simply counting the number of iterations in an iterative approximation algorithm, declaring a special integer type is probably overkill. The predefined exponentiation operators ** require an integer as the type of its right operand.

You should use the predefined types Natural and Positive for manipulating certain kinds of values in the predefined language environment. The types String and Wide_String use an index of type Positive. If your code indexes into a string using an incompatible integer type, you will be forced to do type conversion, reducing its readability. If you are performing operations like slices and concatenation, the subtype of your numeric array index is probably insignificant and you are better off using a predefined subtype. On the other hand, if your array represents a table (e.g., a hash table), then your index subtype is significant, and you should declare a distinct index type.

notes

There is an alternative that this guideline permits. As Guideline 7.1.5 suggests, implementation dependencies can be encapsulated in packages intended for that purpose. This could include the definition of a 32-bit integer type. It would then be possible to derive additional types from that 32-bit type.

7.2.2   Accuracy Model

guideline

- Use an implementation that supports the Numerics Annex (Ada Reference Manual 1995, Annex G) when performance and accuracy are overriding concerns.

rationale

The Numerics Annex defines the accuracy and performance requirements for floating- and fixed-point arithmetic. The Annex provides a "strict" mode in which the compiler must support these requirements. To guarantee that your program's numerical performance is portable, you should compile and link in the strict mode. If your program relies upon the numeric properties of the strict mode, then it will only be portable to other environments that support the strict numerics mode.

The accuracy of floating-point numbers is based on what machine numbers can be represented exactly in storage. A computational result in a register can fall between two machine numbers when the register contains more bits than storage. You can step through the machine numbers using the attributes 'Pred and 'Succ. Other attributes return values of the mantissa, exponent, radix, and other characteristics of floating- and fixed-point numbers.

7.2.3   Accuracy Analysis

guideline

- Carefully analyze what accuracy and precision you really need.

rationale

Floating-point calculations are done with the equivalent of the implementation's predefined floating-point types. The effect of extra "guard" digits in internal computations can sometimes lower the number of digits that must be specified in an Ada declaration. This may not be consistent over implementations where the program is intended to be run. It may also lead to the false conclusion that the declared types are sufficient for the accuracy required.

You should choose the numeric type declarations to satisfy the lowest precision (smallest number of digits) that will provide the required accuracy. Careful analysis will be necessary to show that the declarations are adequate. When you move to a machine with less precision, you probably can use the same type declaration.

7.2.4   Accuracy Constraints

guideline

- Do not press the accuracy limits of the machine(s).

rationale

Just because two different machines use the same number of digits in the mantissa of a floating-point number does not imply they will have the same arithmetic properties. Some Ada implementations may give slightly better accuracy than required by Ada because they make efficient use of the machine. Do not write programs that depend on this.

7.2.5   Comments

guideline

- Comment the analysis and derivation of the numerical aspects of a program.

rationale

Decisions and background about why certain precisions are required in a program are important to program revision or porting. The underlying numerical analysis leading to the program should be commented.

7.2.6   Subexpression Evaluation

guideline

- Anticipate the range of values of subexpressions to avoid exceeding the underlying range of their base type. Use derived types, subtypes, factoring, and range constraints on numeric types (see Guidelines 3.4.1, 5.3.1, and 5.5.3).

example

This example is adapted from the Rationale (1995, §3.3):

```
with Ada.Text_IO;
with Ada.Integer_Text_IO;
procedure Demo_Overflow is
```

```
-- assume the predefined type Integer has a 16-bit range
X : Integer := 24_000;
Y : Integer;

begin   -- Demo_Overflow

    y := (3 * X) / 4;  -- raises Constraint_Error if the machine registers used are 16-bit

    -- mathematically correct intermediate result if 32-bit registers
    Ada.Text_IO.Put ("(");
    Ada.Integer_Text_IO.Put (X);
    Ada.Text_IO.Put (" * 3 ) / 4 = ");
    Ada.Integer_Text_IO.Put (Y);

exception
    when Constraint_Error =>
        Ada.Text_IO.Put_Line ("3 * X too big for register!");
end Demo_Overflow;
```

rationale

The Ada language does not require that an implementation perform range checks on subexpressions within an expression. Ada does require that overflow checks be performed. Thus, depending on the order of evaluation and the size of the registers, a subexpression will either overflow or produce the mathematically correct result. In the event of an overflow, you will get the exception Constraint_Error. Even if the implementation on your program's current target does not result in an overflow on a subexpression evaluation, your program might be ported to an implementation that does.

7.2.7   Relational Tests

guideline

* Consider using <= and >= to do relational tests on real valued arguments, avoiding the <, >, =, and /= operations.
* Use values of type attributes in comparisons and checking for small values.

example

The following examples test for (1) absolute "equality" in storage, (2) absolute "equality" in computation, (3) relative "equality" in storage, and (4) relative "equality" in computation:

```
abs (X - Y) <= Float_Type'Model_Small              -- (1)

abs (X - Y) <= Float_Type'Base'Model_Small         -- (2)

abs (X - Y) <= abs X * Float_Type'Model_Epsilon    -- (3)

abs (X - Y) <= abs X * Float_Type'Base'Model_Epsilon -- (4)
```

And, specifically, for "equality" to 0:

```
abs X <= Float_Type'Model_Small                    -- (1)

abs X <= Float_Type'Base'Model_Small               -- (2)

abs X <= abs X * Float_Type'Model_Epsilon          -- (3)

abs X <= abs X * Float_Type'Base'Model_Epsilon     -- (4)
```

rationale

Strict relational comparisons (<, >, =, /=) are a general problem with computations involving real numbers. Because of the way comparisons are defined in terms of model intervals, it is possible for the values of the comparisons to depend on the implementation. Within a model interval, the result of comparing two values is nondeterministic if the values are not model numbers. In general, you should test for proximity rather than equality as shown in the examples. See also Rationale (1995, §§G.4.1 and G.4.2.).

Type attributes are the primary means of symbolically accessing the implementation of the Ada numeric model. When the characteristics of the model numbers are accessed by type attributes, the source code is portable. The appropriate model numbers of any implementation will then be used by the generated code.

Although 0 is technically not a special case, it is often overlooked because it looks like the simplest and, therefore, safest case. But in reality, each time comparisons involve small values, you should evaluate the situation to determine which technique is appropriate.

notes

Regardless of language, real-valued computations have inaccuracy. That the corresponding mathematical operations have algebraic properties usually introduces some confusion. This guideline explains how Ada deals with the problem that most languages face.

7.2.8 Decimal Types and the Information Systems Annex

guideline

- In information systems, declare different numeric decimal types to correspond to different scales (Brosgol, Eachus, and Emery 1994).

- Create objects of different decimal types to reflect different units of measure (Brosgol, Eachus, and Emery 1994).

- Declare subtypes of the appropriately scaled decimal type to provide appropriate range constraints for application-specific types.

- Encapsulate each measure category in a package (Brosgol, Eachus, and Emery 1994).

- Declare as few decimal types as possible for unitless data (Brosgol, Eachus, and Emery 1994).

- For decimal calculations, determine whether the result should be truncated toward 0 or rounded.

- Avoid decimal types and arithmetic on compilers that do not support the Information Systems Annex (Ada Reference Manual 1995, Annex F) in full.

example

```
-- The salary cap today is $500,000; however this can be expanded to $99,999,999.99.
type Executive_Salary is delta 0.01 digits 10 range 0 .. 500_000.00;

-----------------------------------------------------------------------------

package Currency is

   type Dollars is delta 0.01 digits 12;

   type Marks   is delta 0.01 digits 12;

   type Yen     is delta 0.01 digits 12;

   function To_Dollars (M : Marks)  return Dollars;
   function To_Dollars (Y : Yen)    return Dollars;

   function To_Marks (D : Dollars) return Marks;
   function To_Marks (Y : Yen)     return Marks;

   function To_Yen (D : Dollars) return Yen;
   function To_Yen (M : Marks)   return Yen;

end Currency;
```

rationale

The Ada language does not provide any predefined decimal types. Therefore, you need to declare decimal types for the different scales you will need to use. Differences in scale and precision must be considered in deciding whether or not a common type will suffice (Brosgol, Eachus, and Emery 1994).

You need different types for objects measured in different units. This allows the compiler to detect mismatched values in expressions. If you declare all decimal objects to be of a single type, you forego the benefits of strong typing. For example, in an application that involves several currencies, each currency should be declared as a separate type. You should provide appropriate conversions between different currencies.

You should map data with no particular unit of measure to a small set of types or a single type to avoid the explosion of conversions between numeric types.

Separate the range requirement on a decimal type from its precision, i.e., the number of significant digits required. From the point of view of planning for change and ease of maintenance, you can use the digit's value to accommodate future growth in the values to be stored in objects of the type. For example, you may want to anticipate growth for database values and report formats. You can constrain the values of the type through a range constraint that matches current needs. It is easier to modify the range and avoid redefining databases and reports.

Ada automatically truncates toward 0. If your requirements are to round the decimal result, you must explicitly do so using the 'Round attribute.

The core language defines the basic syntax of and operations on decimal types. It does not specify, however, the minimum number of significant digits that must be supported. Nor does the core language require the compiler to support values of Small other than powers of 2, thus enabling the compiler effectively to reject a decimal declaration (Ada Reference Manual 1995, §3.5.9). The Information Systems Annex provides additional support for decimal types. It requires a minimum of 18 significant digits. It also specifies a Text_IO.Editing package that provides support analogous to the COBOL picture approach.

7.3 STORAGE CONTROL

The management of dynamic storage can vary between Ada environments. In fact, some environments do not provide any deallocation. The following Ada storage control mechanisms are implementation-dependent and should be used with care in writing portable programs.

7.3.1 Representation Clause

guideline

- Do not use a representation clause to specify number of storage units.

rationale

The meaning of the 'Storage_Size attribute is ambiguous; specifying a particular value will not improve portability. It may or may not include space allocated for parameters, data, etc. Save the use of this feature for designs that must depend on a particular vendor's implementation.

notes

During a porting activity, it can be assumed that any occurrence of storage specification indicates an implementation dependency that must be redesigned.

7.3.2 Access-to-Subprogram Values

guideline

- Do not compare access-to-subprogram values.

rationale

The Ada Reference Manual (1995, §3.10.2) explains that an "implementation may consider two access-to-subprogram values to be unequal, even though they designate the same subprogram. This might be because one points directly to the subprogram, while the other points to a special prologue that performs an Elaboration_Check and then jumps to the subprogram." The Ada Reference Manual (1995, §4.5.2) states that it is "unspecified whether two access values that designate the same subprogram but are the result of distinct evaluations of Access attribute references are equal or unequal."

See also Guideline 5.3.4.

exceptions

If you must compare an access-to-subprogram value, you should define a constant using the access to subprogram value and make all future comparisons against the constant. However, if you attempt to compare access-to-subprogram values with different levels of indirection, the values might still be unequal, even if designating the same subprogram.

7.3.3 Storage Pool Mechanisms

guideline

- Consider using explicitly defined storage pool mechanisms.

example

See the Rationale (1995, §13.4) for an example of the use of storage pools.

rationale

There are several alternatives to consider when deciding what storage management technique to use. You should choose as simple a technique as possible that still satisfies your application requirements.

You can use allocators and unchecked deallocation as is. Note that the degree to which explicitly deallocated storage is reclaimed might vary across implementations (Ada Reference Manual 1995, §13.11.2).

You use allocators as before. Instead of using unchecked deallocation, you maintain your own free lists of objects that are no longer in use and available for reuse.

You use allocators and possibly unchecked deallocation; however, you implement a storage pool and associate it with the access type(s) via a `storage_Pool` clause. You can use this technique to implement a mark/release storage management paradigm, which might be significantly faster than an allocate/deallocate paradigm. Some vendors may provide a mark/release package as part of their Ada environment.

You do not use allocators, but instead use unchecked conversion from the address and do all your own default initialization, etc. It is unlikely you would use this last option because you lose automatic default initialization.

7.4   TASKING

The definition of tasking in the Ada language leaves many characteristics of the tasking model up to the implementor. This allows a vendor to make appropriate tradeoffs for the intended application domain, but it also diminishes the portability of designs and code employing the tasking features. In some respects, this diminished portability is an inherent characteristic of concurrency approaches (see Nissen and Wallis 1984, 37).

A discussion of Ada tasking dependencies when employed in a distributed target environment is beyond the scope of this book. For example, multiprocessor task scheduling, interprocessor rendezvous, and the distributed sense of time through package `calendar` are all subject to differences between implementations. For more information, Nissen and Wallis (1984) and ARTEWG (1986) touch on these issues, and Volz et al. (1985) is one of many research articles available.

If the Real-Time Systems Annex is supported, then many concurrency aspects are fully defined and, therefore, a program can rely on these features while still being portable to other implementations that conform to the Real-Time Systems Annex. The following sections provide guidelines based on the absence of this annex.

7.4.1   Task Activation Order

guideline

- Do not depend on the order in which task objects are activated when declared in the same declarative list.

rationale

The order in which task objects are activated is left undefined in the Ada Reference Manual (1995, §9.2). See also Guideline 6.1.5.

7.4.2   Delay Statements

guideline

- Do not depend on a particular delay being achievable (Nissen and Wallis 1984).

- Never use knowledge of the execution pattern of tasks to achieve timing requirements.

rationale

The rationale for this appears in Guideline 6.1.7. In addition, the treatment of `delay` statements varies from implementation to implementation, thereby hindering portability.

Using knowledge of the execution pattern of tasks to achieve timing requirements is nonportable. Ada does not specify the underlying scheduling algorithm, and there is no guarantee that system clock ticks will be consistently precise between different systems. Thus, when you change system clocks, your delay behavior also changes.

7.4.3   Package Calendar, Type Duration, and System.Tick

guideline

- Do not assume a correlation between system.Tick and type Duration (see Guidelines 6.1.7 and 7.4.2).

rationale

Such a correlation is not required, although it may exist in some implementations.

7.4.4   Select Statement Evaluation Order

guideline

- Do not depend on the order in which guard conditions are evaluated or on the algorithm for choosing among several open select alternatives.

rationale

The language does not define the order of these conditions, so assume that they are arbitrary.

7.4.5   Task Scheduling Algorithm

guideline

- Do not assume that tasks execute uninterrupted until they reach a synchronization point.
- Use pragma Priority to distinguish general levels of importance only (see Guideline 6.1.6).

rationale

The Ada tasking model requires that tasks be synchronized only through the explicit means provided in the language (i.e., rendezvous, task dependence, pragma Atomic). The scheduling algorithm is not defined by the language and may vary from time sliced to preemptive priority. Some implementations provide several choices that a user may select for the application.

notes

The number of priorities may vary between implementations. In addition, the manner in which tasks of the same priority are handled may vary between implementations even if the implementations use the same general scheduling algorithm.

exceptions

In real-time systems, it is often necessary to tightly control the tasking algorithm to obtain the required performance. For example, avionics systems are frequently driven by cyclic events with limited asynchronous interruptions. A nonpreemptive tasking model is traditionally used to obtain the greatest performance in these applications. Cyclic executives can be programmed in Ada, as can a progression of scheduling schemes from cyclic through multiple-frame-rate to full asynchrony (MacLaren 1980), although an external clock is usually required.

7.4.6   Abort

guideline

- Avoid using the abort statement.

rationale

The rationale for this appears in Guideline 6.3.3. In addition, treatment of the abort statement varies from implementation to implementation, thereby hindering portability.

7.4.7　Unprotected Shared Variables and Pragmas Atomic and Volatile

guideline

- Do not use unprotected shared variables.
- Consider using protected types to provide data synchronization.
- Have tasks communicate through the rendezvous mechanism.
- Do not use unprotected shared variables as a task synchronization device.
- Consider using protected objects to encapsulate shared data.
- Use pragma `Atomic` or `Volatile` only when you are forced to by run-time system deficiencies.

example

See Guidelines 6.1.1 and 6.1.2.

rationale

The rationale for this appears in Guidelines 6.1.1 and 6.2.4. In addition, the treatment of unprotected shared variables varies from implementation to implementation, thereby hindering portability.

7.5　EXCEPTIONS

You should exercise care when using predefined exceptions because aspects of their treatment may vary between implementations. Implementation-specific exceptions must, of course, be avoided. See Guidelines 4.3 and 5.8 for further information on exceptions. See Guideline 7.1.6 for further information on vendor-supplied features.

7.5.1　Predefined and User-Defined Exceptions

guideline

- Do not depend on the exact locations at which predefined exceptions are raised.
- Do not rely on the behavior of `Ada.Exceptions` beyond the minimum defined in the language.

rationale

The Ada Reference Manual (1995, §11) states that, among implementations, a predefined exception for the same cause may be raised from different locations. You will not be able to discriminate between the exceptions. Further, each of the predefined exceptions is associated with a variety of conditions. Any exception handler written for a predefined exception must be prepared to deal with any of these conditions.

Guideline 5.6.9 discusses the use of blocks to define local exception handlers that can catch exceptions close to their point of origin.

7.5.2　Implementation-Specific Exceptions

guideline

- Do not raise implementation-specific exceptions.
- Convert implementation-specific exceptions within interface packages to visible user-defined exceptions.

rationale

No exception defined specifically by an implementation can be guaranteed to be portable to other implementations whether or not they are from the same vendor. Not only may the names be different, but the range of conditions triggering the exceptions may be different also.

If you create interface packages for the implementation-specific portions of your program, those packages can catch or recognize implementation-specific exceptions and convert them into user-defined exceptions that have been declared in the specification. Do not allow yourself to be forced to find and change the name of every handler you have written for these exceptions when the program is ported.

7.6   REPRESENTATION   CLAUSES   AND   IMPLEMENTATION-DEPENDENT FEATURES

Ada provides many implementation-dependent features that permit greater control over and interaction with the underlying hardware architecture than is normally provided by a high-order language. These mechanisms are intended to assist in systems programming and real-time programming to obtain greater efficiency (e.g., specific size and layout of variables through representation clauses) and direct hardware interaction (e.g., interrupt entries) without having to resort to assembly level programming.

Given the objectives for these features, it is not surprising that you must usually pay a significant price in portability to use them. In general, where portability is the main objective, do not use these features. When you must use these features, encapsulate them in packages that are well-commented as interfacing to the particular target environment. This section identifies the various features and their recommended use with respect to portability.

7.6.1   Representation Clauses

guideline
- Use algorithms that do not depend on the representation of the data and, therefore, do not need representation clauses.
- Consider using representation clauses when accessing or defining interface data or when a specific representation is needed to implement a design.
- Do not assume that sharing source files between programs guarantees the same representation of data types in those files.

rationale

In many cases, it is easy to use representation clauses to implement an algorithm, even when it is not necessary. There is also a tendency to document the original programmer's assumptions about the representation for future reference. But there is no guarantee that another implementation will support the representation chosen. Unnecessary representation clauses also confuse porting or maintenance efforts, which must assume that the programmer depends on the documented representation.

Interfaces to external systems and devices are the most common situations where a representation clause is needed. Uses of pragma Import and address clauses should be evaluated during design and porting to determine whether a representation clause is needed.

Without representation clauses, the language does not require two compilations of an unchanged file to result in the same data representation. Things that can change the representation between compilations include:

- A change in a file earlier in the compilation order
- A change in the optimization strategy or level
- A change in versions of the compiler
- A change in actual compilers
- A change in the availability of system resources

Therefore, two independently linked programs or partitions should only share data that has their representations explicitly controlled.

notes

During a porting effort, all representation clauses can be evaluated as either design artifacts or specifications for accessing interface data that might change with a new implementation.

7.6.2   Package System

guideline
- Avoid using package System constants except in attempting to generalize other machine-dependent constructs.

rationale

Because the values in this package are implementation-provided, unexpected effects can result from their use.

notes

If you must guarantee that physical record layouts will remain the same between implementations, you can express record fields by their first and last bit positions as shown in the Ada Reference Manual (1995, §13.5.1). Static expressions and named numbers should be used to let the compiler compute the endpoints of each range in terms of earlier fields. In this case, greater portability can be achieved by using System.Storage_Unit to let the compiler compute the value of the named number. However, this method might not work for all values of System.Storage_Unit.

exceptions

Do use package System constants to parameterize other implementation-dependent features (see Pappas (1985, §13.7.1).

7.6.3   Machine Code Inserts

guideline

- Avoid machine code inserts.

rationale

The Ada Reference Manual (1995, Annex C) suggests that the package that implements machine code inserts is optional. Additionally, it is not standardized so that machine code inserts are most likely not portable. In fact, it is possible that two different vendors' syntax will differ for an identical target, and differences in lower-level details, such as register conventions, will hinder portability.

exceptions

If machine code inserts must be used to meet another project requirement, recognize and document the portability decreasing effects.

In the declarative region of the body of the routine where machine code inserts are being used, insert comments explaining what functions inserts provide and (especially) why the inserts are necessary. Comment the necessity of using machine code inserts by delineating what went wrong with attempts to use other higher level constructs.

7.6.4   Interfacing to Foreign Languages

guideline

- Use the package Interfaces and its language-defined child packages rather than implementation-specific mechanisms.

- Consider using pragma Import rather than access-to-subprogram types for interfacing to subprograms in other languages.

- Isolate all subprograms employing pragmas Import, Export, and Convention to implementation-specific (interface) package bodies.

example

This example shows how to interface with the following cube root function written in C:

```
double cbrt (double x);
---------------------------------------------------------------------------

package Math_Utilities is

    Argument_Error : exception;

    function Cube_Root (X : Float) return Float;

    ...

end Math_Utilities;
---------------------------------------------------------------------------
```

```
with Interfaces.C;
package body Math_Utilities is

    function Cube_Root (X : Float) return Float is

        function C_Cbrt (X : Interfaces.C.Double) return Interfaces.C.Double;
        pragma Import (Convention   => C,
                       Entity       => C_Cbrt,
                       External_Name => "cbrt");

    begin
        if X < 0.0 then
            raise Argument_Error;
        else
            return Float (C_Cbrt (Interfaces.C.Double (X)));
        end if;
    end Cube_Root;

    ...

end Math_Utilities;
```

rationale

For static interfacing to subprograms in other languages, the pragma Import provides a better solution than access to subprograms because no indirection is required. The pragma Interface (Ada Reference Manual 1983) has been replaced by pragmas Import, Export, and Convention. Annex B of the Rationale (1995) discusses how to use these pragmas in conjunction with the access-to-subprogram types in interfacing to other languages.

Access to subprogram types is useful for implementing callbacks in a separate subsystem, such as the X Window system.

The problems with interfacing to foreign languages are complex. These problems include pragma syntax differences, conventions for linking/binding Ada to other languages, and mapping Ada variables to foreign language variables. By hiding these dependencies within interface packages, the amount of code modification can be reduced.

exceptions

It is often necessary to interact with other languages, if only an assembly language, to reach certain hardware features. In these cases, clearly comment the requirements and limitations of the interface and pragma Import, Export, and Conventions usage.

7.6.5   Implementation-Specific Pragmas and Attributes

guideline

*   Avoid pragmas and attributes added by the compiler implementor.

rationale

The Ada Reference Manual (1995) permits an implementor to add pragmas and attributes to exploit a particular hardware architecture or software environment. These are obviously even more implementation-specific and therefore less portable than an implementor's interpretations of the predefined pragmas and attributes. However, the Ada Reference Manual (1995) defines a set of annexes that have a uniform and consistent approach to certain specialized needs, namely, real-time systems, distributed systems, information systems, numerics, interfacing to foreign languages, and safety and security. You should always prefer the facilities defined in the annexes to any vendor-defined pragmas and attributes.

7.6.6   Unchecked Deallocation

guideline

*   Avoid dependence on Ada.Unchecked_Deallocation (see Guideline 5.9.2).

rationale

The unchecked storage deallocation mechanism is one method for overriding the default time at which allocated storage is reclaimed. The earliest default time is when an object is no longer accessible, for example, when control leaves the scope where an access type was declared (the exact point after this time is implementation-dependent). Any unchecked deallocation of storage performed prior to this may result in an erroneous Ada program if an attempt is made to access the object.

This guideline is stronger than Guideline 5.9.2 because of the extreme dependence on the implementation of Ada.Unchecked_Deallocation. Using it could cause considerable difficulty with portability.

notes

Ada.Unchecked_Deallocation is a supported feature in all Ada implementations. The portability issue arises in that unchecked storage deallocations might cause varying results in different implementations.

exceptions

Using unchecked deallocation of storage can be beneficial in local control of highly iterative or recursive algorithms where available storage may be exceeded.

7.6.7   Unchecked Access

guideline

- Avoid dependence on the attribute Unchecked_Access (see Guideline 5.9.2).

rationale

Access values are subject to accessibility restrictions. Using the attribute Unchecked_Access prevents these rules from being checked, and the programmer runs the risk of having dangling references.

7.6.8   Unchecked Conversion

guideline

- Avoid dependence on Ada.Unchecked_Conversion (see Guideline 5.9.1).

rationale

The unchecked type conversion mechanism is, in effect, a means of bypassing the strong typing facilities in Ada. An implementation is free to limit the types that may be matched and the results that occur when object sizes differ.

exceptions

Unchecked type conversion is useful in implementation-dependent parts of Ada programs where lack of portability is isolated and where low-level programming and foreign language interfacing are the objectives.

If an enumeration representation clause is used, unchecked type conversion is the only language-provided way to retrieve the internal integer code of an enumeration value.

7.6.9   Run-Time Dependencies

guideline

- Avoid the direct invocation of or implicit dependence upon an underlying host operating system or Ada run-time support system, except where the interface is explicitly defined in the language (e.g., Annex C or D of the Ada Reference Manual [1995]).
- Use standard bindings and the package Ada.Command_Line when you need to invoke the underlying run-time support system.
- Use features defined in the Annexes rather than vendor-defined features.

rationale

Features of an implementation not specified in the Ada Reference Manual (1995) will usually differ between implementations. Specific implementation-dependent features are not likely to be provided in other implementations. In addition to the mandatory predefined language environment, the annexes define various packages, attributes, and pragmas to standardize implementation-dependent features for several specialized domains. You enhance portability when you use the features declared in the packages in the Annexes because you can port your program to other vendor environments that implement the same Annexes you have used. Even if a majority of vendors eventually provide similar features, they are unlikely to have identical formulations. Indeed, different vendors may use the same formulation for (semantically) entirely different features.

When coding, try to avoid depending on the underlying operating system. Consider the consequences of including system calls in a program on a host development system. If these calls are not flagged for removal and replacement, the program could go through development and testing only to be unusable when moved to a target environment that lacks the facilities provided by those system calls on the host.

Guideline 7.1.5 discusses the use of the package Ada.Command_Line. If an Ada environment implements a standard binding to operating system services, such as POSIX/Ada, and you write POSIX-compliant calls, your program should be portable across more systems.

exceptions

In real-time, embedded systems, making calls to low-level support system facilities may often be unavoidable. Isolating the uses of these facilities may be too difficult. Comment them as you would machine code inserts (see Guideline 7.6.3); they are, in a sense, instructions for the virtual machine provided by the support system. When isolating the uses of these features, provide an interface for the rest of your program to use, which can be ported through replacement of the interface's implementation.

7.7   INPUT/OUTPUT

I/O facilities in Ada are not a part of the syntactic definition of the language. The constructs in the language have been used to define a set of packages for this purpose. These packages are not expected to meet all the I/O needs of all applications, in particular, embedded systems. They serve as a core subset that may be used on straightforward data and that can be used as examples of building I/O facilities upon the low-level constructs provided by the language. Providing an I/O definition that could meet the requirements of all applications and integrate with the many existing operating systems would result in unacceptable implementation dependencies.

The types of portability problems encountered with I/O tend to be different for applications running with a host operating system versus embedded targets where the Ada run-time is self-sufficient. Interacting with a host operating system offers the added complexity of coexisting with the host file system structures (e.g., hierarchical directories), access methods (e.g., indexed sequential access method [ISAM]), and naming conventions (e.g., logical names and aliases based on the current directory). The section on Input/Output in ARTEWG (1986) provides some examples of this kind of dependency. Embedded applications have different dependencies that often tie them to the low-level details of their hardware devices.

The major defense against these inherent implementation dependencies in I/O is to try to isolate their functionality in any given application. The majority of the following guidelines are focused in this direction.

7.7.1   Name and Form Parameters

guideline

- Use constants and variables as symbolic actuals for the Name and Form parameters on the predefined I/O packages. Declare and initialize them in an implementation dependency package.

rationale

The format and allowable values of these parameters on the predefined I/O packages can vary greatly between implementations. Isolation of these values facilitates portability. Not specifying a Form string or using a null value does not guarantee portability because the implementation is free to specify defaults.

notes

It may be desirable to further abstract the I/O facilities by defining additional Create and Open procedures that hide the visibility of the Form parameter entirely (see Pappas 1985, 54-55).

7.7.2   File Closing

guideline

- Close all files explicitly.

rationale

The Ada Reference Manual (1995, §A.7) does not define what happens to external files after completion of the main subprogram (in particular, if corresponding files have not been closed).

The disposition of a closed temporary file may vary, perhaps affecting performance and space availability (ARTEWG 1986).

7.7.3   Input/Output on Access Types

guideline

*   Avoid performing I/O on access types.

rationale

The Ada Reference Manual (1995, §A.7) does not specify the effects of I/O on access types. When such a value is written, it is placed out of reach of the implementation. Thus, it is out of reach of the reliability-enhancing controls of strong type checking.

Consider the meaning of this operation. One possible implementation of the values of access types is virtual addresses. If you write such a value, how can you expect another program to read that value and make any sensible use of it? The value cannot be construed to refer to any meaningful location within the reader's address space, nor can a reader infer any information about the writer's address space from the value read. The latter is the same problem that the writer would have trying to interpret or use the value if it is read back in. To wit, a garbage collection and/or heap compaction scheme may have moved the item formerly accessed by that value, leaving that value "pointing" at space that is now being put to indeterminable uses by the underlying implementation.

7.7.4   Package Ada.Streams.Stream_IO

guideline

*   Consider using Sequential_IO or Direct_IO instead of Stream_IO unless you need the low-level, heterogeneous I/O features provided by Stream_IO.

rationale

Sequential_IO and Direct_IO are still well suited for processing homogeneous files. Additionally, in cases where the intent is to process homogeneous files, the use of Sequential_IO or Direct_IO has the advantage of enforcing this intent at compile time.

Stream_IO should be reserved for processing heterogeneous files. In this case, a file is not a sequence of objects of all the same type but rather a sequence of objects of varying types. To read a heterogeneous sequence of objects in the correct order requires some application-specific knowledge.

7.7.5   Current Error Files

guideline

*   Consider using Current_Error and Set_Error for run-time error messages.

example

```
with Ada.Text_IO;

...

begin
   Ada.Text_IO.Open (File => Configuration_File,
                     Mode => Ada.Text_IO.In_File,
                     Name => Configuration_File_Name);
exception
   when Ada.Text_IO.Name_Error =>
      Ada.Text_IO.Put_Line (File => Ada.Text_IO.Standard_Error,
                            Item => "Can't open configuration file.");
   ...
end;
```

rationale

The package Text_IO includes the concept of a current error file. You should report errors to the user through the associated subprograms Current_Error and Set_Error instead of the standard output facilities. In interactive applications, using the Text_IO error facilities increases the portability of your user interface.

notes

In a program with multiple tasks for I/O, you need to be careful of two or more tasks trying to set Current_Input, Current_Output, or Current_Error. The potential problem lies in unprotected updates to the "shared" state associated with a package, in this case, the package Text_IO. Guidelines 6.1.1 and 6.2.4 discuss the related issues of unprotected shared variables.

7.8   SUMMARY

fundamentals

- In programs or components intended to have a long life, avoid using the features of Ada declared as "obsolescent" by Annex J of the Ada Reference Manual (1995), unless the use of the feature is needed for backward compatibility with Ada 83 (Ada Reference Manual 1983).

- Document the use of any obsolescent features.

- Avoid using the following features:
  - The short renamings of the packages in the predefined environment (e.g., Text_IO as opposed to Ada.Text_IO)
  - The character replacements of ! for |, : for #, and % for quotation marks
  - Reduced accuracy subtypes of floating-point types
  - The 'Constrained attribute as applied to private types
  - The predefined package ASCII
  - The exception Numeric_Error
  - Various representation specifications, including at clauses, mod clauses, interrupt entries, and the Storage_Size attribute

- Make informed assumptions about the support provided for the following on potential target platforms:
  - Number of bits available for type Integer (range constraints)
  - Number of decimal digits of precision available for floating-point types
  - Number of bits available for fixed-point types (delta and range constraints)
  - Number of characters per line of source text
  - Number of bits for Root_Integer expressions
  - Number of seconds for the range of Duration
  - Number of milliseconds for Duration'Small
  - Minimum and maximum scale for decimal types

- Avoid assumptions about the values and the number of values included in the type Character.

- Use highlighting comments for each package, subprogram, and task where any nonportable features are present.

- For each nonportable feature employed, describe the expectations for that feature.

- Consider using only a parameterless procedure as the main subprogram.

- Consider using Ada.Command_Line for accessing values from the environment, but recognize that this package's behavior and even its specification are nonportable.

- Encapsulate and document all uses of package Ada.Command_Line.

- Create packages specifically designed to isolate hardware and implementation dependencies and designed so that their specification will not change when porting.

- Clearly indicate the objectives if machine or solution efficiency is the reason for hardware or implementation-dependent code.

- For the packages that hide implementation dependencies, maintain different package bodies for different target environments.

- Isolate interrupt receiving tasks into implementation-dependent packages.

- Refer to Annex M of the Ada Reference Manual (1995) for a list of implementation-dependent features.

- Avoid the use of vendor-supplied packages.

- Avoid the use of features added to the predefined packages that are not specified in the Ada language definition or Specialized Needs Annexes.

- Use features defined in the Specialized Needs Annexes rather than vendor-defined features.

- Document clearly the use of any features from the Specialized Needs Annexes (systems programming, real-time systems, distributed systems, information systems, numerics, and safety and security).

- Do not write code whose correct execution depends on the particular parameter passing mechanism used by an implementation (Ada Reference Manual 1995, §6.2; Cohen 1986).

- If a subprogram has more than one formal parameter of a given subtype, at least one of which is [in] out, make sure that the subprogram can properly handle the case when both formal parameters denote the same actual object.

- Avoid depending on the order in which certain constructs in Ada are evaluated.

numeric types and expressions

- Avoid using the predefined numeric types in package standard. Use range and digits declarations and let the implementation pick the appropriate representation.

- For programs that require greater accuracy than that provided by the global assumptions, define a package that declares a private type and operations as needed; see Pappas (1985) for a full explanation and examples.

- Consider using predefined numeric types (Integer, Natural, Positive) for:
  - Indexes into arrays where the index type is not significant, such as type String
  - "Pure" numbers, that is, numbers with no associated physical unit (e.g., exponents)
  - Values whose purpose is to control a repeat or iteration count

- Use an implementation that supports the Numerics Annex (Ada Reference Manual 1995, Annex G) when performance and accuracy are overriding concerns.

- Carefully analyze what accuracy and precision you really need.

- Do not press the accuracy limits of the machine(s).

- Comment the analysis and derivation of the numerical aspects of a program.

- Anticipate the range of values of subexpressions to avoid exceeding the underlying range of their base type. Use derived types, subtypes, factoring, and range constraints on numeric types.

- Consider using <= and >= to do relational tests on real valued arguments, avoiding the <, >, =, and /= operations.

- Use values of type attributes in comparisons and checking for small values.

- In information systems, declare different numeric decimal types to correspond to different scales (Brosgol, Eachus, and Emery 1994).

- Create objects of different decimal types to reflect different units of measure (Brosgol, Eachus, and Emery 1994).

- Declare subtypes of the appropriately scaled decimal type to provide appropriate range constraints for application-specific types.

- Encapsulate each measure category in a package (Brosgol, Eachus, and Emery 1994).

- Declare as few decimal types as possible for unitless data (Brosgol, Eachus, and Emery 1994).

- For decimal calculations, determine whether the result should be truncated toward 0 or rounded.

- Avoid decimal types and arithmetic on compilers that do not support the Information Systems Annex (Ada Reference Manual 1995, Annex F) in full.

storage control

- Do not use a representation clause to specify number of storage units.
- Do not compare access-to-subprogram values.
- Consider using explicitly defined storage pool mechanisms.

tasking

- Do not depend on the order in which task objects are activated when declared in the same declarative list.
- Do not depend on a particular delay being achievable (Nissen and Wallis 1984).
- Never use knowledge of the execution pattern of tasks to achieve timing requirements.
- Do not assume a correlation between System.Tick and type Duration.
- Do not depend on the order in which guard conditions are evaluated or on the algorithm for choosing among several open select alternatives.
- Do not assume that tasks execute uninterrupted until they reach a synchronization point.
- Use pragma Priority to distinguish general levels of importance only.
- Avoid using the abort statement.
- Do not use unprotected shared variables.
- Consider using protected types to provide data synchronization.
- Have tasks communicate through the rendezvous mechanism.
- Do not use unprotected shared variables as a task synchronization device.
- Consider using protected objects to encapsulate shared data.
- Use pragma Atomic or Volatile only when you are forced to by run-time system deficiencies.

exceptions

- Do not depend on the exact locations at which predefined exceptions are raised.
- Do not rely on the behavior of Ada.Exceptions beyond the minimum defined in the language.
- Do not raise implementation-specific exceptions.
- Convert implementation-specific exceptions within interface packages to visible user-defined exceptions.

representation clauses and implementation-dependent features

- Use algorithms that do not depend on the representation of the data and, therefore, do not need representation clauses.
- Consider using representation clauses when accessing or defining interface data or when a specific representation is needed to implement a design.
- Do not assume that sharing source files between programs guarantees the same representation of data types in those files.
- Avoid using package System constants except in attempting to generalize other machine-dependent constructs.
- Avoid machine code inserts.
- Use the package Interfaces and its language-defined child packages rather than implementation-specific mechanisms.
- Consider using pragma Import rather than access-to-subprogram types for interfacing to subprograms in other languages.
- Isolate all subprograms employing pragmas Import, Export, and Convention to implementation-specific (interface) package bodies.
- Avoid pragmas and attributes added by the compiler implementor.
- Avoid dependence on Ada.Unchecked_Deallocation.

- Avoid dependence on the attribute Unchecked_Access.

- Avoid dependence on Ada.Unchecked_Conversion.

- Avoid the direct invocation of or implicit dependence upon an underlying host operating system or Ada run-time support system, except where the interface is explicitly defined in the language (e.g., Annex C or D of the Ada Reference Manual [1995]).

- Use standard bindings and the package Ada.Command_Line when you need to invoke the underlying run-time support system.

- Use features defined in the Annexes rather than vendor-defined features.

input/output

- Use constants and variables as symbolic actuals for the Name and Form parameters on the predefined I/O packages. Declare and initialize them in an implementation dependency package.

- Close all files explicitly.

- Avoid performing I/O on access types.

- Consider using Sequential_IO or Direct_IO instead of Stream_IO unless you need the low-level, heterogeneous I/O features provided by Stream_IO.

- Consider using Current_Error and Set_Error for run-time error messages.

CHAPTER 8
Reusability

Reusability is the extent to which code can be used in different applications with minimal change. As code is reused in a new application, that new application partially inherits the attributes of that code. If the code is maintainable, the application is more maintainable. If it is portable, then the application is more portable. So this chapter's guidelines are most useful when all of the other guidelines in this book are also applied.

Several guidelines are directed at the issue of maintainability. Maintainable code is easy to change to meet new or changing requirements. Maintainability plays a special role in reuse. When attempts are made to reuse code, it is often necessary to change it to suit the new application. If the code cannot be changed easily, it is less likely to be reused.

There are many issues involved in software reuse: whether to reuse parts, how to store and retrieve reusable parts in a library, how to certify parts, how to maximize the economic value of reuse, how to provide incentives to engineers and entire companies to reuse parts rather than reinvent them, and so on. This chapter ignores these managerial, economic, and logistic issues to focus on the single technical issue of how to write software parts in Ada to increase reuse potential. The other issues are just as important but are outside of the scope of this book.

One of the design goals of Ada was to facilitate the creation and use of reusable parts to improve productivity. To this end, Ada provides features to develop reusable parts and to adapt them once they are available. Packages, visibility control, and separate compilation support modularity and information hiding (see guidelines in Sections 4.1, 4.2, 5.3, and 5.7). This allows the separation of application-specific parts of the code, maximizes the general purpose parts suitable for reuse, and allows the isolation of design decisions within modules, facilitating change. The Ada type system supports localization of data definitions so that consistent changes are easy to make. The Ada inheritance features support type extension so that data definitions and interfaces may be customized for an application. Generic units directly support the development of general purpose, adaptable code that can be instantiated to perform specific functions. The Ada 95 improvements for object-oriented techniques and abstraction support all of the above goals. Using these features carefully and in conformance to the guidelines in this book, produces code that is more likely to be reusable.

Reusable code is developed in many ways. Code may be scavenged from a previous project. A reusable library of code may be developed from scratch for a particularly well-understood domain, such as a math library. Reusable code may be developed as an intentional byproduct of a specific application. Reusable code may be developed a certain way because a design method requires it. These guidelines are intended to apply in all of these situations.

The experienced programmer recognizes that software reuse is much more a requirements and design issue than a coding issue. The guidelines in this section are intended to work within an overall method for developing reusable code. This section will not deal with artifacts of design, testing, etc. Some research into reuse issues related specifically to the Ada language can be found in AIRMICS (1990), Edwards (1990), and Wheeler (1992).

Regardless of development method, experience indicates that reusable code has certain characteristics, and this chapter makes the following assumptions:

- Reusable parts must be understandable. A reusable part should be a model of clarity. The requirements for commenting reusable parts are even more stringent than those for parts specific to a particular application.

- Reusable parts must be of the highest possible quality. They must be correct, reliable, and robust. An error or weakness in a reusable part may have far-reaching consequences, and it is important that other programmers can have a high degree of confidence in any parts offered for reuse.

- Reusable parts must be adaptable. To maximize its reuse potential, a reusable part must be able to adapt to the needs of a wide variety of users.

- Reusable parts should be independent. It should be possible to reuse a single part without also adopting many other parts that are apparently unrelated.

In addition to these criteria, a reusable part must be easier to reuse than to reinvent, must be efficient, and must be portable. If it takes more effort to reuse a part than to create one from scratch or if the reused part is simply not efficient enough, reuse does not occur as readily. For guidelines on portability, see Chapter 7.

This chapter should not be read in isolation. In many respects, a well-written, reusable component is simply an extreme example of a well-written component. All of the guidelines in the previous chapters and in Chapter 9 apply to reusable components as well as components specific to a single application. As experience increases with the 1995 revision to the Ada standard, new guidelines may emerge while others may change. The guidelines listed here apply specifically to reusable components.

Guidelines in this chapter are frequently worded "consider . . ." because hard and fast rules cannot apply in all situations. The specific choice you can make in a given situation involves design tradeoffs. The rationale for these guidelines is intended to give you insight into some of these tradeoffs.

8.1   UNDERSTANDING AND CLARITY

It is particularly important that parts intended for reuse should be easy to understand. What the part does, how to use it, what anticipated changes might be made to it in the future, and how it works are facts that must be immediately apparent from inspection of the comments and the code itself. For maximum readability of reusable parts, follow the guidelines in Chapter 3, some of which are repeated more strongly below.

8.1.1   Application-Independent Naming

guideline
- Select the least restrictive names possible for reusable parts and their identifiers.
- Select the generic name to avoid conflicting with the naming conventions of instantiations of the generic.
- Use names that indicate the behavioral characteristics of the reusable part, as well as its abstraction.

example

General-purpose stack abstraction:

```
---------------------------------------------------------------------
generic

   type Item is private;

package Bounded_Stack is

   procedure Push (New_Item    : in     Item);
   procedure Pop  (Newest_Item :    out Item);
   ...

end Bounded_Stack;
---------------------------------------------------------------------
```

Renamed appropriately for use in current application:

```
with Bounded_Stack;

...

   type Tray is ...

   package Tray_Stack is
      new Bounded_Stack (Item => Tray);
```

rationale

Choosing a general or application-independent name for a reusable part encourages its wide reuse. When the part is used in a specific context, it can be instantiated (if generic) or renamed with a more specific name.

When there is an obvious choice for the simplest, clearest name for a reusable part, it is a good idea to leave that name for use by the reuser of the part, choosing a longer, more descriptive name for the reusable part. Thus, Bounded_Stack is a better name than Stack for a generic stack package because it leaves the simpler name Stack available to be used by an instantiation.

Include indications of the behavioral characteristics (but not indications of the implementation) in the name of a reusable part so that multiple parts with the same abstraction (e.g., multiple stack packages) but with different restrictions (bounded, unbounded, etc.) can be stored in the same Ada library and used as part of the same Ada program.

8.1.2   Abbreviations

guideline

- Do not use abbreviations in identifier or unit names.

example

```
--------------------------------------------------------------------------
with Ada.Calendar;
package Greenwich_Mean_Time is

    function Clock return Ada.Calendar.Time;
    ...

end Greenwich_Mean_Time;
--------------------------------------------------------------------------
```

The following abbreviation may not be clear when used in an application:

```
with Ada.Calendar;
with Greenwich_Mean_Time;
...

    function Get_GMT return Ada.Calendar.Time renames
            Greenwich_Mean_Time.Clock;
```

rationale

This is a stronger guideline than Guideline 3.1.4. However well commented, an abbreviation may cause confusion in some future reuse context. Even universally accepted abbreviations, such as GMT for Greenwich Mean Time, can cause problems and should be used only with great caution.

The difference between this guideline and Guideline 3.1.4 involves issues of domain. When the domain is well-defined, abbreviations and acronyms that are accepted in that domain will clarify the meaning of the application. When that same code is removed from its domain-specific context, those abbreviations may become meaningless.

In the example above, the package, Greenwich_Mean_Time, could be used in any application without loss of meaning. But the function Get_GMT could easily be confused with some other acronym in a different domain.

notes

See Guideline 5.7.2 concerning the proper use of the renames clause. If a particular application makes extensive use of the Greenwich_Mean_Time domain, it may be appropriate to rename the package GMT within that application:

```
with Greenwich_Mean_Time;
...

    package GMT renames Greenwich_Mean_Time;
```

8.1.3   Generic Formal Parameters

guideline

- Document the expected behavior of generic formal parameters just as you document any package specification.

example

The following example shows how a very general algorithm can be developed but must be clearly documented to be used:

```
------------------------------------------------------------------------
generic
     -- Index provides access to values in a structure.  For example,
     -- an array, A.
     type Index is (<>);

     type Element is private;
     type Element_Array is array (Index range <>) of Element;

     -- The function, Should_Precede, does NOT compare the indexes
     -- themselves; it compares the elements of the structure.
     -- The function Should_Precede is provided rather than a "Less_Than" function
     -- because the sort criterion need not be smallest first.
     with function Should_Precede (Left  : in     Element;
                                   Right : in     Element)
       return Boolean;

     -- This procedure swaps values of the structure (the mode won't
     -- allow the indexes themselves to be swapped!)
     with procedure Swap (Index1 : in     Index;
                          Index2 : in     Index;
                          A      : in out Element_Array);

     -- After the call to Quick_Sort, the indexed structure will be
     -- sorted:
     --      For all i,j in First..Last : i<j  =>  A(i) < A(j).

procedure Quick_Sort (First : in     Index := Index'First;
                      Last  : in     Index := Index'Last);
------------------------------------------------------------------------
```

rationale

The generic capability is one of Ada's strongest features because of its formalization. However, not all of the assumptions made about generic formal parameters can be expressed directly in Ada. It is important that any user of a generic know exactly what that generic needs in order to behave correctly.

In a sense, a generic specification is a contract where the instantiator must supply the formal parameters and, in return, receives a working instance of the specification. Both parties are best served when the contract is complete and clear about all assumptions.

8.2 ROBUSTNESS

The following guidelines improve the robustness of Ada code. It is easy to write code that depends on an assumption that you do not realize that you are making. When such a part is reused in a different environment, it can break unexpectedly. The guidelines in this section show some ways in which Ada code can be made to automatically conform to its environment and some ways in which it can be made to check for violations of assumptions. Finally, some guidelines are given to warn you about errors that Ada does not catch as soon as you might like.

8.2.1 Named Numbers

guideline

- Use named numbers and static expressions to allow multiple dependencies to be linked to a small number of symbols.

example

```
------------------------------------------------------------------------
procedure Disk_Driver is

     -- In this procedure, a number of important disk parameters are
     -- linked.
     Number_Of_Sectors  : constant :=     4;
     Number_Of_Tracks   : constant :=   200;
     Number_Of_Surfaces : constant :=    18;
     Sector_Capacity    : constant := 4_096;

     Track_Capacity   : constant := Number_Of_Sectors  * Sector_Capacity;
     Surface_Capacity : constant := Number_Of_Tracks   * Track_Capacity;
     Disk_Capacity    : constant := Number_Of_Surfaces * Surface_Capacity;
```

```
type Sector_Range  is range 1 .. Number_Of_Sectors;
type Track_Range   is range 1 .. Number_Of_Tracks;
type Surface_Range is range 1 .. Number_Of_Surfaces;

type Track_Map    is array (Sector_Range)  of ...;
type Surface_Map  is array (Track_Range)   of Track_Map;
type Disk_Map     is array (Surface_Range) of Surface_Map;

begin  -- Disk_Driver
...
end Disk_Driver;
```

rationale

To reuse software that uses named numbers and static expressions appropriately, just one or a small number of constants need to be reset, and all declarations and associated code are changed automatically. Apart from easing reuse, this reduces the number of opportunities for error and documents the meanings of the types and constants without using error-prone comments.

8.2.2   Unconstrained Arrays

guideline

- Use unconstrained array types for array formal parameters and array return values.

- Make the size of local variables depend on actual parameter size, where appropriate.

example

```
...
type Vector is array (Vector_Index range <>) of Element;
type Matrix is array
       (Vector_Index range <>, Vector_Index range <>) of Element;
...
```

```
procedure Matrix_Operation (Data : in     Matrix) is

   Workspace   : Matrix (Data'Range(1), Data'Range(2));
   Temp_Vector : Vector (Data'First(1) .. 2 * Data'Last(1));
...
```

rationale

Unconstrained arrays can be declared with their sizes dependent on formal parameter sizes. When used as local variables, their sizes change automatically with the supplied actual parameters. This facility can be used to assist in the adaptation of a part because necessary size changes in local variables are taken care of automatically.

8.2.3   Minimizing and Documenting Assumptions

guideline

- Minimize the number of assumptions made by a unit.

- For assumptions that cannot be avoided, use subtypes or constraints to automatically enforce conformance.

- For assumptions that cannot be automatically enforced by subtypes, add explicit checks to the code.

- Document all assumptions.

- If the code depends upon the implementation of a specific Special Needs Annex for proper operation, document this assumption in the code.

example

The following poorly written function documents but does not check its assumption:

```
-- Assumption:  BCD value is less than 4 digits.
function Binary_To_BCD (Binary_Value : in     Natural)
   return BCD;
```

The next example enforces conformance with its assumption, making the checking automatic and the comment unnecessary:

```
subtype Binary_Values is Natural range 0 .. 9_999;

function Binary_To_BCD (Binary_Value : in     Binary_Values)
   return BCD;
```

The next example explicitly checks and documents its assumption:

```
-----------------------------------------------------------------------
-- Out_Of_Range raised when BCD value exceeds 4  digits.
function Binary_To_BCD (Binary_Value : in     Natural)
   return BCD is

   Maximum_Representable : constant Natural := 9_999;

begin  -- Binary_To_BCD
   if Binary_Value > Maximum_Representable then
      raise Out_Of_Range;
   end if;

   ...
end Binary_To_BCD;
-----------------------------------------------------------------------
```

rationale

Any part that is intended to be used again in another program, especially if the other program is likely to be written by other people, should be robust. It should defend itself against misuse by defining its interface to enforce as many assumptions as possible and by adding explicit defensive checks on anything that cannot be enforced by the interface. By documenting dependencies on a Special Needs Annex, you warn the user that he should only reuse the component in a compilation environment that provides the necessary support.

notes

You can restrict the ranges of values of the inputs by careful selection or construction of the subtypes of the formal parameters. When you do so, the compiler-generated checking code may be more efficient than any checks you might write. Indeed, such checking is part of the intent of the strong typing in the language. This presents a challenge, however, for generic units where the user of your code selects the types of the parameters. Your code must be constructed to deal with any value of any subtype the user may choose to select for an instantiation.

8.2.4   Subtypes in Generic Specifications

guideline

- Use first subtypes when declaring generic formal objects of mode in out.

- Beware of using subtypes as subtype marks when declaring parameters or return values of generic formal subprograms.

- Use attributes rather than literal values.

example

In the following example, it appears that any value supplied for the generic formal object Object would be constrained to the range 1..10. It also appears that parameters passed at run-time to the Put routine in any instantiation and values returned by the Get routine would be similarly constrained:

```
subtype Range_1_10 is Integer range 1 .. 10;

-----------------------------------------------------------------------
generic

   Object : in out Range_1_10;
   with procedure Put (Parameter : in     Range_1_10);
   with function  Get return Range_1_10;

package Input_Output is
   ...
end Input_Output;
-----------------------------------------------------------------------
```

However, this is not the case. Given the following legal instantiation:

```
subtype Range_15_30 is Integer range 15 .. 30;
Constrained_Object : Range_15_30 := 15;

procedure Constrained_Put (Parameter : in     Range_15_30);
function  Constrained_Get return Range_15_30;
```

```
package Constrained_Input_Output is
   new Input_Output (Object => Constrained_Object,
                     Put    => Constrained_Put,
                     Get    => Constrained_Get);

   ...
```

`Object`, `Parameter`, and the return value of `Get` are constrained to the range `15..30`. Thus, for example, if the body of the generic package contains an assignment statement:

```
Object := 1;
```

`Constraint_Error` is raised when this instantiation is executed.

rationale

The language specifies that when constraint checking is performed for generic formal objects and parameters and return values of generic formal subprograms, the constraints of the actual subtype (not the formal subtype) are enforced (Ada Reference Manual 1995, §§12.4 and 12.6).Thus, the subtype specified in a formal in out object parameter and the subtypes specified in the profile of a formal subprogram need not match those of the actual object or subprogram.

Thus, even with a generic unit that has been instantiated and tested many times and with an instantiation that reported no errors at instantiation time, there can be a run-time error. Because the subtype constraints of the generic formal are ignored, the Ada Reference Manual (1995, §§12.4 and 12.6) suggests using the name of a base type in such places to avoid confusion. Even so, you must be careful not to assume the freedom to use any value of the base type because the instantiation imposes the subtype constraints of the generic actual parameter. To be safe, always refer to specific values of the type via symbolic expressions containing attributes like `'First`, `'Last`, `'Pred`, and `'Succ` rather than via literal values.

For generics, attributes provide the means to maintain generality. It is possible to use literal values, but literals run the risk of violating some constraint. For example, assuming that an array's index starts at 1 may cause a problem when the generic is instantiated for a zero-based array type.

notes

Adding a generic formal parameter that defines the subtype of the generic formal object does not address the ramifications of the constraint checking rule discussed in the above rationale. You can instantiate the generic formal type with any allowable subtype, and you are not guaranteed that this subtype is the first subtype:

```
generic
   type Object_Range is range <>;
   Objects : in out Object_Range;
   ...
package X is
   ...
end X;
```

You can instantiate the subtype `Object_Range` with any `Integer` subtype, for example, `Positive`. However, the actual variable `Object` can be of `Positive'Base`, i.e., `Integer` and its value are not guaranteed to be greater than 0.

8.2.5   Overloading in Generic Units

guideline

*   Be careful about overloading the names of subprograms exported by the same generic package.

example

```
-------------------------------------------------------------------------
generic
   type Item is limited private;

package Input_Output is

   procedure Put (Value : in     Integer);
   procedure Put (Value : in     Item);

end Input_Output;
-------------------------------------------------------------------------
```

rationale

If the generic package shown in the example above is instantiated with Integer (or any subtype of Integer) as the actual type corresponding to generic formal Item, then the two Put procedures have identical interfaces, and all calls to Put are ambiguous. Therefore, this package cannot be used with type Integer. In such a case, it is better to give unambiguous names to all subprograms. See the Ada Reference Manual (1995, §12.3) for more information.

8.2.6 Hidden Tasks

guideline

- Within a specification, document any tasks that would be activated by with'ing the specification and by using any part of the specification.
- Document which generic formal parameters are accessed from a task hidden inside the generic unit.
- Document any multithreaded components.

rationale

The effects of tasking become a major factor when reusable code enters the domain of real-time systems. Even though tasks may be used for other purposes, their effect on scheduling algorithms is still a concern and must be clearly documented. With the task clearly documented, the real-time programmer can then analyze performance, priorities, and so forth to meet timing requirements, or, if necessary, he can modify or even redesign the component.

Concurrent access to data structures must be carefully planned to avoid errors, especially for data structures that are not atomic (see Chapter 6 for details). If a generic unit accesses one of its generic formal parameters (reads or writes the value of a generic formal object or calls a generic formal subprogram that reads or writes data) from within a task contained in the generic unit, then there is the possibility of concurrent access for which the user may not have planned. In such a case, the user should be warned by a comment in the generic specification.

8.2.7 Exceptions

guideline

- Propagate exceptions out of reusable parts. Handle exceptions within reusable parts only when you are certain that the handling is appropriate in all circumstances.
- Propagate exceptions raised by generic formal subprograms after performing any cleanup necessary to the correct operation of future invocations of the generic instantiation.
- Leave state variables in a valid state when raising an exception.
- Leave parameters unmodified when raising an exception.

example

```
-------------------------------------------------------------------
generic

    type Number is limited private;

    with procedure Get (Value :    out Number);

procedure Process_Numbers;


-------------------------------------------------------------------
procedure Process_Numbers is

    Local : Number;

    procedure Perform_Cleanup_Necessary_For_Process_Numbers is separate;
    ...

begin   -- Process_Numbers
    ...

    Catch_Exceptions_Generated_By_Get:
       begin
          Get (Local);
```

```
        exception
           when others =>
              Perform_Cleanup_Necessary_For_Process_Numbers;
              raise;
        end Catch_Exceptions_Generated_By_Get;

        ...
     end Process_Numbers;
```
----

rationale

On most occasions, an exception is raised because an undesired event (such as floating-point overflow) has occurred. Such events often need to be dealt with entirely differently with different uses of a particular software part. It is very difficult to anticipate all the ways that users of the part may wish to have the exceptions handled. Passing the exception out of the part is the safest treatment.

In particular, when an exception is raised by a generic formal subprogram, the generic unit is in no position to understand why or to know what corrective action to take. Therefore, such exceptions should always be propagated back to the caller of the generic instantiation. However, the generic unit must first clean up after itself, restoring its internal data structures to a correct state so that future calls may be made to it after the caller has dealt with the current exception. For this reason, all calls to generic formal subprograms should be within the scope of a when others exception handler if the internal state is modified, as shown in the example above.

When a reusable part is invoked, the user of the part should be able to know exactly what operation (at the appropriate level of abstraction) has been performed. For this to be possible, a reusable part must always do all or none of its specified function; it must never do half. Therefore, any reusable part that terminates early by raising or propagating an exception should return to the caller with no effect on the internal or external state. The easiest way to do this is to test for all possible exceptional conditions before making any state changes (modifying internal state variables, making calls to other reusable parts to modify their states, updating files, etc.). When this is not possible, it is best to restore all internal and external states to the values that were current when the part was invoked before raising or propagating the exception. Even when this is not possible, it is important to document this potentially hazardous situation in the comment header of the specification of the part.

A similar problem arises with parameters of mode out or in out when exceptions are raised. The Ada language distinguishes between "by-copy" and "by-reference" parameter passing. In some cases, "by-copy" is required; in other cases, "by-reference" is required; and in the remaining cases, either mechanism is allowed. The potential problem arises in those cases where the language does not specify the parameter passing mechanism to use. When an exception is raised, the copy-back does not occur, but for an Ada compiler, which passes parameters by reference (in those cases where a choice is allowed), the actual parameter has already been updated. When parameters are passed by copy, the update does not occur. To reduce ambiguity, increase portability, and avoid situations where some but not all of the actual parameters are updated when an exception is raised, it is best to treat values of out and in out parameters like state variables, updating them only after it is certain that no exception will be raised.

See also Guideline 7.1.8.

notes

A reusable part could range from a low-level building block (e.g., data structure, sorting algorithm, math function) to a large reusable subsystem. The lower level the building block, the less likely that the reusable part will know how to handle exceptions or produce meaningful results. Thus, the low-level parts should propagate exceptions. A large reusable subsystem, however, should be able to handle any anticipated exceptions independently of the variations across which it is reused.

8.3   ADAPTABILITY

Reusable parts often need to be changed before they can be used in a specific application. They should be structured so that change is easy and as localized as possible. One way of achieving adaptability is to create general parts with complete functionality, only a subset of which might be needed in a given application. Another way to achieve adaptability is to use Ada's generic construct to produce parts that can be appropriately instantiated with different parameters. Both of these approaches avoid the error-prone process of adapting a part by changing its code but have limitations and can carry some overhead.

Anticipated changes, that is, changes that can be reasonably foreseen by the developer of the part, should be provided for as far as possible. Unanticipated changes can only be accommodated by carefully structuring a part to be adaptable. Many of the considerations pertaining to maintainability apply. If the code is of high quality, clear, and conforms to well-established design principles such as information hiding, it is easier to adapt in unforeseen ways.

8.3.1   Complete Functionality

guideline

- Provide core functionality in a reusable part or set of parts so that the functionality in this abstraction can be meaningfully extended by its reusers.

- More specifically, provide initialization and finalization procedures for every data structure that may contain dynamic data.

- For data structures needing initialization and finalization, consider deriving them, when possible, from the types `Ada.Finalization.Controlled` or `Ada.Finalization.Limited_Controlled`.

example

```
Incoming : Queue;
...
Set_Initial (Incoming);    -- initialization operation
...
if Is_Full (Incoming) then  -- query operation
   ...
end if;
...
Clean_Up (Incoming);       -- finalization operation
```

rationale

This functionality is particularly important in designing/programming an abstraction. You have to balance the completeness of the abstraction against its extensibility. Completeness ensures that you have configured the abstraction correctly, without built-in assumptions about its execution environment. It also ensures the proper separation of functions so that they are useful to the current application and, in other combinations, to other applications. Extensibility ensures that reusers can add functionality by extension, using tagged type hierarchies (see Guideline 8.4.8 and Chapter 9) or child library packages (see Guidelines 4.1.6, 8.4.1, and 9.4.1).

In designing for reuse, you need to think in terms of clean abstractions. If you provide too little functionality and rely on your reusers to extend the abstraction, they risk having an abstraction that lacks cohesion. This hodgepodge abstraction has inherited many operations, not all of which are necessary or work together.

When a reusable part can be implemented reasonably using dynamic data, then any application that must control memory can use the initialization and finalization routines to guard against memory leakage. Then, if data structures become dynamic, the applications that are sensitive to these concerns can be easily adapted.

The predefined types `Ada.Finalization.Controlled` or `Ada.Finalization.Limited_Controlled` provide automatic, user-definable initialization, adjustment, and finalization procedures. When you declare controlled types and objects, you are guaranteed that the compiler will insert the necessary calls to initialization, adjustment, and finalization, making your code less error-prone and more maintainable. When overriding the `Initialize` and `Finalize` routines on the controlled types, make sure to call the parent `Initialize` or `Finalize`.

notes

The example illustrates end condition functions. An abstraction should be automatically initialized before its user gets a chance to damage it. When that is not possible, it should be supplied with initialization operations. In any case, it needs finalization operations. One way to supply the initialization and finalization operations is to derive the abstraction from the predefined types `Ada.Finalization.Controlled` or `Ada.Finalization.Limited_Controlled`. Wherever possible, query operations should be provided to determine when limits are about to be exceeded, so that the user can avoid causing exceptions to be raised.

It is also useful to provide reset operations for many objects. To see that a reset and an initiation can be different, consider the analogous situation of a "warm boot" and a "cold boot" on a personal computer.

Even if all of these operations are not appropriate for the abstraction, the exercise of considering them aids in formulating a complete set of operations, others of which may be used by another application.

Some implementations of the language link all subprograms of a package into the executable file, ignoring whether they are used or not, making unused operations a liability (see Guideline 8.4.5). In such cases, where the overhead is significant, create a copy of the fully functional part and comment out the unused operations with an indication that they are redundant in this application.

8.3.2   Generic Units

guideline

- Use generic units to avoid code duplication.
- Parameterize generic units for maximum adaptability.
- Reuse common instantiations of generic units, as well as the generic units themselves.

rationale

Ada does not allow data types to be passed as actual parameters to subprograms during execution. Such parameters must be specified as generic formal parameters to a generic unit when it is instantiated. Therefore, if you want to write a subprogram for which there is variation from call to call in the data type of objects on which it operates, then you must write the subprogram as a generic unit and instantiate it once for each combination of data type parameters. The instantiations of the unit can then be called as regular subprograms.

You can pass subprograms as actual parameters either by declaring access-to-subprogram values or generic formal subprogram parameters. See Guideline 5.3.4 for a discussion of the tradeoffs.

If you find yourself writing two very similar routines differing only in the data type they operate on or the subprograms they call, then it is probably better to write the routine once as a generic unit and instantiate it twice to get the two versions you need. When the need arises later to modify the two routines, the change only needs to be made in one place. This greatly facilitates maintenance.

Once you have made such a choice, consider other aspects of the routine that these two instances may have in common but that are not essential to the nature of the routine. Factor these out as generic formal parameters. When the need arises later for a third similar routine, it can be automatically produced by a third instantiation if you have foreseen all the differences between it and the other two. A parameterized generic unit can be very reusable.

It may seem that the effort involved in writing generic rather than nongeneric units is substantial. However, making units generic is not much more difficult or time-consuming than making them nongeneric once you become familiar with the generic facilities. It is, for the most part, a matter of practice. Also, any effort put into the development of the unit will be recouped when the unit is reused, as it surely will be if it is placed in a reuse library with sufficient visibility. Do not limit your thinking about potential reuse to the application you are working on or to other applications with which you are very familiar. Applications with which you are not familiar or future applications might be able to reuse your software.

After writing a generic unit and placing it in your reuse library, the first thing you are likely to do is to instantiate it once for your particular needs. At this time, it is a good idea to consider whether there are instantiations that are very likely to be widely used. If so, place each such instantiation in your reuse library so that they can be found and shared by others.

See also Guideline 9.3.5.

8.3.3   Formal Private and Limited Private Types

guideline

- Consider using a limited private type for a generic formal type when you do not need assignment on objects of the type inside the generic body.
- Consider using a nonlimited private type for a generic formal type when you need normal assignment on objects of the type inside the body of the generic.

- Consider using a formal tagged type derived from `Ada.Finalization.Controlled` when you need to enforce special assignment semantics on objects of the type in the body of the generic.

- Export the least restrictive type that maintains the integrity of the data and abstraction while allowing alternate implementations.

- Consider using a limited private abstract type for generic formal types of a generic that extends a formal private tagged type.

example

The first example shows a case of a template providing only a data structure, a case in which assignment is clearly not needed in the body of the generic:

```
------------------------------------------------------------------------
generic
    type Element_Type is limited private;
package Generic_Doubly_Linked_Lists is
    type Cell_Type;
    type List_Type is access all Element_Type;
    type Cell_Type is
        record
            Data     : Element_Type;
            Next     : List_Type;
            Previous : List_Type;
        end record;
end Generic_Doubly_Linked_Lists;
```

The second example shows a template that composes new operations out of (nonassignment) operations passed as generic formal parameters:

```
generic
    type Element_Type is limited private;
    with procedure Process_Element (X : in out Element_Type);
    type List_Type is array (Positive range <>) of Element_Type;
procedure Process_List (L : in out List_Type);

procedure Process_List (L : in out List_Type) is
begin -- Process_List
    for I in L'Range loop
        Process_Element (L(I));
    end loop;
end Process_List;
------------------------------------------------------------------------
generic
    type Domain_Type is limited private;
    type Intermediate_Type is limited private;
    type Range_Type is limited private;
    with function Left (X : Intermediate_Type) return Range_Type;
    with function Right (X : Domain_Type) return Intermediate_Type;
function Generic_Composition (X : Domain_Type) return Range_Type;
-- the function Left o Right

function Generic_Composition (X : Domain_Type) return Range_Type is
begin  -- generic_Composition
    return Left (Right (X));
end Generic_Composition;
```

The third example shows how to use Ada's controlled types to provide special assignment semantics:

```
with Ada.Finalization;
generic
    type Any_Element is new Ada.Finalization.Controlled with private;
    Maximum_Stack_Size : in Natural := 100;
package Bounded_Stack is
    type Stack is private;

    procedure Push (On_Top      : in out Stack;
                    New_Element : in     Any_Element);
    procedure Pop  (From_Top    : in out Stack;
                    Top_Element :    out Any_Element);
    Overflow  : exception;
    Underflow : exception;
    ...
private
    type Stack_Information;
    type Stack is access Stack_Information;
end Bounded_Stack;
```

rationale

For a generic component to be usable in as many contexts as possible, it should minimize the assumptions that it makes about its environment and should make explicit any assumptions that are necessary. In Ada, the assumptions made by generic units can be stated explicitly by the types of the generic formal parameters. A limited private generic formal type prevents the generic unit from making any assumptions about the structure of objects of the type or about operations defined for such objects. A private (nonlimited) generic formal type allows the assumption that assignment and equality comparison operations are defined for the type. Thus, a limited private data type cannot be specified as the actual parameter for a private generic formal type.

In general, you should choose the private or limited private generic formal type based on the need for assignment inside a generic. Limited private types should be used for abstractions that do not need assignment, as in the first two examples above. In the third example, where assignment is needed, a type derived from a controlled type is specified to ensure that the correct assignment semantics will be available. If you need equality in the body of the generic, you may need to redefine equality as well to get the correct semantics; you would then need to include a formal generic subprogram parameter for the = function.

The situation is reversed for types exported by a reusable part. For exported types, the restrictions specified by limited and limited private are restrictions on the user of the part, not on the part itself. To provide maximum capability to the user of a reusable part, export types with as few restrictions as possible. Apply restrictions as necessary to protect the integrity of the exported data structures and the abstraction for the various implementations envisioned for that generic.

Because they are so restrictive, limited private types are not always the best choice for types exported by a reusable part. In a case where it makes sense to allow the user to make copies of and compare data objects, and when the underlying data type does not involve access types (so that the entire data structure gets copied or compared), then it is better to export a (nonlimited) private type. In a case where it makes sense to allow the user to make copies of and compare data objects and when the underlying data type involves access types (so that the entire data structure gets copied or compared), then it is better to export a controlled type and an (overridden) equality operation. In cases where it does not detract from the abstraction to reveal even more about the type, then a nonprivate type (e.g., a numeric, enumerated, record, or array type) should be used.

One use of generic units is to create a mixin generic (see Guideline 8.3.8) to extend a tagged type. In this situation, you want to use the most restrictive type as the generic formal type, that is, a formal type that is both limited and abstract. When you instantiate the generic, if the actual type is nonlimited, the type extension will also be nonlimited. In the generic package, you must declare the type extension as abstract. The instantiator of the generic can then extend the type again to achieve the desired mixin configuration.

notes

The predefined packages, Sequential_IO and Direct_IO, take private types. This will complicate I/O requirements for limited private types and should be considered during design.

There are also some cases where you must use a limited private formal type. These cases arise when the formal type has an access discriminant, or the formal is used as the parent type in defining a type extension that itself includes a component of a limited type (e.g., task type), or the formal defines a new discriminant part with an access discriminant.

8.3.4 Using Generic Units to Encapsulate Algorithms

guideline

• Use generic units to encapsulate algorithms independently of data type.

example

This is the specification of a generic sort procedure:

```
-----------------------------------------------------------------------------
generic
    type Element is private;
    type Data     is array (Positive range <>) of Element;
    with function Should_Precede (Left  : in      Element;
                                  Right : in      Element)
             return Boolean is <>;
```

```
      with procedure Swap (Left  : in out Element;
                           Right : in out Element) is <>;
   procedure Generic_Sort (Data_To_Sort : in out Data);
------------------------------------------------------------------------
```

The generic body looks just like a regular procedure body and can make full use of the generic formal parameters in implementing the sort algorithm:

```
------------------------------------------------------------------------
   procedure Generic_Sort (Data_To_Sort : in out Data) is
   begin
      ...
      for I in Data_To_Sort'Range loop
         ...

            ...
            if Should_Precede (Data_To_Sort(J), Data_To_Sort(I)) then
               Swap(Data_To_Sort(I), Data_To_Sort(J));
            end if;

            ...
         ...
      end loop;

      ...
   end Generic_Sort;
------------------------------------------------------------------------
```

The generic procedure can be instantiated as:

```
      type Integer_Array is array (Positive range <>) of Integer;

      function Should_Precede (Left  : in     Integer;
                               Right : in     Integer)
         return Boolean;

      procedure Swap (Left  : in out Integer;
                      Right : in out Integer);

      procedure Sort is
         new Generic_Sort (Element => Integer,
                           Data    => Integer_Array);
```

or:

```
      subtype String_80   is String (1 .. 80);
      type    String_Array is array (Positive range <>) of String_80;

      function Should_Precede (Left  : in     String_80;
                               Right : in     String_80)
         return Boolean;

      procedure Swap (Left  : in out String_80;
                      Right : in out String_80);

      procedure Sort is
         new Generic_Sort (Element => String_80,
                           Data    => String_Array);
```

and called as:

```
      Integer_Array_1 : Integer_Array (1 .. 100);
      ...
      Sort (Integer_Array_1);
```

or:

```
      String_Array_1  : String_Array  (1 .. 100);
      ...
      Sort (String_Array_1);
```

rationale

A sort algorithm can be described independently of the data type being sorted. This generic procedure takes the Element data type as a generic limited private type parameter so that it assumes as little as possible about the data type of the objects actually being operated on. It also takes Data as a generic formal parameter so that instantiations can have entire arrays passed to them for sorting. Finally, it explicitly requires the two operators that it needs to do the sort: Should_Precede and Swap. The sort algorithm is encapsulated without reference to any data type. The generic can be instantiated to sort an array of any data type.

8.3.5   Using Generic Units for Data Abstraction

guideline

- Consider using abstract data types (not to be confused with Ada's abstract types) in preference to abstract data objects.

- Consider using generic units to implement abstract data types independently of their component data type.

example

This example presents a series of different techniques that can be used to generate abstract data types and objects. A discussion of the merits of each follows in the rationale section below. The first is an abstract data object (ADO), which can be used to encapsulate an abstract state machine. It encapsulates one stack of integers:

```
------------------------------------------------------------------------
package Bounded_Stack is

    subtype Element is Integer;
    Maximum_Stack_Size : constant := 100;

    procedure Push (New_Element : in      Element);
    procedure Pop  (Top_Element :     out Element);

    Overflow  : exception;
    Underflow : exception;
    ...

end Bounded_Stack;
------------------------------------------------------------------------
```

The second example is an abstract data type (ADT). It differs from the ADO by exporting the Stack type, which allows the user to declare any number of stacks of integers. Because multiple stacks may now exist, it is necessary to specify a Stack argument on calls to Push and Pop:

```
------------------------------------------------------------------------
package Bounded_Stack is

    subtype Element is Integer;
    type    Stack   is limited private;

    Maximum_Stack_Size : constant := 100;

    procedure Push (On_Top      : in out Stack;
                    New_Element : in      Element);
    procedure Pop  (From_Top    : in out Stack;
                    Top_Element :     out Element);

    Overflow  : exception;
    Underflow : exception;

    ...
private
    type Stack_Information;
    type Stack is access Stack_Information;

end Bounded_Stack;
------------------------------------------------------------------------
```

The third example is a parameterless generic abstract data object (GADO). It differs from the ADO (the first example) simply by being generic, so that the user can instantiate it multiple times to obtain multiple stacks of integers:

```
------------------------------------------------------------------------
generic
package Bounded_Stack is

    subtype Element is Integer;

    Maximum_Stack_Size : constant := 100;

    procedure Push (New_Element : in      Element);
    procedure Pop  (Top_Element :     out Element);

    Overflow  : exception;
    Underflow : exception;
    ...

end Bounded_Stack;
------------------------------------------------------------------------
```

The fourth example is a slight variant on the third, still a GADO but with parameters. It differs from the third example by making the data type of the stack a generic parameter so that stacks of data types other than `Integer` can be created. Also, `Maximum_Stack_Size` has been made a generic parameter that defaults to 100 but can be specified by the user, rather than a constant defined by the package:

```
-------------------------------------------------------------------------
generic

    type Element is private;

    Maximum_Stack_Size : in Natural := 100;

package Bounded_Stack is

    procedure Push (New_Element : in      Element);
    procedure Pop  (Top_Element :     out Element);

    Overflow  : exception;
    Underflow : exception;
    ...

end Bounded_Stack;
-------------------------------------------------------------------------
```

The fifth example is a generic abstract data type (GADT). It differs from the GADO in the fourth example in the same way that the ADT in the second example differed from the ADO in the first example; it exports the `Stack` type, which allows the user to declare any number of stacks:

```
-------------------------------------------------------------------------
generic

    type Element is private;

    Maximum_Stack_Size : in Natural := 100;

package Bounded_Stack is

    type Stack is private;

    procedure Push (On_Top      : in out Stack;
                    New_Element : in      Element);
    procedure Pop  (From_Top    : in out Stack;
                    Top_Element :     out Element);

    Overflow  : exception;
    Underflow : exception;
    ...

private
    type Stack_Information;
    type Stack is access Stack_Information;
end Bounded_Stack;
-------------------------------------------------------------------------
```

rationale

The biggest advantage of an ADT over an ADO (or a GADT over a GADO) is that the user of the package can declare as many objects as desired with an ADT. These objects can be declared as standalone variables or as components of arrays and records. They can also be passed as parameters. None of this is possible with an ADO, where the single data object is encapsulated inside of the package. Furthermore, an ADO provides no more protection of the data structure than an ADT. When a private type is exported by the ADT package, as in the example above, then for both the ADO and ADT, the only legal operations that can modify the data are those defined explicitly by the package (in this case, `Push` and `Pop`). For these reasons, an ADT or GADT is almost always preferable to an ADO or GADO, respectively.

A GADO is similar to an ADT in one way: it allows multiple objects to be created by the user. With an ADT, multiple objects can be declared using the type defined by the ADT package. With a GADO (even a GADO with no generic formal parameters, as shown in the third example), the package can be instantiated multiple times to produce multiple objects. However, the similarity ends there. The multiple objects produced by the instantiations suffer from all restrictions described above for ADOs; they cannot be used in arrays or records or passed as parameters. Furthermore, the objects are each of a different type, and no operations are defined to operate on more than one of them at a time. For example, there cannot be an operation to compare two such objects or to assign one to another. The multiple objects declared using the type defined by an ADT package suffer from no such restrictions; they can be used in arrays and records and can be passed as parameters. Also, they are all declared to be of the same type, so that it is possible for the ADT package to provide operations to assign, compare, copy, etc. For these reasons, an ADT is almost always preferable to a parameterless GADO.

The biggest advantage of a GADT or GADO over an ADT or ADO, respectively, is that the GADT and GADO are generic and can thus be parameterized with types, subprograms, and other configuration information. Thus, as shown above, a single generic package can support bounded stacks of any data type and any stack size, while the ADT and ADO above are restricted to stacks of Integer, no more than 100 in size. For this reason, a GADO or GADT is almost always preferable to an ADO or ADT.

The list of examples above is given in order of increasing power and flexibility, starting with an ADO and ending with a GADT. These advantages are not expensive in terms of complexity or development time. The specification of the GADT above is not significantly harder to write or understand than the specification of the ADO. The bodies are also nearly identical.

Compare the body for the simplest version, the ADO:

```
----------------------------------------------------------------------
package body Bounded_Stack is

    type Stack_Slots is array (Natural range <>) of Element;

    type Stack_Information is
        record
            Slots : Stack_Slots (1 .. Maximum_Stack_Size);
            Index : Natural := 0;
        end record;

    Stack : Stack_Information;
----------------------------------------------------------------------
    procedure Push (New_Element : in    Element) is
    begin
        if Stack.Index >= Maximum_Stack_Size then
            raise Overflow;
        end if;

        Stack.Index := Stack.Index + 1;
        Stack.Slots(Stack.Index) := New_Element;
    end Push;
----------------------------------------------------------------------
    procedure Pop (Top_Element :    out Element) is
    begin
        if Stack.Index <= 0 then
            raise Underflow;
        end if;

        Top_Element := Stack.Slots(Stack.Index);
        Stack.Index := Stack.Index - 1;
    end Pop;
----------------------------------------------------------------------
    ...
end Bounded_Stack;
----------------------------------------------------------------------
```

with the body for the most powerful and flexible version, the GADT:

```
----------------------------------------------------------------------
package body Bounded_Stack is

    type Stack_Slots is array (Natural range <>) of Element;

    type Stack_Information is
        record
            Slots : Stack_Slots (1 .. Maximum_Stack_Size);
            Index : Natural := 0;
        end record;
----------------------------------------------------------------------
    procedure Push (On_Top     : in out Stack;
                    New_Element : in    Element) is
    begin
        if On_Top.Index >= Maximum_Stack_Size then
            raise Overflow;
        end if;

        On_Top.Index := On_Top.Index + 1;
        On_Top.Slots(On_Top.Index) := New_Element;
    end Push;
```

```
-------------------------------------------------------------------
procedure Pop (From_Top    : in out Stack;
               Top_Element :    out Element) is
begin
   if From_Top.Index <= 0 then
      raise Underflow;
   end if;

   Top_Element := From_Top.Slots(From_Top.Index);

   From_Top.Index := From_Top.Index - 1;
end Pop;
-------------------------------------------------------------------
   ...
end Bounded_Stack;
-------------------------------------------------------------------
```

There is only one difference. The ADO declares a local object called stack, while the GADT has one additional parameter (called stack) on each of the exported procedures Push and Pop.

8.3.6   Iterators

guideline

- Provide iterators for traversing complex data structures within reusable parts.
- Consider providing both active and passive iterators.
- Protect the iterators from errors due to modification of the data structure during iteration.
- Document the behavior of the iterators when the data structure is modified during traversal.

example

Ada provides several mechanisms for building reusable iterators. The following examples discuss the alternatives of "simple" generics, access discriminants, and type extension. The terms active and passive are used to differentiate whether the iteration mechanism (i.e., the way in which the complex data structure is traversed) is exposed or hidden. A passive iterator hides the traversal (e.g., looping mechanism) and consists of a single operation, iterate, that is parameterized by the processing you do on each element of the data structure. By contrast, an active iterator exposes the primitive operations by which you traverse the data structure (Booch 1987).

The first example shows a generic package that defines an abstract list data type, with both active and passive iterators for traversing a list:

```
-------------------------------------------------------------------
generic
   type Element is limited private;
   ...
package Unbounded_List is
   type List is limited private;
   procedure Insert (New_Element : in     Element;
                     Into        : in out List);
   -- Passive (generic) iterator.
   generic
      with procedure Process (Each : in out Element);
   procedure Iterate (Over : in     List);
   -- Active iterator
   type Iterator is limited private;

   procedure Initialize (Index        : in out Iterator;
                         Existing_List : in     List);

   function  More       (Index        : in     Iterator)
      return Boolean;

   -- The procedure Get_Next combines an "Advance" and "Current" function
   procedure Get_Next   (Index           : in out Iterator;
                         Current_Element :    out Element);
   ...
private
   ...
end Unbounded_List;
-------------------------------------------------------------------
```

After instantiating the generic package and declaring a list as:

```
with Unbounded_List;
procedure List_User is

   type Employee is ...;

   package Roster is
      new Unbounded_List (Element => Employee, ...);

   Employee_List : Roster.List;
```

the passive iterator is instantiated, specifying the name of the routine that should be called for each list element when the iterator is called.

```
procedure Process_Employee (Each : in out Employee) is
begin
   ...
   -- Perform the required action for EMPLOYEE here.
end Process_Employee;

procedure Process_All is
   new Roster.Iterate (Process => Process_Employee);
```

The passive iterator can then be called as:

```
begin  -- List_User
   Process_All (Employee_List);
end List_User;
```

Alternatively, the active iterator can be used without the second instantiation required by the passive iterator:

```
Iterator         : Roster.Iterator;
Current_Employee : Employee;

procedure Process_Employee (Each : in     Employee) is separate;

begin  -- List_User
   Roster.Initialize (Index         => Iterator,
                       Existing_List => Employee_List);

   while Roster.More (Iterator) loop

      Roster.Get_Next (Index         => Iterator,
                       Current_Element => Current_Employee);

      Process_Employee (Current_Employee);

   end loop;
end List_User;
```

The second example shows a code excerpt from Rationale (1995, §3.7.1) on how to construct iterators using access discriminants:

```
generic
   type Element is private;
package Sets is

   type Set is limited private;
   ... -- various set operations
   type Iterator (S : access Set) is limited private;
   procedure Start (I : Iterator);
   function Done (I : Iterator) return Boolean;
   procedure Next (I : in out Iterator);
   ... -- other iterator operations
private
   type Node;
   type Ptr is access Node;
   type Node is
      record
         E    : Element;
         Next : Ptr;
      end record;
   type Set is new Ptr;

   type Iterator (S : access Set) is
      record
         This : Ptr;
      end record;
end Sets;
```

```
package body Sets is
   ...  -- bodies of the various set operations

   procedure Start (I : in out Iterator) is
   begin
      I.This := Ptr(I.S.all);
   end Start;

   function Done (I : Iterator) return Boolean is
   begin
      return I.This = null;
   end Done;

   procedure Next (I : in out Iterator) is
   begin
      I.This := I.This.Next;
   end Next;

   ...
end Sets;
```

The iterator operations allow you to iterate over the elements of the set with the component This of the iterator object accessing the current element. The access discriminant always points to the enclosing set to which the current element belongs.

The third example uses code fragments from Rationale (1995, §4.4.4) to show an iterator using type extension and dispatching:

```
type Element is ...

package Sets is
   type Set is limited private;
   -- various set operations
   type Iterator is abstract tagged null record;
   procedure Iterate (S : in Set; IC : in out Iterator'Class);
   procedure Action (E : in out Element;
                     I : in out Iterator) is abstract;
private
   -- definition of Node, Ptr (to Node), and Set
end Sets;

package body Sets is
   ...

   procedure Iterate (S : in Set; IC : in out Iterator'Class) is
      This : Ptr := Ptr (S);
   begin
      while This /= null loop
         Action (This.E, IC);  -- dispatch
         This := This.Next;
      end loop;
   end Iterate;
end Sets;
```

The general purpose iterator looks like this:

```
package Sets.Something is
   procedure Do_Something (S : Set; P : Parameters);
end Sets.Something;

package body Sets.Something is

   type My_Iterator is new Iterator with
      record
         -- components for parameters and workspace
      end record;

   procedure Action (E : in out Element;
                     I : in out My_Iterator) is
   begin
      -- do something to element E using data from iterator I
   end Action;

   procedure Do_Something (S : Set; P : Parameters) is
      I : My_Iterator;
   begin  -- Do_Something
      ...  -- copy parameters into iterator
      Iterate (S, I);
      ... copy any results from iterator back to parameters
   end Do_Something;

end Sets.Something;
```

rationale

Iteration over complex data structures is often required and, if not provided by the part itself, can be difficult to implement without violating information hiding principles.

Active and passive iterators each have their advantages, but neither is appropriate in all situations. Therefore, it is recommended that both be provided to give the user a choice of which to use in each situation.

Passive iterators are simpler and less error-prone than active iterators, in the same way that the `for` loop is simpler and less error-prone than the `while` loop. There are fewer mistakes that the user can make in using a passive iterator. Simply instantiate it with the routine to be executed for each list element, and call the instantiation for the desired list. Active iterators require more care by the user. Care must be taken to invoke the iterator operations in the proper sequence and to associate the proper iterator variable with the proper list variable. It is possible for a change made to the software during maintenance to introduce an error, perhaps an infinite loop.

On the other hand, active iterators are more flexible than passive iterators. With a passive iterator, it is difficult to perform multiple, concurrent, synchronized iterations. For example, it is much easier to use active iterators to iterate over two sorted lists, merging them into a third sorted list. Also, for multidimensional data structures, a small number of active iterator routines may be able to replace a large number of passive iterators, each of which implements one combination of the active iterators. Finally, active iterators can be passed as generic formal parameters while passive iterators cannot because passive iterators are themselves generic, and generic units cannot be passed as parameters to other generic units.

For either type of iterator, semantic questions can arise about what happens when the data structure is modified as it is being iterated. When writing an iterator, be sure to consider this possibility, and indicate with comments the behavior that occurs in such a case. It is not always obvious to the user what to expect. For example, to determine the "closure" of a mathematical "set" with respect to some operation, a common algorithm is to iterate over the members of the set, generating new elements and adding them to the set. In such a case, it is important that elements added to the set during the iteration be encountered subsequently during the iteration. On the other hand, for other algorithms, it may be important that the iterated set is the same set that existed at the beginning of the iteration. In the case of a prioritized list data structure, if the list is iterated in priority order, it may be important that elements inserted at lower priority than the current element during iteration not be encountered subsequently during the iteration but that elements inserted at a higher priority should be encountered. In any case, make a conscious decision about how the iterator should operate, and document that behavior in the package specification.

Deletions from the data structure also pose a problem for iterators. It is a common mistake for a user to iterate over a data structure, deleting it piece by piece during the iteration. If the iterator is not prepared for such a situation, it is possible to end up dereferencing a null pointer or committing a similar error. Such situations can be prevented by storing extra information with each data structure, which indicates whether it is currently being iterated, and using this information to disallow any modifications to the data structure during iteration. When the data structure is declared as a `limited private` type, as should usually be the case when iterators are involved, the only operations defined on the type are declared explicitly in the package that declares the type, making it possible to add such tests to all modification operations.

The Rationale (1995, §4.4.4) notes that the access discriminant and type extension techniques are inversions of each other. In the access discriminant approach, you have to write out the looping mechanism for each action. In the type extension approach, you write one loop and dispatch to the desired action. Thus, an iterator that uses the access discriminant technique would be considered active, while an iterator that uses the type extension technique would be considered passive.

notes

You can use an access to subprogram type as an alternative to generic instantiation, using a nongeneric parameter as a pointer to subprogram. You would then apply the referenced subprogram to every element in a collection (Rationale 1995, §3.7.2). There are drawbacks to this approach, however, because you cannot use it to create a general purpose iterator. Anonymous access to subprogram parameters is not allowed in Ada; thus, the following fragment is illegal:

```
procedure Iterate (C      : Collection;
                    Action : access procedure (E : in out Element));
```

The formal parameter `Action` must be of a named access subtype, as in:

```
type Action_Type is access procedure (E : in out Element);
procedure Iterate (C       : Collection;
                   Action : Action_Type);
```

In order for this to work, you must make sure that the action subprogram is in scope and not defined internal to another subprogram. If it is defined as a nested procedure, it would be illegal to access it. See the Rationale (1995, §4.4.4) for a more complete example.

For further discussion of passive and active iterators, see the Rationale (1995, §3.7.1 and §4.4.4), Ross (1989), and Booch (1987).

8.3.7   Decimal Type Output and Information Systems Annex

guideline

- Localize the currency symbol, digits separator, radix mark, and fill character in picture output.

- Consider using the # character in picture layouts so that the edited numeric output lengths are invariant across currency symbols of different lengths.

example

```
with Ada.Text_IO.Editing;
package Currency is

    type Dollars is delta 0.01 digits 10;
    type Marks   is delta 0.01 digits 10;

    package Dollar_Output is
        new Ada.Text_IO.Editing.Decimal_Output
            (Num                => Dollars,
             Default_Currency   => "$",
             Default_Fill       => '*',
             Default_Separator  => ',',
             Default_Radix_Mark => '.');

    package Mark_Output is
        new Ada.Text_IO.Editing.Decimal_Output
            (Num                => Marks,
             Default_Currency   => "DM",
             Default_Fill       => '*',
             Default_Separator  => '.',
             Default_Radix_Mark => ',');

end Currency;

with Ada.Text_IO.Editing;
with Currency;  use Currency;
procedure Test_Picture_Editing is

    DM_Amount     : Marks;
    Dollar_Amount : Dollars;

    Amount_Picture : constant Ada.Text_IO.Editing.Picture
        := Ada.Text_IO.Editing.To_Picture ("##ZZ_ZZZ_ZZ9.99");

begin   -- Test_Picture_Editing

    DM_Amount     := 1_234_567.89;
    Dollar_Amount := 1_234_567.89;

    DM_Output.Put (Item => DM_Amount,
                   Pic  => Amount_Picture);

    Dollar_Output.Put (Item => Dollar_Amount,
                       Pic  => Amount_Picture);

end Test_Picture_Editing;
```

rationale

Currencies differ in how they are displayed in a report. Currencies use different symbols of different lengths (e.g., the American $, the German DM, and the Austrian ÖS). They use different symbols to separate digits. The United States and the United Kingdom use the comma to separate groups of thousands, whereas Continental Europe uses the period. The United States and the United Kingdom use a period as a decimal point; Continental Europe uses the comma. For a program involving financial calculations that is to be reused across countries, you need to take these differences into account. By encapsulating them, you limit the impact of change in adapting the financial package.

8.3.8   Implementing Mixins

guideline

- Consider using abstract tagged types and generics to define reusable units of functionality that can be "mixed into" core abstractions (also known as mixins).

example

Note the use of an abstract tagged type as a generic formal parameter and as the exported extended type in the pattern that follows, excerpted from the Rationale (1995, §4.6.2):

```
generic
   type S is abstract tagged private;
package P is
   type T is abstract new S with private;
   -- operations on T
private
   type T is abstract new S with
      record
         -- additional components
      end record;
end P;
```

The following code shows how the generic might be instantiated to "mixin" the desired features in the final type extension. See also Guideline 9.5.1 for a related example of code.

```
-- Assume that packages P1, P2, P3, and P4 are generic packages which take a tagged
-- type as generic formal type parameter and which export a tagged type T
package Q is
   type My_T is new Basic_T with private;
   ... -- exported operations
private
   package Feature_1 is new P1 (Basic_T);
   package Feature_2 is new P2 (Feature_1.T);
   package Feature 3 is new P3 (Feature_2.T);
   package Feature_4 is new P4 (Feature_3.T);
   -- etc.
   type My_T is new Feature_4.T with null record;
end Q;
```

rationale

The Rationale (1995, §4.6.2) discusses the use of a generic template to define the properties to be mixed in to your abstraction:

The generic template defines the mixin. The type supplied as generic actual parameter determines the parent . . . the body provides the operations and the specification exports the extended type.

If you have defined a series of generic mixin packages, you would then serialize the instantiations. The actual parameter to the next instantiation is the exported tagged type from the previous instantiation. This is shown in the second code segment in the example. Each extension is derived from a previous extension, so you have a linearized succession of overriding subprograms. Because they are linearized, you have a derivation order you can use to resolve any conflicts.

You should encapsulate one extension (and related operations) per generic package. This provides a better separation of concerns and more maintainable, reusable components.

See Guideline 9.5.1 for a full discussion of the use of mixins.

8.4   INDEPENDENCE

A reusable part should be as independent as possible from other reusable parts. A potential user is less inclined to reuse a part if that part requires the use of other parts that seem unnecessary. The "extra baggage" of the other parts wastes time and space. A user would like to be able to reuse only that part that is perceived as useful.

The concept of a "part" is intentionally vague here. A single package does not need to be independent of each other package in a reuse library if the "parts" from that library that are typically reused are entire subsystems. If the entire subsystem is perceived as providing a useful function, the entire subsystem is reused. However, the subsystem should not be tightly coupled to all the other subsystems in the reuse library so that it is difficult or impossible to reuse the subsystem without reusing the entire library. Coupling between reusable parts should only occur when it provides a strong benefit perceptible to the user.

8.4.1   Subsystem Design

guideline

- Consider structuring subsystems so that operations that are only used in a particular context are in different child packages than operations used in a different context.
- Consider declaring context-independent functionality in the parent package and context-dependent functionality in child packages.

rationale

The generic unit is a basic building block. Generic parameterization can be used to break dependencies between program units so that they can be reused separately. However, it is often the case that a set of units, particularly a set of packages, are to be reused together as a subsystem. In this case, the packages can be collected into a hierarchy of child packages, with private packages to hide internal details. The hierarchy may or may not be generic. Using the child packages allows subsystems to be reused without incorporating too many extraneous operations because the unused child packages can be discarded in the new environment.

See also Guidelines 4.1.6 and 8.3.1.

8.4.2   Using Generic Parameters to Reduce Coupling

guideline

- Minimize with clauses on reusable parts, especially on their specifications.
- Consider using generic parameters instead of with statements to reduce the number of context clauses on a reusable part.
- Consider using generic formal package parameters to import directly all the types and operations defined in an instance of a preexisting generic.

example

A procedure like the following:

```
-----------------------------------------------------------------
with Package_A;
procedure Produce_And_Store_A is
   ...
begin   -- Produce_And_Store_A
   ...
   Package_A.Produce (...);
   ...
   Package_A.Store (...);
   ...
end Produce_And_Store_A;
-----------------------------------------------------------------
```

can be rewritten as a generic unit:

```
-----------------------------------------------------------------
generic
   with procedure Produce (...);
   with procedure Store   (...);
procedure Produce_And_Store;
-----------------------------------------------------------------
procedure Produce_And_Store is
   ...
begin   -- Produce_And_Store
   ...
   Produce (...);
   ...
   Store   (...);
   ...
end Produce_And_Store;
-----------------------------------------------------------------
```

and then instantiated:

```
with Package_A;
with Produce_And_Store;
procedure Produce_And_Store_A is
    new Produce_And_Store (Produce => Package_A.Produce,
                           Store   => Package_A.Store);
```

rationale

Context (with) clauses specify the names of other units upon which this unit depends. Such dependencies cannot and should not be entirely avoided, but it is a good idea to minimize the number of them that occur in the specification of a unit. Try to move them to the body, leaving the specification independent of other units so that it is easier to understand in isolation. Also, organize your reusable parts in such a way that the bodies of the units do not contain large numbers of dependencies on each other. Partitioning your library into independent functional areas with no dependencies spanning the boundaries of the areas is a good way to start. Finally, reduce dependencies by using generic formal parameters instead of with statements, as shown in the example above. If the units in a library are too tightly coupled, then no single part can be reused without reusing most or all of the library.

The first (nongeneric) version of Produce_And_Store_A above is difficult to reuse because it depends on Package_A that may not be general purpose or generally available. If the operation Produce_And_Store has reuse potential that is reduced by this dependency, a generic unit and an instantiation should be produced as shown above. The with clause for Package_A has been moved from the Produce_And_Store generic procedure, which encapsulates the reusable algorithm to the Produce_And_Store_A instantiation. Instead of naming the package that provides the required operations, the generic unit simply lists the required operations themselves. This increases the independence and reusability of the generic unit.

This use of generic formal parameters in place of with clauses also allows visibility at a finer granularity. The with clause on the nongeneric version of Produce_And_Store_A makes all of the contents of Package_A visible to Produce_And_Store_A, while the generic parameters on the generic version make only the Produce and Store operations available to the generic instantiation.

Generic formal packages allow for "safer and simpler composition of generic abstractions" (Rationale 1995, §12.6). The generic formal package allows you to group a set of related types and their operations into a single unit, avoiding having to list each type and operation as an individual generic formal parameter. This technique allows you to show clearly that you are extending the functionality of one generic with another generic, effectively parameterizing one abstraction with another.

8.4.3   Coupling Due to Pragmas

guideline

• In the specification of a generic library unit, use pragma Elaborate_Body.

example

```
generic
    ...
package Stack is

    pragma Elaborate_Body (Stack); -- in case the body is not yet elaborated

    ...

end Stack;

with Stack;
package My_Stack is
    new Stack (...);

package body Stack is
begin
    ...
end Stack;
```

rationale

The elaboration order of compilation units is only constrained to follow the compilation order. Furthermore, any time you have an instantiation as a library unit or an instantiation in a library package, Ada requires that you elaborate the body of the generic being instantiated before elaborating the instantiation itself. Because a generic library unit body may be compiled after an instantiation of that generic, the body may not necessarily be elaborated at the time of the instantiation, causing a Program_Error. Using pragma Elaborate_Body avoids this by requiring that the generic unit body be elaborated immediately after the specification, whatever the compilation order.

When there is clear requirement for a recursive dependency, you should use pragma Elaborate_Body. This situation arises, for example, when you have a recursive dependency (i.e., package A's body depends on package B's specification and package B's body depends on package A's specification).

notes

Pragma Elaborate_All controls the order of elaboration of one unit with respect to another. This is another way of coupling units and should be avoided when possible in reusable parts because it restricts the number of configurations in which the reusable parts can be combined. Recognize, however, that pragma Elaborate_All provides a better guarantee of elaboration order because if using this pragma uncovers elaboration problems, they will be reported at link time (as opposed to a run-time execution error).

Any time you call a subprogram (typically a function) during the elaboration of a library unit, the body of the subprogram must have been elaborated before the library unit. You can ensure this elaboration happens by adding a pragma Elaborate_Body for the unit containing the function. If, however, that function calls other functions, then it is safer to put a pragma Elaborate_All on the unit containing the function.

For a discussion of the pragmas Pure and Preelaborate, see also the Ada Reference Manual (1995, §10.2.1) and the Rationale (1995, §10.3). If you use either pragma Pure or Preelaborate, you will not need the pragma Elaborate_Body.

The idea of a registry is fundamental to many object-oriented programming frameworks. Because other library units will need to call it during their elaboration, you need to make sure that the registry itself is elaborated early. Note that the registry should only depend on the root types of the type hierarchies and that the registry should only hold "class-wide" pointers to the objects, not more specific pointers. The root types should not themselves depend on the registry. See Chapter 9 for a more complete discussion of the use of object-oriented features.

8.4.4 Part Families

guideline

* Create families of generic or other parts with similar specifications.

example

The Booch parts (Booch 1987) are an example of the application of this guideline.

rationale

Different versions of similar parts (e.g., bounded versus unbounded stacks) may be needed for different applications or to change the properties of a given application. Often, the different behaviors required by these versions cannot be obtained using generic parameters. Providing a family of parts with similar specifications makes it easy for the programmer to select the appropriate one for the current application or to substitute a different one if the needs of the application change.

notes

A reusable part that is structured from subparts that are members of part families is particularly easy to tailor to the needs of a given application by substitution of family members.

Guideline 9.2.4 discusses the use of tagged types in building different versions of similar parts (i.e., common interface, multiple implementations).

8.4.5   Conditional Compilation

guideline

• Structure reusable code to take advantage of dead code removal by the compiler.

example

```
-----------------------------------------------------------------------
package Matrix_Math is

   ...
   type Algorithm is (Gaussian, Pivoting, Choleski, Tri_Diagonal);

   generic
      Which_Algorithm : in       Algorithm := Gaussian;
   procedure Invert ( ... );

end Matrix_Math;
-----------------------------------------------------------------------
package body Matrix_Math is
   ...
   -----------------------------------------------------------------------
   procedure Invert ( ... ) is
      ...
   begin   -- Invert
      case Which_Algorithm is
         when Gaussian     => ... ;
         when Pivoting     => ... ;
         when Choleski     => ... ;
         when Tri_Diagonal => ... ;
      end case;

   end Invert;
   -----------------------------------------------------------------------

end Matrix_Math;
-----------------------------------------------------------------------
```

rationale

Some compilers omit object code corresponding to parts of the program that they detect can never be executed. Constant expressions in conditional statements take advantage of this feature where it is available, providing a limited form of conditional compilation. When a part is reused in an implementation that does not support this form of conditional compilation, this practice produces a clean structure that is easy to adapt by deleting or commenting out redundant code where it creates an unacceptable overhead.

This feature should be used when other factors prevent the code from being separated into separate program units. In the above example, it would be preferable to have a different procedure for each algorithm. But the algorithms may differ in slight but complex ways to make separate procedures difficult to maintain.

caution

Be aware of whether your implementation supports dead code removal, and be prepared to take other steps to eliminate the overhead of redundant code if necessary.

8.4.6   Table-Driven Programming

guideline

• Write table-driven reusable parts wherever possible and appropriate.

example

The epitome of table-driven reusable software is a parser generation system. A specification of the form of the input data and of its output, along with some specialization code, is converted to tables that are to be "walked" by preexisting code using predetermined algorithms in the parser produced. Other forms of "application generators" work similarly.

rationale

Table-driven (sometimes known as data-driven) programs have behavior that depends on data with'ed at compile time or read from a file at run-time. In appropriate circumstances, table-driven programming provides a very powerful way of creating general-purpose, easily tailorable, reusable parts.

See Guideline 5.3.4 for a short discussion of using access-to-subprogram types in implementing table-driven programs.

notes

Consider whether differences in the behavior of a general-purpose part could be defined by some data structure at compile- or run-time, and if so, structure the part to be table-driven. The approach is most likely to be applicable when a part is designed for use in a particular application domain but needs to be specialized for use in a specific application within the domain. Take particular care in commenting the structure of the data needed to drive the part.

Table-driven programs are often more efficient and easier to read than the corresponding `case` or `if-elsif-else` networks to compute the item being sought or looked up.

8.4.7   String Handling

guideline

• Use the predefined packages for string handling.

example

Writing code such as the following is no longer necessary in Ada 95:

```
function Upper_Case (S : String) return String is

    subtype Lower_Case_Range is Character range 'a'..'z';

    Temp : String := S;
    Offset : constant := Character'Pos('A') - Character'Pos('a');

begin
    for Index in Temp'Range loop
        if Temp(Index) in Lower_Case_Range then
            Temp(Index) := Character'Val (Character'Pos(Temp(Index)) + Offset);
        end if;
    end loop;
    return Temp;
end Upper_Case;


with Ada.Characters.Latin_1;
function Trim (S : String) return String is
    Left_Index  : Positive := S'First;
    Right_Index : Positive := S'Last;
    Space : constant Character := Ada.Characters.Latin_1.Space;
begin
    while (Left_Index < S'Last) and then (S(Left_Index) = Space) loop
        Left_Index := Positive'Succ(Left_Index);
    end loop;

    while (Right_Index > S'First) and then (S(Right_Index) = Space) loop
        Right_Index := Positive'Pred(Right_Index);
    end loop;

    return S(Left_Index..Right_Index);
end Trim;
```

Assuming a variable s of type string, the following expression:

```
Upper_Case(Trim(S))
```

can now be replaced by more portable and preexisting language-defined operations such as:

```
with Ada.Characters.Handling;  use Ada.Characters.Handling;
with Ada.Strings;              use Ada.Strings;
with Ada.Strings.Fixed;        use Ada.Strings.Fixed;

...
To_Upper (Trim (Source => S, Side => Both))
```

rationale

The predefined Ada language environment includes string handling packages to encourage portability. They support different categories of strings: fixed length, bounded length, and unbounded length. They also support subprograms for string construction, concatenation, copying, selection, ordering, searching, pattern matching, and string transformation. You no longer need to define your own string handling packages.

8.4.8   Tagged Type Hierarchies

guideline

- Consider using hierarchies of tagged types to promote generalization of software for reuse.
- Consider using a tagged type hierarchy to decouple a generalized algorithm from the details of dependency on specific types.

example

```
with Wage_Info;
package Personnel is
   type Employee is abstract tagged limited private;
   type Employee_Ptr is access all Employee'Class;
   ...
   procedure Compute_Wage (E : Employee) is abstract;
private
   type Employee is tagged limited record
      Name  : ...;
      SSN   : ... ;
      Rates : Wage_Info.Tax_Info;
      ...
   end record;
end Personnel;

package Personnel.Part_Time is
   type Part_Timer is new Employee with private;
   ...
   procedure Compute_Wage (E : Part_Timer);
private
   ...
end Personnel.Part_Time;

package Personnel.Full_Time is
   type Full_Timer is new Employee with private;
   ...
   procedure Compute_Wage (E : Full_Timer);
private
   ...
end Personnel.Full_Time;
```

Given the following array declaration:

```
type Employee_List is array (Positive range <>) of Personnel.Employee_Ptr;
```

you can write a procedure that computes the wage of each employee, regardless of the different types of employees that you create. The Employee_List consists of an array of pointers to the various kinds of employees, each of which has an individual Compute_Wage procedure. (The primitive Compute_Wage is declared as an abstract procedure and, therefore, must be overridden by all descendants.) You will not need to modify the payroll code as you specialize the kinds of employees:

```
procedure Compute_Payroll (Who : Employee_List) is
begin -- Compute_Payroll
   for E in Who'Range loop
      Compute_Wage (Who(E).all);
   end loop;
end Compute_Payroll;
```

rationale

The general algorithm can depend polymorphically on objects of the class-wide type of the root tagged type without caring what specialized types are derived from the root type. The generalized algorithm does not need to be changed if additional types are added to the type hierarchy. See also Guideline 5.4.2. Furthermore, the child package hierarchy then mirrors the inheritance hierarchy.

A general root tagged type can define the common properties and have common operations for a hierarchy of more specific types. Software that depends only on this root type will be general, in that it can be used with objects of any of the more specific types. Further, the general algorithms of clients of the root type do not have to be changed as more specific types are added to the type hierarchy. This is a particularly effective way to organize object-oriented software for reuse.

Separating the hierarchy of derived tagged types into individual packages enhances reusability by reducing the number of items in package interfaces. It also allows you to `with` only the capabilities needed.

See also Guidelines 9.2, 9.3.1, 9.3.5, and 9.4.1.

8.5   SUMMARY

understanding and clarity

- Select the least restrictive names possible for reusable parts and their identifiers.
- Select the generic name to avoid conflicting with the naming conventions of instantiations of the generic.
- Use names that indicate the behavioral characteristics of the reusable part, as well as its abstraction.
- Do not use abbreviations in identifier or unit names.
- Document the expected behavior of generic formal parameters just as you document any package specification.

robustness

- Use named numbers and static expressions to allow multiple dependencies to be linked to a small number of symbols.
- Use unconstrained array types for array formal parameters and array return values.
- Make the size of local variables depend on actual parameter size, where appropriate.
- Minimize the number of assumptions made by a unit.
- For assumptions that cannot be avoided, use subtypes or constraints to automatically enforce conformance.
- For assumptions that cannot be automatically enforced by subtypes, add explicit checks to the code.
- Document all assumptions.
- If the code depends upon the implementation of a specific Special Needs Annex for proper operation, document this assumption in the code.
- Use first subtypes when declaring generic formal objects of mode `in out`.
- Beware of using subtypes as subtype marks when declaring parameters or return values of generic formal subprograms.
- Use attributes rather than literal values.
- Be careful about overloading the names of subprograms exported by the same generic package.
- Within a specification, document any tasks that would be activated by `with`'ing the specification and by using any part of the specification.
- Document which generic formal parameters are accessed from a task hidden inside the generic unit.
- Document any multithreaded components.
- Propagate exceptions out of reusable parts. Handle exceptions within reusable parts only when you are certain that the handling is appropriate in all circumstances.
- Propagate exceptions raised by generic formal subprograms after performing any cleanup necessary to the correct operation of future invocations of the generic instantiation.
- Leave state variables in a valid state when raising an exception.
- Leave parameters unmodified when raising an exception.

adaptability

- Provide core functionality in a reusable part or set of parts so that the functionality in this abstraction can be meaningfully extended by its reusers.
- More specifically, provide initialization and finalization procedures for every data structure that may contain dynamic data.

- For data structures needing initialization and finalization, consider deriving them, when possible, from the types `Ada.Finalization.Controlled` or `Ada.Finalization.Limited_Controlled`.
- Use generic units to avoid code duplication.
- Parameterize generic units for maximum adaptability.
- Reuse common instantiations of generic units, as well as the generic units themselves.
- Consider using a limited private type for a generic formal type when you do not need assignment on objects of the type inside the generic body.
- Consider using a nonlimited private type for a generic formal type when you need normal assignment on objects of the type inside the body of the generic.
- Consider using a formal tagged type derived from `Ada.Finalization.Controlled` when you need to enforce special assignment semantics on objects of the type in the body of the generic.
- Export the least restrictive type that maintains the integrity of the data and abstraction while allowing alternate implementations.
- Consider using a limited private abstract type for generic formal types of a generic that extends a formal private tagged type.
- Use generic units to encapsulate algorithms independently of data type.
- Consider using abstract data types (not to be confused with Ada's abstract types) in preference to abstract data objects.
- Consider using generic units to implement abstract data types independently of their component data type.
- Provide iterators for traversing complex data structures within reusable parts.
- Consider providing both active and passive iterators.
- Protect the iterators from errors due to modification of the data structure during iteration.
- Document the behavior of the iterators when the data structure is modified during traversal.
- Localize the currency symbol, digits separator, radix mark, and fill character in picture output.
- Consider using the # character in picture layouts so that the edited numeric output lengths are invariant across currency symbols of different lengths.
- Consider using abstract tagged types and generics to define reusable units of functionality that can be "mixed into" core abstractions (also known as mixins).
- Consider structuring subsystems so that operations that are only used in a particular context are in different child packages than operations used in a different context.
- Consider declaring context-independent functionality in the parent package and context-dependent functionality in child packages.

Independence

- Minimize `with` clauses on reusable parts, especially on their specifications.
- Consider using generic parameters instead of `with` statements to reduce the number of context clauses on a reusable part.
- Consider using generic formal package parameters to import directly all the types and operations defined in an instance of a preexisting generic.
- In the specification of a generic library unit, use pragma `Elaborate_Body`.
- Create families of generic or other parts with similar specifications.
- Structure reusable code to take advantage of dead code removal by the compiler.
- Write table-driven reusable parts wherever possible and appropriate.
- Use the predefined packages for string handling.
- Consider using hierarchies of tagged types to promote generalization of software for reuse.
- Consider using a tagged type hierarchy to decouple a generalized algorithm from the details of dependency on specific types.

CHAPTER 9
Object-Oriented Features

This chapter recommends ways of using Ada's object-oriented features. Ada supports inheritance and polymorphism, providing the programmer some effective techniques and building blocks. Disciplined use of these features will promote programs that are easier to read and modify. These features also give the programmer flexibility in building reusable components.

The following definitions are provided in order to make this chapter more understandable. The essential characteristics of object-oriented programming are encapsulation, inheritance, and polymorphism. These are defined as follows in the Rationale (1995, §§4.1 and III.1.2):

> Inheritance. A means for incrementally building new abstractions from an existing one by "inheriting" their properties without disturbing the implementation of the original abstraction or the existing clients.

> Multiple Inheritance. The means of inheriting components and operations from two or more parent abstractions.

> Mixifn Inheritance. Multiple inheritance in which one or more of the parent abstractions cannot have instances of their own and exist only to provide a set of properties for abstractions inheriting from them.

> Polymorphism. A means of factoring out the differences among a collection of abstractions, such that programs may be written in terms of the common properties.

> Static polymorphism is provided through the generic parameter mechanism whereby a generic unit may be instantiated at compile time with any type from a class of types.

> Dynamic polymorphism is provided through the use of so-called class-wide types and the distinction is then made at runtime on the basis of the value of the tag ("effectively a hidden discriminant identifying the type" [Rationale 1995, §II.1]).

As stated in the Ada Reference Manual (1995, Annex N):

> A type has an associated set of values and a set of primitive operations that implement the fundamental aspects of its semantics.

> A class is a set of types that is closed under derivation, which means that if a given type is in the class, then all types derived from that type are also in the class. The set of types of a class share common properties, such as their primitive operations. The semantics of a class include expected behavior and exceptions.

> An object is either a constant or variable defined from a type (class). An object contains a value. A subcomponent of an object is itself an object.

Guidelines in this chapter are frequently worded "consider . . ." because hard and fast rules cannot apply in all situations. The specific choice you make in a given situation involves design tradeoffs. The rationale for these guidelines is intended to give you insight into some of these tradeoffs.

9.1   OBJECT-ORIENTED DESIGN

You will find it easier to take advantage of many of the concepts in this chapter if you have done an object-oriented design. The results of an object-oriented design would include a set of meaningful abstractions and hierarchy of classes. The abstractions need to include the definition of the design objects, including structure and state, the operations on the objects, and the intended encapsulation for each object. The details on designing these abstractions and the hierarchy of classes are beyond the scope of this book. A number of good sources exist for this detail, including Rumbaugh et al. (1991), Jacobson et al. (1992), Software Productivity Consortium (1993), and Booch (1994).

An important part of the design process is deciding on the overall organization of the system. Looking at a single type, a single package, or even a single class of types by itself is probably the wrong place to start. The appropriate level to start is more at the level of "subsystem" or "framework." You should use child packages (Guidelines 4.1.1 and 4.2.2) to group sets of abstractions into subsystems representing reusable frameworks. You should distinguish the "abstract" reusable core of the framework from the particular "instantiation" of the framework. Presuming the framework is constructed properly, the abstract core and its instantiation can be separated into distinct subsystems within the package hierarchy because the internals of an abstract reusable framework probably do not need to be visible to a particular instantiation of the framework.

9.2   TAGGED TYPE HIERARCHIES

You should use inheritance primarily as a mechanism for implementing a class hierarchy from an object-oriented design. A class hierarchy should be a generalization/specialization ("is-a") relationship. This relationship may also be referred to as "is-a-kind-of," not to be confused with "is an instance of." This "is-a" usage of inheritance is in contrast to other languages in which inheritance is used also to provide the equivalent of the Ada context clauses with and use. In Ada, you first identify the external modules of interest via with clauses and then choose selectively whether to make only the name of the module (package) visible or its contents (via a use clause).

9.2.1   Tagged Types

guideline

- Consider using type extension when designing an is-a (generalization/specialization) hierarchy.
- Use tagged types to preserve a common interface across differing implementations (Taft 1995a).
- When defining a tagged type in a package, consider including a definition of a general access type to the corresponding class-wide type.
- In general, define only one tagged type per package.

example

Consider the type structure for a set of two-dimensional geometric objects positioned in a Cartesian coordinate system (Barnes 1996). The ancestor or root type Object is a tagged record. The components common to this type and all its descendants are an x and y coordinate. Various descendant types include points, circles, and arbitrary shapes. Except for points, these descendant types extend the root type with additional components; for example, the circle adds a radius component:

```
type Object is tagged
   record
      X_Coord : Float;
      Y_Coord : Float;
   end record;

type Circle is new Object with
   record
      Radius : Float;
   end record;

type Point is new Object with null record;

type Shape is new Object with
   record
      -- other components
      ...
   end record;
```

The following is an example of general access type to the corresponding class-wide type:

```
package Employee is
   type Object is tagged limited private;
   type Reference is access all Object'class;
   ...
private
   ...
end Employee;
```

rationale

You can derive new types from both tagged and untagged types, but the effects of this derivation are different. When you derive from an untagged type, you are creating a new type whose implementation is identical to the parent. Values of the derived types are subject to strong type checking; thus, you cannot mix the proverbial apples and oranges. When you derive a new type from an untagged type, you are not allowed to extend it with new components. You are effectively creating a new interface without changing the underlying implementation (Taft 1995a).

In deriving from a tagged type, you can extend the type with new components. Each descendant can extend a common interface (the parent's). The union of a tagged type and its descendants form a class, and a class offers some unique features not available to untagged derivations. You can write class-wide operations that can be applied to any object that is a member of the class. You can also provide new implementations for the descendants of tagged types, either by overriding inherited primitive operations or by creating new primitive operations. Finally, tagged types can be used as the basis for multiple inheritance building blocks (see Guideline 9.5.1).

Reference semantics are very commonly used in object-oriented programming. In particular, heterogeneous polymorphic data structures based on tagged types require the use of access types. It is convenient to have a common definition for such a type provided to any client of the package defining the tagged type. A heterogeneous polymorphic data structure is a composite data structure (such as an array) whose elements have a homogeneous interface (i.e., an access to class-wide type) and whose elements' implementations are heterogeneous (i.e., the implementation of the elements uses different specific types). See also Guidelines 9.3.5 on polymorphism and 9.4.1 on managing visibility of tagged type hierarchies.

In Ada, the primitive operations of a type are implicitly associated with the type through scoping rules. The definition of a tagged type and a set of operations corresponds together to the "traditional" object-oriented programming concept of a "class." Putting these into a package provides a clean encapsulation mechanism.

exceptions

If the root of the hierarchy does not define a complete set of values and operations, then use an abstract tagged type (see Guideline 9.2.4). This abstract type can be thought of as the least common denominator of the class, essentially a conceptual and incomplete type.

If a descendant needs to remove one of the components or primitive operations of its ancestor, it may not be appropriate to extend the tagged type.

An exception to using reference semantics is when a type is exported that would not be used in a data structure or made part of a collection.

If the implementation of two tagged types requires mutual visibility and the two types are generally used together, then it may be best to define them together in one package, though thought should be given to using child packages instead (see Guideline 9.4.1). Also, it can be convenient to define a small hierarchy of (completely) abstract types (or a small part of a larger hierarchy) all in one package specification; however, the negative impact on maintainability may outweigh the convenience. You do not provide a package body in this situation unless you have declared nonabstract operations on members of the hierarchy.

9.2.2   Properties of Dispatching Operations

guideline

- The implementation of the dispatching operations of each type in a derivation class rooted in a tagged type T should conform to the expected semantics of the corresponding dispatching operations of the class-wide type T'Class.

example

The key point of both of the alternatives in the following example is that it must be possible to use the class-wide type `Transaction.Object'Class` polymorphically without having to study the implementations of each of the types derived from the root type `Transaction.Object`. In addition, new transactions can be added to the derivation class without invalidating the existing transaction processing code. These are the important practical consequences of the design rule captured in the guideline:

```
with Database;
package Transaction is

    type Object (Data : access Database.Object'Class) is abstract tagged limited
        record
            Has_Executed : Boolean := False;
        end record;

    function Is_Valid (T : Object) return Boolean;
    -- checks that Has_Executed is False

    procedure Execute (T : in out Object);
    -- sets Has_Executed to True

    Is_Not_Valid : exception;

end Transaction;
```

The precondition of `Execute(T)` for all `T` in `Transaction.Object'Class` is that `Is_Valid(T)` is `True`. The postcondition is the `T.Has_Executed = True`. This model is trivially satisfied by the root type `Transaction.Object`.

Consider the following derived type:

```
with Transaction;
with Personnel;
package Pay_Transaction is

    type Object is new Transaction.Object with
        record
            Employee     : Personnel.Name;
            Hours_Worked : Personnel.Time;
        end record;

    function Is_Valid (T : Object) return Boolean;
    -- checks that Employee is a valid name, Hours_Worked is a valid
    -- amount of work time and Has_Executed = False

    procedure Has_Executed (T : in out Object);
    -- computes the pay earned by the Employee for the given Hours_Worked
    -- and updates this in the database T.Data, then sets Has_Executed to True

end Pay_Transaction;
```

The precondition for the specific operation `Pay_Transaction.Execute(T)` is that `Pay_Transaction.Is_Valid(T)` is `True`, which is the same precondition as for the dispatching operation `Execute` on the class-wide type. (The actual validity check is different, but the statement of the "precondition" is the same.) The postcondition for `Pay_Transaction.Execute(T)` includes `T.Has_Executed = True` but also includes the appropriate condition on `T.Data` for computation of pay.

The class-wide transaction type can then be properly used as follows:

```
type Transaction_Reference is access all Transaction.Object'Class;
type Transaction_List is array (Positive range <>) of Transaction_Reference;
procedure Process (Action : in Transaction_List) is
begin

    for I in Action'Range loop
    -- Note that calls to Is_Valid and Execute are dispatching

        if Transaction.Is_Valid(Action(I).all) then
            -- the precondition for Execute is satisfied
            Transaction.Execute(Action(I).all);
            -- the postcondition Action(I).Has_Executed = True is
            -- guaranteed to be satisfied (as well as any stronger conditions
            -- depending on the specific value of Action(I))

        else
            -- deal with the error
            ...
        end if;
    end loop;
end Process;
```

If you had not defined the operation Is_Valid on transactions, then the validity condition for pay computation (valid name and hours worked) would have to directly become the precondition for Pay_Transaction.Execute. But this would be a "stronger" precondition than that on the class-wide dispatching operation, violating the guideline. As a result of this violation, there would be no way to guarantee the precondition of a dispatching call to Execute, leading to unexpected failures.

An alternative resolution to this problem is to define an exception to be raised by an Execute operation when the transaction is not valid. This behavior becomes part of the semantic model for the class-wide type: the precondition for Execute(T) becomes simply True (i.e., always valid), but the postcondition becomes "either" the exception is not raised and Has_Executed = True "or" the exception is raised and Has_Executed = False. The implementations of Execute in all derived transaction types would then need to satisfy the new postcondition. It is important that the "same" exception be raised by "all" implementations because this is part of the expected semantic model of the class-wide type.

With the alternative approach, the above processing loop becomes:

```
procedure Process (Action : in Transaction_List) is
begin

    for I in Action'Range loop

        Process_A_Transaction:
            begin

                -- there is no precondition for Execute
                Transaction.Execute (Action(I).all);
                -- since no exception was raised, the postcondition
                -- Action(I).Has_Executed = True is guaranteed (as well as
                -- any stronger condition depending on the specific value of
                -- Action(I))

            exception
                when Transaction.Is_Not_Valid =>
                    -- the exception was raised, so Action(I).Has_Executed = False

                    -- deal with the error
                    ...

            end Process_A_Transaction;

    end loop;

end Process;
```

rationale

All the properties expected of a class-wide type by clients of that type should be meaningful for any specific types in the derivation class of the class-wide type. This rule is related to the object-oriented programming "substitutability principle" for consistency between the semantics of an object-oriented superclass and its subclasses (Wegner and Zdonik 1988). However, the separation of the polymorphic class-wide type T'Class from the root specific type T in Ada 95 clarifies this principle as a design rule on derivation classes rather than a correctness principle for derivation itself.

When a dispatching operation is used on a variable of a class-wide type T'Class, the actual implementation executed will depend dynamically on the actual tag of the value in the variable. In order to rationally use T'Class, it must be possible to understand the semantics of the operations on T'Class without having to study the implementation of the operations for each of the types in the derivation class rooted in T. Further, a new type added to this derivation class should not invalidate this overall understanding of T'Class because this could invalidate existing uses of the class-wide type. Thus, there needs to be an overall set of semantic properties of the operations of T'Class that is preserved by the implementations of the corresponding dispatching operations of all the types in the derivation class.

One way to capture the semantic properties of an operation is to define a "precondition" that must be true before the operation is invoked and a "postcondition" that must be true (given the precondition) after the operation has executed. You can (formally or informally) define pre- and postconditions for each operation of T'Class without reference to the implementations of dispatching operations of specific types. These semantic properties define the "minimum" set of properties common to all types in the derivation class. To preserve this minimum set of properties, the implementation of the dispatching operations of all the types in the derivation class rooted in T (including the root type T) should have (the same or) weaker preconditions than the corresponding operations of T'Class and (the same or) stronger postconditions than the T'Class operations. This means that any invocation of a dispatching operation on T'Class will result in the execution of an implementation that requires no more than what is expected of the dispatching operation in general (though it could require less) and delivers a result that is no less than what is expected (though it could do more).

exceptions

Tagged types and type extension may sometimes be used primarily for type implementation reasons rather than for polymorphism and dispatching. In particular, a nontagged private type may be implemented using a type extension of a tagged type. In such cases, it may not be necessary for the implementation of the derived type to preserve the semantic properties of the class-wide type because the membership of the new type in the tagged type derivation class will not generally be known to clients of the type.

9.2.3   Controlled Types

guideline

- Consider using a controlled type whenever a type allocates resources that must be deallocated or otherwise "cleaned up" on destruction or overwriting.

- Use a derivation from a controlled type in preference to providing an explicit "cleanup" operation that must be called by clients of the type.

- When overriding the adjustment and finalization procedures derived from controlled types, define the finalization procedure to undo the effects of the adjustment procedure.

- Derived type initialization procedures should call the initialization procedure of their parent as part of their type-specific initialization.

- Derived type finalization procedures should call the finalization procedure of their parent as part of their type-specific finalization.

- Consider deriving a data structure's components rather than the enclosing data structure from a controlled type.

example

The following example demonstrates the use of controlled types in the implementation of a simple linked list. Because the Linked_List type is derived from Ada.Finalization.Controlled, the Finalize procedure will be called automatically when objects of the Linked_List type complete their scope of execution:

```
with Ada.Finalization;
package Linked_List_Package is
    type Iterator is private;
    type Data_Type is ...
    type Linked_List is new Ada.Finalization.Controlled with private;
    function Head (List : Linked_List) return Iterator;
    procedure Get_Next (Element  : in out Iterator;
                        Data     :     out Data_Type);
    procedure Add (List     : in out Linked_List;
                   New_Data : in      Data_Type);
    procedure Finalize (List : in out Linked_List); -- reset Linked_List structure
    -- Initialize and Adjust are left to the default implementation.
private
    type Node;
    type Node_Ptr is access Node;
    type Node is
        record
            Data . Data_Type;
            Next : Node_Ptr;
        end record;
    type Iterator is new Node_Ptr;
    type Linked_List is new Ada.Finalization.Controlled with
        record
            Number_Of_Items : Natural := 0;
            Root            : Node_Ptr;
        end record;
end Linked_List_Package;
```

```
package body Linked_List_Package is

    function Head (List : Linked_List) return Iterator is
        Head_Node_Ptr : Iterator;
    begin
        Head_Node_Ptr := Iterator (List.Root);
        return Head_Node_Ptr;   -- Return the head element of the list
    end Head;

    procedure Get_Next (Element : in out Iterator;
                        Data    :    out Data_Type) is
    begin
        --
        -- Given an element, return the next element (or null)
        --
    end Get_Next;

    procedure Add (List     : in out Linked_List;
                   New_Data : in     Data_Type) is
    begin
        --
        -- Add a new element to the head of the list
        --
    end Add;

    procedure Finalize (List : in out Linked_List) is
    begin
        -- Release all storage used by the linked list
        --    and reinitialize.
    end Finalize;

end Linked_List_Package;
```

rationale

The three controlling operations, Initialize, Adjust, and Finalize, serve as automatically called procedures that control three primitive activities in the life of an object (Ada Reference Manual 1995, §7.6). When an assignment to an object of a type derived from Controlled occurs, adjustment and finalization work in tandem. Finalization cleans up the object being overwritten (e.g., reclaims heap space), then adjustment finishes the assignment work once the value being assigned has been copied (e.g., to implement a deep copy).

You can ensure that the derived type's initialization is consistent with that of the parent by calling the parent type's initialization from the derived type's initialization.

You can ensure that the derived type's finalization is consistent with that of the parent by calling the parent type's finalization from the derived type's finalization.

In general, you should call parent initialization before descendant-specific initialization. Similarly, you should call parent finalization after descendant-specific finalization. (You may position the parent initialization and/or finalization at the beginning or end of the procedure.)

9.2.4   Abstract Types

guideline

- Consider using abstract types and operations in creating classification schemes, for example, a taxonomy, in which only the leaf objects will be meaningful in the application.

- Consider declaring root types and internal nodes in a type tree as abstract.

- Consider using abstract types for generic formal derived types.

- Consider using abstract types to develop different implementations of a single abstraction.

example

In a banking application, there are a wide variety of account types, each with different features and restrictions. Some of the variations are fees, overdraft protection, minimum balances, allowable account linkages (e.g., checking and savings), and rules on opening the account. Common to all bank accounts are ownership attributes: unique account number, owner name(s), and owner tax identification number(s). Common operations across all types of accounts are opening, depositing, withdrawing, providing current balance, and closing. The common attributes and operations describe the conceptual bank account. This idealized bank account can form the root of a generalization/specialization hierarchy that describes the bank's array of products. By using abstract tagged types, you ensure that only account objects corresponding to a specific product will be created. Because any abstract operations must be overridden with each derivation, you ensure that any restrictions for a specialized account are implemented (e.g., how and when the account-specific fee structure is applied):

```
---------------------------------------------------------------------------
package Bank_Account_Package is

    type Bank_Account_Type is abstract tagged limited private;
    type Money is delta 0.01 digits 15;

    -- The following abstract operations must be overridden for
    --   each derivation, thus ensuring that any restrictions
    --   for specialized accounts will be implemented.

    procedure Open (Account : in out Bank_Account_Type) is abstract;

    procedure Close (Account : in out Bank_Account_Type) is abstract;

    procedure Deposit (Account : in out Bank_Account_Type;
                       Amount  : in     Money) is abstract;

    procedure Withdraw (Account : in out Bank_Account_Type;
                        Amount  : in     Money) is abstract;

    function Balance (Account : Bank_Account_Type)
      return Money is abstract;

private
    type Account_Number_Type is ...
    type Account_Owner_Type  is ...
    type Tax_ID_Number_Type  is ...

    type Bank_Account_Type is abstract tagged limited
        record
            Account_Number : Account_Number_Type;
            Account_Owner  : Account_Owner_Type;
            Tax_ID_Number  : Tax_ID_Number_Type;
        end record;
end Bank_Account_Package;


---------------------------------------------------------------------------
-- Now, other specialized accounts such as a savings account can
-- be derived from Bank_Account_Type as in the following example.
-- Note that abstract types are still used to ensure that only
-- account objects corresponding to specific products will be
-- created.with Bank_Account_Package;
with Bank_Account_Package;
package Savings_Account_Package is
    type Savings_Account_Type is abstract
        new Bank_Account_Package.Bank_Account_Type with private;
    -- We must override the abstract operations provided
    --   by Bank_Account_Package.  Since we are still declaring
    --   these operations to be abstract, they must also be
    --   overridden by the specializations of Savings_Account_Type.
    procedure Open (Account : in out Savings_Account_Type) is abstract;
    procedure Close (Account : in out Savings_Account_Type) is abstract;

    procedure Deposit (Account : in out Savings_Account_Type;
                       Amount  : in     Bank_Account_Package.Money) is abstract;


    procedure Withdraw (Account : in out Savings_Account_Type;
                        Amount  : in     Bank_Account_Package.Money) is abstract;

    function Balance (Account : Savings_Account_Type)
      return Bank_Account_Package.Money is abstract;

private
    type Savings_Account_Type is abstract
        new Bank_Account_Package.Bank_Account_Type with
            record
                Minimum_Balance : Bank_Account_Package.Money;
            end record;
end Savings_Account_Package;


---------------------------------------------------------------------------
```

See the abstract set package in Guideline 9.5.1 for an example of creating an abstraction with a single interface and the potential for multiple implementations. The example only shows one possible implementation; however, you could provide an alternate implementation of the Hashed_Set abstraction using other data structures.

rationale

In many classification schemes, for example, a taxonomy, only objects at the leaves of the classification tree are meaningful in the application. In other words, the root of the hierarchy does not define a complete set of values and operations for use by the application. The use of "abstract" guarantees that there will be no objects of the root or intermediate nodes. Concrete derivations of the abstract types and subprograms are required so that the leaves of the tree become objects that a client can manipulate.

You can only declare abstract subprograms when the root type is also abstract. This is useful as you build an abstraction that forms the basis for a family of abstractions. By declaring the primitive subprograms to be abstract, you can write the "common class-wide parts of a system . . . without being dependent on the properties of any specific type at all" (Rationale 1995, §4.2).

Abstract types and operations can help you resolve problems when your tagged type hierarchy violates the expected semantics of the class-wide type dispatching operations. The Rationale (1995, §4.2) explains:

> When building an abstraction that is to form the basis of a class of types, it is often convenient not to provide actual subprograms for the root type but just abstract subprograms which can be replaced when inherited. This is only allowed if the root type is declared as abstract; objects of an abstract type cannot exist. This technique enables common class-wide parts of a system to be written without being dependent on the properties of any specific type at all. Dispatching always works because it is known that there can never be any objects of the abstract type and so the abstract subprograms could never be called.

See Guidelines 8.3.8 and 9.2.1.

The multiple inheritance techniques discussed in Guideline 9.5.1 make use of abstract tagged types. The basic abstraction is defined using an abstract tagged (limited) private type (whose full type declaration is a null record) with a small set of abstract primitive operations. While abstract operations have no bodies and thus cannot be called, they are inherited. Derivatives of the abstraction then extend the root type with components that provide the data representation and override the abstract operations to provide callable implementations (Rationale 1995, §4.4.3). This technique allows you to build multiple implementations of a single abstraction. You declare a single interface and vary the specifics of the data representation and operation implementation.

notes

When you use abstract data types as described in this guideline, you can have multiple implementations of the same abstraction available to you within a single program. This technique differs from the idea of writing multiple package bodies to provide different implementations of the abstraction defined in a package specification because with the package body technique, you can only include one of the implementations (i.e., bodies) in your program.

9.3   TAGGED TYPE OPERATIONS

You can use three options when you define the operations on a tagged type and its descendants. These categories are primitive abstract, primitive nonabstract, and class-wide operations. An abstract operation must be overridden for a nonabstract derived type. A nonabstract operation may be redefined for a subclass. A class-wide operation cannot be overridden by a subclass definition. A class-wide operation can be redefined for the derivation class rooted in the derived type; however, this practice is discouraged because of the ambiguities it introduces in the code.

Through careful usage of these options, you can ensure that your abstractions preserve class-wide properties, as discussed in Guideline 9.2.1. As stated above, this principle requires that any type that is visibly derived from some parent type must fully support the semantics of the parent type.

9.3.1 Primitive Operations and Redispatching

guideline

- Consider declaring a primitive abstract operation based on the absence of a meaningful "default" behavior.

- Consider declaring a primitive nonabstract operation based on the presence of a meaningful "default" behavior.

- When overriding an operation, the overriding subprogram should not raise exceptions that are not known to the users of the overridden subprogram.

- If redispatching is used in the implementation of the operations of a type, with the specific intent that some of the redispatched-to operations be overridden by specializations for the derived types, then document this intent clearly in the specification as part of the "interface" of a parent type with its derived types.

- When redispatching is used (for any reason) in the implementation of a primitive operation of a tagged type, then document (in some project-consistent way) this use in the body of the operation subprogram so that it can be easily found during maintenance.

example

This example (Volan 1994) is intended to show a clean derivation of a square from a rectangle. You do not want to derive `Square` from `Rectangle` because `Rectangle` has semantics that are inappropriate for `Square`. (For instance, you can make a rectangle with any arbitrary height and width, but you should not be able to make a square this way.) Instead, both `Square` and `Rectangle` should be derived from some common abstract type, such as:

```
Any_Rectangle:

type Figure is abstract tagged
   record
      ...
   end record;

type Any_Rectangle is abstract new Figure with private;
-- No Make function for this; it's abstract.
function Area (R: Any_Rectangle) return Float;
   -- Overrides abstract Area function inherited from Figure.
   -- Computes area as Width(R) * Height(R), which it will
   -- invoke via dispatching calls.
function Width (R: Any_Rectangle) return Float is abstract;
function Height (R: Any_Rectangle) return Float is abstract;

type Rectangle is new Any_Rectangle with private;
function Make_Rectangle (Width, Height: Float) return Rectangle;
function Width (R: Rectangle) return Float;
function Height (R: Rectangle) return Float;
-- Area for Rectangle inherited from Any_Rectangle

type Square is new Any_Rectangle with private;
function Make_Square (Side_Length: Float) return Square;
function Side_Length (S: Square) return Float;
function Width (S: Square) return Float;
function Height (S: Square) return Float;
-- Area for Square inherited from Any_Rectangle

   ...

-- In the body, you could just implement Width and Height for
-- Square as renamings of Side_Length:
function Width (S: Square) return Float renames Side_Length;
function Height (S: Square) return Float renames Side_Length;

function Area (R: Any_Rectangle) return Float is
begin
   return Width(Any_Rectangle'Class(R)) * Height(Any_Rectangle'Class(R));
   -- Casting [sic, i.e., converting] to the class-wide type causes the function calls to
   -- dynamically dispatch on the 'Tag of R.
   -- [sic, i.e., redispatch on the tag of R.]
end Area;
```

Alternatively, you could just wait until defining types `Rectangle` and `Square` to provide actual `Area` functions:

```
type Any_Rectangle is abstract new Figure with private;
-- Inherits abstract Area function from Figure,
-- but that's okay, Any_Rectangle is abstract too.
function Width (R: Any_Rectangle) return Float is abstract;
function Height (R: Any_Rectangle) return Float is abstract;

type Rectangle is new Any_Rectangle with private;
function Make_Rectangle (Width, Height: Float) return Rectangle;
function Width (R: Rectangle) return Float;
function Height (R: Rectangle) return Float;
function Area (R: Rectangle) return Float; -- Overrides Area from Figure

type Square is new Any_Rectangle with private;
function Make_Square (Side_Length: Float) return Square;
function Side_Length (S: Square) return Float;
function Width (S: Square) return Float;
function Height (S: Square) return Float;
function Area (S: Square) return Float;  -- Overrides Area from Figure
...

function Area (R: Rectangle) return Float is
begin
   return Width(R) * Height(R); -- Non-dispatching calls
end Area;

function Area (S: Square) return Float is
begin
   return Side_Length(S) ** 2;
end Area;
```

rationale

The behavior of a nonabstract operation can be interpreted as the expected behavior for all members of the class; therefore, the behavior must be a meaningful default for all descendants. If the operation must be tailored based on the descendant abstraction (e.g., computing the area of a geometric shape depends on the specific shape), then the operation should be primitive and possibly abstract. The effect of making the operation abstract is that it guarantees that each descendant must define its own version of the operation. Thus, when there is no acceptable basic behavior, an abstract operation is appropriate because a new version of the operation must be provided with each derivation.

All operations declared in the same package as the tagged type and following the tagged type's declaration but before the next type declaration are considered its primitive operations. Therefore, when a new type is derived from the tagged type, it inherits the primitive operations. If there are any operations that you do not want to be inherited, you must choose whether to declare them as class-wide operations (see Guideline 9.3.2) or to declare them in a separate package (e.g., a child package).

Exceptions are part of the semantics of the class. By modifying the exceptions, you are violating the semantic properties of the class-wide type (see Guideline 9.2.1).

There are (at least) two distinct users of a tagged type and its primitives. The "ordinary" user uses the type and its primitives without enhancement. The "extending" user extends the type by deriving a type based on the existing (tagged) type. Extending users and maintainers must determine the ramifications of a possibly incorrect extension. The guidelines here try to strike a balance between too much documentation (that can then easily get out of synch with the actual code) and an appropriate level of documentation to enhance the maintainability of the code.

One of the major maintenance headaches associated with inheritance and dynamic binding relates to undocumented interdependencies among primitive (dispatching) operations of tagged types (the equivalent of "methods" in typical object-oriented terminology). If a derived type inherits some and overrides other primitive operations, there is the question of what indirect effects on the inherited primitives are produced. If no redispatching is used, the primitives may be inherited as "black boxes." If redispatching is used internally, then when inherited, the externally visible behavior of an operation may change, depending on what other primitives are overridden. Maintenance problems (here, finding and fixing bugs) occur when someone overrides incorrectly (on purpose or by accident) an operation used in redispatching. Because this overriding can invalidate the functioning of another operation defined perhaps several levels of inheritance up from the incorrect operation, it can be extremely difficult to track down.

In the object-oriented paradigm, redispatching is often used to parameterize abstractions. In other words, certain primitives are intended to be overridden precisely because they are redispatching. These primitives may even be declared as abstract, requiring that they be overridden. Because they are redispatching, they act as "parameters" for the other operations. Although in Ada much of this parameterization can be done using generics, there are cases where the redispatching approach leads to a clearer object-oriented design. When you document the redispatching connection between the operations that are to be overridden and the operations that use them, you make the intended use of the type much clearer.

Hence, any use of redispatching within a primitive should be considered part of the "interface" of the primitive, at least as far as any inheritor, and requires documentation at the specification level. The alternative (i.e., not providing such documentation in the specification) is to have to delve deep into the code of all the classes in the derivation hierarchy in order to map out the redispatching calls. Such detective work compromises the black-box nature of object-oriented class definitions. Note that if you follow Guideline 9.2.1 on preserving the semantics of the class-wide dispatching operations in the extensions of derived types, you will minimize or avoid the problems discussed here about redispatching.

9.3.2   Class-Wide Operations

guideline

- Consider using a class-wide operation (i.e., an operation with parameter[s] of a class-wide type) when an operation can be written, compiled, and tested without knowing all the possible descendants of a given tagged type (Barnes 1996).

- Consider using a class-wide operation when you do not want an operation to be inherited and/or overridden.

example

The following example is adapted from Barnes (1996) using the geometric objects from the example of Guideline 9.2.1 and declaring the following functions as primitives in the package specification:

```
function Area (O : in Object) return Float;

function Area (C : in Circle) return Float;

function Area (S : in Shape) return Float;
```

A function for computing the moment of a force about a fulcrum can now be created using a class-wide type as follows:

```
function Moment (OC : Object'Class) return Float is
begin
   return OC.X_Coord*Area(OC);
end Moment;
```

Because Moment accepts the class-wide formal parameter of Object'Class, it can be called with an actual parameter that is any derivation of type Object. Assuming that all derivations of type object have defined a function for Area, Moment will dispatch to the appropriate function when called. For example:

```
C : Circle;
M : Float;

...

-- Moment will dispatch to the Area function for the Circle type.
M := Moment(C);
```

rationale

The use of class-wide operations avoids unnecessary duplication of code. Run-time dispatching may be used where necessary to invoke appropriate type-specific operations based on an operand's tag.

See also Guideline 8.4.3 for a discussion of class-wide pointers in an object-oriented programming framework registry.

9.3.3   Constructors

Ada does not define a unique syntax for constructors. In Ada a constructor for a type is defined as an operation that produces as a result a constructed object, i.e., an initialized instance of the type.

guideline

- Avoid declaring a constructor as a primitive abstract operation.
- Use a primitive abstract operation to declare an initialization function or constructor only when objects of the inheriting derived types will not require additional parameters for initialization.
- Consider using access discriminants to provide parameters to default initialization.
- Use constructors for explicit initialization.
- Consider splitting the initialization and construction of an object.
- Consider declaring a constructor operation in a child package.
- Consider declaring a constructor operation to return an access value to the constructed object (Dewar 1995).

example

The following example illustrates the declaration of a constructor in a child package:

```
-------------------------------------------------------------------------
package Game is
   type Game_Piece is tagged ...
   ...

end Game;
-------------------------------------------------------------------------
package Game.Constructors is
   function Make_Piece return Game_Piece;
   ...
end Game.Constructors;
-------------------------------------------------------------------------
```

The following example shows how to split the initialization and construction of an object:

```
type Vehicle is tagged ...

procedure Initialize (Self : in out Vehicle;
                      Make : in     String);

...


type Car is new Vehicle with ... ;
type Car_Ptr is access all Car'Class;

...


procedure Initialize (Self  : in out Car_Ptr;
                      Make  : in     String;
                      Model : in     String) is
begin -- Initialize
   Initialize (Vehicle (Self.all), Make);
   ...
   -- initialization of Car
end Initialize;

function Create (Make  : in String;
                 Model : in String) return Car_Ptr is
   Temp_Ptr : Car_Ptr;
begin -- Create
   Temp_Ptr := new Car;
   Initialize (Temp_Ptr, Make, Model);
   return Temp_Ptr;
end Create;
```

rationale

Constructor operations for the types in a type hierarchy (assuming tagged types and their derivatives) usually differ in their parameter profiles. The constructor will typically need more parameters because of the added components in the descendant types. You run into a problem when you let constructor operations be inherited because you now have operations for which there is no meaningful implementation (default or overridden). Effectively, you violate the class-wide properties (see Guideline 9.2.1) because the root constructor will not successfully construct a descendant object. Inherited operations cannot add parameters to their parameter profile, so these are inappropriate to use as constructors.

214 Ada 95 QUALITY AND STYLE

You cannot initialize a limited type at its declaration, so you may need to use an access discriminant and rely on default initialization. For a tagged type, however, you should not assume that any default initialization is sufficient, and you should declare constructors. For limited types, the constructors must be separate procedures or functions that return an access to the limited type.

The example shows using a constructor in a child package. By declaring constructor operations in either a child package or a nested package, you avoid the problems associated with making them primitive operations. Because they are no longer primitive operations, they cannot be inherited. By declaring them in a child package (see also Guidelines 4.1.6 and 4.2.2 on using child packages versus nested packages), you gain the ability to change them without affecting the clients of the parent package (Taft 1995b).

You should put the construction logic and initialization logic in distinct subprograms so that you are able to call the initialization routine for the parent tagged type.

notes

When you extend a tagged type (regardless whether it is an abstract type), you can choose to declare as abstract some of the additional operations. Doing so, however, means that the derived type must also be declared as abstract. If this newly derived type has inherited any functions that name it as the return type, these inherited functions now also become abstract (Barnes 1996). If one of these primitive functions served as the constructor function, you have now violated the first guideline in that the constructor has become a primitive abstract operation.

9.3.4   Equality

guideline

• When you redefine the "=" operator on a tagged type, make sure that it has the expected behavior in extensions of this type and override it if necessary.

example

The following example is adapted from the discussion of equality and inheritance in Barnes (1996):

```
--------------------------------------------------------------------------
package Object_Package is

    Epsilon : constant Float := 0.01;

    type Object is tagged
        record
            X_Coordinate : Float;
            Y_Coordinate : Float;
        end record;

    function "=" (A, B : Object) return Boolean;

end Object_Package;

--------------------------------------------------------------------------
package body Object_Package is

    -- redefine equality to be when two objects are located within a delta
    -- of the same point
    function "=" (A, B : Object) return Boolean is
    begin
        return (A.X_Coordinate - B.X_Coordinate) ** 2
               + (A.Y_Coordinate - B.Y_Coordinate) ** 2 < Epsilon**2;
    end "=";

end Object_Package;

--------------------------------------------------------------------------

with Object_Package;  use Object_Package;
package Circle_Package_1 is
    type Circle is new Object with
        record
            Radius : Float;
        end record;
    function "=" (A, B : Circle) return Boolean;
end Circle_Package_1;
--------------------------------------------------------------------------
```

```
package body Circle_Package_1 is

    -- Equality is overridden, otherwise two circles must have exactly
    -- equal radii to be considered equal.
    function "=" (A, B : Circle) return Boolean is
    begin
        return (Object(A) = Object(B)) and
               (abs (A.Radius - B.Radius) < Epsilon);
    end "=";

end Circle_Package_1;
----------------------------------------------------------------------------
with Object_Package;  use Object_Package;
package Circle_Package_2 is

    type Circle is new Object with
        record
            Radius : Float;
        end record;

    -- don't override equality in this package

end Circle_Package_2;
----------------------------------------------------------------------------
with Object_Package;
with Circle_Package_1;
with Circle_Package_2;
with Ada.Text_IO;
procedure Equality_Test is

    use type Object_Package.Object;
    use type Circle_Package_1.Circle;
    use type Circle_Package_2.Circle;

    Object_1 : Object_Package.Object;
    Object_2 : Object_Package.Object;

    Circle_1 : Circle_Package_1.Circle;
    Circle_2 : Circle_Package_1.Circle;

    Circle_3 : Circle_Package_2.Circle;
    Circle_4 : Circle_Package_2.Circle;

begin
    Object_1 := (X_Coordinate => 1.000, Y_Coordinate => 2.000);
    Object_2 := (X_Coordinate => 1.005, Y_Coordinate => 2.000);
    -- These Objects are considered equal.  Equality has been redefined to be
    -- when two objects are located within a delta of the same point.
    if Object_1 = Object_2 then
        Ada.Text_IO.Put_Line ("Objects equal.");
    else
        Ada.Text_IO.Put_Line ("Objects not equal.");
    end if;
    Circle_1 := (X_Coordinate => 1.000, Y_Coordinate => 2.000, Radius => 5.000);
    Circle_2 := (X_Coordinate => 1.005, Y_Coordinate => 2.000, Radius => 5.005);
    -- These Circles are considered equal.  Equality has been redefined to be
    -- when the X-Y locations of the circles and their radii are both within
    -- the delta.
    if Circle_1 = Circle_2 then
        Ada.Text_IO.Put_Line ("Circles equal.");
    else
        Ada.Text_IO.Put_Line ("Circles not equal.");
    end if;
    Circle_3 := (X_Coordinate => 1.000, Y_Coordinate => 2.000, Radius => 5.000);
    Circle_4 := (X_Coordinate => 1.005, Y_Coordinate => 2.000, Radius => 5.005);
    -- These Circles are not considered equal because predefined equality of
    -- the extension component Radius will evaluate to False.
    if Circle_3 = Circle_4 then
        Ada.Text_IO.Put_Line ("Circles equal.");
    else
        Ada.Text_IO.Put_Line ("Circles not equal.");
    end if;
end Equality_Test;
```

rationale

Equality is applied to all components of a record. When you extend a tagged type and compare two objects of the derived type for equality, the parent components as well as the new extension components will be compared. Therefore, when you redefine equality on a tagged type and define extensions on this type, the parent components are compared using the redefined equality. The extension components are also compared, using either predefined equality or some other redefined equality if appropriate. The behavior of inherited equality differs from the behavior of other inherited operations. When other primitives are inherited, if you do not override the inherited primitive, it can only operate on the parent components of the object of the extended type. Equality, on the other hand, generally does the right thing.

9.3.5   Polymorphism

guideline

- Consider using class-wide programming to provide run-time, dynamic polymorphism when constructing larger, reusable, extensible frameworks.

- When possible, use class-wide programming rather than variant records.

- Use class-wide programming to provide a consistent interface across the set of types in the tagged type hierarchy (i.e., class).

- Consider using generics to define a new type in terms of an existing type, either as an extension or as a container, collection, or composite data structure.

- Avoid using type extensions for parameterized abstractions when generics provide a more appropriate mechanism.

example

```
generic
   type Element is private;
package Stack is
   ...
end Stack;
```

is preferable to:

```
package Stack is
   type Element is tagged null record;
   -- Elements to be put on the stack must be of a descendant type
   -- of this type.
   ...
end Stack;
```

rationale

Both generics and class-wide types allow a single algorithm to be applicable to multiple, specific types. With generics, you achieve polymorphism across unrelated types because the type used in the instantiation must match the generic formal part. You specify required operations using generic formal subprograms, constructing them as needed for a given instantiation. Generics are ideal for capturing relatively small, reusable algorithms and programming idioms, for example, sorting algorithms, maps, bags, and iterators. As generics become large, however, they become unwieldy, and each instantiation may involve additional generated code. Class-wide programming, including class-wide types and type extension, is more appropriate for building a large subsystem because you avoid the additional generated code and unwieldy properties of generics.

Class-wide programming enables you to take a set of heterogeneous data structures and provide a homogeneous-looking interface across the whole set. See also Guideline 9.2.1 on using tagged types to describe heterogeneous polymorphic data.

In object-oriented programming languages without generic capabilities, it was common to use inheritance to achieve much the same effect. However, this technique is generally less clear and more cumbersome to use than the equivalent explicit generic definition. The nongeneric, inheritance approach can always be recovered using a specific instantiation of the generic. Also see Guidelines 5.3.2 and 5.4.7 for a discussion of self-referential data structures.

9.4 MANAGING VISIBILITY

9.4.1 Derived Tagged Types

guideline

- Consider giving derived tagged types the same visibility to the parent type as other clients of the parent.

- Define a derived tagged type in a child of the package that defines the base type if the implementation of the derived type requires greater visibility into the implementation of the base type than other clients of the base type require.

example

The following example illustrates the need for a derived type to have greater visibility into the implementation of the base type than other clients of the base type. In this example of a stack class hierarchy, Push and Pop routines provide a homogeneous interface for all variations of stacks. However, the implementation of these operations requires greater visibility into the base types due to the differences in the data elements. This example is adapted from Barbey, Kempe, and Strohmeier (1994):

```
generic
   type Item_Type is private;
package Generic_Stack is

   type Abstract_Stack_Type is abstract tagged limited private;

   procedure Push (Stack : in out Abstract_Stack_Type;
                   Item  : in      Item_Type) is abstract;

   procedure Pop (Stack : in out Abstract_Stack_Type;
                  Item  :     out Item_Type) is abstract;

   function Size (Stack : Abstract_Stack_Type) return Natural;

   Full_Error  : exception; -- May be raised by Push
   Empty_Error : exception; -- May be raised by Pop

private

   type Abstract_Stack_Type is abstract tagged limited
      record
         Size : Natural := 0;
      end record;

end Generic_Stack;

package body Generic_Stack is

   function Size (Stack : Abstract_Stack_Type)
      return Natural is
   begin
      return Stack.Size;
   end Size;

end Generic_Stack;

--
-- Now, a bounded stack can be derived in a child package as follows:
--
----------------------------------------------------------------------

generic
package Generic_Stack.Generic_Bounded_Stack is

   type Stack_Type (Max : Positive) is
      new Abstract_Stack_Type with private;

   -- override all abstract subprograms

   procedure Push (Stack : in out Stack_Type;
                   Item  : in      Item_Type);

   procedure Pop (Stack : in out Stack_Type;
                  Item  :     out Item_Type);

private

   type Table_Type is array (Positive range <>) of Item_Type;

   type Stack_Type (Max : Positive) is new Abstract_Stack_Type with
      record
         Table : Table_Type (1 .. Max);
      end record;

end Generic_Stack.Generic_Bounded_Stack;
----------------------------------------------------------------------
```

```
package body Generic_Stack.Generic_Bounded_Stack is

    procedure Push (Stack : in out Stack_Type;
                    Item  : in     Item_Type) is
    begin

        -- The new bounded stack needs visibility into the base type
        --    in order to update the Size element of the stack type
        --    when adding or removing items.

        if (Stack.Size = Stack.Max) then
            raise Full_Error;
        else
            Stack.Size := Stack.Size + 1;
            Stack.Table(Stack.Size) := Item;
        end if;
    end Push;

    procedure Pop (Stack : in out Stack_Type;
                   Item  :    out Item_Type) is
    begin
        ...
    end Pop;

end Generic_Stack.Generic_Bounded_Stack;
```

rationale

If the derived type can be defined without any special visibility of the base type, this provides for the best possible decoupling of the implementation of the derived type from changes in the implementation of the base type. On the other hand, the operations of an extension of a tagged type may need additional information from the base type that is not commonly needed by other clients.

When the implementation of a derived tagged type requires visibility of the implementation of the base type, use a child package to define the derived type. Rather than providing additional public operations for this information, it is better to place the definition of the derived type in a child package. This gives the derived type the necessary visibility without risking misuse by other clients.

This situation is likely to arise when you build a data structure with a homogeneous interface but whose data elements have a heterogeneous implementation. See also Guidelines 8.4.8, 9.2.1, and 9.3.5.

9.5   MULTIPLE INHERITANCE

Ada provides several mechanisms to support multiple inheritance, where multiple inheritance is a means for incrementally building new abstractions from existing ones, as defined at the beginning of this chapter. Specifically, Ada supports multiple inheritance module inclusion (via multiple with/use clauses), multiple inheritance "is-implemented-using" via private extensions and record composition, and multiple inheritance mixins via the use of generics, formal packages, and access discriminants (Taft 1994).

9.5.1   Multiple Inheritance Techniques

guideline

- Consider using type composition for implementation, as opposed to interface, inheritance.
- Consider using a generic to "mix in" functionality to a derivative of some core abstraction.
- Consider using access discriminants to support "full" multiple inheritance where an object must be referenceable as an entity of two or more distinct unrelated abstractions.

example

Both examples that follow are taken directly from Taft (1994). The first shows how to use multiple inheritance techniques to create an abstract type whose interface inherits from one type and whose implementation inherits from another type. The second example shows how to enhance the functionality of a basic abstraction by mixing in new features.

The abstract type set_of_strings provides the interface to inherit:

```
type Set_Of_Strings is abstract tagged limited private;
type Element_Index is new Natural;  -- Index within set.

No_Element : constant Element_Index := 0;

Invalid_Index : exception;

procedure Enter(
   -- Enter an element into the set, return the index
   Set : in out Set_Of_Strings;
   S : String;
   Index : out Element_Index) is abstract;

procedure Remove(
   -- Remove an element from the set; ignore if not there
   Set : in out Set_Of_Strings;
   S : String) is abstract;

procedure Combine(
   -- Combine Additional_Set into Union_Set
   Union_Set : in out Set_Of_Strings;
   Additional_Set : Set_Of_Strings) is abstract;

procedure Intersect(
   -- Remove all elements of Removal_Set from Intersection_Set
   Intersection_Set : in out Set_Of_Strings;
   Removal_Set : Set_Of_Strings) is abstract;

function Size(Set : Set_Of_Strings) return Element_Index
   is abstract;
   -- Return a count of the number of elements in the set

function Index(
   -- Return the index of a given element;
   -- return No_Element if not there.
   Set : Set_Of_Strings;
   S : String) return Element_Index is abstract;

function Element(Index : Element_Index) return String is abstract;
   -- Return element at given index position
   -- raise Invalid_Index if no element there.
private
   type Set_Of_Strings is abstract tagged limited ...
```

The type Hashed_Set derives its interface from Set_of_Strings and its implementation from an existing (concrete) type Hash_Table:

```
type Hashed_Set(Table_Size : Positive) is
   new Set_Of_Strings with private;

-- Now we give the specs of the operations being implemented
procedure Enter(
   -- Enter an element into the set, return the index
   Set : in out Hashed_Set;
   S : String;
   Index : out Element_Index);

procedure Remove(
   -- Remove an element from the set; ignore if not there
   Set : in out Hashed_Set;
   S : String);
   -- . . . etc.

private
   type Hashed_Set(Table_Size : Positive) is
      new Set_Of_Strings with record
         Table : Hash_Table(1..Table_Size);
      end record;
```

In the package body, you define the bodies of the operations (i.e., Enter, Remove, Combine, Size, etc.) using the operations available on Hash_Table. You must also provide any necessary "glue" code.

In this second example, the type Basic_Window responds to various events and calls:

```
type Basic_Window is tagged limited private;
procedure Display(W : Basic_Window);
procedure Mouse_Click(W        : in out Basic_Window;
                      Where :        Mouse_Coords);
   . . .
```

You use mixins to add features such as labels, borders, menu bar, etc:

```
generic
  type Some_Window is new Window with private;
  -- take in any descendant of Window
package Label_Mixin is
  type Window_With_Label is new Some_Window with private;
    -- Jazz it up somehow.

  -- Overridden operations:
  procedure Display(W : Window_With_Label);

  -- New operations:
  procedure Set_Label(W : in out Window_With_Label; S : String);
    -- Set the label
  function Label(W : Window_With_Label) return String;
    -- Fetch the label
private
  type Window_With_Label is
    new Some_Window with record
      Label : String_Quark := Null_Quark;
        -- An XWindows-Like unique ID for a string
    end record;
```

In the generic body, you implement any overridden operations as well as the new operations. For example, you could implement the overridden Display operation using some of the inherited operations:

```
procedure Display(W : Window_With_Label) is
begin
    Display(Some_Window(W));
      -- First display the window normally,
      -- by passing the buck to the parent type.

    if W.Label /= Null_Quark then
      -- Now display the label if it is not null
        Display_On_Screen(XCoord(W), YCoord(W)-5, Value(W.Label));
          -- Use two inherited functions on Basic_Window
          -- to get the coordinates where to display the label.
    end if;
end Display;
```

Assuming you have defined several generics with these additional features, to create the desired window, you use a combination of generic instantiations and private type extension, as shown in the following code:

```
type My_Window is new Basic_Window with private;
. . .
private
  package Add_Label is new Label_Mixin(Basic_Window);
  package Add_Border is
    new Border_Mixin(Add_Label.Window_With_Label);
  package Add_Menu_Bar is
    new Menu_Bar_Mixin(Add_Border.Window_With_Border);

  type My_Window is
    new Add_Menu_Bar.Window_With_Menu_Bar with null record;
      -- Final window is a null extension of Window_With_Menu_Bar.
      -- We could instead make a record extension and
      -- add components for My_Window over and above those
      -- needed by the mixins.
```

The following example shows "full" multiple inheritance.

Assume previous definition of packages for Savings_Account and Checking_Account. The following example shows the definition of an interest-bearing checking account (NOW account):

```
with Savings_Account;
with Checking_Account;
package NOW_Account is

    type Object is tagged limited private;

    type Savings (Self : access Object'Class) is
      new Savings_Account.Object with null record;

    -- These need to be overridden to call through to "Self"
    procedure Deposit (Into_Account : in out Savings; ...);
    procedure Withdraw (...);
    procedure Earn_Interest (...);
    function Interest (...) return Float;
    function Balance (...) return Float;
```

```
    type Checking (Self : access Object'Class) is
        new Checking_Account.Object with null record;

    procedure Deposit (Into_Account : in out Checking; ...);
    ...
    function Balance (...) return Float;

    -- These operations will call-through to Savings_Account or
    -- Checking_Account operations. "Inherits" in this way all savings and
    -- checking operations

    procedure Deposit (Into_Account : in out Object; ...);
    ...
    procedure Earn_Interest (...);
    ...
    function Balance (...) return Float;

private

    -- Could alternatively have Object be derived from either
    -- Savings_Account.Object or Checking_Account.Object
    type Object is tagged
        record
            As_Savings  : Savings (Object'Access);
            As_Checking : Checking (Object'Access);
        end record;

end NOW_Account;
```

Another possibility is that the savings and checking accounts are both implemented based on a common Account abstraction, resulting in inheriting a Balance state twice for NOW_Account.Object. To resolve this ambiguity, you need to use an abstract type hierarchy for the multiple inheritance of interface and separate mixins for the multiple inheritance of implementation.

rationale

In other languages such as Eiffel and C++, multiple inheritance serves many purposes. In Eiffel, for instance, you must use inheritance both for module inclusion and for inheritance itself (Taft 1994). Ada provides context clauses for module inclusion and child libraries for finer modularization control. Ada does not provide a separate syntax for multiple inheritance. Rather, it provides a set of building blocks in type extension and composition that allow you to mix in additional behaviors.

A library of mixins allows the client to mix and match in order to develop an implementation. Also see Guideline 8.3.8 about implementing mixins.

You should not use multiple inheritance to derive an abstraction that is essentially unrelated to its parent(s). Thus, you should not try to derive a menu abstraction by inheriting from a command line type and a window type. However, if you have a basic abstraction such as a window, you can use multiple inheritance mixins to create a more sophisticated abstraction, where a mixin is the package containing the type(s) and operations that will extend the parent abstraction.

Use self-referential data structures to implement types with "full" multiple inheritance ("multiple polymorphism").

A common mistake is to use multiple inheritance for parts-of relations. When a type is composed of several others types, you should use heterogeneous data structuring techniques, discussed in Guideline 5.4.2.

9.6   SUMMARY

tagged type hierarchies

- Consider using type extension when designing an is-a (generalization/specialization) hierarchy.
- Use tagged types to preserve a common interface across differing implementations (Taft 1995a).
- When defining a tagged type in a package, consider including a definition of a general access type to the corresponding class-wide type.
- In general, define only one tagged type per package.

- The implementation of the dispatching operations of each type in a derivation class rooted in a tagged type T should conform to the expected semantics of the corresponding dispatching operations of the class-wide type T'Class.

- Consider using a controlled type whenever a type allocates resources that must be deallocated or otherwise "cleaned up" on destruction or overwriting.

- Use a derivation from a controlled type in preference to providing an explicit "cleanup" operation that must be called by clients of the type.

- When overriding the adjustment and finalization procedures derived from controlled types, define the finalization procedure to undo the effects of the adjustment procedure.

- Derived type initialization procedures should call the initialization procedure of their parent as part of their type-specific initialization.

- Derived type finalization procedures should call the finalization procedure of their parent as part of their type-specific finalization.

- Consider deriving a data structure's components rather than the enclosing data structure from a controlled type.

- Consider using abstract types and operations in creating classification schemes, for example, a taxonomy, in which only the leaf objects will be meaningful in the application.

- Consider declaring root types and internal nodes in a type tree as abstract.

- Consider using abstract types for generic formal derived types.

- Consider using abstract types to develop different implementations of a single abstraction.

tagged type operations

- Consider declaring a primitive abstract operation based on the absence of a meaningful "default" behavior.

- Consider declaring a primitive nonabstract operation based on the presence of a meaningful "default" behavior.

- When overriding an operation, the overriding subprogram should not raise exceptions that are not known to the users of the overridden subprogram.

- If redispatching is used in the implementation of the operations of a type, with the specific intent that some of the redispatched-to operations be overridden by specializations for the derived types, then document this intent clearly in the specification as part of the "interface" of a parent type with its derived types.

- When redispatching is used (for any reason) in the implementation of a primitive operation of a tagged type, then document (in some project-consistent way) this use in the body of the operation subprogram so that it can be easily found during maintenance.

- Consider using a class-wide operation (i.e., an operation with parameter[s] of a class-wide type) when an operation can be written, compiled, and tested without knowing all the possible descendants of a given tagged type (Barnes 1996).

- Consider using a class-wide operation when you do not want an operation to be inherited and/or overridden.

- Avoid declaring a constructor as a primitive abstract operation.

- Use a primitive abstract operation to declare an initialization function or constructor only when objects of the inheriting derived types will not require additional parameters for initialization.

- Consider using access discriminants to provide parameters to default initialization.

- Use constructors for explicit initialization.

- Consider splitting the initialization and construction of an object.

- Consider declaring a constructor operation in a child package.

- Consider declaring a constructor operation to return an access value to the constructed object (Dewar 1995).

- When you redefine the "=" operator on a tagged type, make sure that it has the expected behavior in extensions of this type and override it if necessary.

- Consider using class-wide programming to provide run-time, dynamic polymorphism when constructing larger, reusable, extensible frameworks.

- When possible, use class-wide programming rather than variant records.

- Use class-wide programming to provide a consistent interface across the set of types in the tagged type hierarchy (i.e., class).

- Consider using generics to define a new type in terms of an existing type, either as an extension or as a container, collection, or composite data structure.

- Avoid using type extensions for parameterized abstractions when generics provide a more appropriate mechanism.

managing visibility

- Consider giving derived tagged types the same visibility to the parent type as other clients of the parent.

- Define a derived tagged type in a child of the package that defines the base type if the implementation of the derived type requires greater visibility into the implementation of the base type than other clients of the base type require.

multiple inheritance

- Consider using type composition for implementation, as opposed to interface, inheritance.

- Consider using a generic to "mix in" functionality to a derivative of some core abstraction.

- Consider using access discriminants to support "full" multiple inheritance where an object must be referenceable as an entity of two or more distinct unrelated abstractions.

CHAPTER 10
Improving Performance

In many ways, performance is at odds with maintainability and portability. To achieve improved speed or memory usage, the most clear algorithm sometimes gives way to confusing code. To exploit special purpose hardware or operating system services, nonportable implementation dependencies are introduced. When concerned about performance, you must decide how well each algorithm meets its performance and maintainability goals. Use the guidelines in this chapter with care; they may be hazardous to your software.

The best way to build a system that satisfies its performance requirements is through good design. You should not assume that speeding up your code will result in a visible increase in system execution. In most applications, the overall throughput of the system is not defined by the execution speed of the code but by the interaction between concurrent processes and the response time of the system peripherals.

Most of the guidelines in this chapter read ". . . when measured performance indicates." "Indicates" means that you have determined that the benefit in increased performance to your application in your environment outweighs the negative side effects on understandability, maintainability, and portability of the resulting code. Many of the guideline examples show the alternatives that you will need to measure in order to determine if the guideline is indicated.

10.1   PERFORMANCE ISSUES

Performance has at least four aspects: execution speed, code size, compilation speed, and linking speed. Although all four are important, most people think of execution speed when performance is mentioned, and most of the guidelines in this chapter focus on execution speed.

Performance is influenced by many factors, including the compilation software, hardware, system load, and coding style. While only coding style is typically under the control of the programmer, the other factors have so much influence that it is impossible to make flat statements such as "case statements are more efficient than if-then-else structures." When performance is critical, you cannot assume that a coding style that proves more efficient on one system will also be more efficient on another. *Decisions made for the sake of performance must be made on the basis of testing the alternatives on the actual system on which the application will be fielded.*

10.2   PERFORMANCE MEASUREMENT

While most well-known tools for measuring performance are stand-alone programs that concentrate on execution speed, there is a comprehensive tool that covers all four aspects of performance. The Ada Compiler Evaluation System (ACES) is the result of merging two earlier products: the United States Department of Defense's Ada Compiler Evaluation Capability and the United Kingdom Ministry of Defence's Ada Evaluation System. It offers a comprehensive set of nearly 2,000 performance tests along with automated setup, test management, and analysis software. This system reports (and statistically analyzes) compilation time, linking time, execution time, and code size. The analysis tools make comparisons among multiple compilation-execution systems and also provide comparisons of the run-time performance of tests using different coding styles to achieve similar purposes.

Version 2.0 of the ACES, released in March of 1995, includes a Quick-Look facility that is meant to replace the Performance Issues Working Group (PIWG) suite. The Quick-Look facility is advertised as being easy to download, install, and execute in less than a day, while providing information that is as useful as that generated by the PIWG suite. In addition, Version 2.0 contains a limited number of Ada 95 tests (all of which are also included in the Quick-Look subset). Version 2.1, including broad coverage of the "core" Ada 95 language, is scheduled for release in March 1996.

At the time of this writing, the ACES software and documentation can be obtained via anonymous FTP from the host `sw-eng.falls-church.va.us`, directory `/public/AdaIC/testing/aces`. For World Wide Web access, use the following uniform resource locator (URL): `http://sw-eng.falls-church.va.us/AdaIC/testing/aces/`.

While measuring performance may seem to be a relatively straightforward matter, there are significant issues that must be addressed by any person or toolset planning to do such measurement. For detailed information, see the following sources: ACES (1995a, 1995b, 1995c); Clapp, Mudge, and Roy (1990); Goforth, Collard, and Marquardt (1990); Knight (1990); Newport (1995); and Weidermann (1990).

10.3 PROGRAM STRUCTURE

10.3.1 Blocks

guideline

- Use blocks (see Guideline 5.6.9) to introduce late initialization when measured performance indicates.

example

```
    ...
    Initial : Matrix;

begin  -- Find_Solution

    Initialize_Solution_Matrix:
        for Row in Initial'Range(1) loop
            for Col in Initial'Range(2) loop
                Initial (Row, Col) := Get_Value (Row, Col);
            end loop;
        end loop Initialize_Solution_Matrix;

    Converge_To_The_Solution:
        declare

            Solution      : Matrix                := Identity;
            Min_Iterations : constant Natural := ...;

        begin  -- Converge_To_The_Solution
            for Iterations in 1 .. Min_Iterations loop
                Converge (Solution, Initial);
            end loop;

        end Converge_To_The_Solution;

    ...
end Find_Solution;
```

rationale

Late initialization allows a compiler more choices in register usage optimization. Depending on the circumstance, this may introduce a significant performance improvement.

Some compilers incur a performance penalty when declarative blocks are introduced. Careful analysis and timing tests by the programmer may identify those declarative blocks that should be removed.

notes

It is difficult to accurately predict through code inspections which declarative blocks improve performance and which degrade performance. However, with these general guidelines and a familiarity with the particular implementation, performance can be improved.

10.4   DATA STRUCTURES

10.4.1   Dynamic Arrays

guideline

- Use constrained arrays when measured performance indicates.

rationale

If array bounds are not known until run-time, then calculations of these bounds may affect run-time performance. Using named constants or static expressions as array bounds may provide better performance than using variables or nonstatic expressions. Thus, if the values of Lower and Upper are not determined until run-time, then:

```
... is array (Lower .. Upper) of ...
```

may cause address and offset calculations to be delayed until run-time, introducing a performance penalty. See NASA (1992) for a detailed discussion of the tradeoffs and alternatives.

10.4.2   Zero-Based Arrays

guideline

- Use zero-based indexing for arrays when measured performance indicates.

rationale

For some compilers, offset calculations for an array whose lower bound is 0 (either the integer zero or the first value of an enumeration type) are simplified. For other compilers, optimization is more likely if the lower bound is 1.

10.4.3   Unconstrained Records

guideline

- Use fixed-size components for records when measured performance indicates.

example

```
subtype Line_Range   is Integer range 0 .. Max_Lines;
subtype Length_Range is Integer range 0 .. Max_Length;

-- Note that Max_Lines and Max_Length need to be static
type Paragraph_Body is array (Line_Range range <>, Length_Range range <>) of Character;

type Paragraph (Lines : Line_Range := 0; Line_Length : Length_Range := 0) is
   record
      Text : Paragraph_Body (1 .. Lines, 1 .. Line_Length);
   end record;
```

rationale

Determine the size and speed impact of unconstrained records having components depending on discriminants. Some compilers will allocate the maximum possible size to each object of the type; others will use pointers to the dependent components, incurring a possible heap performance penalty. Consider the possibility of using fixed-size components.

10.4.4   Records and Arrays

guideline

- Define arrays of records as parallel arrays when measured performance indicates.

example

```
-- Array of records
Process (Student (Index).Name, Student (Index).Grade);

-- Record of arrays
Process (Student.Name (Index), Student.Grade (Index));

-- Parallel arrays
Process (Name (Index), Grade (Index));
```

rationale

Determine the impact of structuring data as arrays of records, records containing arrays, or parallel arrays. Some implementations of Ada will show significant performance differences among these examples.

10.4.5   Record and Array Aggregates

guideline

*   Use a sequence of assignments for an aggregation when measured performance indicates.

rationale

Determine the impact of using an aggregate versus a sequence of assignments. Using an aggregate generally requires the use of a temporary variable. If the aggregate is "static" (i.e., its size and components are known at compile- or link-time, allowing link-time allocation and initialization), then it will generally be more efficient than a sequence of assignments. If the aggregate is "dynamic," then a series of assignments may be more efficient because no temporary variable is needed.

See Guideline 5.6.10 for a discussion of aggregates from the point of view of readability and maintainability.

See Guideline 10.6.1 for a discussion of extension aggregates.

10.5   ALGORITHMS

10.5.1   Mod and rem Operators

guideline

*   Use incremental schemes instead of mod and rem when measured performance indicates.

example

```
-- Using mod
for I in 0 .. N loop
    Update (Arr (I mod Modulus));
end loop;

-- Avoiding mod
J := 0;
for I in 0 .. N loop
    Update (Arr (J));
    J := J + 1;
    if J = Modulus then
        J := 0;
    end if;
end loop;
```

rationale

Determine the impact of using the mod and rem operators. One of the above styles may be significantly more efficient than the other.

10.5.2   Short-Circuit Operators

guideline

*   Use the short-circuit control form when measured performance indicates.

example

```
-- Nested "if"
if Last >= Target_Length then
   if Buffer (1 .. Target_Length) = Target then
       ...
   end if;
end if;

-- "and then"
if Last >= Target_Length and then Buffer (1 .. Target_Length) = Target then
    ...
end if;
```

rationale

Determine the impact of using nested if statements versus using the and then or or else operator. One of the above may be significantly more efficient than the other.

10.5.3   Case Statement Versus elsif

guideline

- Use the case statement when measured performance indicates.

example

```
subtype Small_Int is Integer range 1 .. 5;
Switch : Small_Int;
...

-- Case statement
case Switch is
   when 1 => ...
   when 2 => ...
   when 3 => ...
   when 4 => ...
   when 5 => ...
end case;

-- "elsif construct"
if Switch = 1 then
   ...
elsif Switch = 2 then
   ...
elsif Switch = 3 then
   ...
elsif Switch = 4 then
   ...
elsif Switch = 5 then
   ...
end if;
```

rationale

Determine the impact of using case statements versus the elsif construct. If the case statement is implemented using a small jump table, then it may be significantly more efficient than the if .. then .. elsif construct.

See also Guideline 8.4.6 for a discussion of the table-driven programming alternative.

10.5.4   Checking for Constraint Errors

guideline

- Use hard-coded constraint checking when measured performance indicates.

example

```
subtype Small_Int is Positive range Lower .. Upper;
Var : Small_Int;
...

-- Using exception handler
Double:
   begin
      Var := 2 * Var;
   exception
      when Constraint_Error =>
         ...
   end Double;

   -- Using hard-coded check
   if Var > Upper / 2 then
      ...
   else
      Var := 2 * Var;
   end if;
```

rationale

Determine the impact of using exception handlers to detect constraint errors. If the exception handling mechanism is slow, then hard-coded checking may be more efficient.

10.5.5   Order of Array Processing

guideline

- Use column-first processing of two-dimensional arrays when measured performance indicates.

example

```
type Table_Type is array (Row_Min .. Row_Max, Col_Min .. Col_Max) of ...
Table : Table_Type;
...

-- Row-order processing
for Row in Row_Min .. Row_Max loop
   for Col in Col_Min .. Col_Max loop
      -- Process Table (Row, Col)
   end loop;
end loop;
-- Column-order processing
for Col in Col_Min .. Col_Max loop
   for Row in Row_Min .. Row_Max loop
      -- Process Table (Row, Col)
   end loop;
end loop;
```

rationale

Determine the impact of processing two-dimensional arrays in row-major order versus column-major order. While most Ada compilers are likely to use row-major order, it is not a requirement. In the presence of good optimization, there may be no significant difference in the above examples. Using static array bounds is also likely to be significant here. See Guidelines 10.4.1 and 10.4.2.

10.5.6   Assigning Alternatives

guideline

- Use overwriting for conditional assignment when measured performance indicates.

example

```
-- Using "if .. else"
if Condition then
   Var := One_Value;
else
   Var := Other_Value;
end if;
```

```
-- Using overwriting
Var := Other_Value;
if Condition then
    Var := One_Value;
end if;
```

rationale

Determine the impact of styles of assigning alternative values. The examples illustrate two common methods of doing this; for many systems, the performance difference is significant.

10.5.7   Packed Boolean Array Shifts

guideline

• When measured performance indicates, perform packed Boolean array shift operations by using slice assignments rather than repeated bit-wise assignment.

example

```
subtype Word_Range is Integer range 0 .. 15;
type Flag_Word is array (Word_Range) of Boolean;
pragma Pack (Flag_Word);
Word : Flag_Word;
...

-- Loop to shift by one bit
for Index in 0 .. 14 loop
    Word (Index) := Word (Index + 1);
end loop;
Word (15) := False;

-- Use slice assignment to shift by one bit
Word (0 .. 14) := Word (1 .. 15);
Word (15) := False;
```

rationale

Determine the impact of slice manipulation when shifting packed Boolean arrays. For Ada 83 implementations using packed Boolean arrays, shift operations may be much faster when slice assignments are used as opposed to for loop moving one component at a time. For Ada 95 implementations, consider using modular types instead (see Guideline 10.6.3).

10.5.8   Subprogram Dispatching

guideline

• Use static subprogram dispatching when measured performance indicates.

example

The term "static dispatching" in this example refers to the use of if/elsif sequences to explicitly determine which subprograms to call based on certain conditions:

```
-- (1) Dispatching where tag is not known at compile time
--      (See ACES V2.0 test "a9_ob_class_wide_dynamic_01")

-- Object_Type is a tagged type
-- The_Pointer designates Object_Type'Class;
-- Subclass1_Pointer designates Subclass1 (derived from Object_Type)
-- Subclass2_Pointer designates Subclass2 (derived from Subclass1)
-- Subclass3_Pointer designates Subclass3 (derived from Subclass2)
Random_Value := Simple_Random; -- Call to a random number generator
if Random_Value < 1.0/3.0 then
    The_Pointer := Subclass1_Pointer;
elsif Random_Value > 2.0/3.0 then
    The_Pointer := Subclass2_Pointer;
else
    The_Pointer := Subclass3_Pointer;
end if;
Process (The_Pointer.all);   -- Tag is unknown

-- (2) Tag is determinable at compile time (static dispatching)
--      (See ACES V2.0, test "a9_ob_class_wide_static_01")
```

```
-- Object_Type is a tagged type
-- The_Pointer designates Object_Type'Class;
-- Subclass1_Pointer designates Subclass1 (derived from Object_Type)
-- Subclass2_Pointer designates Subclass2 (derived from Subclass1)
-- Subclass3_Pointer designates Subclass3 (derived from Subclass2)
Random_Value := Simple_Random; -- Call to a random number generator
if Random_Value < 1.0/3.0 then
    Process (Subclass1_Pointer.all);
elsif Random_Value > 2.0/3.0 then
    Process (Subclass2_Pointer.all);
else
    Process (Subclass3_Pointer.all);
end if;

-- (3) No tagged types are involved (no dispatching)
--     (See ACES V2.0, test "ap_ob_class_wide_01")

-- Object_type is a discriminated type with variants; possible
-- discriminant values are Subclass1, Subclass2, and Subclass3
-- All the pointers designate values of Object_Type
-- Subclass1_Pointer := new Object_Type (Subclass1);
-- Subclass2_Pointer := new Object_Type (Subclass2);
-- Subclass3_Pointer := new Object_Type (Subclass3);
-- There is only one "Process" procedure (operating on Object_Type)
Random_Value := Simple_Random; -- Call to a random number generator
if Random_Value < 1.0/3.0 then
    Process (Subclass1_Pointer.all);
elsif Random_Value > 2.0/3.0 then
    Process (Subclass2_Pointer.all);
else
    Process (Subclass3_Pointer.all);
end if;
```

rationale

Determine the impact of dynamic and static subprogram dispatching. The compiler may generate much more efficient code for one form of dispatching than the other.

notes

Dynamic dispatching will almost certainly be more efficient than an explicit if . . . elsif sequence. However, you should be aware of any optimizing decisions made by a compiler that might affect this situation.

10.6   TYPES

10.6.1   Aggregates for Type Extensions

guideline

• Use only simple aggregates when measured performance indicates.

example

```
type Parent is tagged
    record
        C1 : Float;
        C2 : Float;
    end record;

type Extension is new Parent with
    record
        C3 : Float;
        C4 : Float;
    end record;

Parent_Var : Parent := (C1 => Float_Var1, C2 => Float_Var2);
Exten_Var  : Extension;
...

-- Simple aggregate
-- (See ACES V2.0, test "a9_ob_simp_aggregate_02")
Exten_Var := (C1 => Float_Var1, C2 => Float_Var2,
              C3 => Float_Var3, C4 => Float_Var4);

-- Extension aggregate
-- (See ACES V2.0, test "a9_ob_ext_aggregate_02")
Exten_Var := (Parent_Var with C3 => Float_Var3, C4 => Float_Var4);
```

rationale

Determine the impact of using extension aggregates. There may be a significant performance difference between evaluation of simple aggregates and evaluation of extension aggregates.

10.6.2   Protected Types

guideline

- For mutual exclusion, when measured performance indicates, use protected types as an alternative to tasking rendezvous.

- To implement an interrupt handler, when performance measurement indicates, use a protected procedure.

example

```
-- (1) Using protected objects
--      (See ACES V2.0, test "a9_pt_prot_access_02")

protected Object is
   function Read return Float;
   procedure Write (Value : in Float);
private
   Data : Float;
end Object;

protected body Object is
   function Read return Float is
   begin
      return Data;
   end Read;

   procedure Write (Value : in Float) is
   begin
      Data := Value;
   end Write;
end Object;

task type Modify is
end Modify;

type Mod_Bunch is array (1 .. 5) of Modify;

task body Modify is
   ...
begin -- Modify
   for I in 1 .. 200 loop
      The_Value := Object.Read;
      Object.Write (The_Value - 0.125);
      if The_Value < -1.0E7 then
         The_Value := 1.0;
      end if;
   end loop;
end Modify;
...

-- Block statement to be timed
declare
   Contending_Tasks : array (1 .. 5) of Modify;
begin
   null; -- 5 tasks contend for access to protected data
end;

--------------------------------------------------------------------------

-- (2) Using monitor task
--      (See ACES V2.0, test "tk_rz_entry_access_02")

Task Object is
   entry Write (Value : in      Float);
   entry Read  (Value :    out Float);
end Object;
```

```
task body Object is
   Data : Float;
begin -- Object
   loop
      select
         accept Write (Value : in      Float) do
            Data := Value;
         end Write;
      or
         accept Read  (Value :     out Float) do
            Value := Data;
         end Read;
      or
         terminate;
      end select;
   end loop;
end Object;

-- Task type Modify declared as above
-- Block statement to be timed as above
```

rationale

Protected objects are meant to be much faster than tasks used for the same purpose (see Guideline 6.1.1). Determine the impact of using protected objects to provide access safely to encapsulated data in a concurrent program.

10.6.3   Bit Operations on Modular Types

guideline

- Use modular types rather than packed Boolean arrays when measured performance indicates.

example

```
-- (1) Packed Boolean arrays
--      (See ACES V2.0, test "dr_ba_bool_arrays_11")

type Set is array (0 .. 15) of Boolean;
pragma Pack (Set);

S1     : Set;
S2     : Set;
Empty  : Set := (Set'Range => False);
Result : Boolean;

   ...

-- Is S1 a subset of S2?
Result := ((S1 and not S2) = Empty);

-----------------------+-----------------------------------------

-- (2) Modular types
--      (See ACES V2.0, test "a9_ms_modular_oper_02")

type Set is mod 16;

S1     : Set;
S2     : Set;
Empty  : Set := 0;
Result : Boolean;

   ...

-- Is S1 a subset of S2?
Result := ((S1 and not S2) = Empty);
```

rationale

Determine the impact of performing bit-wise operations on modular types. The performance of these operations may be significantly different from similar operations on packed Boolean arrays. See also Guideline 10.5.7.

10.6.4   Bounded Strings

guideline

- Use the predefined bounded strings when predictable performance is an issue and measured performance indicates.

rationale

The unbounded strings may be allocated on the heap. If bounded strings are not allocated on the heap, then they may provide better performance. Determine the impact of using the string type declared in instantiations of Ada.Strings.Bounded.Generic_Bounded_Length versus the type declared in Ada.Strings.Unbounded.

The predefined Ada 95 language environment defines packages that support both bounded and unbounded strings. Using bounded strings may avoid the unpredictable duration of delays associated with using heap storage.

10.6.5   String Handling Subprograms

guideline

- Use the procedural form of the string handling subprograms when measured performance indicates.

rationale

Determine the relative performance cost of functions and procedures having the same name and functionality in Ada.Strings.Fixed, Ada.Strings.Bounded, Ada.Strings.Unbounded and the corresponding child packages whose names include Wide.

While functional notation typically leads to clearer code, it may cause the compiler to generate additional copying operations.

10.6.6   Constraint Checking

guideline

- Use strong typing with carefully selected constraints to reduce run-time constraint checking when measured performance indicates.

example

In this example, two potential constraint checks are eliminated. If the function Get_Response returns String, then the initialization of the variable Input would require constraint checking. If the variable Last is type Positive, then the assignment inside the loop would require constraint checking:

```
...
subtype Name_Index is Positive range 1 .. 32;
subtype Name      is String (Name_Index);
...
function Get_Response return Name is separate;
...
begin
...
Find_Last_Period:
   declare
      -- No Constraint Checking needed for initialization
      Input      : constant Name      := Get_Response;
      Last_Period :        Name_Index := 1;

   begin  -- Find_Last_Period
      for I in Input'Range loop
         if Input(I) = '.' then
            -- No Constraint Checking needed in  this `tight' loop
            Last_Period := I;
         end if;

      end loop;
      ...
   end Find_Last_Period;
```

rationale

Because run-time constraint checking is associated with slow performance, it is not intuitive that the addition of constrained subtypes could actually improve performance. However, the need for constraint checking appears in many places regardless of the use of constrained subtypes. Even assignments to variables that use the predefined subtypes may need constraint checks. By consistently using constrained subtypes, many of the unnecessary run-time checking can be eliminated. Instead, the checking is usually moved to less frequently executed code involved in system input. In the example, the function Get_Response may need to check the length of a user-supplied string and raise an exception.

Some compilers can do additional optimizations based on the information provided by constrained subtypes. For example, although an unconstrained array does not have a fixed size, it has a maximum size that can be determined from the range of its index. Performance can be improved by limiting this maximum size to a "reasonable" number. Refer to the discussion on unconstrained arrays found in NASA (1992).

10.6.7   Real-Time System Annex

guideline

- For cases where both rendezvous and protected types are inefficient, consider the use of the Real-Time Systems Annex (Ada Reference Manual 1995, Annex D).

rationale

The packages Ada.Synchronous_Task_Control and Ada.Asynchronous_Task_Control have been defined to provide an alternative to tasking and protected types for use in applications where a minimal run-time is desired (Ada Reference Manual 1995, Annex D).

10.7   PRAGMAS

10.7.1   Pragma Inline

guideline

- When measured performance indicates, use pragma Inline when calling overhead is a significant portion of the routine's execution time.

example

```
procedure Assign (Variable : in out Integer;
                  Value    : in     Integer);
pragma Inline (Assign);

...
procedure Assign (Variable : in out Integer;
                  Value    : in     Integer) is
begin
   Variable := Value;
end Assign;
```

rationale

If calling overhead is a significant portion of a subprogram's execution time, then using pragma Inline may reduce execution time.

Procedure and function invocations include overhead that is unnecessary when the code involved is very small. These small routines are usually written to maintain the implementation hiding characteristics of a package. They may also simply pass their parameters unchanged to another routine. When one of these routines appears in some code that needs to run faster, either the implementation-hiding principle needs to be violated or a pragma Inline can be introduced.

The use of pragma Inline does have its disadvantages. It can create compilation dependencies on the body; that is, when the specification uses a pragma Inline, both the specification and corresponding body may need to be compiled before the specification can be used. As updates are made to the code, a routine may become more complex (larger) and the continued use of a pragma Inline may no longer be justified.

exceptions

Although it is rare, inlining code may increase code size, which can lead to slower performance caused by additional paging. A pragma Inline may actually thwart a compiler's attempt to use some other optimization technique, such as register optimization.

When a compiler is already doing a good job of selecting routines to be inlined, the pragma may accomplish little, if any, improvement in execution speed.

10.7.2 Pragma Restrictions

guideline

* Use pragma Restrictions to express the user's intent to abide by certain restrictions.

rationale

This may facilitate the construction of simpler run-time environments (Ada Reference Manual 1995, §§13.12, D.7, and H.4).

10.7.3 Pragma Preelaborate

guideline

* Use pragma Preelaborate where allowed.

rationale

This may reduce memory write operations after load time (Ada Reference Manual 1995, §§10.2.1 and C.4).

10.7.4 Pragma Pure

guideline

* Use pragma Pure where allowed.

rationale

This may permit the compiler to omit calls on library-level subprograms of the library unit if the results are not needed after the call (Ada Reference Manual 1995, §10.2.1).

10.7.5 Pragma Discard_Names

guideline

* Use pragma Discard_Names when the names are not needed by the application and data space is at a premium.

rationale

This may reduce the memory needed to store names of Ada entities, where no operation uses those names (Ada Reference Manual 1995, §C.5).

10.7.6 Pragma Suppress

guideline

* Use pragma Suppress where necessary to achieve performance requirements.

rationale

See Guideline 5.9.5.

10.7.7 Pragma Reviewable

guideline

* Use pragma Reviewable to aid in the analysis of the generated code.

rationale

See the Ada Reference Manual (1995, Annex H).

10.8   SUMMARY

Use the guidelines in this chapter with care; they may be hazardous to your software.

program structure

- Use blocks to introduce late initialization when measured performance indicates.

data structures

- Use constrained arrays when measured performance indicates.
- Use zero-based indexing for arrays when measured performance indicates.
- Use fixed-size components for records when measured performance indicates.
- Define arrays of records as parallel arrays when measured performance indicates.
- Use a sequence of assignments for an aggregation when measured performance indicates.

algorithms

- Use incremental schemes instead of mod and rem when measured performance indicates.
- Use the short-circuit control form when measured performance indicates.
- Use the case statement when measured performance indicates.
- Use hard-coded constraint checking when measured performance indicates.
- Use column-first processing of two-dimensional arrays when measured performance indicates.
- Use overwriting for conditional assignment when measured performance indicates.
- When measured performance indicates, perform packed Boolean array shift operations by using slice assignments rather than repeated bit-wise assignment.
- Use static subprogram dispatching when measured performance indicates.

types

- Use only simple aggregates when measured performance indicates.
- For mutual exclusion, when measured performance indicates, use protected types as an alternative to tasking rendezvous.
- To implement an interrupt handler, when measured performance indicates, use a protected procedure.
- Use modular types rather than packed Boolean arrays when measured performance indicates.
- Use the predefined bounded strings when predictable performance is an issue and measured performance indicates.
- Use the procedural form of the string handling subprograms when measured performance indicates.
- Use strong typing with carefully selected constraints to reduce run-time constraint checking when measured performance indicates.
- For cases where both rendezvous and protected types are inefficient, consider the use of the Real-Time Systems Annex (Ada Reference Manual 1995, Annex D).

pragmas

- When measured performance indicates, use pragma Inline when calling overhead is a significant portion of the routine's execution time.
- Use pragma Restrictions to express the user's intent to abide by certain restrictions.
- Use pragma Preelaborate where allowed.
- Use pragma Pure where allowed.
- Use pragma Discard_Names when the names are not needed by the application and data space is at a premium.

- Use pragma `Suppress` where necessary to achieve performance requirements.
- Use pragma `Reviewable` to aid in the analysis of the generated code.

CHAPTER 11
Complete Example

This chapter presents an elaborate implementation of Edsger Dijkstra's famous Dining Philosophers; a classical demonstration of deadlock problems in concurrent programming. This example demonstrates the portability of Ada packages and tasking and illustrates many of the Ada 95 quality and style guidelines. Since many of the guidelines leave the program writer to decide what is best, there is no single best or correct example of how to use Ada. Instead, you will find several styles that differ from your own that may deserve consideration.

11.1 PORTABLE DINING PHILOSOPHERS EXAMPLE

This version of the Dining Philosophers example was provided by Dr. Michael B. Feldman of the George Washington University and Bjorn Kallberg of CelciusTech Systems, Sweden. This example was compiled using the GNAT Ada 95 compiler, version 2.07, on a Sun platform.

```
--::::::::::::
--random_generic.ads
--::::::::::::
generic
  type Result_Subtype is (<>);
package Random_Generic is

  -- Simple integer pseudo-random number generator package.
  -- Michael B. Feldman, The George Washington University,
  -- June 1995.

  function Random_Value return Result_Subtype;

end Random_Generic;
```

```
--:::::::::::
--screen.ads
--:::::::::::
package Screen is

   -- simple ANSI terminal emulator
   -- Michael Feldman, The George Washington University
   -- July, 1995

   ScreenHeight : constant Integer := 24;
   ScreenWidth  : constant Integer := 80;

   subtype Height is Integer range 1 .. ScreenHeight;
   subtype Width  is Integer range 1 .. ScreenWidth;

   type Position is record
      Row    : Height := 1;
      Column : Width  := 1;
   end record;

   procedure Beep;
   -- Pre:  none
   -- Post: the terminal beeps once

   procedure ClearScreen;
   -- Pre:  none
   -- Post: the terminal screen is cleared

   procedure MoveCursor (To : in Position);
   -- Pre:  To is defined
   -- Post: the terminal cursor is moved to the given position

end Screen;
```

```
--::::::::::
--windows.ads
--::::::::::
with Screen;
package Windows is

    -- manager for simple, nonoverlapping screen windows
    -- Michael Feldman, The George Washington University
    -- July, 1995

    type Window is private;

    function Open (UpperLeft : Screen.Position;
                   Height    : Screen.Height;
                   Width     : Screen.Width) return Window;
    -- Pre:  W, Height, and Width are defined
    -- Post: returns a Window with the given upper-left corner,
    --    height, and width

    procedure Title (W     : in out Window;
                     Name  : in     String;
                     Under : in     Character);
    -- Pre:  W, Name, and Under are defined
    -- Post: Name is displayed at the top of the window W, underlined
    -- with the character Under.

    procedure Borders (W      : in out Window;
                       Corner : in     Character
                       Down   : in     Character
                       Across : in     Character);
    -- Pre:  All parameters are defined
    -- Post: Draw border around current writable area in window with
    -- characters specified.  Call this BEFORE Title.

    procedure MoveCursor (W : in out Window;
                          P : in     Screen.Position);
    -- Pre:  W and P are defined, and P lies within the area of W
    -- Post: Cursor is moved to the specified position.
    --    Coordinates are relative to the
    --    upper left corner of W, which is (1, 1)

    procedure Put (W  : in out Window;
                   Ch : in     Character);
    -- Pre:  W and Ch are defined.
    -- Post: Ch is displayed in the window at
    --    the next available position.
    --    If end of column, go to the next row.
    --    If end of window, go to the top of the window.

    procedure Put (W : in out Window;
                   S : in     String);
    -- Pre:  W and S are defined
    -- Post: S is displayed in the window, "line-wrapped" if necessary

    procedure New_Line (W : in out Window);
    -- Pre:  W is defined
    -- Post: Cursor moves to beginning of next line of W;
    --    line is not blanked until next character is written

private
    type Window is record
        First   : Screen.Position; -- coordinates of upper left
        Last    : Screen.Position; -- coordinates of lower right
        Current : Screen.Position; -- current cursor position
    end record;

end Windows;
```

```
--:::::::::::
--Picture.ads
--:::::::::::
with Windows;
with Screen;
package Picture is

    -- Manager for semigraphical presentation of the philosophers
    -- i.e. more application oriented windows, build on top of
    -- the windows package.
    -- Each picture has an orientation, which defines which borders
    -- top-bottom, bottom-top, left-right, or right-left correspond
    -- to the left and right hand of the philosopher.
    --
    -- Bjorn Kallberg, CelsiusTech Systems, Sweden
    -- July, 1995

    type Root is abstract tagged private;
    type Root_Ptr is access Root'Class;

    procedure Open (W          : in out Root;
                    UpperLeft  : in      Screen.Position;
                    Height     : in      Screen.Height;
                    Width      : in      Screen.Width);
    -- Pre:  Not opened
    -- Post: An empty window exists

    procedure Title (W     : in out Root;
                     Name  : in      String);
    -- Pre:  An empty window
    -- Post: Name and a border is drawn.

    procedure Put_Line (W : in out Root;
                        S : in      String);

    procedure Left_Fork  (W    : in out Root;
                          Pick : in      Boolean) is abstract;
    procedure Right_Fork (W    : in out Root;
                          Pick : in      Boolean) is abstract;
    -- left and right relates to philosopher position around table

    type North is new Root with private;
    type South is new Root with private;
    type East  is new Root with private;
    type West  is new Root with private;

private
    type Root is abstract tagged record
        W : Windows.Window;
    end record;

    type North is new Root with null record;
    type South is new Root with null record;
    type East  is new Root with null record;
    type West  is new Root with null record;

    procedure Left_Fork  (W    : in out North;
                          Pick : in      Boolean);
    procedure Right_Fork (W    : in out North;
                          Pick : in      Boolean);

    procedure Left_Fork  (W    : in out South;
                          Pick : in      Boolean);
    procedure Right_Fork (W    : in out South;
                          Pick : in      Boolean);

    procedure Left_Fork  (W    : in out East;
                          Pick : in      Boolean);
    procedure Right_Fork (W    : in out East;
                          Pick : in      Boolean);

    procedure Left_Fork  (W    : in out West;
                          Pick : in      Boolean);
    procedure Right_Fork (W    : in out West;
                          Pick : in      Boolean);

end Picture;
```

```
--:::::::::::
--chop.ads
--:::::::::::
package Chop is

   -- Dining Philosophers - Ada 95 edition
   -- Chopstick is an Ada 95 protected type
   -- Michael B. Feldman, The George Washington University,
   -- July, 1995.

   protected type Stick is
     entry Pick_Up;
     procedure Put_Down;
   private
     In_Use: Boolean := False;
   end Stick;

end Chop;


--:::::::::::
--society.ads
--:::::::::::
package Society is

   -- Dining Philosophers - Ada 95 edition
   -- Society gives unique ID's to people, and registers their names
   -- Michael B. Feldman, The George Washington University,
   -- July, 1995.

   subtype Unique_DNA_Codes is Positive range 1 .. 5;

   Name_Register : array (Unique_DNA_Codes) of String (1 .. 18) :=

       ("Edsger Dijkstra    ",
        "Bjarne Stroustrup  ",
        "Chris Anderson     ",
        "Tucker Taft        ",
        "Jean Ichbiah       ");

end Society;

--:::::::::::
--phil.ads
--:::::::::::
with Society;
package Phil is

   -- Dining Philosophers - Ada 95 edition
   -- Philosopher is an Ada 95 task type with discriminant
   -- Michael B. Feldman, The George Washington University,
   -- July 1995
   --
   -- Revisions:
   -- July 1995. Bjorn Kallberg, CelsiusTech
   --            Reporting left or right instead of first stick

   task type Philosopher (My_ID : Society.Unique_DNA_Codes) is

      entry Start_Eating (Chopstick1 : in Positive;
                          Chopstick2 : in Positive);

   end Philosopher;

   type States is (Breathing, Thinking, Eating, Done_Eating,
                   Got_Left_Stick, Got_Right_Stick, Got_Other_Stick, Dying);

end Phil;
```

```
--:::::::::::
--room.ads
--:::::::::::
with Chop;
with Phil;
with Society;
package Room is

   -- Dining Philosophers - Ada 95 edition

   -- Room.Maitre_D is responsible for assigning seats at the
   --    table, "left" and "right" chopsticks, and for reporting
   --    interesting events to the outside world.

   -- Michael B. Feldman, The George Washington University,
   -- July, 1995.

   Table_Size : constant := 5;
   subtype Table_Type is Positive range 1 .. Table_Size;

   Sticks : array (Table_Type) of Chop.Stick;

   task Maitre_D is
     entry Start_Serving;
     entry Report_State (Which_Phil : in Society.Unique_DNA_Codes;
                         State      : in Phil.States;
                         How_Long   : in Natural := 0;
                         Which_Meal : in Natural := 0);
   end Maitre_D;

end Room;

--:::::::::::
--random_generic.adb
--:::::::::::
with Ada.Numerics.Discrete_Random;
package body Random_Generic is

   -- Body of random number generator package.
   -- Uses Ada 95 random number generator; hides generator parameters
   -- Michael B. Feldman, The George Washington University,
   -- June 1995.

   package Ada95_Random is new Ada.Numerics.Discrete_Random
     (Result_Subtype => Result_Subtype);

   G : Ada95_Random.Generator;

   function Random_Value return Result_Subtype is
   begin
     return Ada95_Random.Random (Gen => G);
   end Random_Value;

begin -- Random_Generic

   Ada95_Random.Reset (Gen => G);   -- time-dependent initialization

end Random_Generic;
```

```
--:::::::::::
--screen.adb
--:::::::::::
with Text_IO;
package body Screen is

   -- simple ANSI terminal emulator
   -- Michael Feldman, The George Washington University
   -- July, 1995

   -- These procedures will work correctly only if the actual
   -- terminal is ANSI compatible. ANSI.SYS on a DOS machine
   -- will suffice.

   package Int_IO is new Text_IO.Integer_IO (Num => Integer);

   procedure Beep is
   begin
      Text_IO.Put (Item => ASCII.BEL);
   end Beep;

   procedure ClearScreen is
   begin
      Text_IO.Put (Item => ASCII.ESC);
      Text_IO.Put (Item => "[2J");
   end ClearScreen;

   procedure MoveCursor (To : in Position) is
   begin
      Text_IO.New_Line;
      Text_IO.Put (Item => ASCII.ESC);
      Text_IO.Put ("[");
      Int_IO.Put (Item => To.Row, Width => 1);
      Text_IO.Put (Item => ';');
      Int_IO.Put (Item => To.Column, Width => 1);
      Text_IO.Put (Item => 'f');
   end MoveCursor;

end Screen;
```

```
--:::::::::::
--windows.adb
--:::::::::::
with Text_IO, with Screen;
package body Windows is

   -- manager for simple, nonoverlapping screen windows
   -- Michael Feldman, The George Washington University
   -- July, 1995

   function Open (UpperLeft : Screen.Position;
                  Height    : Screen.Height;
                  Width     : Screen.Width) return Window is
      Result : Window;
   begin
      Result.Current := UpperLeft;
      Result.First   := UpperLeft;
      Result.Last    := (Row    => UpperLeft.Row + Height - 1,
                         Column => UpperLeft.Column + Width - 1);
      return Result;
   end Open;

   procedure EraseToEndOfLine (W : in out Window) is
   begin
      Screen.MoveCursor (W.Current);
      for Count in W.Current.Column .. W.Last.Column loop
         Text_IO.Put (' ');
      end loop;
      Screen.MoveCursor (W.Current);
   end EraseToEndOfLine;

   procedure Put (W  : in out Window;
                  Ch : in     Character) is
   begin

      -- If at end of current line, move to next line
      if W.Current.Column > W.Last.Column then
         if W.Current.Row = W.Last.Row then
            W.Current.Row := W.First.Row;
         else
            W.Current.Row := W.Current.Row + 1;
         end if;
         W.Current.Column := W.First.Column;
      end if;

      -- If at First char, erase line
      if W.Current.Column = W.First.Column then
         EraseToEndOfLine (W);
      end if;

      Screen.MoveCursor (To => W.Current);

      -- here is where we actually write the character!
      Text_IO.Put (Ch);
      W.Current.Column := W.Current.Column + 1;

   end Put;

   procedure Put (W : in out Window;
                  S : in     String) is
   begin
      for Count in S'Range loop
         Put (W, S (Count));
      end loop;
   end Put;

   procedure New_Line (W : in out Window) is
   begin
      if W.Current.Column = 1 then
         EraseToEndOfLine (W);
      end if;
      if W.Current.Row = W.Last.Row then
         W.Current.Row := W.First.Row;
      else
         W.Current.Row := W.Current.Row + 1;
      end if;
      W.Current.Column := W.First.Column;
   end New_Line;
```

```
   procedure Title (W     : in out Window;
                    Name  : in     String;
                    Under : in     Character) is
   begin
     -- Put name on top line
     W.Current := W.First;
     Put (W, Name);
     New_Line (W);
     -- Underline name if desired, and reduce the writable area
     -- of the window by one line
     if Under = ' ' then    -- no underlining
       W.First.Row := W.First.Row + 1;
     else                   -- go across the row, underlining
       for Count in W.First.Column .. W.Last.Column loop
         Put (W, Under);
       end loop;
       New_Line (W);
       W.First.Row := W.First.Row + 2; -- reduce writable area
     end if;
   end Title;

   procedure Borders (W      : in out Window;
                      Corner : in     Character
                      Down   : in     Character
                      Across : in     Character is

   begin
     -- Put top line of border
     Screen.MoveCursor (W.First);
     Text_IO.Put (Corner);
     for Count in W.First.Column + 1 .. W.Last.Column - 1 loop
       Text_IO.Put (Across);
     end loop;
     Text_IO.Put (Corner);

     -- Put the two side lines
     for Count in W.First.Row + 1 .. W.Last.Row - 1 loop
       Screen.MoveCursor ((Row => Count, Column => W.First.Column));
       Text_IO.Put (Down);
       Screen.MoveCursor ((Row => Count, Column => W.Last.Column));
       Text_IO.Put (Down);
     end loop;

     -- Put the bottom line of the border
     Screen.MoveCursor ((Row => W.Last.Row, Column => W.First.Column));
     Text_IO.Put (Corner);
     for Count in W.First.Column + 1 .. W.Last.Column - 1 loop
       Text_IO.Put (Across);
     end loop;
     Text_IO.Put (Corner);

     -- Make the Window smaller by one character on each side
     W.First   := (Row => W.First.Row + 1, Column => W.First.Column + 1);
     W.Last    := (Row => W.Last.Row - 1,  Column => W.Last.Column - 1);
     W.Current := W.First;
   end Borders;

   procedure MoveCursor (W : in out Window;
                         P : in     Screen.Position) is
     -- Relative to writable Window boundaries, of course
   begin
     W.Current.Row    := W.First.Row + P.Row;
     W.Current.Column := W.First.Column + P.Column;
   end MoveCursor;

begin -- Windows

   Text_IO.New_Line;
   Screen.ClearScreen;
   Text_IO.New_Line;

end Windows;
```

```
--------------------
package Windows.Util is
  --
  -- Child package to change the borders of an existing window
  -- Bjorn Kallberg, CelsiusTech Systems, Sweden
  -- July, 1995.

  -- call these procedures after border and title
  procedure Draw_Left   (W  : in out Window;
                         C  : in      Character);
  procedure Draw_Right  (W  : in out Window;
                         C  : in      Character);
  procedure Draw_Top    (W  : in out Window;
                         C  : in      Character);
  procedure Draw_Bottom (W  : in out Window;
                         C  : in      Character);

end Windows.Util;
--------------------

with Text_IO;
package body Windows.Util is

  -- Bjorn Kallberg, CelsiusTech Systems, Sweden
  -- July, 1995.

  -- When making borders and titles, the size has shrunk, so
  -- we must now draw outside the First and Last points


  procedure Draw_Left (W  : in out Window;
                       C  : in      Character) is
  begin
    for R in W.First.Row - 3 .. W.Last.Row + 1 loop
      Screen.MoveCursor ((Row => R, Column => W.First.Column-1));
      Text_IO.Put (C);
    end loop;
  end;

  procedure Draw_Right (W  : in out Window;
                        C  : in      Character) is
  begin
    for R in W.First.Row - 3 .. W.Last.Row + 1 loop
      Screen.MoveCursor ((Row => R, Column => W.Last.Column + 1));
      Text_IO.Put (C);
    end loop;
  end;

  procedure Draw_Top (W  : in out Window;
                      C  : in      Character) is
  begin
    for I in W.First.Column - 1 .. W.Last.Column + 1 loop
      Screen.MoveCursor ((Row => W.First.Row - 3, Column => I));
      Text_IO.Put (C);
    end loop;
  end;

  procedure Draw_Bottom (W  : in out Window;
                         C  : in      Character) is
  begin
    for I in W.First.Column - 1 .. W.Last.Column + 1 loop
      Screen.MoveCursor ((Row => W.Last.Row + 1, Column => I));
      Text_IO.Put (C);
    end loop;
  end;

end Windows.Util;
```

```
--:::::::::::
--Picture.adb
--:::::::::::
with Windows.Util;
package body Picture is
   --
   -- Bjorn Kallberg, CelsiusTech Systems, Sweden
   -- July, 1995

   function Vertical_Char (Stick : Boolean) return Character is
   begin
      if Stick then
         return '#';
      else
         return ':';
      end if;
   end;

   function Horizontal_Char (Stick : Boolean) return Character is
   begin
      if Stick then
         return '#';
      else
         return '-';
      end if;
   end;

   procedure Open (W         : in out Root;
                   UpperLeft : in      Screen.Position;
                   Height    : in      Screen.Height;
                   Width     : in      Screen.Width) is
   begin
      W.W := Windows.Open (UpperLeft, Height, Width);
   end;


   procedure Title (W    : in out Root;
                    Name : in      String) is
   -- Pre:  An empty window
   -- Post: Name and a boarder is drawn.

   begin
      Windows.Borders (W.W, '+', ':', '-');
      Windows.Title (W.W, Name,'-');
   end;

   procedure Put_Line (W : in out Root;
                       S : in      String) is
   begin
      Windows.Put (W.W, S);
      Windows.New_Line (W.W);
   end;


   -- North
   procedure Left_Fork  (W    : in out North;
                         Pick : in      Boolean) is
   begin
      Windows.Util.Draw_Right (W.W, Vertical_Char (Pick));
   end;

   procedure Right_Fork (W    : in out North;
                         Pick : in      Boolean) is
   begin
      Windows.Util.Draw_Left (W.W, Vertical_Char (Pick));
   end;


   -- South
   procedure Left_Fork  (W    : in out South;
                         Pick : in      Boolean) is
   begin
      Windows.Util.Draw_Left (W.W, Vertical_Char (Pick));
   end;

   procedure Right_Fork (W    : in out South;
                         Pick : in      Boolean) is
   begin
      Windows.Util.Draw_Right (W.W, Vertical_Char (Pick));
   end;
```

```
-- East
procedure Left_Fork  (W    : in out East;
                       Pick : in     Boolean) is
begin
   Windows.Util.Draw_Bottom (W.W, Horizontal_Char (Pick));
end;
procedure Right_Fork (W    : in out East;
                       Pick : in     Boolean) is
begin
   Windows.Util.Draw_Top (W.W, Horizontal_Char (Pick));
end;


-- West
procedure Left_Fork  (W    : in out West;
                       Pick : in     Boolean) is
begin
   Windows.Util.Draw_Top (W.W, Horizontal_Char (Pick));
end;

procedure Right_Fork (W    : in out West;
                       Pick : in     Boolean) is
begin
   Windows.Util.Draw_Bottom (W.W, Horizontal_Char (Pick));
end;


end Picture;


--::::::::::::
--chop.adb
--::::::::::::
package body Chop is

   -- Dining Philosophers - Ada 95 edition
   -- Chopstick is an Ada 95 protected type
   -- Michael B. Feldman, The George Washington University,
   -- July, 1995.

   protected body Stick is

      entry Pick_Up when not In_Use is
      begin
         In_Use := True;
      end Pick_Up;

      procedure Put_Down is
      begin
         In_Use := False;
      end Put_Down;

   end Stick;

end Chop;
```

```
--:::::::::::
--phil.adb
--:::::::::::
with Society;
with Room;
with Random_Generic;
package body Phil is

   -- Dining Philosophers - Ada 95 edition
   -- Philosopher is an Ada 95 task type with discriminant.

   -- Chopsticks are assigned by a higher authority, which
   --    can vary the assignments to show different algorithms.
   -- Philosopher always grabs First_Grab, then Second_Grab.
   -- Philosopher is oblivious to outside world, but needs to
   --    communicate is life-cycle events the Maitre_D.
   -- Chopsticks assigned to one philosopher must be
   -- consecutive numbers, or the first and last chopstick.

   -- Michael B. Feldman, The George Washington University,
   -- July, 1995.
   -- Revisions:
   -- July, 1995. Bjorn Kallberg, CelsiusTech

   subtype Think_Times is Positive range 1 .. 8;
   package Think_Length is
     new Random_Generic (Result_Subtype => Think_Times);

   subtype Meal_Times is Positive range 1 .. 10;
   package Meal_Length is
     new Random_Generic (Result_Subtype => Meal_Times);

   task body Philosopher is  -- My_ID is discriminant

      subtype Life_Time is Positive range 1 .. 5;

      Who_Am_I     : Society.Unique_DNA_Codes := My_ID; -- discriminant
      First_Grab   : Positive;
      Second_Grab  : Positive;
      Meal_Time    : Meal_Times;
      Think_Time   : Think_Times;
      First_Stick  : States;

   begin
         -- get assigned the first and second chopsticks here
      accept Start_Eating (Chopstick1 : in Positive;
                           Chopstick2 : in Positive) do
        First_Grab   := Chopstick1;
        Second_Grab := Chopstick2;
        if (First_Grab mod Room.Table_Type'Last) + 1 = Second_Grab then
           First_Stick := Got_Right_Stick;
        else
           First_Stick := Got_Left_Stick;
        end if;
      end Start_Eating;
      Room.Maitre_D.Report_State (Who_Am_I, Breathing);

      for Meal in Life_Time loop
        Room.Sticks (First_Grab).Pick_Up;
        Room.Maitre_D.Report_State (Who_Am_I, First_Stick, First_Grab);
        Room.Sticks (Second_Grab).Pick_Up;
        Room.Maitre_D.Report_State (Who_Am_I, Got_Other_Stick, Second_Grab);
        Meal_Time := Meal_Length.Random_Value;
        Room.Maitre_D.Report_State (Who_Am_I, Eating, Meal_Time, Meal);
        delay Duration (Meal_Time);
        Room.Maitre_D.Report_State (Who_Am_I, Done_Eating);
        Room.Sticks (First_Grab).Put_Down;
        Room.Sticks (Second_Grab).Put_Down;
        Think_Time := Think_Length.Random_Value;
        Room.Maitre_D.Report_State (Who_Am_I, Thinking, Think_Time);
        delay Duration (Think_Time);
      end loop;
      Room.Maitre_D.Report_State (Who_Am_I, Dying);
   end Philosopher;
end Phil;
```

```
--::::::::::
--room.adb
--::::::::::
with Picture;
with Chop;
with Phil;
with Society;
with Calendar;
pragma Elaborate (Phil);
package body Room is

   -- Dining Philosophers, Ada 95 edition
   -- A line-oriented version of the Room package
   -- Michael B. Feldman, The George Washington University,
   -- July, 1995.
   -- Revisions
   -- July, 1995. Bjorn Kallberg, CelsiusTech Systems, Sweden.
   --             Pictorial display of stick in use

   -- philosophers sign into dining room, giving Maitre_D their DNA code

   Dijkstra   : aliased Phil.Philosopher (My_ID => 1);
   Stroustrup : aliased Phil.Philosopher (My_ID => 2);
   Anderson   : aliased Phil.Philosopher (My_ID => 3);
   Taft       : aliased Phil.Philosopher (My_ID => 4);
   Ichbiah    : aliased Phil.Philosopher (My_ID => 5);

   type Philosopher_Ptr is access all Phil.Philosopher;

   Phils      : array (Table_Type) of Philosopher_Ptr;
   Phil_Pics  : array (Table_Type) of Picture.Root_Ptr;
   Phil_Seats : array (Society.Unique_DNA_Codes) of Table_Type;

   task body Maitre_D is

      T          : Natural;
      Start_Time : Calendar.Time;
      Blanks     : constant String := "      ";


   begin

      accept Start_Serving;

      Start_Time := Calendar.Clock;

      -- now Maitre_D assigns phils to seats at the table

      Phils :=
         (Dijkstra'Access,
          Anderson'Access,
          Ichbiah'Access,
          Taft'Access,
          Stroustrup'Access);

      -- Which seat each phil occupies.
      for I in Table_Type loop
         Phil_Seats (Phils(I).My_Id) := I;
      end loop;

      Phil_Pics :=
         (new Picture.North,
          new Picture.East,
          new Picture.South,
          new Picture.South,
          new Picture.West);

      Picture.Open (Phil_Pics(1).all,( 1, 24), 7, 30);
      Picture.Open (Phil_Pics(2).all,( 9, 46), 7, 30);
      Picture.Open (Phil_Pics(3).all,(17, 41), 7, 30);
      Picture.Open (Phil_Pics(4).all,(17,  7), 7, 30);
      Picture.Open (Phil_Pics(5).all,( 9,  2), 7, 30);


      -- and assigns them their chopsticks.

      Phils (1).Start_Eating (1, 2);
      Phils (3).Start_Eating (3, 4);
      Phils (2).Start_Eating (2, 3);
      Phils (5).Start_Eating (1, 5);
      Phils (4).Start_Eating (4, 5);
```

```
      loop
         select
            accept Report_State (Which_Phil : in Society.Unique_DNA_Codes;
                                 State       : in Phil.States;
                                 How_Long    : in Natural := 0;
                                 Which_Meal  : in Natural := 0) do

            T := Natural (Calendar."-" (Calendar.Clock, Start_Time));

            case State is

               when Phil.Breathing =>
                  Picture.Title (Phil_Pics (Phil_Seats (Which_Phil)).all,
                          Society.Name_Register (Which_Phil));
                  Picture.Put_line (Phil_Pics (Phil_Seats (Which_Phil)).all,
                          "T =" & Integer'Image (T) & " "
                          & "Breathing...");

               when Phil.Thinking =>
                  Picture.Put_line (Phil_Pics (Phil_Seats (Which_Phil)).all,
                          "T =" & Integer'Image (T) & " "
                          & "Thinking"
                          & Integer'Image (How_Long) & " seconds.");

               when Phil.Eating =>
                  Picture.Put_line (Phil_Pics (Phil_Seats (Which_Phil)).all,
                          "T =" & Integer'Image (T) & " "
                          & "Meal"
                          & Integer'Image (Which_Meal)
                          & ","
                          & Integer'Image (How_Long) & " seconds.");

               when Phil.Done_Eating =>
                  Picture.Put_line (Phil_Pics (Phil_Seats (Which_Phil)).all,
                          "T =" & Integer'Image (T) & " "
                          & "Yum-yum (burp)");
                  Picture.Left_Fork (Phil_Pics (Phil_Seats (Which_Phil)).all, False);
                  Picture.Right_Fork (Phil_Pics (Phil_Seats (Which_Phil)).all, False);

               when Phil.Got_Left_Stick =>
                  Picture.Put_line (Phil_Pics (Phil_Seats (Which_Phil)).all,
                          "T =" & Integer'Image (T) & " "
                          & "First chopstick"
                          & Integer'Image (How_Long));
                  Picture.Left_Fork (Phil_Pics (Phil_Seats (Which_Phil)).all, True);

               when Phil.Got_Right_Stick =>
                  Picture.Put_line (Phil_Pics (Phil_Seats (Which_Phil)).all,
                          "T =" & Integer'Image (T) & " "
                          & "First chopstick"
                          & Integer'Image (How_Long));
                  Picture.Right_Fork (Phil_Pics (Phil_Seats (Which_Phil)).all, True);

               when Phil.Got_Other_Stick =>
                  Picture.Put_line (Phil_Pics (Phil_Seats (Which_Phil)).all,
                          "T =" & Integer'Image (T) & " "
                          & "Second chopstick"
                          & Integer'Image (How_Long));
                  Picture.Left_Fork (Phil_Pics (Phil_Seats (Which_Phil)).all, True);
                  Picture.Right_Fork (Phil_Pics (Phil_Seats (Which_Phil)).all, True);

               when Phil.Dying =>
                  Picture.Put_line (Phil_Pics (Phil_Seats (Which_Phil)).all,
                          "T =" & Integer'Image (T) & " "
                          & "Croak");

            end case; -- State

         end Report_State;

      or
         terminate;
      end select;

   end loop;

   end Maitre_D;

end Room;
```

```
--:::::::::::
--diners.adb
--:::::::::::
with Text_IO;
with Room;
procedure Diners is

   -- Dining Philosophers - Ada 95 edition

   -- This is the main program, responsible only for telling the
   --   Maitre_D to get busy.

   -- Michael B. Feldman, The George Washington University,
   -- July, 1995.

begin
   --Text_IO.New_Line;      -- artifice to flush output buffer
   Room.Maitre_D.Start_Serving;
end Diners;
```

APPENDIX A
Map From *Ada 95 Reference Manual* to Guidelines

REFERENCES

ACES 1995a	*Ada Compiler Evaluation System Primer*, version 2.0. Wright-Patterson Air Force Base, Ohio: High Order Language Control Facility (88 CG/SCTL).
1995b	*Ada Compiler Evaluation System Reader's Guide*, version 2.0. Wright-Patterson Air Force Base, Ohio: High Order Language Control Facility (88 CG/SCTL).
1995c	*Ada Compiler Evaluation System User's Guide*, version 2.0. Wright-Patterson Air Force Base, Ohio: High Order Language Control Facility (88 CG/SCTL).
Ada Reference Manual 1983	*Reference Manual for the Ada Programming Language.* Department of Defense, ANSI/MIL-STD-1815A.
Ada Reference Manual 1995	*Ada 95 Reference Manual*, ISO/8652-1995 Cambridge, Massachusetts: Intermetrics, Inc.
AIRMICS 1990	*Software Reuse Guidelines*, ASQB-GI-90-015. U.S. Army Institute for Research in Management Information, Communications, and Computer Sciences.
Anderson, T., and R.W. Witty 1978	Safe Programming. *BIT (Tidscrift Nordisk for Informations Behandling)* 18:1-8.
ARTEWG 1986	*Catalogue of Ada Runtime Implementation Dependencies.* Draft version. Association for Computing Machinery, Special Interest Group for Ada, Ada Run-Time Environments Working Group.
Baker, Henry G. 1991	"A Heavy Thought . . ." *Ada Letters.* 11,2:45.
Barbey, S., M. Kempe, and A. Strohmeier 1994	"Advanced Object-Oriented Programming With Ada 9X." *TRI-Ada '94 Tutorial Proceedings*, pp. 373-467.
Barnes, J.G.P. 1989	*Programming in Ada.* 3d ed. Reading, Massachusetts: Addison-Wesley.
1996	*Programming in Ada 95.* Reading, Massachusetts: Addison-Wesley.
Booch, G. 1986	*Software Engineering With Ada.* 2d ed. Menlo Park, California: The Benjamin/Cummings Publishing Company, Inc.

1987   *Software Components With Ada-Structures, Tools and Subsystems.* Menlo
                             Park, California: The Benjamin/Cummings Publishing Company, Inc.

1994   *Object-Oriented Analysis and Design.* 2d ed. Menlo Park, California: The
                             Benjamin/Cummings Publishing Company, Inc.

Brosgol, B., R. Eachus,   *Ada for Information Systems: A Style Guide.* Bedford, Massachusetts:
and D. Emery   MITRE.
1994

CECOM   CECOM "Final Report—Catalogue of Ada Runtime Implementation
1989   Dependencies," CIN; C02092JNB0001.

Charette, R.N.   *Software Engineering Environments Concepts and Technology.* Intertext
1986   Publications Inc. New York, New York: McGraw-Hill Inc.

Clapp, R.M, T. Mudge,   "Rationale," *Ada Letters.* 10,3.
and D.M. Roy
1990

Cohen, N.H.   *Ada as a Second Language.* New York, New York: McGraw-Hill Inc.
1986

1996   *Ada as a Second Language.* 2nd edition. New York, New York:
                             McGraw-Hill Inc.

Cohen, N., M. Kamrad,   "Ada 9X as a Second Ada." *TRI-Ada '93 Tutorial Proceedings,*
E. Schonberg, and R. Dewar   pp. 1115-1196.
1993

Conti, R.A.   Critical Run-Time Design Tradeoffs in an Ada Implementation. *Proceedings*
1987   *of the Joint Ada Conference, Fifth National Conference on Ada Technology*
                             and Washington Ada Symposium. pp. 486-495.

Dewar, R.   Newsgroup discussion on *comp.lang.ada.* February 11, 1994. Subject:
1995   Constructor in ADA9X.

Edwards, S.   *An Approach for Constructing Reusable Software Components in Ada,* IDA
1990   Paper P-2378. Institute for Defense Analyses.

Goforth, A., P. Collard,   "Performance Measurement of Parallel Ada," *Ada Letters.* 10,3.
and M. Marquardt
1990

Gonzalez, Dean W.   "ʼ▪ʼ Considered Harmful," *Ada Letters.* 11,2:56.
1991

Goodenough, J., and   *The Priority Ceiling Protocol: A Method for Minimizing the Blocking of*
L. Sha   *High Priority Ada Tasks,* Tech. Rep. SEI-SSR-4. Pittsburgh, Pennsylvania:
1988   Software Engineering Institute.

Griest 1989	"Limitations on the Portability of Real Time Ada Programs," Proceedings of the 1989 Tri-Ada Conference, Tom Griest.
Hefley, W., J. Foreman, C. Engle, and J. Goodenough 1992	*Ada Adoption Handbook: A Program Manager's Guide*, version 2.0. CMU/SEI-92-TR-29. Pittsburgh, Pennsylvania: Software Engineering Institute.
Honeywell 1986	*A Guidebook for Writing Reusable Source Code in Ada.* Corporate Systems Development Division. Version 1.1. CSC-86-3:8213.
IEEE Dictionary 1984	IEEE Standard Dictionary of Electrical and Electronics Terms. ANSI/IEEE STD 100-1984.
Intermetrics 1995	*Changes to Ada-1987 to 1995*, version 6.0. ISO/IEC 8652:1995(E), 1995.
Jacobson, I. et al. 1992	*Object-Oriented Software Engineering.* Reading, Massachusetts: Addison-Wesley.
Knight, J. 1990	"On the Assessment of Ada Performance," *Ada Letters.* 10,3.
MacLaren, L. 1980	Evolving Toward Ada in Real Time Systems. *ACM Sigplan Notices.* 15(11):146-155.
Matthews, E.R. 1987	Observations on the Portability of Ada I/O. *ACM Ada Letters.* VII(5): 100–103.
Melliar-Smith, P.M., and B. Randell 1987	Software Reliability: The Role of Programmed Exception Handling. *ACM Sigplan Notices.* 12(3):95-100.
NASA 1987	*Ada Style Guide.* Version 1.1, SEL-87-002. Greenbelt, Maryland: NASA, Goddard Space Flight Center.
1992	Ada Efficiency Guide. Technical Note 552-FDD-91/068R0UD0. Greenbelt, Maryland: NASA, Goddard Space Flight Center.
Newport, J.R. 1995	"A Performance Model for Real-Time Systems," *Ada Letters.* 15,2.
Nissen, J., and P. Wallis 1984	*Portability and Style in Ada.* Cambridge University Press.
Pappas, F. 1985	*Ada Portability Guidelines.* DTIC/NTIS #AD-A160 390.
Pyle, I.C. 1985	*The Ada Programming Language.* 2d ed. United Kingdom: Prentice-Hall International.
Rationale 1995	*Ada 95 Rationale*, Cambridge, Massachusetts: Intermetrics, Inc.

Rosen, J.P.
1987

In Defense of the 'Use' Clause. *ACM Ada Letters.* VII(7):77-81.

1995

A Naming Convention for Classes in Ada 9X. *ACM Ada Letters.* VXV(2):54-58.

Ross, D.
1989

The Form of a Passive Iterator. *ACM Ada Letters.* IX(2):102-105.

Rumbaugh, J., M. Blaha,
W. Premerlani, F. Eddy,
and W. Lorensen
1991

Object-Oriented Modeling and Design. Englewood Cliffs, New Jersey: Prentice-Hall.

Sanden, B.
1994

Software Systems Construction With Examples in Ada. Englewood Cliffs, New Jersey: Prentice-Hall.

Schneiderman, B.
1986

Empirical Studies of Programmers: The Territory, Paths and Destinations. *Empirical Studies of Programmers*, edited by E. Soloway and S. Iyengar. Norwood, NJ: Ablex Publishing Corp. pp. 1-12.

Software Productivity
Consortium
1992

Ada Quality and Style: Guidelines for Professional Programmers, SPC-91061-CMC, version 02.01.01. Herndon, Virginia: Software Productivity Consortium.

1993

ADARTS ⓢ *Guidebook*, SPC-91104-MC, version 03.00.09. 2 vols. Herndon, Virginia: Software Productivity Consortium.

Soloway, E., J. Pinto,
S. Fertig, S. Letovsky,
R. Lampert, D. Littman,
and K. Ewing
1986

Studying Software Documentation From a Cognitive Perspective: A Status Report. *Proceedings of the Eleventh Annual Software Engineering Workshop.* Report SEL-86-006, Software Engineering Laboratory. Greenbelt, Maryland: NASA, Goddard Space Flight Center.

Taft, S.T.
1994

Multiple Inheritance in Ada 9X. Cambridge, Massachusetts: Intermetrics, Inc.

1995a

Newsgroup discussion on *comp.lang.ada.* January 22, 1995. Subject: Ada.strings.bounded problems?

1995b

Newsgroup discussion on *comp.lang.ada.* February 11, 1995. Subject: Constructor in ADA9X.

Taylor, B.
1995

Ada Compatibility Guide, version 6.0. United Kingdom: Transition Technology Limited.

United Technologies
1987

CENC Programmer's Guide. Appendix A: Ada Programming Standards.

Volan, J.
1994

Newsgroup discussion on *comp.lang.ada.* December 9, 1995. Subject: Type extension vs. inheritance.

Volz, R.A., Mudge, Naylor, and Mayer
1985

Some Problems in Distributing Real-Time Ada Programs Across Machines. *Ada in Use, Proceedings of the Ada International Conference.* pp. 14–16. Paris.

Wegner, P., and S.B. Zdonik
1988

Inheritance as an Incremental Modification Mechanism or What Like Is and Isn't Like. *Proceedings of the European Conference on Object-Oriented Programming.* LNCS 322. Springer-Verlag.

Weidermann, N.
1990

"Hartstone: Synthetic Benchmark Requirements for Hard Real-Time Applications," *Ada Letters.* 10,3.

Wheeler, David A.
1992

Analysis and Guidelines for Reusable Ada Software. IDA Paper P-2765. Alexandria, Virginia: Institute for Defense Analyses.

BIBLIOGRAPHY

BIBLIOGRAPHY

ACVC (Ada Compiler Validation Capability). Ada Validation Facility, ASD/SIOL. Wright-Patterson Air Force Base, Ohio.

AIRMICS. *Software Reuse Guidelines*, ASQB-GI-90-015. U.S. Army Institute for Research in Management Information, Communications, and Computer Sciences, 1990.

Ausnit, C., and K.A. Johnson. "Ada 95 Quality and Style." In *Proceedings of the Thirteenth Annual National Conference on Ada Technology*, March 1995.

Bardin, Thompson. "Composable Ada Software Components and the Re-Export Paradigm." *ACM Ada Letters*. VIII(1) (January/February 1988):58–79.

Bardin, Thompson. "Using the Re-Export Paradigm to Build Composable Ada Software Components." *ACM Ada Letters*. VIII(2) (March–April 1988):39–54.

Brooks, F.B. *The Mythical Man-Month*. Essays on Software Engineering. Reading, Massachusetts: Addison-Wesley, 1975.

Cristian, F. "Correct and Robust Programs." *IEEE Transactions on Software Engineering*. SE-10(2) (March 1984):163–174.

Department of Defense, Ada Joint Program Office. *Rationale for the Design of the Ada Programming Language*, 1984.

Department of Defense, Ada Joint Program Office. *Reference Manual for the Ada Programming Language*. ANSI/MIL-STD-1815A, January 1983.

Foreman, J., and J. Goodenough. *Ada Adoption Handbook: A Program Manager's Guide*. Version 1.0, CMU/SEI-87-TR-9 ESD-TR-87-110. Pittsburgh, Pennsylvania: Software Engineering Institute, May 1987.

Gary, B., and D. Pokrass. *Understanding Ada: A Software Engineering Approach*. John Wiley & Sons, 1985.

Goodenough, J. B. A Sample of Ada Programmer Errors. *Unpublished draft resident in the Ada Repository under file name* PD2:<ADA.EDUCATION>PROGERRS.DOC.2, March 1986.

Herr, C.S. Compiler Validation and Reusable Software. St. Louis, Missouri: A Report from the CAMP Project, McDonnell Douglas Astronautics Company, August 1987.

International Workshop on Real-Time Ada Issues. *ACM Ada Letters*. VII(6). Mortonhampstead, Devon, U.K., 1987.

International Workshop on Real-Time Ada Issues II. *ACM Ada Letters*. VIII(6). Mortonhampstead, Devon, U.K., 1988.

Kempe, M. Ada Programmer's Frequently Asked Questions (FAQ), 1995.

Kernighan, B., and P.J. Plauger. The Elements of Programming Style. New York, New York: McGraw-Hill, Inc., 1978.

MacLaren, L. "Evolving Toward Ada in Real Time Systems." *ACM Sigplan Notices.* 15(11) (November 1980):146–155.

Mowday, B.L., and E. Normand. *Ada Programming Standards.* General Dynamics Data Systems Division Departmental Instruction 414.717, November 1986.

Nissen, J.C.D., P. Wallis, B.A. Wichmann, et al. "Ada-Europe Guidelines for the Portability of Ada Programs." *ACM Ada Letters.* I(3)(1982):44–61.

Rymer, J., and T. McKeever. *The FSD Ada Style Guide.* IBM Federal Systems Division Ada Coordinating Group, September 1986.

SofTech Inc. *ISEC Reusability Guidelines.* Report 3285-4-247/2. Also U.S. Army Information Systems Engineering Command. Waltham, Massachusetts, December 1985.

Stark M., and E. Seidewitz. Towards A General Object-Oriented Ada Lifecycle. In *Proceedings of the Joint Ada Conference.* Fifth National Conference on Ada Technology and Washington Ada Symposium, pp. 213–222, March 1987.

St. Dennis, R. *A Guidebook for Writing Reusable Source Code in Ada,* version 1.1. Report CSC-86-3:8213. Golden Valley, Minnesota: Honeywell Corporate Systems Development Division, May 1986.

VanNeste, K.F. "Ada Coding Standards and Conventions." *ACM Ada Letters.* VI(1) (January/February 1986): 41–48.

INDEX

erroneous execution, 102
propagation, 101, 112, 176, 198
rendezvous, 126
reusability, 176
Storage_Error, 78, 109
suppress, 105
Tasking_Error, 125, 126, 138
user-defined, 101, 111

execution pattern
portable, 155, 166

exit statement, 67, 89, 90, 110
conditional, 86
in loop, 65, 89, 110

exit status
setting, 137, 139

export
overloading in generic, 175, 198

expression, 83, 110
aggregate, 94
alignment, 13, 15
evaluation
portability, 151
function calls in, 51
logical, 85
nesting, 86, 110
numeric, 149, 165
order dependency, 149, 165
parenthesis, 84
relational, 84, 85, 110
slice, 87
spacing, 10
static, 30, 45, 172, 198
use named association, 68, 108

F

family of parts, 194

file
closing, 162
header, 33
naming convention, 48
naming conventions, 47, 62
organization, 47, 62

finalization, 178, 206, 207, 222
complete functionality, 178, 198

fixed point
in relational expression, 86
precision, 143, 164

flag
in complex loop, 90
in while loop, 90
naming, 84, 110

floating point
accuracy, 151
affects equality, 98
arithmetic, 150, 165
in relational expression, 86
precision, 143, 151, 164
relational expression, 152, 165

flow of control, 99

for loop, 89, 110
indentation, 11
is bounded, 92

foreign code, 148

Form
parameter in predefined I/O, 162

formal parameter, 68, 108
anonymous, 72
generic, 171
name, 68, 108

formatter, 10, 13, 14, 15, 16, 17, 18, 19, 21, 23

FORTRAN, 76
equivalence, 104, 112

fraction, 22

free list, 79

function
access, 55
body
indentation, 12
call
in declaration, 105, 112
named association, 68, 108
recursive, 91, 110
spacing, 9
default parameter, 69, 108
end statement, 67, 108
generic, 179, 192, 199
Inline, 236, 238
interrogative
to avoid exception, 60, 64
name, 28, 45
overload, 97, 111
parameter list, 68, 108
return, 92
side effect, 50, 62

U

Springer
and the
environment

At Springer we firmly believe that an international science publisher has a special obligation to the environment, and our corporate policies consistently reflect this conviction.
We also expect our business partners – paper mills, printers, packaging manufacturers, etc. – to commit themselves to using materials and production processes that do not harm the environment. The paper in this book is made from low- or no-chlorine pulp and is acid free, in conformance with international standards for paper permanency.

Springer

Lecture Notes in Computer Science

For information about Vols. 1–1265

please contact your bookseller or Springer-Verlag